AF792092

Shaping Internet Governance: Regulatory Challenges

Rolf H. Weber

Shaping Internet Governance: Regulatory Challenges

in collaboration with Mirina Grosz
and Romana Weber

Springer

Professor Dr. Rolf H. Weber
Professor for Civil, Business
and European Law
Faculty of Law
University of Zürich
Rämistr. 74/38
CH-8001 Zürich
rolf.weber@rwi.uzh.ch

ISBN 978-3-642-04619-3 e-ISBN 978-3-642-04620-9
DOI 10.1007/978-3-642-04620-9
Springer Heidelberg Dordrecht London New York

Library of Congress Control Number: 2009943299

Copyright © Schulthess Juristische Medien AG, Zurich – Basel – Geneva 2009
ISBN 978-3-7255-5891-9
www.schulthess.com

Published by Springer-Verlag Berlin Heidelberg 2010
This work is subject to copyright. All rights are reserved, whether the whole or part of the material is concerned, specifically the rights of translation, reprinting, reuse of illustrations, recitation, broadcasting, reproduction on microfilm or in any other way, and storage in data banks. Duplication of this publication or parts thereof is permitted only with permission of the copyright holder.
The use of general descriptive names, registered names, trademarks, etc. in this publication does not imply, even in the absence of a specific statement, that such names are exempt from the relevant protective laws and regulations and therefore free for general use.

Cover design: WMXDesign GmbH

Printed on acid-free paper

Springer is part of Springer Science+Business Media (www.springer.com)

Preface

The information society is a key issue in everyday life and a phenomenon encompassing social, cultural, economic, and legal facettes. Currently, an information society's legal framework is gradually crystallizing under the newly introduced term of "Internet governance".

During the last few years, intensive discussions about the contents of Internet governance have addressed manifold aspects of a possible regulatory regime. In light of the general comprehension that an international treaty structure is missing and that self-regulation as a normative model does not suffice in all respects, new architectural and constitutional theories have been developed; furthermore, the international body of the Internet Governance Forum (IGF) came to life. Notwithstanding the available literature on IGF, however, a thorough and systematic study shedding light on the main topics of Internet governance (such as legitimacy, transparency, accountability, and participation) and on the key regulatory issues (for example critical Internet resources, access, protection of civil liberties/human rights, realization of security, safety and privacy standards, as well as the overcoming of the digital divide) from a legal perspective is not yet at hand. The present publication aims at discussing these legal challenges.

This book has benefited from many inputs and encouragements from colleagues that I am deeply grateful for. In particular, I am indebted to the very meaningful discussions and valuable support in the preparation of the publication by my research assistants lic. iur. Mirina Grosz and lic. iur. Romana Weber, to lic. iur. Karen Grossmann for the review of the manuscript and to lic. iur. Stephanie Volz for her assistance in the completion of the book. Furthermore, I am grateful to the Ecoscentia Foundation for financially supporting the publication of the book.

Any comments and suggestions from readers would be highly appreciated (rolf.weber@rwi.uzh.ch).

Zurich, May 2009 — Rolf H. Weber

Contents

Bibliography XIII

Materials XXIX

Abbreviations XXXV

I. Introduction 1

A. Perceptions of Governance 1

1. Cyberspace and Governance 1
2. Governance and Internet's Legal Framework 3
3. Mapping of Governance Issues 7

B. Perceptions of Information Society 9

C. Regulatory Approaches 10

1. International Agreements and Cooperation 11
   1.1 Forms, Strengths and Weaknesses of International Law 11
      a) Introduction 11
      b) International Conventions 13
      c) Customary Rules 14
      d) General Legal Principles 15
   1.2 Future Prospects 16
2. Self-Regulation 17
   2.1 Background 17
   2.2 Forms and Legal Quality of Self-Regulation 18
      a) Forms of Self-Regulation 18
      b) Legal Quality of Self-Regulation 20
   2.3 Strengths and Weaknesses of Self-Regulation 21
      a) Strengths of Self-Regulation 21
      b) Weaknesses of Self-Regulation 21
3. Concluding Remarks 23

II. Historical Developments 25

A. From McBride to WSIS 25

B. From ICANN to WSIS 28

1. First Steps towards the Internet's Institutionalization 28
2. Internet Corporation for Assigned Names and Numbers (ICANN) 29

3. World Summit on the Information Society and Internet Governance Forum 31
3.1 First Phase: Geneva 2003 31
3.2 Working Group on Internet Governance (WGIG) 33
3.3 Second Phase: Tunis 2005 35
3.4 IGF Meetings 36

III. Organizational Framework in Internet Governance 39

A. Overview 39
B. Policy and Technology Organizations 40
1. International Telecommunication Union 40
2. Internet Engineering Task Force and Internet Architecture Board 42
3. Internet Society 43
4. World Wide Web Consortium 47
C. Internet Corporation for Assigned Names and Numbers 51
1. Basic Framework and Development 51
2. Membership and Financing 54
3. Organizational Structure 55
3.1 Board of Directors 55
a) Composition 55
b) Meetings 56
c) Duties 56
d) Committees 57
3.2 Officers 57
3.3 Ombudsman 58
3.4 Advisory Mechanisms 58
a) Advisorory Committees 58
b) External Expert Advice 59
c) Technical Supporting Group 59
3.5 Supporting Organizations 60
4. Discussions about the Role of ICANN 60
4.1 ICANN's Significance for the Governance of the Internet 60
4.2 Points of International Criticism 61
a) Public Policy Set by a Private Entity 61
b) US Influence 62
c) Democratic Legitimacy 62
4.3 Possible Adaptations 64
5. Outlook 65

D. World Summits of the Information Society and Internet Governance Forum 66
E. European Dialogue on Internet Governance 71

IV. Philosophical and Sociological Environment 73

A. Philosophical Concepts of a Social Contract for the Internet Community 73
1. Introduction 73
2. Philosophical Concept of the Social Contract 74
2.1 Form of Integration 74
2.2 Necessity of Overall Approval 75
3. Adaptability of the Social Contract Concept 76
3.1 Inclusion of Civil Society in All Areas 77
a) Bottom-up Approach 77
b) Realization of an Open Society 78
3.2 No Authority of one Individual through the Creation of a Social Contract 79
3.3 Application of the General Will (Volonté Générale) 80
a) Derived from Everyone 80
b) Aimed at Everyone's Welfare 83
4. Enshrinement of Fundamental Rights 84
4.1 Right to Freedom 84
a) Continuing Freedom for Everyone 84
b) Socialization and Right to Freedom 85
4.2 Equity and Equality 86
4.3 Fairness 86
5. Outlook 87

B. Multi-Stakeholderism in Internet Governance 88
1. Introduction 88
2. Architectural and Constitutional Principles 89
3. Theories of Global Rulemaking 92
3.1 Processes of International Regime Formation 92
3.2 Creation of Government Networks 94
4. Milestones for Multi-Stakeholderism in Internet Governance 96
4.1 Improvement of ICANN's Democratic Legitimacy 96
4.2 Need for Better Transparency and Accountability 98
4.3 Creation of an International Internet Governance Body 99
a) Appropriateness and Framework 99
b) Governing Structures within a New Entity 102

V. **Discussion Topics of Internet Governance** 105
A. **Introduction** 105
B. **Legitimacy** 105
1. Introduction 105
2. Present Problems with Legitimacy 106
2.1 Criticism on Internet Governance Organizations' Legitimacy .. 106
2.2 Adherence to Democracy as a Remedy? 107
3. Linking Legitimacy and Democracy? 109
3.1 Attempts towards framing Legitimacy 109
3.2 Perceptions of Democracy 112
3.3 Assessment 114
4. New Approaches 115
4.1 Conceptual Shifts in addressing Democracy and Legitimacy in International Governance 115
4.2 Framing the Stakeholders 116
4.3 Legitimacy through Fair Processes of Consensus-Making 118
4.4 Architectural Principles 119
5. Outlook 120
C. **Transparency** 121
1. Introduction 121
2. Assessing Guiding Principles of Transparency 121
3. Addressing Transparency in Other Markets 124
3.1 Transparency in the WTO Framework 124
3.2 Transparency in the IMF/World Bank Framework 125
3.3 Transparency in the EU Framework 126
4. Enhancing Transparency for the Future of Internet Governance 127
4.1 Tackling Controversies over ICANN 127
4.2 Further Developments 129
5. Outlook 131
D. **Accountability** 132
1. Introduction 132
2. Notion and Importance of Accountability 133
3. Accountability in Internet Governance at Present 134
3.1 Accountability in ICANN's Documentation 134
3.2 Relevant Accountability Types 135
4. Evaluation of Accountability Elements 137
4.1 Organization Level Aspects 137
4.2 Project Level Aspects 138
4.3 Policy Level Aspects 139

5. Approaches for Improving Accountability ... 140
   5.1 Extended Consultation of Civil Society ... 140
   5.2 Improved Inclusion of Civil Society ... 141
   5.3 Intergovernmental Supervision ... 143
   5.4 Market-Oriented Accountability ... 145
6. Outlook ... 146

E. Participation ... 148

1. Introduction ... 148
   1.1 Desirability of Public Participation in the Internet ... 148
   1.2 Comparable Developments in Environmental Law ... 149
      a) Justification for Comparison ... 149
      b) Aarhus Convention—Background and Contents ... 150
2. Access to Information ... 151
   2.1 Modalities of Publication of Information ... 152
   2.2 Passive Authentication ... 153
   2.3 People Entitled to Be Informed ... 155
   2.4 Extent of the Obligation to Inform ... 155
   2.5 Exceptions to the Obligation to Inform ... 156
   2.6 Time Limit ... 159
   2.7 Language (Translating Efforts) ... 160
   2.8 Charges for Supplying Information ... 161
   2.9 Establishment of the Necessary Requirements for the Requested Information ... 162
3. Participation and Involvement of Civil Society ... 162
   3.1 Participation Procedures ... 163
      a) Overview ... 163
      b) Decision-Making Processes ... 164
      c) Development of Plans, Programs and Policies ... 166
      d) Preparation of Law, Rules and Legally Binding Norms ... 167
   3.2 Exceptions to the Right of Participation ... 168
   3.3 People Entitled to Participate ... 168
   3.4 Form of Participation ... 169
   3.5 Time Frame for Participation ... 170
   3.6 Taking Account of the Results of Public Participation ... 170
4. Recognition and Support of the Bodies Promoting Internet Governance ... 171
5. Access to Jurisdiction ... 171
6. Outlook ... 172

VI. Regulatory Issues 175

A. Introduction 175

B. Critical Resources and Access 176

1. Internet Governance and Critical Resources 176
1.1 Notion of "Critical Resources" 177
1.2 Technical Occurrence of Critical Resources 178
a) Overview 178
b) Root Servers 179
c) Backbone Structures 180
d) Broadband Access 180
e) Internet System of Names and Numbers 181
1.3 Protection of Scarce Resources in International Law 181
a) Allocation of Water Resources 182
b) Avoidance of Technical Risks 183
c) Protection against Cyber-Attacks 183
d) Resolution of Interstate Conflicts 184
e) Prohibition of Child Labor 185
f) Access to Cultural Expressions 185
g) Preliminary Evaluation 186
2. Transition from IPv4 to IPv6 in Particular 186
2.1 Introduction 186
2.2 Transition from IPv4 to IPv6 187
2.3 Technical Framework 189
a) Problem of Restricted Capacity 189
b) Technical Standards 190
c) Interoperability and Security 191
2.4 Specific Issues Regarding the Transition Period 193
a) Time Factor 193
b) Compatibility 194
2.5 Challenges for IPv6 Deployment 196
a) Allocation of "Critical Resources" 196
b) Open Technical Access 196
c) Administration of Scarce Resources 197
d) Availability of Resources—Financing Mechanisms 199
2.6 Outlook 202
3. Access 202
3.1 Introduction 202
3.2 Net Neutrality 203
3.3 Access and Development 205

C. Protection of Civil Liberties and Humanization of Internet Governance 207
1. Notion and Functions of Human Rights 207
2. Existing Legal Framework for Human Rights 209
2.1 Global Level 209
2.2 Regional Level 212
3. Characteristics of Human Rights Protection 213
3.1 Contents of Human Rights 213
a) Dignity, Integrity and Equality 213
b) Freedom of Expression and Information 214
c) Privacy 215
3.2 Scope of Human Rights Application 216
3.3 Human Rights Transition from the Traditional to the New Online World 218
4. New Approaches for a Comprehensive Human Rights Architecture 219
4.1 Ongoing Activities 219
a) Context of the WSIS 219
b) Private Bodies 223
4.2 Perspectives for a Humanization of Internet Governance 224
a) General Developments 224
b) Specific Initiatives 225
c) Long-term Expectations 229
D. Security: Assuring Safety, Trust, and Reliability 231
1. Safety 231
1.1 Security Threats 231
1.2 Regulatory Framework 233
2. Trust and Reliability 237
2.1 Privacy 237
a) Meaning and Functions of Privacy 237
b) Regulatory Framework 239
c) Relation between Security and Privacy 240
d) Future Approaches 241
2.2 Data Security 245
a) General Guidelines 245
b) Cryptography 246
c) Electronic Signature 247

E. Bridging the Digital Divide 248
1. Introduction 248
2. Digital Divide Problematic 249
2.1 Factual Situation 249
2.2 Relevant Aspects of the Digital Divide 250
3. Financing Strategies 252
3.1 Financing Needs 252
3.2 Political Initiatives 254
a) Monterrey Consensus 254
b) World Summits on the Information Society 257
3.3 Financial Mechanisms 259
3.4 Financing Strategies' Legal Framework 261
4. Outlook 264

VII. Concluding Obervations 267

Index 273

Bibliography

Alvestrand Harald/Lie Hakon Wium, Development of Core Internet Standards: The Work of IETF and W3C, in: Bygrave/Bing (eds), Internet Governance: Infrastructure and Institutions, Oxford 2009, 126–146

Amtenbrink Fabian, The Three Pillars of Central Bank Governance – Towards a Model Central Bank Law or a Code of Good Governance, presentation during an IMF LEG Workshop on Central Banking, Washington DC, March 2004, available at <http://www.imf.org/external/np/leg/sem/2004/cdmfl/eng/amtenb.pdf>

Amoretti Francesco (ed.), Electronic Constitution – Social, Cultural and Political Implications, Salerno 2009

Anderson Kenneth, Book Review: Squaring the Circle? Reconciling Sovereignty and Global Governance through Global Government Networks, Harvard Law Review, Vol. 118, 2005, 1255–1312

Antonova Slavka, Powerscape of Internet Governance, Saarbrücken 2008

Aristotle, The Politics of Aristotle, translated into English with introduction, marginal analysis, essays, notes and incises by B. Jowett, Vol. 1, Oxford 1885, available at <http://oll.libertyfund.org/title/579>

Aristotle, Nicomachean Ethics, translated by F. H. Peter, 5th ed. London 1893, available at <http://oll.libertyfound.org/title/903>

Ashforth Blake E./Gibbs Barrie W., The Double-Edge of Organizational Legitimation, Organization Science, Vol. 1, 1990, 177–194, available at <http://www.jstor.org/stable/2635061>

Baird Zoë, Governing the Internet, Foreign Affairs, Vol. 81, 2002, 15–20

Basho Kalinda, The Licensing of Our Personal Information: Is It a Solution to Internet Privacy?, California Law Review, Vol. 88, 2000, 1507–1545

Bendrath Ralf/Jørgensen Rikke Frank, The World Summit on the Information Society – Privacy not Found?, SCRIPT-ed, Vol. 3, 2006, 355–369

Barth James R./Caprio Gerard Jr./Levine Ross, Rethinking Bank Regulation, Cambridge 2006

Benedek Wolfgang, Internet Governance and Human Rights, in: Benedek/Bauer/Kettemann (eds), Internet Governance and the Information Society, Utrecht 2008, 31–49 (Benedek, Human Rights)

Benedek Wolfgang (ed.), Understanding Human Rights, Manual on Human Rights Education, Vienna/Berlin/Antwerp 2006

Benedek Wolfgang/ Kettemann Matthias C./Senges Max, The Humanization of Internet Governance: A Roadmap Towards a Comprehensive Global (Human) Rights Architecture for the Internet, available at <http://giganet.igloogroups.org/annualsymp>

Benkler Yochai, The Wealth of Networks: How Social Production Transforms Markets and Freedom, New Haven/London 2006

BENZ ARTHUR, Einleitung: Governance – Modebegriff oder nützliches sozialwissenschaftliches Konzept?, in: Benz (ed.), Governance – Regieren in komplexen Regelsystemen, Wiesbaden 2004, 11–28

BERLE ADOLF/MEANS GARDINER, The Modern Corporation and Private Property, Cambridge/Mass. 1932

BERNERS-LEE TIM, Weaving the Web, The Original Design and Ultimate Destiny of the World Wide Web by its Inventor, San Francisco 1999 (BERNERS-LEE, Weaving the Web)

BERNERS-LEE TIM, Information Management: A Proposal, March 1989/May 1990, available at <http://www.w3.org/History/1989/proposal.html> (BERNERS-LEE, Information Management)

BIEGEL STUART, Beyond Our Control?, Confronting the Limits of Our Legal System in the Age of Cyberspace, Cambridge/Mass. 2001

BIRKINSHAW PATRICK, Freedom of Information and Openness: Fundamental Human Rights?, Administrative Law Review, Vol. 58, 2006, 177–218

BLACK JULIA, Constitutionalizing Self-Regulation, The Modern Law Review, Vol. 59, 1996, 24–55

BLOEM RENATE, Multi-Stakeholderism and Civil Society, in: Stauffacher/Kleinwächter (eds), The World Summit on the Information Society: Moving from the Past into the Future, New York 2005, 99–103

BRADY KATY, Aarhus Convention Signed, Environmental Policy and Law, Vol. 28, 1998, 171–181 (BRADY, Aarhus Convention)

BRADY KATY, New Convention on Access to Information and Public Participation in Environmental Matters, in: Environmental Policy and Law, Vol. 28, 1998, 69–75 (BRADY, New Convention)

BRANDEIS LOUIS, The Others Peoples Money and How the Bank Use It, New York 1914

BRANSCOMB ANNE WELLS, Anonymity, Autonomy, and Accountability: Challenges to the First Amendment in Cyberspace, Yale Law Journal, Vol. 104, 1995, 1639–1679

BRATT STEVE, World-wide Participation in the World Wide Web Consortium, 7th June 2007, available at <http://www.w3.org/2005/02/W3C-Global-Focus.html>

BROWNLIE IAN, Principles of Public International Law, 7th ed., Oxford/New York 2008

BROWNSWORD ROGER/LEWIS DOUGLAS, Preface in MacLeod (ed.), Global Governance and the Quest for Justice, Volume II: Corporate Governance, Oxford/Portland (Oregon) 2006, vii-ix

BUCHANAN ALLEN/KEOHANE ROBERT O., The Legitimacy of Global Governance Institutions, in: Wolfrum/Röben (eds), Legitimacy in International Law, Berlin/Heidelberg/New York 2008, 25–62

BUCKLEY STEVE, Whose Information Society? Communication Rights and the WSIS, in: Möller/Amouroux (eds), OSCE Representative on Freedom of the Media, The Media Freedom Internet Cookbook, Vienna 2004, 230–241

BUERGENTHAL THOMAS/MURPHY SEAN D., Public International Law in a Nutshell, 4th ed., St. Paul, MN 2007

Burnstein Matthew R., Conflicts on the Net: Choice of Law in Transnational Cyberspace, Vanderbilt Journal of Transnational Law, Vol. 29, 1996, 75–116

Bush Vannevar, As We May Think, Atlantic Monthly, July 1945, available at <http://www.theatlantic.com/doc/194507/bush>

Bygrave Lee A./Bing Jon (eds), Internet Governance: Infrastructure and Institutions, Oxford 2009

Bygrave Lee A./Michaelsen Terje, Governors of Internet, in: Bygrave/Bing (eds), Internet Governance: Infrastructure and Institutions, Oxford 2009, 92–125.

Campbell Angela, Self-Regulation and the Media, Federal Communications Law Journal, Vol. 51, 1999, 711–772

Caral Jose Ma. Emmanuel A., Lessons from ICANN: Is self-regulation on the Internet fundamentally flawed?, International Journal of Law and Information Technology, Vol. 12, 2004, 1–31

Casacuberta David/Senges Max, Basic Considerations on the Governance of Cyberspace, Committee for a Democratic U.N., Working Paper, available at <http://kdun.org/en/documents/igf_oct2006.pdf>

Cerf Vinton G., Looking Towards the Future, October 2007, available at <http://www.icann.org/documents/vint_cerf/lttf.htm> (Cerf, Looking Towards the Future)

Cerf Vinton G., IETF and ISOC, 1995, available at <http://www.isoc.org/internet/history/ietfhis.shtml> (Cerf, IETF and ISOC)

Cerf Vinton G./Kahn Bob/Chapin Lyman, Announcing ISOC, 1992, available at <http://www.isoc.org/internet/history/isochistory.shtml>

Charnovitz Steve, WTO Cosmopolitics, New York University Journal of International Law and Politics, Vol. 34, 2002, 299–354

Cheung Anne S.Y./Weber Rolf H., Internet Governance and the Responsibility of Internet Service Providers, Wisconsin International Law Journal, Vol. 26, 2008, 403–477

Chik Warren B., Lord of Your Domain, But Master of None: The Need to Harmonize and Recalibrate the Domain Name Regime of Ownership and Control, International Journal of Law and Information Technology, Vol. 16, 2007, 8–72

Clapham Andrew, Human Rights Obligations of Non-State Actors, Oxford/New York 2006

Clark Ian, Legitimacy in International Society, New York 2005

Crampton Jeremy W., The Political Mapping of Cyberspace, Chicago/Edinburgh 2003

Dany Charlotte, Civil Society Participation under Most Favorable Conditions: Assessing the Deliberative Quality of the WSIS, in: Steffek/Kissling/Nanz (eds), Civil Society Participation in European and Global Governance, Palgrave 2008, 53–70

De la Chapelle Bertrand, The Internet Governance Forum: How a United Nations Summit Produced a New Governance Paradigm for the Internet Age, in: Möller/Amouroux (eds), Governing the Internet – Freedom and Regulation in the OSCE Region, Vienna 2007, 19–27 (de la Chapelle, Governance Paradigm)

De la Chapelle Bertrand, Towards Multi-Stakeholder Governance – The Internet Governance Forum as Laboratory, in: Kleinwächter (ed.), The Power of Ideas, Berlin 2007, 256–270

DeNardis Laura, Protocol Politics: The Globalization of Internet Governance, Cambridge/Mass. 2009 (DeNardis, Protocol Politics)

DeNardis Laura, Open Standards and Global Politics, International Journal of Communications Law & Policy, Vol. 13, 2009, 70–86 (DeNardis, Open Standards)

De Vey Mestdagh Kees/Rijgersberg Rudolf W., Rethinking Accountability in Cyberspace: A New Perspective on ICANN, International Review of Law, Computers & Technology, Vol. 21, 2007, 27–38

Donges Patrick, Medienpolitik und Media Governance, in: Donges (ed.), Von der Medienpolitik zur Media Governance?, Köln 2007, 7–23

Doria Avri/Kleinwächter Wolfgang (eds), Internet Governance Forum (IGF): The First Two Years, a UNESCO Publication for the World Summit of the Information Society – Special issue co-produced with ITU and UNDESA, December 2008, available at <http://www.intgovforum.org/cms/index.php/component/content/article/57-2008igf/311-internet-governance-forum-the-first-two-years>

Dörr Oliver, Privatisierung des Völkerrechts, Juristenzeitung 2005, 905–916

Drake William J., Encouraging Implementation of WSIS Principles on Internet Governance Procedures, in: Kleinwächter (ed.), The Power of Ideas, Berlin 2007, 271–280 (Drake, Implementation)

Drake William J., Reframing Internet Governance Discourse: Fifteen Baseline Propositions, in: MacLean (ed.), Internet Governance: A Grand Collaboration, New York 2004, 122–161, available at <http://www.citi.columbia.edu/affiliates/wdrake.htm> (Drake, Discourse)

Drake William J./Jørgensen Rikke Frank, Introduction, in: Jørgensen (ed.), Human Rights in the Global Information Society, Cambridge/Mass. 2006, 1–49

Drezner Daniel W., All Politics is Global, Explaining International Regulatory Regimes, Princeton/Oxford 2007

Drissel David, Internet Governance in a Multipolar World: Challenging American Hegemony, Cambridge Review of International Affairs, Vol. 19, 2006, 105–120

Dupuy René Jean, Declaratory Law and Programmatory Law: From Revolutionary Custom to "Soft Law", in: Akkerman/Krieken/Pannenborg (eds), Declaration on Principles, Leyden 1977, 247–257

Dwivedi O. P./Jabbra Joseph G., Introduction: Public Service Responsibility and Accountability, in Dwivedi/Jabbra (eds), Public Service Accountability, West Hartford, Connecticut 1989, 1–16

Ebrahim Alnoor/Herz Steve, Accountability in Complex Organizations: World Bank Responses to Civil Society, John F. Kennedy School of Government, Harvard University, December 2007, RWP 07-060, available at <http://ksgnotes1.harvard.edu/Research/wpaper.nsf/rwp/RWP07-060>

EDDY NATHALIE, Public Participation in CDM and JI Projects, in: Freestone/Streck (eds), Legal Aspects of Implementing the Kyoto Mechanisms: Making Kyoto Work, Oxford 2005, 71–104

ELLICKSON ROBERT C., Order Without Law: How Neighbors Settle Disputes, Cambridge/Mass. 1991

ELSIG MANFRED, The World Trade Organization's Legitimacy Crisis: What Does the Beast Look Like?, Journal of World Trade, Vol. 41, 2007, 75–98

EPINEY ASTRID/SCHEYLI MARTIN, Die Aarhus-Konvention: Rechtliche Tragweite und Implikationen für das schweizerische Recht, Freiburg 2000, 13–24 (EPINEY/SCHEYLI, Aarhus-Konvention)

EPINEY ASTRID/SCHEYLI MARTIN, Umweltvölkerrecht, Bern 2000 (EPINEY/SCHEYLI, Umweltvölkerrecht)

ESTERHUYSEN ANRIETTE/CURRIE WILLIE, Open, Universal, and Affordable Access to the Internet, in: Kleinwächter (ed.), The Power of Ideas, Berlin 2007, 60–67

FAWCETT AMELIA C., Examining the Objectives of Financial Regulation – Will the New Regime Succeed? A Practitioner's View in: Ferran/Goodhart (eds), Regulating Financial Services and Markets in the 21th Century, Oxford 2001, 37–56

FAY MARIANNE/YEPES TITO, Investing in Infrastructure: What is needed from 2000 to 2010?, World Bank Policy Research Working Paper 3102, July 2003

FRANCK THOMAS M., Democracy, Legitimacy and the Rule of Law: Linkages, in: Public Law and Legal Theory Working Paper Series, Working Paper 2, 1999, 1–20, available at <http://papers.ssrn.com> (FRANCK, Democracy, Legitimacy and the Rule of Law)

FRANCK THOMAS M., Fairness in International Law and Institutions, Oxford 1995 (FRANCK, Fairness)

FREDMAN SANDRA, Human Rights Transformed, Positive Rights and Positive Duties, Oxford/New York 2008

FRIEDMANN WOLFGANG, The Uses of "General Principles" in the Development of International Law, American Journal of International Law, Vol. 57, 1963, 279–299

FROOMKIN A. MICHAEL, International and National Regulation of the Internet, in: Dommering/van Eijk (eds), The Round Table Expert Group on Telecommunications Laws: Conference Papers 2005, Amsterdam 2005, available at <http://law.tm/docs/International-regulation.pdf> (FROOMKIN, International and National Regulation)

FROOMKIN A. MICHAEL, Form and Substance in Cyberspace, Journal of Small and Emerging Business Law, Vol. 6, 2002, 93–124 (FROOMKIN, Form and Substance)

FROOMKIN A. MICHAEL, Wrong turn in cyberspace: using ICANN to route around the APA and the constitution, Duke Law Journal, Vol. 50, 2000, 17–184 (FROOMKIN, Wrong turn in cyberspace)

FROOMKIN A. MICHAEL, The Death of Privacy?, Stanford Law Review, Vol. 52, 2000, 1461–1543 (FROOMKIN, Privacy)

FROOMKIN A. MICHAEL, Of Governments and Governance, Berkeley Technology Law Journal, Vol. 14, 1999, 617–633 (FROOMKIN, Governance)

GIBBONS LLEWELLYN JOSEPH, No Regulation, Government Regulation, or Self-Regulation: Social Enforcement or Social Contracting for Governance in Cyberspace, Cornell Journal of Law and Public Policy, Vol. 6, 1996–1997, 475–551

GIBSON WILLIAM, Neuromance, New York 1984

GOLDSMITH JACK L./WU TIM, Who Controls the Internet? Illusions of a Borderless World, Oxford 2006

GOODHART CHARLES A. E., Regulating the Regulator – An Economist's Perspective on Accountability and Control in: Ferran/Goodhart (eds), Regulating Financial Services and Markets in the 21th Century, Oxford 2001, 151–164

GRANT RUTH W./KEOHANE ROBERT O., Accountability and Abuses of Power in World Politics, American Political Science Review, Vol. 99, 2005, 29–43

GREWLICH KLAUS W., Konstitutionalisierung des "Cyberspace", Zwischen europarechtlicher Regulierung und völkerrechtlicher Governance, Baden-Baden 2001 (GREWLICH, Konstitutionalisierung des „Cyberspace")

GREWLICH KLAUS W., Governance in "cyberspace": access and public interest in global communications, The Hague etc. 1999 (GREWLICH, Governance)

GROSZ MIRINA, Internet Society (ISOC), in: Tietje/Brouder (eds), Handbook of Transnational Economic Governance Regimes, Leiden, forthcoming 2009 (GROSZ, ISOC)

GROSZ MIRINA, The World Wide Web Consortium (W3C), in: Tietje/ Brouder (eds), Handbook of Transnational Economic Governance Regimes, Leiden, forthcoming 2009 (GROSZ, W3C)

HABERMAS JÜRGEN, Faktizität und Geltung, Beiträge zur Diskurstheorie des Rechts und des demokratischen Rechtsstaats, Frankfurt a.M. 1992

HACOHEN MALACHI HAIM, Karl Popper – The Formative Years, 1902–1945, London 2000

HAGEN SYLVIA, IPv6 Essentials, 2nd ed., Beijing 2006, available at <http://proquest.safaribooksonline.com/0596100582>

HALLER WALTER/KÖLZ ALFRED/GÄCHTER THOMAS, Allgemeines Staatsrecht, 4th ed., Basel 2008

HAQUE INAAMUL/BURDESCU RUXANDRA, Monterrey Consensus on Financing for Development: Response Sought from International Economic Law, Boston College International and Comparative Law Review, Vol. 27, 2004, 219–285

HART HERBERT, The Concept of Law, 2nd ed., Oxford 1997

HARVARD LAW SCHOOL, Developments – The Law of Cyberspace, Harvard Law Review, Vol. 112, 1999, 1574–1704

HEALD DAVID, Varieties of Transparency, in: Hood/Heald (eds), Transparency. The Key to Better Governance?, Oxford 2006, 25–43

HELD DAVID, Democracy and the Global Order, From the Modern State to Cosmopolitan Governance, Cambridge/Oxford 1995

HELD DAVID/MCGREW ANTHONY, Introduction, in: Held/McGrew (eds), Governing Globalization: power, authority and global governance, Cambridge 2002, 1–21

Hemmati Minu, Multi-Stakeholder Processes for Governance and Sustainability – Beyond Deadlock and Conflict, London/Sterling (VA) 2002

Herb Karlfriedrich, Jean-Jacques Rousseau – Ein Moderner mit antiker Seele, in: Kreimendahl (ed.), Philosophen des 18. Jahrhunderts, Darmstadt 2000, 141–156

Hubbard Amanda/Bygrave Lee A, Internet Governance Goes Global, in: Bygrave/Bing (eds), Internet Governance: Infrastructure and Institutions, Oxford 2009, 213–235

Hobbes Thomas, The English Works of Thomas Hobbes of Malmesbury (Leviathan), Vol. 3, ed. by Sir W. Molesworth, London 1839–45, available at <http://oll.libertyfund.org/title/585>

Hoffmann Jeanette, Internet Governance. A Regulatory Idea in Flux (2005), available at <http://duplox.wzb.eu/people/jeanette/texte/Internet%20Governance%20english%20version.pdf>

Holder Jane/Lee Maria, Environmental Protection, Law and Policy, 2nd ed., Cambridge 2007

Hood Christopher, Beyond Exchanging First Principles? Some Closing Comments, in: Hood/Heald (eds), Transparency. The Key to Better Governance?, Oxford 2006, 211–225 (Hood, Beyond Exchanging First Principles?)

Hood Christopher, Transparency in Historical Perspective, in: Hood/Heald (eds), Transparency. The Key to Better Governance?, Oxford 2006, 3–23 (Hood, Transparency)

Hosein Gus, Privacy as Freedom, in: Jørgensen (ed.), Human Rights in the Global Information Society, Cambridge/Mass. 2006, 121–147

Hubbard Amanda/Bygrave Lee A., Internet governance goes global, in: Bygrave/Bing (eds), Internet Governance: Infrastructure and Institutions, Oxford 2009, 213–235

Hughes David/Jewell Tim/Lowther Jason/Parpworth Neil/de Prez Paula, Environmental Law, 4th ed., London 2002

Hunter Dan, ICANN and the Concept of Democratic Deficit, Loyola of Los Angeles Law Review, Vol. 36, 2003, 1149–1183

Huston Geoff, On the Hunt for "Critical Internet Resources, available at <http://www.circleid.com/posts/cricial_internet_resources>

Ipsen Knut, Völkerrecht, 3rd ed., Zurich 2007

Irion Kristina, Separated Together: The International Telecommunications Union and Civil Society, International Journal of Communications Law & Policy, Vol. 13, 2009, 87–105

Janis Mark W., An Introduction to International Law, 3rd ed., Gaithersburg 1999

Johnson David R./Post David G., Law and Borders – The Rise of Law in Cyberspace, Stanford Law Review, Vol. 48, 1996, 1367–1402

Jørgensen Rikke Frank, The freedom to express oneself and to seek information, in: Jørgensen (ed.), Human Rights in the Global Information Society, Cambridge/Mass. 2006, 53–71

JØRGENSEN RIKKE FRANK/MARZOUKI MERYEM, Human Rights: The Missing Link, in: Droussou/Jensen (eds), Vision in Process II – The World Summit on the Information Society, Geneva 2003 to Tunis 2005, Berlin 2005, 17–23

KANG JERRY, Information Privacy in Cyberspace Transactions, Stanford Law Review, Vol. 50, 1998, 1193–1294

KANT IMMANUEL, Metaphysics of Ethics, translated by J. W. Semple, 3rd ed., Edinburgh 1886, available at <http://files.libertyfund.org/files/1443/0332_Bk.pdf>

KEOHANE ROBERT O., Governance in a Partially Globalized World, American Political Science Review, Vol. 95, 2001, 1–13

KERSTING WOLFGANG, John Rawls – Verteilungsgerechtigkeit und politischer Liberalismus, in: Henningfeld/Jansohn (eds), Philosophen der Gegenwart, Darmstadt 2005, 142–159

KETTEMANN MATTHIAS C., E-Inclusion as a Means to Bridge the Digital Divides: Conceptual Issues and International Approaches, in: Benedek/Bauer/Kettemann (eds), Internet Governance and the Information Society, Utrecht 2008, 51–61

KISS ALEXANDRE/SHELTON DINAH, International Environmental Law, 2nd ed., Ardsley/New York 2000

KLEIN HANS, The Right to Political Participation and the Information Society, in: Jørgensen (ed.), Human Rights in the Global Information Society, Cambridge/Mass. 2006, 185–196

KLEIN HANS/MUELLER MILTON, What to do about ICANN: A Proposal for Structural Reform, Concept Paper by the Internet Governance Project, 5th April 2005, available at <http://internetgovernance.org>

KLEINSTEUBER HANS J., The Internet between Regulation and Governance, in: Möller/Amouroux (eds), OSCE Representative on Freedom of the Media, The Media Freedom Internet Cookbook, Vienna 2004, 61–75

KLEINWÄCHTER WOLFGANG, Multi-Stakeholder Internet Governance: the Role of Governments, in: Benedek/Bauer/Kettemann (eds), Internet Governance and the Information Society, Utrecht 2008, 9–29 (KLEINWÄCHTER, Multi-Stakeholder)

KLEINWÄCHTER WOLFGANG (ed.), The Power of Ideas, Internet Governance in a Multi-Stakeholder Environment, Berlin 2007 (KLEINWÄCHTER, Power of Ideas)

KLEINWÄCHTER WOLFGANG, Internet Governance: Auf dem Weg zu einem strukturierten Dialog, in: Klumpp/Kubicek/Rossnagel/Schulz (eds), Medien, Ordnung und Innovation, Berlin/Heidelberg/New York 2006, 215–226 (KLEINWÄCHTER, Internet Governance)

KLEINWÄCHTER WOLFGANG, Internet Governance – die Kontroverse des WSIS. Eine globale Ressource im Spannungsfeld nationaler Interessen, Medienheft Dossier 24, 14th November 2005, 29–39 (KLEINWÄCHTER, Kontroverse des WSIS)

KLEINWÄCHTER WOLFGANG, A New Diplomacy for the 21st Century? Multi-Stakeholder Approach and Bottom-Up Policy Development in the Information Society, in: Stauffacher/Kleinwächter (eds), The World Summit on the Information Society: Moving from the Past into the Future, New York 2005, 110–113 (KLEINWÄCHTER, New Diplomacy)

KLEINWÄCHTER WOLFGANG, Beyond ICANN vs. ITU? How WSIS tries to enter the new territory of Internet Governance, Gazette: The International Journal for Communication Studies, Vol. 66, 2004, 233–251 (KLEINWÄCHTER, Beyond ICANN vs. ITU)

KLEINWÄCHTER WOLFGANG, Global Governance in the Information Age: GBDe and ICANN as "Pilot Projects" for co-regulation and a new trilateral policy?, Center for Internet Research, University of Aarhus, Copenhagen 2001 (KLEINWÄCHTER, Global Governance)

KLEINWÄCHTER WOLFGANG, ICANN as the "United Nations" of the Global Information Society?: The Long Road Towards Self-Regulation of the Internet, International Communication Gazette Vol. 62, 2000, 451–476, available at <http://gaz.sagepub.com/cgi/content/abstract/62/6/451> (KLEINWÄCHTER, ICANN as the "United Nations")

KLUTH WINFRIED, Die demokratische Legitimation der Europäischen Union, Berlin 1995

KOBACH KRIS W., The Referendum: Direct Democracy in Switzerland, Aldershot/Brookfield USA/Hong Kong/Singapore/Sidney 1993

KOCH IDA ELISABETH, Dichotomies, Trichotomies, or Waves of Duties? in Human Rights Law Review, Vol. 5, 2005, 81–103, available at <http://hrlr.oxfordjournals.org/cgi/content/full/5/1/81>

KOMAITIS KONSTANTINOS, Aristotle, Europe and Internet Governance, Pacific McGeorge Global Business & Development Law Journal, Vol. 21, 2008, 57–77

KUNZ JOSEF L., Natural-Law Thinking in the Modern Science of International Law, American Journal of International Law, Vol. 55, 1961, 951–958

KURBALIJA JOVAN, Internet Governance and International Law, in: Drake (ed.), Reforming Internet Governance: Perspectives from the Working Group on Internet Governance (WGIG), New York 2005, 105–115, available at <http://www.unicttaskforce.org/perl/documents.pl?id=1572>

LANGE STEFAN/SCHIMANK UWE, Governance und gesellschaftliche Integration, in: Lange/Schimank (eds), Governance und gesellschaftliche Integration, Wiesbaden 2004, 9–44

LANGHART ALBRECHT, Rahmengesetz und Selbstregulierung, Diss. Zurich 1993

LASTRA ROSA M./SHAMS HEBA, Public Accountability in the Financial Sector, in: Ferran/Goodhart (eds), Regulating Financial Services and Markets in the 21th Century, Oxford 2001, 165–188

LATIF LATID, Widening the Internet Address Space, in: Kleinwächter (ed.), The Power of Ideas, Berlin 2007, 227–242

LEAFFER MARSHALL, Domain Names, Globalization, and Internet Governance, Indiana Journal of Global Legal Studies, Vol. 6, 1998–1999, 139–165

LEINER BARRY M./CERF VINTON G./CLARK DAVID D./KAHN ROBERT E./KLEINROCK LEONARD/LYNCH DANIEL C./POSTEL JAN/ROBERTS LARRY G./WOLFF STEPHEN, A Brief History of the Internet, available at <http://www.isoc.org/internet/history/brief.shtml> (LEINER/CERF/CLARK ET AL.)

LESSIG LAWRENCE, Code version 2.0, New York 2006 (LESSIG, version 2.0)

LESSIG LAWRENCE, The Future of Ideas, New York 2001 (LESSIG, Future of Ideas)

LESSIG LAWRENCE, Code and other Laws of Cyberspace, New York 1999 (LESSIG, Code)

LIU JOSEPH P., Legitimacy and Authority in Internet Coordination: A Domain Name Case Study, Indiana Law Journal, Vol. 74, 1999, 587–626

LOCKE JOHN, The Works of John Locke in Nine Volumes, Vol. 4 Economic Writings and Two Treatises of Government, 12th ed., London 1824, available at <http://oll.libertyfund.org/title/1725>

LOCKE CHRISTOPHER/LEVINE RICK/SEARLS DOC, The Cluetrain Manifesto: the End of Business as Usual, Cambridge/Mass. 1999

LUHMANN NIKLAS, Legitimation durch Verfahren, 2nd ed., Darmstadt/Neuwied 1975

MACBRIDE-REPORT, Many Voices One World, Report of the MacBride Commission, Paris 1979, available at <http://unesdoc.unesco.org/images/0004/000400/040066eb.pdf>

MACLEAN DON, Herding Schrödinger's Cats: Some Conceptual Tools for Thinking about Internet Governance, available at <http://www.itu.int/osg/spu/forum/intgov04/contributions/itu-workshop-feb-04-internet-governance-background.pdf>

MALCOLM JEREMY, Appraising the Success of the Internet Governance Forum (21st November 2008), available at <http://www.internetgovernance.org> (MALCOLM, Success)

MALCOLM JEREMY, Multi-Stakeholder Governance and the Internet Governance Forum, Perth 2008 (MALCOLM, Governance)

MALCOLM JEREMY, The Space Law Analogy to Internet Governance, Journal of Law, Information and Science, Vol. 17, 2006, 1–43 (MALCOLM, The Space Law Analogy)

MARKS SUSAN, Democracy and International Governance, in: Coicaud/Heiskanen (eds), The Legitimacy of International Organizations, Tokyo/New York/Paris 2001, 45–68

MARSDEN CHRISTOPHER T., Co- and Self-regulation in European Media and Internet Sectors: The Results of Oxford University's Study, in: Möller/Amouroux (eds), OSCE Representative on Freedom of the Media, The Media Freedom Internet Cookbook, Vienna 2004, 76–100

MASANGO CHENGETAI, The Internet Governance Forum: its Development, Function and Future, in: Benedek/Bauer/Kettemann (eds), Internet Governance and the Information Society, Utrecht 2008, 63–77

MAYER PETER, Civil Society Participation in International Security Organizations: The Cases of the NATO and the OSCE, in: Steffek/Kissling/Nanz (eds), Civil Society Participation in European and Global Governance, Basingstoke 2008, 116–139

MAYER-SCHÖNBERGER VIKTOR/ZIEWITZ MALTE, Jefferson Rebuffed: The United States and the Future of Internet Governance, The Columbia Science and Technology Law Review, Vol. 8, 2007, 188–228

MCLUHAN MARSHALL, The Gutenberg Galaxy: The Making of Typographic Man, Toronto 1962

MARZOUKI MERYEM, The «Guarantee Rights» for Realizing the Rule of Law, in: Jørgensen (ed.), Human Rights in the Global Information Society, Cambridge/Mass. 2006, 197 – 218

MICHAEL DOUGLAS C., Federal Agency Use of Audited Self-Regulation as a Regulatory Technique, Administrative Law Review, Vol. 47, 1995, 171–250

MITCHELL RONALD B., Sources of Transparency: Information Systems in International Regimes, International Studies Quarterly, Vol. 42, 1998, 109–130

MOCK WILLIAM, The Centrality of Information Law: A Rational Choice Discussion of Information Law and Transparency, John Marshall Journal of Computer & Information Law, Vol. 17, 1999, 1069–1100

MÖLLER CHRISTIAN, Internet Governance in the OSCE Region: Media Freedom, Human Security and the Multi-Stakeholder Approach, in: Benedek/Bauer/Kettememann (eds), Internet Governance and the Information Society, Utrecht 2008, 95–106

MÖLLER CHRISTIAN/AMOUROUX ARNAUD (eds), OSCE Representative on Freedom of the Media, The Media Freedom Internet Cookbook, Vienna 2004

MONTES IO, Legal Framework for Domain Names, Diss. Zurich 2005

MONTESQUIEU, De L'Esprit Des Lois, Introduction, des Notes et des Variantes par Gonzague Truc, Tome Permier, Paris 1944/45

MUELLER MILTON, Securing Internet Freedom: Security, Privacy, and Global Governance, Delft 2008 (MUELLER, Securing Internet Freedom)

MUELLER MILTON, Net Neutrality as Global Principle for Internet Governance (3rd November 2007), available at <http://www.internetgovernance.org/pdf/NetNeutralityGlobalPrinciple.pdf> (MUELLER, Net Neutrality)

MUELLER MILTON, Ruling the Root, Cambridge/Mass. 2002 (MUELLER, Ruling the Root)

MUELLER MILTON, ICANN and internet governance, in: info – the journal of policy, regulation and strategy for telecommunications information and media, Vol. 1, December 1999, 497–520, available at <http://ssrn.com/abstract=203973> (MUELLER, ICANN)

NEGROPONTE NICHOLAS, Being Digital, London 1996

NETANEL NEIL WEINSTOCK, Cyberspace Self-Governance: A Skeptical View from Liberal Democratic Theory, California Law Review, Vol. 88, 2000, 395–498

NIEBLING CHRISTIAN, Das Staatsrecht in der Rechtslehre Kants, München 2005

NOWAK MANFRED, Introduction to the International Human Rights Regime, Leiden 2003

O'HARA KIERON/STEVENS DAVID, inequality.com – Power, Poverty and the Digital Divide, Oxford 2006

OWENS RICHARD C., Human Rights and the Internet, CRi 2008, 161–168

PADOVANI CLAUDIA/PAVAN ELENA, Diversity Reconsidered in a Global Multi-Stakeholder Environment: Insights from the Online World, in: Kleinwächter (ed.), The Power of Ideas, Berlin 2007, 99–109

PAGE ALAN, Regulating the Regulator – A Lawyer's Perspective on Accountability and Control, in: Ferran/Goodhart (eds), Regulating Financial Services and Markets in the 21th Century, Oxford 2001, 127–149

PARÉ DANIEL J., Internet Governance in Transition: Who is the Master of this Domain?, Lanham 2003

PEAKE ADAM, Internet governance and the World Summit on the Information Society (WSIS), prepared for the Association for Progressive Communications (APC), June 2004, available at <http://www.itu.int/wsis/documents/background.asp?lang=en& theme=ip>

PERRITT HENRY H. JR., The Internet is Changing the Public International Legal System, Kentucky Law Journal, Vol. 88, 1999–2000, 885–955 (PERRITT, Internet)

PERRITT HENRY H. JR., The Internet as a Threat to Sovereignty? Thoughts on the Internet's Role in Strenghtening National and Global Convergence, Indiana Journal of Global Legal Studies, Vol. 5, 1998, 423–442 (PERRITT, Threat)

POPPER KARL, The Open Society and Its Enemies, London 1945

PRADA FERNANDO, A Systemic Vision for Financing the Information Society as a Global Public Good, in: Instituto del Tercer Mundo (ITeM), Information Society for the South: Vision or Hallucination?, Briefing Papers towards the World Summit of the Information Society, Montevideo November 2005, 47–70 (PRADA, Vision)

PRADA FERNANDO, Mechanisms for Financing the Information Society from a Global Public Goods Perspective, Instituto del Tercer Mundo (ITeM) WSIS Papers, revised version July 2005, available at <http://wsispapers.choike.org//papers/eng/fernando_is_gpg.pdf> (PRADA, Mechanisms)

PRICE MONROE E./VERHULST STEFAAN G., Selbstregulierung und Verhaltenskodizes als Grundlage von Internet-Politik, in: Waltermann/Machill (eds), Verantwortung im Internet – Selbstregulierung und Jugendschutz, Gütersloh 2000, 141–209

PUTTERMAN ETHAN, Rousseau on Agenda-Setting and Majority Rule, in: American Political Science Review, Vol. 97, 2003, 459–469

RAUSTIALA KAL, The Architecture of International Cooperation: Transgovernmental Networks and the Future of International Law, Virginia Journal of International Law, Vol. 43, 2002, 1–92

RAWLS JOHN, A Theory of Justice, Cambridge/Mass. 1971 (revised ed. 4th printing 2001)

REIDENBERG JOEL R., Resolving Conflicting International Data Privacy Rules in Cyberspace, Stanford Law Review, Vol. 52, 2000, 1315–1371

REINISCH AUGUST, The Changing International Legal Framework for Dealing with Non-State Actors, in: Alston (ed.), Non-State Actors and Human Rights, Oxford/New York 2005, 37–89

ROUSSEAU JEAN-JACQUES, The Social Contract and Discourses by Jean-Jacques Rousseau, translated with an Introduction by G. D. H. Cole, London/Toronto 1923, available at <http//oll.libertyfund.org>

RUGGIE JOHN GERARD, Reconstituting the Global Public Domain – Issues, Actors and Practices, European Journal of International Relations, 2004, 499–531 (RUGGIE, Global Public Domain)

RUGGIE JOHN GERARD, International Responses to Technology: Concepts and Trends, International Organization, Vol. 29, 1975, 557–583 (RUGGIE, Concepts)

SADOWSKY GEORGE, Internet Governance: The Importance of Access, in: Kleinwächter (ed.), The Power of Ideas, Berlin 2007, 68–74 (SADOWSKY, Importance of Access)

SADOWSKY GEORGE, Paving the Way for Internet-Rich Environments in Developing Nations, the Internet Society's Network Training Workshops, eOTI article, 2001, available at <http://www.isoc.org/oti/articles/0401/sadowsky.html> (SADOWSKY, Paving the Way)

SALAMUN KURT, Karl R. Popper – Aufklärungsethos und kritische Rationalität, in: Henningfeld/Jansohn (eds), Philosophen der Gegenwart, Darmstadt 2005, 49–67

SAMUELSON PAMELA, Privacy as Intellectual Property?, Stanford Law Review, Vol. 52, 2000, 1125–1173

SANO HANS-OTTO, Good Governance, Accountability and Human Rights, in: Sano/Alfredsson (eds), Human Rights and Good Governance, Building Bridges, The Hague 2002, 123–146

SAUL GRAHAM, Transparency and Accountability in International Financial Institutions, Washington D.C. 2003

SAYLE AMBER JENE, Net Nation and the Digital Revolution: Regulation of Offensive Material for a New Community, Wisconsin International Law Journal, Vol. 18, 2000, 257–285

SCHARPF FRITZ W., Regieren in Europa, Effektiv und demokratisch?, Frankfurt a.M./New York 1999

SCHMIDT MOGENS/COUDRAY SILVIE, Future Challenges to Building Knowledge Societies, in: Möller/Amouroux (eds), OSCE Representative on Freedom of the Media, The Media Freedom Internet Cookbook, Vienna 2004, 221–263

SCHNEIDER THOMAS, IGF: Neues Modell für einen Multi-Stakeholder Policy Dialog?, Medialex, 2007, 8–9

SCHWALB EGON, Some Aspects of International Jus Cogens as Formulated by the International Law Committee, American Journal of International Law, Vol. 61, 1967, 946–975

SCHWEIGHOFER ERICH, Role and Perspectives of ICANN, in: Benedek/Bauer/Kettemann (eds), Internet Governance and the Information Society, Utrecht 2008, 79–92 (SCHWEIGHOFER, Role and Perspectives of ICANN)

SCHWEIGHOFER ERICH, A Review of the Uniform Dispute Resolution Policy of the Internet Corperation for Assigned Names and Numbers (ICANN), Austrian Review of International and European Law, Vol. 6, 2001, 91–122 (SCHWEIGHOFER, Review of the UDRP)

SINGH J.P., Negotiation and the Global Information Economy, Cambridge/Mass. 2009

SLAUGHTER ANNE-MARIE, A New World Order, Princeton/Oxford 2004

SLOMANSON WILLIAM R., Fundamental Perspectives on International Law, 3rd ed., Wadsworth 2000

SOLUM LAWRENCE B., Models of Internet Governance, in: Bygrave/Bing (eds), Internet Governance: Infrastructure and Institutions, Oxford 2009, 48–91.

SOMMER JOSEPH H., Against Cyberlaw, Berkeley Technology Law Journal, Vol. 15, 2000, 1145–1232

SOUTER DAVID, The View from the Summit: A Report on the Outcomes of the World Summit on the Information Society, info – the journal of policy, regulation and strategy for telecommunications, Vol. 6, 2004, 6–11

SREENIVASAN GOPAL, What Is the General Will?, Philosophical Review, Vol. 109, 2000, 545–581

STEFFEK JENS/NANZ PATRIZIA, Emergent Patterns of Civil Society Participation in Global and European Governance, in: Steffek/Kissling/Nanz (eds), Civil Society Participation in European and Global Governance, Palgrave 2008, 1–29

STOOKES PAUL, A Practical Approach to Environmental Law, Oxford 2005

SUBEDI SURYA, The International Conference on Financing for Development, Monterrey Mexico 18–22 March 2002, International Law Forum du droit international, Vol. 4, 2002, 52–53

SUNSTEIN CASS, Republic.com, Princeton/Oxford 2001

TEGGE ANDREAS, Die Internationale Telekommunikations-Union, Baden-Baden 1994

THÜRER DANIEL, The Emergence of Non-Governmental Organizations and Transnational Enterprises in International Law and the Changing Role of the State, in: Hoffmann/Geissler (eds), Non-State Actors as New Subjects of International Law, Veröffentlichungen des Walther-Schücking-Instituts für Internationales Recht an der Universität Kiel, Band 125, Berlin, 1999, 37–58 (THÜRER, Changing Role of the State)

THÜRER DANIEL, "Soft Law" – eine neue Form von Völkerrecht, Zeitschrift für Schweizerisches Recht, Vol. 104, 1985, 429–453 (THÜRER, Soft Law)

THURNHERR DANIELA, Öffentlichkeit und Geheimhaltung von Umweltinformationen, Diss. Zurich 2003

TOMUSCHAT CHRISTIAN, Human Rights, Between Idealism and Realism, 2nd ed., Oxford/New York 2008

VAN DEN BOSSCHE PETER, The Law and Policy of the World Trade Organization, Cambridge/New York/Melbourne et al. 2005

VERDROSS ALFRED, Jus Dispositivum and Jus Cogens in International Law, American Journal of International Law, Vol. 60, 1966, 55–63 (VERDROSS, Jus Dispositivum and Jus Cogens)

VERDROSS ALFRED, Forbidden Treaties in International Law, American Journal of International Law, Vol. 31, 1937, 571–577 (VERDROSS, Forbidden Treaties)

WACKS RAYMOND, Law, Morality, and the Private Domain, Hong Kong 2000

WALKER CLIVE/WALL DAVID/AKDENIZ YAMAN, The Internet, law and society, in: Akdeniz/Walker/Wall (eds), The Internet, Law and Society, Longman 2000, 1–5

WEBER MAX, Wirtschaft und Gesellschaft, Grundriss der verstehenden Soziologie, 5th ed., Tübingen 1976

WEBER ROLF H., Internet Corporation for Assigned Names and Numbers (ICANN), in: Tietje/Brouder (eds), Handbook of Transnational Economic Governance Regimes, Leiden, forthcoming 2009 (WEBER, ICANN)

WEBER ROLF H., Accountability in Internet Governance, International Journal of Communications Law & Policy (IJCLP), Vol. 13, 2009, 144–159 (WEBER, Accountability)

WEBER ROLF H., Transparency and the Governance of the Internet, Computer Law & Security Report, Vol. 24, 2008, 342–348 (WEBER, Transparency)

WEBER ROLF H., International E-Trade, The International Lawyer, Vol. 41, 2007, 845–872 (WEBER, International E-Trade)

WEBER ROLF H., Looking ahead: more harmonization in the domain name system?, International Journal of Intercultural Information Management, Vol. 1, 2007, 74–84 (WEBER, More harmonization in the DNS)

WEBER ROLF H., Media Governance, Qualitätssicherung und öffentlich-rechtlicher Rundfunk, Jusletter of 16th July 2007, available at <http://www.weblaw.ch> (WEBER, Media Governance)

WEBER ROLF H., The Enhancement of Transparency in Internet Governance, in: Mercado Kierkegaard (ed.), Cyberlaw, Security & Privacy, Bejing 2007, 312–320 (and Ankara 2007, 515–529) (WEBER, Enhancement of Transparency)

WEBER ROLF H., From "Many Voices One World" to "Information Society", Experiences with and lessons from the MacBride-Report for the future of the WSIS-Principles, Computer Law Review International (CRi), 2004/4, 97–104 (WEBER, MacBride-Report)

WEBER ROLF H., Governance of Information Quality in Enterprises, in: Gasser (ed.), Information Quality Regulation: Foundations, Perspectives, and Applications, Baden-Baden 2004, 165–186 (WEBER, Governance of Information Quality)

WEBER ROLF H., Selbstregulierung und Selbstorganisation bei den elektronischen Medien, Medialex 2004, 211–217 (WEBER, Selbstregulierung und Selbstorganisation)

WEBER ROLF H., Towards a Legal Framework for the Information Society, Zurich 2003 (WEBER, Towards a Legal Framework)

WEBER ROLF H., Regulatory Models for the Online World, Zurich/Basel/Geneva 2002 (WEBER, Regulatory Models)

WEBER ROLF H./DÖRR BIANKA S., Digitale Verbreitung von Rundfunkprogrammen und Meinungsvielfalt, Zurich 2001

WEBER ROLF H./GROSZ MIRINA, Legitimate Governing of the Internet, International Journal of Private Law (IJPL), Vol. 2, 2009, 316–330 (WEBER/GROSZ, Legitimate Governing of the Internet) (also published in: Mercado Kierkegaard (ed.), Synergies and Conflicts in Cyberlaw, 3rd International Conference on Legal, Security and Privacy Issues in IT, Prague 2008, 300–313)

WEBER ROLF H./GROSZ MIRINA, Internet Governance – From Vague Ideas to Realistic Implementation, Medialex 2007, 119–135 (WEBER/GROSZ, Vague Ideas)

WEBER ROLF H./MENOUD VALÉRIE, The Information Society and the Digital Divide, Legal Strategies to Finance Global Access, Zurich/Basel/Geneva 2008

WEBER ROLF H./WEBER ROMANA, Social Contract for the Internet Community? Historical and Philosophical Theories as Basis for the Inclusion of Civil Society in Internet Governance?, SCRIPT-ed, Vol. 6, 2009, 90–105 (WEBER/WEBER, Social Contract)

WEBER ROLF H./WEBER ROMANA, Inclusion of the Civil Society in the Governance of the Internet, Can Lessons be Drawn from the Environmental Legal Framework?, Computer Law Review International (CRi) Vol. 1, 2009, 9–15 (WEBER/WEBER, Civil Society)

WEBER ROLF H./WEBER ROMANA, International ordre public for terrorism-related Internet content?, Humboldt Forum Recht, Vol. 4, 2009, 52–73 (WEBER/WEBER, ordre public)

WEINBERG JONATHAN, ICANN and the Problem of Legitimacy, Duke Law Journal, Vol. 50, 2000, 187–260

WEIRICH PAUL, Rousseau on Proportional Majority Rule, Philosophy and Phenomenological Research, Vol. 47, 1986, 111–126

WOLFRUM RÜDIGER, Legitimacy of International Law from a Legal Perspective: Some Introductory Considerations, in: Wolfrum/Röben (eds), Legitimacy in International Law, Berlin/Heidelberg/New York 2008, 1–24

WONG MARY W.S., Terrorism and technology: policy challenges and current responses, in: Ramraj/Hor/Roach (eds), Global Anti-Terrorism Law and Policy, Cambridge 2005, 199–224.

YU PETER K., Bridging the Digital Divide: Equality in the Information Age, Cardozo Arts & Entertainment Law Journal, Vol. 20, 2002, 1–52, available at <http://ssrn.com/abstract-ID=309841>

ZITTRAIN JONATHAN, The Future of the Internet and How to Stop It, London 2008

ZSCHIESCHE MICHAEL, Die Aarhus-Konvention – mehr Bürgerbeteiligung durch umweltrechtliche Standards?, Zeitschrift für Umweltrecht, Vol. 12, 2001, 177–183

Weblinks have been last checked on 29th April 2009.

Materials

The following documents listed here will not be cited anew in the footnotes

Weblinks have been last checked on 29th April 2009

United Nations

Aarhus Convention: UN/ECE Convention on Access to Information, Public Participation in Decision Making and Access to Justice, signed in Aarhus, Denmark on 25th June 1998; available at <http://www.unece.org/env/pp/documents/cep43e.pdf> (hereinafter: Aarhus Convention)

Economic Commission for Europe, The Aarhus Convention: An Implementation Guide, New York/Geneva 2000, available at <http://www.unece.org/env/pp/acig.pdf> (hereinafter: Economic Commission for Europe, Aarhus Convention Implementation Guide)

Exploratory report on the concept and possible scope of a code of good practice on participation, access to information and transparency in Internet governance, written on behalf of UNECE, the Council of Europe and APC by Professor David Souter for discussion at a workshop in Geneva on 23th May 2008, available at <http://www.unece.org/env/pp/electronictools/UNECE_CoE_APC_draft_report02.pdf, 16/17> (hereinafter: Exploratory report on the concept and possible scope of a code of good practice on participation)

Resolution 73 of the ITU Plenipotentiary Conference, Minneapolis, available at <http://www.itu.int/wsis> (hereinafter: Resolution 73 of the ITU Plenipotentiary Conference)

Monterrey Consensus of the International Conference on Financing for Development is entailed in: UN, Report of the International Conference on Financing for Development, Monterrey, Mexico, 2002, UN Doc A/CONF.198/11 (hereinafter: Monterrey Consensus)

Vienna Convention on the Law of Treaties, 23rd May 1969, UN Doc. A/Conf.39/27, 1155 UNTS 331, 8 ILM 679 (1969)

Council of Europe:

Democracy, Human Rights and the Rule of Law in the Information Society, Contribution by the Council of Europe to the 2nd Preparatory Committee for the World Summit on the Information Society (2003) (hereinafter: Council of Europe Contribution to the 2nd Preparatory Committee for the WSIS, Democracy, Human Rights and the Rule of Law in the Information Society)

Internet governance and critical internet resources, a report prepared by the Council of Europe secretariat, April 2009 (hereinafter: Council of Europe, Internet governance)

European Union (EU):

Commission of the European Communities, Advancing the Internet, Action Plan for the deployment of Internet Protocol version 6 (IPv6) in Europe, Brussels, 27th May 2008, COM(208) 313, available at <http://ec.europa.eu/information_society/policy/ipv6/

docs/european_day/comm-ipv6-final_en.pdf> (hereinafter: EU Commission, Advancing the Internet)

EC Directive 95/46/EC of the European Parliament and of the Council of 24th October 1995 on the protection of individuals with regard to the processing of personal data and on the free movement of such data, OJ L 281/31 (hereinafter: EC Directive on the Protection of Personal Data)

Internet Corporation for Assigned Names and Numbers (ICANN):

ICANN Adopted Budget: Fiscal Year 2009 ending 30th June 2009, 17th May 2008, version 3, updated 25th June 2008, available at <http://www.icann.org/en/financials/adopted-opplan-budget-v3-fy09-25jun08-en.pdf> (hereinafter: ICANN, Adopted Budget 2009)

ICANN Announcement, Biggest Expansion in gTLDs Approved for Implementation, 26th June 2008, available at <http://www.icann.org/en/announcements/announcement-4-26jun08-en.htm>

ICANN Announcement, ICANN Concludes Successful 32nd Meeting in Paris, 26th June 2008, available at <http://www.icann.org/en/announcements/announcement-3-26jun08-en.htm>

Annual Report 2005–2006, available at <http://www.icann.org/annualreport> (hereinafter: ICANN, Annual Report 2005–2006)

Annual Report 2008, available at <http://www.icann.org/annualreport> (hereinafter: ICANN, Annual Report 2008)

Bylaws for Internet Corporation for Assigned Names and Numbers, 15th February 2008 available at <http://www.icann.org/general/bylaws.htm> (hereinafter: ICANN Bylaws)

Bylaws for Internet Corporation for Assigned Names and Numbers, 15th December 2002, available at <http://www.icann.org/en/general/archive-bylaws> (hereinafter: ICANN Bylaws 2002)

Bylaws for Internet Corporation for Assigned Names and Numbers, 16th July 2000, available at <http://www.icann.org/general/archive-bylaws> (hereinafter: ICANN Bylaws July 2000)

Bylaws for Internet Corporation for Assigned Names and Numbers, 10th March 2000, available at <http://www.icann.org/general/archive-bylaws> (hereinafter: ICANN Bylaws March 2000)

Fact Sheet, last modified 7th April 2008, available at <http://www.icann.org/en/factsheets/fact-sheet.html> (hereinafter: ICANN, Fact Sheet)

Improving Institutional Confidence in ICANN, 16th June 2008, available at <http://www.icann.org/psc/iic/improving-confidence-en.pdf> (hereinafter: ICANN, Improving Institutional Confidence in ICANN)

Joint Project Agreement between the US Department of Commerce and the Internet Corporation for Assigned Names and Numbers, 29th September 2006, available at <http://www.ntia.doc.gov/ntiahome/domainname/agreements/jpa/ICANNJPA_09292006.htm> (hereinafter: Joint Project Agreement)

Management Operating Principles on Accountability & Transparency, Frameworks and Principles (Draft), 1st January 2008, available at <http://www.icann.org/ transparency> (hereinafter: ICANN, Management Operating Principles, Accountability & Transparency)

Memorandum of Understanding between the Department of Commerce and the Internet Corporation for Assigned Names and Numbers (ICANN), available at <http://www.ntia.doc.gov/ntiahome/domainname/icann.htm> (hereinafter: Memorandum of Understanding)

Internet Society (ISOC):

ISOC Advisory Council Charter, 30th October 2005, available at <http://www.isoc.org/orgs/ac/cms/index.php?page=advisory-council-charter> (hereinafter: ISOC Advisory Council Charter)

ISOC Annual Report 2007, available at <http://www.isoc.org/isoc/reports/ar2007> (hereinafter: ISOC, Annual Report 2007)

ISOC Articles of Incorporation, 2001, available at <http://www.isoc.org/isoc/general/trustees/incorp.shtml> (hereinafter: ISOC Articles of Incorporation)

ISOC Bylaws, 11th February 2001, available at <http://www.isoc.org/isoc/general/trustees/bylaws.shtml> (hereinafter: ISOC Bylaws)

ISOC Strategic Operating Plan of the Internet Society, 5th August 2005, available at <http://www.isoc.org/isoc/mission> (hereinafter: ISOC, Strategic Operating Plan).

United States (US):

United States Department of Commerce, Improvement of Technical Management of Internet Names and Addresses, Doc. Nr. 980212036-8036-01, 20th February 1998, available at <http://www.ntia.doc.gov/ntiahome/domainname/background.htm> (hereinafter: US Green Paper)

United States Department of Commerce, Management of Internet Names and Addresses, Doc. Nr. 980212036-8146-02, 4th June 1998, available at <http://www.ntia.doc.gov/ntiahome/domainname /background.htm> (hereinafter: US White Paper)

World Summit on Information Society (WSIS):

European Union (UK), Proposal for Addition to Chair's Paper Sub-Com A Internet Governance on Paragraph 5 "Follow-up and Possible Arrangements", Doc. WSIS-II/PC-3/DT/21-E, 30th September 2005, available at <http://www.itu.int/wsis/docs2/pc3/working/dt21.pdf> (hereinafter: European Proposal)

Human Rights in the Information Society (HRIS) Caucus, Towards an Information and Communication Society Respectful of Civil and Political Rights, as well as Economic, Social and Cultural Rights of Citizens, 31st Mai 2003, available at <http://www.iris.sgdg.org/actions/smsi/hr-wsis/hris-caucus-input.html> (hereinafter: HRIS Caucus, Towards a Respectful Information and Communication Society)

Working Group on Internet Governance (WGIG), Report of the WGIG, Working Group on Internet Governance (WGIG), June 2005, paras. 29–48, available at <http://www.wgig.org/docs/WGIGREPORT.pdf> (hereinafter: Report of the WGIG)

World Summit on Information Society (WSIS), Geneva Declaration of Principles, 12th December 2003, Doc. WSIS-03/GENEVA/DOC/4-E, available at <http://www.itu.int/wsis> (hereinafter: WSIS, Geneva Declaration of Principles)

World Summit on Information Society (WSIS), Geneva Plan of Action, 12th December 2003, Doc. WSIS-03/GENEVA/DOC/0005, 12, available at <http://www.itu.int/wsis> (hereinafter: WSIS, Geneva Plan of Action)

World Summit on Information Society (WSIS), Tunis Agenda for the Information Society, 18th November 2005, Doc. WSIS-05/TUNIS/DOC/7–E, available at <http://www.itu.int/wsis> (hereinafter: WSIS, Tunis Agenda)

World Summit on Information Society (WSIS), Tunis Commitment, 18th November 2005, Doc. WSIS-05/TUNIS/DOC/7, available at <http://www.itu.int/wsis>(hereinafter: WSIS, Tunis Commitment)

World Wide Web Consortium (W3C):

World Wide Web Consortium (W3C), Appendix 1, available at <http://www.w3.org/2005/03/Appendix.html> (hereinafter: W3C, Appendix 1)

World Wide Web Consortium (W3C) Member Agreement, available at <http://www.w3.org/2005/03/Member-Agreement> (hereinafter: W3C, Member Agreement)

World Wide Web Consortium (W3C), Process Document, 14th October 2005, Ian Jacobs, W3C (ed.), available at <http://www.w3.org/2005/10/Process-20051014/cover.html#toc> (hereinafter: W3C, Process Document)

RFC's (available at <http://www.rfc-editor.org>)

Vinton Cerf, The Internet Activities Board, May 1990, RFC 1160

Internet Engineering Task Force (IETF) of The Internet Society, Architectural Principles of the Internet, June 1996, RFC 1958

Internet Engineering Task Force (IETF), Internet Standards Process, October 1996, RFC 2026

Erik Huizer, IETF – ISOC Relationship, October 1996, RFC 2031

Network Working Group, Internet Transparency, February 2000, RFC 2775

Charter of the Internet Architecture Board, May 2000, RFC 2850

Paul Hoffman/Scott Bradner, Defining the IETF, February 2002, RFC 3233

Harald Alvestrand, Mission Statement for the IETF, October 2004, RFC 3935

Network Working Group, Structure of the IETF Administrative Support Activity (IASA), April 2005, RFC 4071

Network Working Group, RFC 3978 Update to Recognize the IETF Trust, October 2006, RFC 4748

Network Working Group, RFC 4181 Update to Recognize the IETF Trust, March 2007, RFC 4841

Network Working Group, Reflections on Internet Transparency, July 2007, RFC 4924, available at <http://www.rfc-editor.org>

Abbreviations

ACHR	American Convention on Human Rights
ALAC	(ICANN's) At-Large Advisory Comittee
APC	Accociation for Progressive Communications
approx.	approximately
Art.	Article
AS	Autonomous system (numbers)
ASO	(ICANN's) Address Supporting Organization
CA/Browser Forum	Certification Authority Browser Forum
ccNSO	(ICANN's) Country-Code Names Supporting Organization
ccTLDs	Country code Top-Level Domains
CEO	Chief Executive Officer
CESCR	Committee on Social, Economic and Cultural Rights
CETS	Council of Europe Treaty Series
CHF	Swiss franc
CFO	Chief Financial Officer
COM	(European) Commission Document
CORE	Council of Registrars
CSAIL	(MIT) Computer Science and Artificial Intelligence Laboratory
DARPA	US Defense Advanced Research Projects Agency
DHCPv6	Dynamic Host Configuration Protocol for IPv6
DIDP	(ICANN's) Documentary Information Disclosure Policy
DNS	Domain Name System
DNSSEC	Domain Name System Security Extensions
Doc.	Document
DSF	Digital Solidarity Fund
ECHR	European Convention for the Protection of Human Rights and Fundamental Freedoms
ECJ	European Court of Justice
ECOSOC	Economic and Social Council
ECT	Treaty establishing the European Community (consolidated text), OJ C 325 of 24th December 2002, 33–184
ed./eds	editor/editors
e.g.	for example
ERCIM	European Research Consortium for Informatics and Mathematics
ETS	European Treaty Series
ETSI	European Telecommunications Standards Institute
EuroDig	European Dialogue on Internet Governance
e2e	end-to-end (principle)

fn.	footnote
FSF	Financial Stability Forum
HRIS	Human Rights in the Information Society
GAC	(ICANN's) General Advisory Committee
GATS	General Agreement on Trade in Services (WTO)
GATT	General Agreement on Tariffs and Trade (GATT)
GDP	Gross Domestic Product
GNSO	(ICANN's) Generic Names Supporting Organization
GPC	(ISOC's) Global Policy Council
GPG	Global Public Goods
gTLDs	Generic Top-Level Domains
gTLD-MoU	Memorandum of Understanding for the gTLDs
HRIS	Human Rights in the Information Society (Caucus)
HTML	Hypertext Markup Language
IAB	Internet Architecture Board
IAHC	International Ad Hoc Committee
IANA	Internet Assigned Numbers Association
IARS	International Accounting Rate System
IASA	IETF Administration Support Activity
IBR	Internet Bill of Rights
ICANN	Internet Corporation for Assigned Names and Numbers
ICANN ACs	Internet Corporation for Assigned Names and Numbers Advisory Committees
ICANN SOs	Internet Corporation for Assigned Names and Numbers Supporting Organizations
ICC	International Chamber of Commerce
ICCPR	International Covenant on Civil and Political Rights
ICESCR	International Covenant on Economic, Social and Cultural Rights
ICMPv6	Internet Control Message Protocol Version 6
ICT	Information and Communication Technologies
ID	Identification
i.e.	that is; Latin abbreviation for "id est"
IETF	Internet Engineering Task Force
IFWP	International Forum on the White Paper
IGF	Internet Governance Forum
ILC	International Law Commission
ILM	International Legal Materials
IMF	International Monetary Fund
INRIA	Institut national de Recherche on Informatique et Automatique
INTA	International Trademark Association
IP	Internet Protocol

IPv4/IPv6	Internet Protocol version 4/6
IRP	Independent Review Panel
ISI	(US Department of Post and Telecommunications') Information Sciences Institute
ISOC	Internet Society
ISPs	Internet Services Providers
IT	Information Technology
ITR	International Terrestrial Reference System
ITU	International Telecommunciations Union
ITU-R	International Telecommunications Union's Radiocommunciation Sector
ITU-T	International Telecommunications Union's Telecommunication Standardization Sector
IXP	Internet Exchange Points
JPA	Joint Project Agreement
Jr.	Junior
LAP	London Action Plan
LDC	Least Developed Country
MAC	Media Access Control
MIT/LCS	Massachusetts Institute of Technolgy, Laboratory for Computer Science
MoU	Memorandum of Understanding
NAT	Network Address Translation
NGOs	Nongovernmental Organizations
No.	Number
NSF	US National Science Foundation
NSI	Network Solution Inc.
NTIA	National Telecommunications and Information Administration
NWIO	New World Information Order
OAS	Organization of American States
OAU	Organization of African Union
ODA	Official Development Assistance
OECD	Organization for Economic Cooperation and Development
OJ	Official Journal of the European Union
OSCE	Organization for Security and Cooperation in Europe
p/pp	page/pages
PAC	Policy Advisory Committee
para./paras.	paragraph/paragraphs
PETs	Privacy Enhancing Technologies
PIC	Platform for Internet Content Selection
POC	Policy Oversight Committee
PPP	Point-to-Point Protocol

PPP	Public-Private Partnership
PrepCom	(WSIS) Preparatory Committee
PSEC	IETF IP Security Protocol Working Group
P3P	Platform for Privacy Preferences
RALO's	(ICANN's) Regional At-Large Organizations
RFCs	Request for Comments
RIFs	Regional Internet Registries
RPAG	(ISOC's) Regional Policy Advisory Groups
RSSAC	(ICANN's) Root Server System Advisory Committee
R&D	Research and Development
S/MIME	Secure/Multipurpose Internet Mail Extensions
SMTP	Simple Mail Transfer Protocol
SR	Systematische Sammlung des (Schweizerischen) Bundesrechts
SSAC	(ICANN's) Security and Stability Advisory Committee
TAG	(W3C's) Technical Architecture Group
TCP/IP	Transfer Control Protocol/Internet Protocol
TFFM	Task Force on Financial Mechanism
TLDs	Top-level Domains
TLG	(ICANN's) Technical Liaison Group
TRIPS	Agreement on Trade-Related Aspects of Intellectual Property Rights (WTO)
UDHR	Universal Declaration of Human Rights
UDRP	(ICANN's) Uniform Domain Name Dispute Resolution Policy
UK	United Kingdom
UN	United Nations
UNCITRAL	United Nations Commission on International Trade Law
UNCTAD	United Nations Conference on Trade and Development
UNDESA	United Nations Department of Economic and Social Affairs
UNDP	United Nations Development Programme
UNECE	United Nations Economic Commission for Europe
UNESCO	United Nations Educational, Scientific and Cultural Organization
UNTS	United Nations Treaty Series
US	United States of America
USD	United States Dollar
VoIP	Voice over IP
Vol.	Volume
VPN	Virtual Private Networks
vs.	versus
WGIG	Working Group on Internet Governance
WIPO	World Intellectual Property Organization
W3C	World Wide Web Consortium

WSIS	World Summit on the Information Society
WTO	World Trade Organization
WWW	World Wide Web
XHTML	Extensible Hypertext Markup Language
XML	Extensible Markup Language

I. Introduction

A. Perceptions of Governance

1. Cyberspace and Governance

Almost 20 years ago, in July 1990, John Perry Barlow, together with Mitchell Kapor, wrote a first manifesto, entitled "Across the Electronic Frontier", containing the following "regulatory" appreciation:[1]

> "Over the last 50 years, the people of the developed world have begun to cross into a landscape unlike any which humanity has experienced before. It is a region without physical shape or form. It exists, like a standing wave, in the vast web of our electronic communication systems. It consists of electron states, microwaves, magnetic fields, light pulses and thought itself. (…)
>
> What it is eventually called, it is the homeland of the Information Age, the place where the future is destined to dwell."

In February 1996, John Perry Barlow issued a manifesto called "A Declaration of the Independence of Cyberspace", containing the following emphatic pronouncements:[2]

> "Governments of the Industrial World, you weary giants of flesh and steel, I come from Cyberspace, the new home of Mind. On behalf of the future, I ask you of the past to leave us alone. You are not welcome among us. You have no sovereignity where we gather. …
>
> I declare the global space we are building to be naturally independent of the tyrannies you seek to impose on us. You have no moral right to rule us nor do you possess any methods of enforcement we have true reason to fear.
>
> Governments derive their just powers from the consent of the governed. You have neither solicited nor received ours. We did not invite you. You do not know us, nor do you know our world. Cyberspace does not lie within your borders (…)
>
> Where there are real conflicts, where there are wrongs, we will identify them by our means. We are forming our own Social Contract. This governance will arise according to the conditions of our world, not yours. Our world is different."

---

1 Available at <http://www.eff.org/pub/Publication/John_Perry_Barlow/html/html/eff.html>.

2 Available at <http://www.eff.org/pub/Publication/John_Perry_Barlow/barlow0296.declaration>.

Copyright © Schulthess Juristische Medien AG, Zurich – Basel – Geneva 2009.
Published by Springer-Verlag GmbH Berlin Heidelberg 2010. All Rights Reserved

Subsequently, scholars of different disciplines have taken up BARLOW's ideas and have assigned attributes of independence to this new "province" of the world.[3] For example, it has been argued that the participants in cyberspace have created a "net nation",[4] based on the analogy that most laws were conceived in and for a world of atoms rather than bits.[5] On the legal side, the following description may serve as an example:[6]

> "There is no regulatory body, and computer users are capable of anything. The Internet is a place where anyone is welcome, regardless of gender, age, race, or association. (…) Since there is no regulatory body policing the Internet, the extent to which an individual is capable of speaking without restriction is an enigma."

In the meantime, scholars have become less euphoric about the independence of (and particularly the lack of a legal framework in) cyberspace. Critical voices do not find "cyberlaw" a useful concept;[7] moreover, they opine that defining a body of law in terms of technology would not be appropriate.[8] Nevertheless, hectic legislative activities during the past 15 years have shown that governments are indeed concerned about the "legalization" of cyberspace.[9]

As the acknowledgement of legal interests in the "structuring" of cyberspace and the Internet have increased, discussions about "governance" and its implications have also become more popular within the legal doctrine in the last 15 years.[10] "Governance" can be traced back to the Greek term "kybernetes", the "steersman", and the Latin word "gubernator" leading to the English notion "governor" and therefore addressing aspects of steering or governing behavior.

Different disciplines have addressed governance issues which, in a nutshell, can be summarized as the discussion on the appropriate allocation of duties and responsibilities as well as the proper structuring of the concerned "organs", thereby balancing performance-based strategic management and financial/economic con-

---

3 See also WEBER, Regulatory Models, 26; on the effects of BARLOW in general see GOLDSMITH/WU, 17 ss.

4 See SAYLE, 281 ss (with further references).

5 NEGROPONTE, 237.

6 BARBARA M. RYGA, Cyberspace: Contemplating the First Amendment in Cyberspace, Seton Hall Constitutional Law Journal, Vol. 6, 1995, 221, 223.

7 See SOMMER, 1147 and 1157 with further references; SOMMER, 1150, even points to the "perils of cyberlaw".

8 SOMMER, 1151, 1154.

9 On the "rise (and fall?)" of cyberspace in more details see WEBER, Regulatory Models, 26–29 with further references; see also BIEGEL, 31 ss; JOHNSON/POST, 1367, 1370, 1378; GIBSON, 485, 489; generally to the "production of cyberspace" see CRAMPTON, 14 ss.

10 The following text in the subsections I.A.1 and I.A.2 has been partly taken (and revised) from WEBER/GROSZ, Vague Ideas, 119 ss.

trol.[11] Or in other words: "Governance, at whatever level of social organization it may take place, refers to conducting the public's business—to the constellation of authoritative rules, institutions and practices by means of which any collectivity manages its affairs".[12]

What had first started out in the private domain under the well-known concept of "corporate governance" has eventually expanded to further regulatory structures, including the public sector, at both the national and the international level. Thereby, different governance theories have been developed, of which the so called "transgovernmentalism"[13] as well as concepts of "democratic governance",[14] taking particular account of aspects of fairness, are of special interest for the present topic of Internet governance and will subsequently be outlined in more detail.[15]

When sheding light on the central questions such as: who rules the Internet?, in whose interests?, by which mechanisms? and for which purposes?,[16] the concept of "co-regulation"[17] is of major importance in the field of the media in general. The original governance theories reflected the traditional view that strictly distinguished the State (public law) from society (civil law). These theories have been adapted to overarching networks and negotiation systems between these two sectors, thus forming a "cooperative approach to governance" that includes the whole of society, hence dividing responsibilities between public and private actors.[18]

As a form of global governance with reference to an international framework, Internet governance has to be seen in connection with the globalization of governmental relationships. Its aim is to provide a conceptual setting which describes the combination of rulemaking systems, political coordination and problem solving, making global Internet governance a highly ambitious and complex undertaking.

2. Governance and Internet's Legal Framework

As mentioned, originally the Internet developed beyond a regulatory legal framework and was mainly based on self-regulation by its users since the assumption prevailed that cyberspace was an independent new "province" in the world, not

11 For a sociological point of view see LANGE/SCHIMANK, 19; a political science approach is given by BENZ, 25; see also SIGH, 291 ss.
12 RUGGIE, Global Public Domain, 504.
13 For an introduction see SLAUGHTER, 15–27; for a further discussion see below IV.B.3.2.
14 See FRANCK, Fairness, 85–89.
15 For an overview on governance perceptions and developments see WEBER, Media Governance, nos. 5–11; DONGES, 10; DREZNER, 93/94.
16 HELD/MCGREW, 8.
17 On the term "co-regulation" see below I.C.2.2 a) (i).
18 WEBER, Media Governance, no. 9; MARSDEN, 76–100.

governed by laws in the legal sense, but rather by "codes" defining the Internet as parameters resulting from technical protocols, standards, and procedures.[19] Indeed, when addressing Internet governance, the particularities of the technical network have to be taken into account. In the meantime, however, the Internet as a subject to governance mechanisms is no longer challenged in principle, but the notion of "Internet governance" remains a fluid term with varying definitions.[20]

The necessity of the Internet's regulation by law seems clear: Since cyberspace cannot be entirely dissociated from real (physical) space, activities on the Internet inevitably have an influence on individuals and other entities in the real world; the citizen entering cyberspace and becoming a netizen cannot escape the national legal system.[21] Furthermore, the Internet has become too important for various stakeholders so as not to be regulated. As a prominent example, the success of electronic commercial transactions depends on the stability of the legal framework; only if the legal consequences of certain activities can be properly foreseen, is it possible for cross-border transactional e-business to come to life; for example it is imperative to establish a stable legal framework for e-trade.[22]

Indeed, it should not be overlooked that various aspects of the Internet are already managed by a number of different organizations, such as ICANN, WIPO, etc. The Domain Name System (DNS), in particular, was of major importance for the functioning and the regulation of the Internet and the beginnings of its governance.[23] Therefore, some scholars argue that in such a complex sociotechnical system as the Internet, control takes the form of institutions, not commands.[24]

---

19 On codes as the law in the Internet see LESSIG, Code; regarding its critical appraisal as well as the myth of independence of cyberspace and the role of law see WEBER, Regulatory Models, 25–26 and 93–99; on the decentralized standard-setting process see LIU, 587–588 and 595–604; PERRITT, 885–888; DREZNER, 107 ss; see also KLEINWÄCHTER, Kontroverse des WSIS, 29/30; GREWLICH, Governance, 53–56; MALCOLM, Governance, 50–69; SOLUM, 58.

20 For an overview of definitions see the paper of HOFFMANN; see also SOLUM, 52 ss.

21 KLEINWÄCHTER, Kontroverse des WSIS, 30; see also KURBALIJA, 105/06.

22 WEBER, International E-Trade, 852/53, 872; see also below VI.D.2.2.

23 An individual or an enterprise needs to have a specific address which allows him or it to be present world-wide on global networks. Domain names serve to identify the destination of communications, strengthen the organizational identity of the addressee, increase accessibility to information, and may have an economic value as substitutes for trademarks. Therefore, their management is of utmost practical, commercial and strategic importance. See WEBER, More harmonization in the DNS, 74–77; FROOMKIN, Wrong turn in cyberspace, 37–50.

24 MUELLER, Ruling the Root, 11; on the possible governance mechanisms see also MALCOLM, Governance, 18–21; on the institutional ecology see BENKLER, 395; on the regulability of the Internet in general see LESSIG, version 2.0, 31 ss.

Consequently, governance needs to address and balance the different interests of the many stakeholders involved when establishing a legal framework. As a rule, private corporations are generally interested in the Internet as an advertising and connecting platform for their businesses. In addition, States have become increasingly interested in their country domain over which they desire sovereign rights and control. The States' involvement on issues such as cybersecurity and stability also call for regulation and were addressed particularly in the light of measures to counteract terrorism. Especially in this context, the Internet has been affected by forms of censorship in various countries through the development of powerful surveillance devices which have been applied to trace the contents of communications and discover the identity of users, subjecting Internet service providers to international criticism.[25]

The Internet, as a system of interconnected computer networks transmitting data, is specially characterized by its world-wide reach, which takes no account of national boundaries. Furthermore, as a public sphere the Internet is generally open to everyone and accessible from everywhere. An adequate concept of governance should therefore have an international realm paying due attention to the globalization of international relations in the sense of global governance theories. In this context it has to be kept in mind that Internet technology itself has an accelerating effect on the process of globalization of legal rules, and (at least) a potential to improve the acknowledgment and reliability of the international law system.[26]

As a consequence, overarching networks between the public and the private law sectors, which encompass approaches of all of the stakeholders concerned in terms of the concept of "co-regulation", seem suitable.[27] Therefore, any definition of Internet governance should not only include technical issues, but also public policy aspects. This fact has been recognized and confirmed by the Geneva Declaration of Principles, released at the occasion of the first World Summit on the Information Society in December 2003: para. 35 expressly points to the public policy issues and the policy authority making it necessary to involve all stakeholders and relevant intergovernmental and international organizations.[28]

In light of such developments, WILLIAM DRAKE is correctly proposing to reframe the Internet governance discourse, based on the definition that Internet governance encompasses collective rules, procedures, and related programs intended to shape social actors' expectations, practices and interactions concerning Internet

25 CHEUNG/WEBER, 406 ss.
26 See WEBER, Regulatory Models, 42.
27 WEBER, Selbstregulierung und Selbstorganisation, 211–217; see also below I.C.2.2 a) (i).
28 Available at <http://www.itu.int/wsis/docs/geneva/official/dop.html>; see also ANTONOVA, 13/14.

infrastructure, transactions and content.[29] In particular, DRAKE refers to the following elements for reframing Internet governance:[30]

(1) The binary distinction between Internet governance matters pertaining to infrastructure and those pertaining to transactions and content should be overcome and replaced by collective rules, procedures and programs.

(2) Technical and policy issues in Internet governance often cannot be neatly separated since techniques rely on social theories.

(3) Internet governance involves much more than the challenges provided by the Internet Corporation for Assigned Names and Numbers (ICANN).

(4) The United Nations are not scheming to control the Internet; such an approach would subject the Internet to whims of bureaucracies and, in view of the majority situations within the UN, eventually to anti-American decision making.

(5) Internet governance should involve a heterogeneous array of formalized public and private sector rules (as described in the form of "co-regulation").

(6) The definitional ambiguities in Internet governance concern informal rules and the character of private sector governance.

(7) Most likely the boundary lines between Internet governance and the wider universe of ICT global governance will blur over time.

(8) Internet governance mechanisms vary widely in their institutional attributes, i.e. institutional forms encompass organizational settings, decision making procedures, different agreement types (treaties, recommendations, guidelines, declarations, memoranda of understanding, or even customs), scopes of topics, strengths, distributional bias, and monitoring compliances.

(9) Efficiency concerns suggest that form should follow function to the extent possible; since one size does not fit all circumstances, topic-specific solutions are to be looked at.

(10) Equity concerns are important and will become even more so as the Internet becomes increasingly pervasive and thus affects a wider range of social interests; therefore, equity concerns should also promote fairness and social justice.

---

29 DRAKE, Discourse, 3.

30 DRAKE, Discourse, 2 ss; the subsequent list summarizes the thoughts of DRAKE and abstains form giving specific comments.

(11) In particular, the effective inclusion of developing countries requires much greater attention; this aspect is mainly covered by the most recent activities of the Internet Governance Forum (IGF).[31]

(12) Similarly, greater attention is needed to come to an inclusion of civil society organizations, small and medium-sized enterprises, and individual users, as in the meantime done by the IGF.[32]

(13) A program of integrative analysis is required in order to reveal weaknesses, gaps and tensions in the Internet governance architecture.

(14) The global community lacks an appropriate institution which can pursue an integrative analysis and dialogue; partly, the IGF has assumed this role since its inauguration in 2006.[33]

(15) According to DRAKE, the World Summit on the Information Society (WSIS) process is unlikely to profoundly affect Internet governance.[34]

The most recent approach of some scholars addressing Internet governance issues puts even more emphasis on the civil liberties than on questions of institutional economics or transnational jurisdiction: In their view, Internet governance should be designed in a way which ensures that the parameters enable technical interoperability and economic competitiveness in light of making decisions about the public's civil liberties online.[35] Since the reflection of these values is of utmost importance, particularly in the field of human rights, such perceptions will be particularly addressed in the context of Internet governance topics.[36]

3. Mapping of Governance Issues

Internet governance issues are very wide and broad; problems occurring in the real world raise corresponding questions in the online world. Therefore, it is not surprising that numerous attempts have been made to achieve a mapping of Internet governance issues.[37]

---

31 See below III.D.

32 See below III.D.

33 See below III.D.

34 Internet governance aspects are indeed no longer dealt with by the WSIS, but since 2006 by the IGF; the activities of the IGF and—in its context or in parallel—of many organizations of civil society had an obvious influence, for example, on the decision-making process within ICANN, as far as the attention to multilingualism is concerned.

35 See DENARDIS, Protocol Politics.

36 See below VI.C.

37 KURBALIJA, 107/08, refers to a "variable geometry approach" in Internet governance.

An interesting approach is chosen by Don MacLean who distinguishes between fora and issues.[38] Accordingly, governance models related to fora can be split into an institutional level, a policy level and an issue level.[39] In respect of the particular issues addressed by Internet governance, the following matrix, highlighting aspects of the potential match or mismatch between different issues and governance tools, has been developed by MacLean:[40]

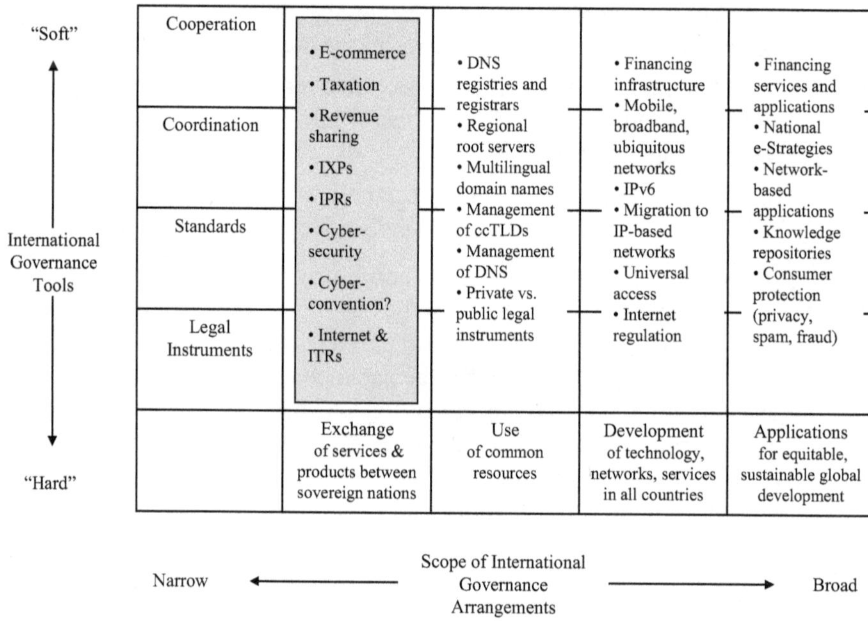

Although this matrix provides a good overview over the manifold issues of Internet governance it is quite complicated and does not correspond to the six main themes as identified by the participants of the Internet Governance Forum, namely openness, security, diversity, access, critical Internet resources, and emerging issues.[41] The Internet governance issues dealt with subsequently have been elected according to the IGF process.[42]

[38] MacLean, 10 ss.
[39] MacLean, 10/11.
[40] MacLean, 14; see also the approach of Kurbalija, 108.
[41] See below III.D.
[42] See below VI.

B. Perceptions of Information Society

During the last decade, terms such as "information age" and "information society" have become common. Indeed, the information society's myriad questions and specific problems can be analyzed from the different perspectives of many disciplines, which provide for their own definitions of "information society"; a universal terminology does not yet exist. But some common characteristics can be outlined as being indicators of the information society:[43]

(1) Information and knowledge are undoubtedly of paramount importance; theoretical knowledge is more than ever at the center of economic and social life.

(2) The information infrastructure that has been put in place to handle the information flow is in constant progress: Information and communication technologies (ICT) proliferate and advance, online services expand.

(3) The access and the use of ICT are fundamental indicators (as well as salient issues) of the information society. ICT are no longer the privilege of certain people, but are generally applied in private and business life; nevertheless, it cannot be overlooked that a large part of the world population (mainly in less developed countries) does not have access to ICT.

The vital role of ICT for national, regional and global economic growth seems quite obvious due to its potential to increase international integration, public sector effectiveness, efficiency, and transparency, all facts which are no longer questioned. New technologies have not only improved the storage, processing and transfer of information, but also created a new "habitat", new virtual spaces, where action, interaction, and exchange of information can take place.[44] The celebrated and visionary expectation of MARSHALL MCLUHAN's "Global Village" is not very far; the Internet, for instance, builds a "single field of experience" and allows "collective interplay".[45]

However, the term "Global Village" has been slightly distorted in the political discussions, shifting away from the original social communications theory approach to a more economic and structural concept, in which ICT are seen as motor of globalization.[46] From this perspective it cannot be overlooked that the "Global Village" is far from being established world-wide; moreover, the so-called "digi-

43 A more detailed description of the information society is given by WEBER/MENOUD, 1–3, on which this subsection is based.

44 O'HARA/STEVENS, 33.

45 MCLUHAN, 5.

46 WEBER/MENOUD, 2.

tal divide"[47] restricts millions of people from participating in the online exchange of information and communication, a fact which will not be overcome within the next few years.[48]

The topic "Internet Governance" is insofar related to the information society as governance issues are increasingly important because the information society is growing. In other words, the improvement and the spread of reliable ICT structures call for policy decisions which take into account the interests of all stakeholders participating in Internet matters. Therefore, the general principles of a sound information society need to be kept in mind for the governance discussions. The information society governance issues should be liaised to the Internet governance policy framework which could lead to the following mapping:[49]

Internet Governance Institutional Framework	**Internet Governance Policy Framework**	**Information Society Governance Issues**
"The international (governance) of the internet should be: • multilateral • transparent • democratic • with the full involvement of governments, the private sector, civil society, and international organizations"	Goals • Equitable distribution of resources • Facilition of access for all • Guarantee of a stable and secure functioning of the Internet, with multilingualism Roles • States: public policy • Private sector: technical & economic development • Civil society: community development • Intergovernmental org's: facilitating coordination of public policy issues • International org's: development technical standards and relevant policies	• Partnership among all stakeholders • Access to infrastructure and services •Access to information and knowledge • Capacity building • Confidence and security in the use of ICTs • Enabling environment • Social and economic applications • Cultural and linguistic diversity • Freedom of communication media • Ethical dimensions • International and regional cooperation

C. Regulatory Approaches

The establishment of an adequate Internet governance framework is a phenomenon giving rise to legal problems. Various regulatory models are available in

47 See below VI.E.1.

48 See also WEBER/MENOUD, 3–7 with further references.

49 MACLEAN, 11.

theory: Apart from the possibility of no regulation at all, the choice is principally between traditional national regulation, international agreements and self-regulation;[50] the latter two models merit to be discussed in more detail with the objective of laying the foundations for a substantive discussion on Internet governance problems.

1. International Agreements and Cooperation

1.1 Forms, Strengths and Weaknesses of International Law

a) Introduction

Structurally, international regulation is an appropriate response to international developments, since this approach is in a position to govern transboundary technical, economic, and legal topics.[51] The attempt to create an international legal framework cannot be successful by simply inducing a national legislator to take an initiative on behalf of the whole world; indeed, the situation is more complicated with regard to international law, which for example lacks a constitution as a fundamental source and basis of law, does not possess a legislative, nor administrative agencies to produce regulations, and does not have a general judiciary in place with plenary jurisdiction over disputes arising under international law.[52] As international regulation requires a collaborative effort by many nations, a majority of the nations whose citizens use the Internet tools would have to participate in the norm-setting process.[53]

In theory, international cooperation can be restricted to certain activities or have a broad scope covering many concerns and/or addressing aspects involving initial legislation as well as jurisdiction and enforcement. Notwithstanding the actual range of application of any international rule, and although the idea of constructing and maintaining an orderly, problem free, global legal framework may be very attractive, the complexities of any legal action a national legislator may have to face are not to be underestimated. Moreover, difficulties in connection with the limits of any legal system in Internet governance might even be compounded in a global context, considering the fact that substantial differences may exist in the value-making processes of the participating nations.[54]

[50] The following subsection is drawn and summarized from WEBER, Regulatory Models, 61–89, containing further references.

[51] Regarding the purpose of legal harmonization see FROOMKIN, Governance, 623/24.

[52] See for example BUERGENTHAL/MURPHY, 18/19.

[53] On the perspectives of international law see also GREWLICH, Governance, 25 and below V.E.

[54] BIEGEL, 158.

According to legal doctrine, international law is traditionally defined as the law that governs relations between States, i.e. originally only States were acknowledged as the subjects of international law.[55] Contemporary international law tends to acknowledge a wider definition of international law, according to which this field is no longer limited merely to relations between nation States but generally accepts the increasing role of other international players such as individual human beings, international organizations or juridical entities.[56] Nevertheless, history has shown that general principles of law somehow related to international law as perceived today have been developed under different social circumstances:

- Roman law recognized the "ius gentium", a linguistic root for the notion of "international law". Roman courts applied this law to foreigners who were not citizens of the Roman empire if the application of generic Roman law seemed inappropriate and the relevant foreign law was unknown.[57] However, ius gentium did not reflect a legal relationship between different subjects of international law, i.e. States at that time, but provided for a law applicable between Romans on the one and non-Romans or foreigners on the other hand, i.e. civil law according to today's understanding.
- Originating in Italian cities in the 11th century, medieval merchants developed the so-called lex mercatoria (law of merchants), consisting of customary legal rules that were applied in trade and other commercial transactions.
- With GROTIUS' oeuvre "De iure belli ac pacis" published in 1620, a paradigm shift was introduced and some principles of "modern" international law developed influenced by the classical tradition and for the first time acknowledging a theoretical system of equilibrium of souvereign States.[58]
- Already in the 19th century, national governments recognized and acknowledged that certain matters (such as postal services, telecommunications, shipping, intellectual property) needed general rules to facilitate transnational trade.

The consent of any State to accept rules of international law of whatever nature, implies a limitation of the discretionary powers of that State and its sovereign decision-making processes. This restriction, however, can make sense if similar

55 BUERGENTHAL/MURPHY, 1.

56 BUERGENTHAL/MURPHY, 2 with further references; on the international legal background see also SLAUGHTER, 506–508.

57 GAIUS, Institutes of Justinian, Book I, Title II, § 9.

58 HUGO GROTUIS, De Jure Belli ac Pacis Libri Tres, Book I, Chapter I, § 14; in 1789 JEREMY BENTHAM declared the law of nations an "international law" (BIEGEL, 159); see also BUERGENTHAL/MURPHY, 12 ss with a historical overview.

rules are applicable in other States, and if entering into such legal regulations helps solving problems.[59]

The statute of the International Court of Justice distinguishes four pertinent provisions of international law, namely (1) international conventions, (2) international customary rules, (3) general principles of law, and (4) judicial decisions as well as "the teachings of the most highly qualified publicists of the various nations".[60] The legal doctrine has generally regarded this enumeration as a list of the "sources" of international law, despite an explicit reference to such an interpretation from the legal text. A strict hierarchy among these sources does not seem to exist in light of the provision's wording, however, in practice the ICJ will be expected to observe the order in which they appear. Furthermore, it is difficult to clearly differentiate between the formal and the material sources of international law.[61]

b) International Conventions

A major source of international law consists in the (mainly written) agreements between States, often called treaties, pacts, protocols, accords, or conventions.[62] These agreements—whether bilateral or multilateral in nature—have a contractual character; the legally binding relations are entered into voluntarily (pacta sunt servanda).[63] Sovereign States have the authority to account for the mandatory character of agreements, and such agreements are legally binding because they have been concluded by sovereign States consenting to be bound;[64] in other words, State sovereignty includes the possibility to negotiate international affairs.[65]

Contrary to national laws, the interpretation of international agreements must often be based on customary law and general legal principles. A good number of such rules has been combined and classified in the Vienna Convention on the Law of Treaties adopted in 1969 and ratified in 1980. This Vienna Convention, containing provisions as to the conclusion, amendment, invalidity, and termination of international relations, is now a major source of the international legal framework between States.[66]

59 Biegel, 159/60.
60 Article 38 para. 1 of the ICJ Statute; Janis, 10 fn. 3.
61 Brownlie, 3–5.
62 Janis, 9–16; Slomanson, 325–328; Kurbalija, 110/11.
63 For analogies Slomanson, 324–325; on the historical background from Machiavelli to Grotius see Janis, 165.
64 Janis, 10.
65 On the problem of the democratic legitimacy of international agreements see Froomkin, Governance, 626.
66 Janis, 14, 19; Biegel, 160/61.

c) Customary Rules

In order to delineate customary rules, two fundamental elements have been distinguished by international legal doctrine. First of all, a uniform, consistent and general practice is a necessary prerequisite for a customary rule to develop. Provided that such practice exists, no particular duration is required. Furthermore, such a practice has to be accompanied by the existence of an "opinion iuris et necessitates", i.e. a "sense of legal obligation, as opposed to motives of courtesy, fairness, or morality".[67]

Although the International Court of Justice is presumed to know the law and to apply a custom as a legal source, even when it has not been expressly pleaded, it will generally be an ambitious task to prove the existence of customary law, and none the less the justifiable expectation of its future observance.[68]

Customary law was already known in Roman times.[69] GROTIUS also pointed out the substantial influence of tradition on legal developments.[70] Furthermore, customary practices in international trade formed the notions of "course of dealing" or "attendant social norms". In the Middle Ages, a specific branch of customary rules in the field of trade was called "lex mercatoria", it was established to govern transnational commerce (law of medieval merchants).[71] Some of these principles have been partly taken over by international organizations and could indeed also play a role in the online world, particularly in regard to e-business.[72]

Beyond their character as a legal source, customary legal rules can also supplement international agreements and cover topics left untouched by them.[73] In and by their international practice, States may implicitly consent to the creation and application of customary rules.[74] The respective "normal" guidelines are often more generally applicable than provisions of international agreements. Nevertheless, a general disadvantage of customary rules consists in the fact that the practice as well as the subjective perception of existing legal obligations will generally not be sufficiently consistent to establish legal predictability.[75] Furthermore, the risk should not be underestimated that different lawmakers and courts will interpret customary rules in different ways.

---

67 BROWNLIE, 7–10.

68 For more details JANIS, 5, 41–54; SLOMANSON, 15–19.

69 Institutes of JUSTINIAN, Book I, Title II, § 9.

70 HUGO GROTIUS, De Jure Belli ac Pacis, Libri Tres, Book 1, Chapter 1, § 14.

71 See BURNSTEIN, 103–105, 108.

72 BIEGEL, 161.

73 JANIS, 42; KURBALIJA, 111/12.

74 JANIS, 42/43.

75 See also JANIS, 53.

With regard to the online world, it is particularly difficult to crystallize a corresponding practice, let alone an opinio iuris. Although habits may evolve and even be generally accepted, it would be difficult to identify them as sufficiently uniform, consistent practices. Indeed, it is deemed difficult for online "rules" to become more or less uniform over time and consistent in such a lively and short-lived environment as cyberspace. In the meantime, however, legal scholars have begun to identify some kinds of implicit rules in cyberspace emerging from customary practice and social behavior in the online world and are partly even advocating that the Internet might improve the coherence of such customary rules.[76] Nevertheless, tradition based on customs can lead to agonizing effects of a "Law of Fashion" (JOHN LOCKE) which was already questioned by PLATO almost 2500 years ago.[77]

d) General Legal Principles

Most States accept the fact that some general principles of law exist, such as good will, equal treatment and fairness in trade, principles of consent and of reciprocity, legal validity of agreements etc. In many cases such general principles may derive from State practice. They can be illustrated as "abstractions from a mass of rules" which have been "so long and so generally accepted as to be no longer *directly* connected with state practice."[78] To some extent, basic legal principles are considered to be an expression of "natural law".[79] Similarly as in view of customary rules, the difficulty in enforcing such principles will differ on a case-by-case basis and may provide for an ambitious task in terms of proof.[80]

Although non-consensual sources such as general legal principles are relatively vague, these rules play an important role in international law. Practically, general legal principles can be so fundamental that they can be found in virtually every legal system[81] and recognized by the individuals and organizations concerned.[82] Such rules, however, are rarely used to reverse or modify existing provisions in international agreements.[83]

---

76 See BIEGEL, 161; PERRITT, Internet, 899; MALCOLM, Governance, 134/135.

77 See KONSTANTINOS KOMAITIS, Internet Governance: Why Plato is still Relevant, International Journal of Communication Law & Policy, Vol. 13, 2009, 126 ss.

78 BROWNLIE, 19, emphasis adopted.

79 JANIS, 59–63.

80 JANIS, 55–59; SLOMANSON, 23/24.

81 Article 38 para.1c) of the Statute of the International Court of Justice restricts the term to "law recognized by civilized nations."

82 For more details FRIEDMANN, 279–299; see also NETANEL, 496/97.

83 The norms can have a gap-filling function (JANIS, 56/57).

Legal scholars have theoretically differentiated between three groups of general principles of law:

- Many legal principles are—following MONTESQUIEU[84]—an expression of natural law[85] or are drawn from its precedents. Natural law is therefore to be found in any community, however, international law based on such a perception threatens to become mere morality.[86]
- General legal principles might establish ius cogens (compelling law), norms believed to be so fundamental that they could even invalidate rules based on international agreements or customary practices.[87] The concept of ius cogens leads to the development of an international public order.[88]
- Equity[89] is a third non-consensual source of international law, recognized as a means to supplement or modify the written provisions of international agreements and customary law. Equity mainly refers to the principle of fairness in global trade.[90]

1.2 Future Prospects

Notwithstanding the difficulties of establishing and implementing international law, this approach should be kept in mind and be subject to further elaboration. Due to the fact that the effects of international agreements are more far-reaching and their problem-solving potential more substantial than national legal approaches, a successful step towards the international regulation of Internet issues is due to have significant importance. Centuries of practice have shown that governments, courts, and private persons have accepted and applied international legal practices that undergo continuous development.[91]

For the time being, international law consists of a patchwork of different legal sources, restricted to the minimal rules which nation States were willing to agree on following tough negotiations and therefore tending to possess a limited scope of application. Nevertheless, even if international implementation may be a challenging undertaking at times, experience with international law has proven that global problems can be tackled by the international community.[92] For the online

84 MONTESQUIEU, 527, 531.
85 On the history see JANIS, 59–61.
86 KUNZ, 951 ss.
87 JANIS, 62; for more details see VERDROSS, Forbidden Treaties, 571 ss.
88 JANIS, 64; see also VERDROSS, Jus Dispositivum and Jus Cogens, 55 ss; SCHWALB, 946 ss.
89 ARISTOTLE, Nicomachean Ethics, Book 5, Ch. 10, refers to what is legally just.
90 JANIS, 66/67.
91 JANIS, 5; PERRITT, Threat, 435.
92 BIEGEL, 184.

world, most certainly a transnational approach is inevitable; national State rules, based on domestic sovereign thinking alone, will not overcome pending problems or offer viable solutions.

At the forefront, the international community will have to strengthen efforts to negotiate and conclude additional treaties.[93] Additionally, customary law could theoretically be a promising approach to form international rules, because of its high degree of acceptance with in the international community and the fact that concerned parties are familiar with their applicable contents. However, developments in cyberspace may not permit enough established practice to form a custom as well as norms that will "consolidate" over time.[94] Nevertheless it should not be underestimated that some customary rules may be applied by analogy to the Internet online world.

Applying general principles of law is a worthwhile approach; in particular, the principle of good will in business might also play a role in the online world. Nevertheless, many problems (for example access or security) cannot be easily solved on the basis of general legal principles. These principles could, however, serve as basis for establishing self-regulation, for example in the form of codes of conduct.[95]

2. Self-Regulation

2.1 Background

As already discussed,[96] early promoters of cyberspace believed that national government rules had no place in the online world because of its geographical extension, and for that reason the Internet deserved autonomous regulation. Even if this approach did not turn out to correspond to reality,[97] it should not be overlooked that autonomous regulation can indeed play a role in the online world. However, cyberspace promoters, especially JOHNSON and POST, do not actually call for an established form of self-regulation, but rather favor "spontaneous" regulation. Such regulatory autonomy[98] means independence from any structured form of rulemaking.[99]

---

93 See also PERRITT, Threat, 437.
94 BIEGEL, 185.
95 See below I.C.2.2 b)
96 See above I.A.1.
97 Particularly critical in this respect NETANEL, 402/03, 446–451.
98 JOHNSON/POST, 1367, 1370 ss.
99 Therefore "spontaneous" regulation does not (fully) correspond to self-regulation.

Traditionally, self-regulation (self-government)[100] follows the principle of subsidiarity, meaning that government intervention should only take place if participants of a specific community are not able to find suitable solutions (structures, behaviors) themselves. Since, however, public law defines the contours of private law it also affects the role of self-regulatory mechanisms.[101]

Self-regulation refers to rules considered by the "governed" people to be adequate guidelines. The legitimacy of self-regulation is based on the fact that private incentives lead to a need-driven rule-setting process.[102] In principle, self-regulation is justified if it is more efficient than State law and if compliance with rules of the community is less likely than compliance with self-regulation.[103] Seen from a broader perspective, self-regulation is "law" which is responsive to changes in the "environment", and which develops and establishes rules independent of the principle of territoriality.[104] The legal doctrine increasingly acknowledges the merits of self-regulation.[105]

2.2 Forms and Legal Quality of Self-Regulation

a) Forms of Self-Regulation

(i) In general, two different *notions* of self-regulation are usually distinguished as follows:[106]

- Self-regulation can be a concept of private groups which—based upon their own initiative—make decisions that limit their own behavior, bound only by broad laws of general application.
- Self-regulation can be a concept occurring within a framework that is set by the government (directed self-regulation);[107] sometimes, this form is called audited self-regulation.[108]

The second self-regulatory approach has gained importance during the last decade: If the government provides for a general framework which can be substantiated by the private sector often the term "co-regulation" is used. "Co-regulation"

---

100 See GIBBONS, 483/84, 509/10; GREWLICH, Governance, 139/40; WEBER, Selbstregulierung und Selbstorganisation, 21 ss.

101 PERRITT, Internet, 892.

102 On the notion of self-regulation in more detail see CAMPBELL, 758 ss; BLACK, 32 ss; KURBALIJA, 112 ss; LANGHART, 93–95.

103 GIBBONS, 509.

104 JOHNSON/POST, 1370.

105 See GIBBONS, 509 ss; GREWLICH, Governance, 139 ss, 291 ss, 323ss.

106 GREWLICH, Governance, 139.

107 See LANGHART, 111–114.

108 See MICHAEL, 174–76.

generally means that the State legislator sets the legal yardsticks and leaves the codification of the given principles into specific rules to private bodies.[109] In addition, the government remains involved in the self-regulatory initiatives at least in a monitoring function supervising the progress and the effectiveness of the initiatives in meeting the perceived objectives.[110] Such kind of mixed approaches can serve legitimate State purposes as well as efforts of the private sector.[111]

(ii) The *scope* and framework of self-regulation obviously depend on practical circumstances of real life. Among others, the following factors can play a role:[112]

- The self-regulatory approach requires a specific design depending on the number of "participants" and the nature of the problems concerned.
- Different self-regulatory approaches need to be established (1) in case participants in the same market segment agree on "private rules",[113] and (2) in case market participants from different segments want to adopt "private rules" in order to balance conflicting interests.[114] In the online world, these two sides of the market are reflected by the Internet industry and the Internet users. Self-regulation can contain either procedural or substantive rules.

(iii) The legal doctrine distinguishes between different *forms* of self-regulation:[115]

- A traditional form of self-regulation can be seen in the so-called collective arrangements within the same market segment or between enterprises of different market segments; in both cases, conflicts with antitrust laws can occur.
- A less strict form of self-regulation is obtained in the case of gentleman's agreements; often these are not directly enforceable, but put the participants under a certain moral pressure to comply and act in accordance with the rules.
- Rules of conduct or behavior aim to induce participants to voluntarily observe certain specified provisions.[116] A kind of code of conduct particularly applicable in the Internet world is called "netiquette".

---

109 WEBER, Selbstregulierung und Selbstorganisation, 212.

110 See Department of Trade and Industry/Department for Culture Media and Sport, A New Future for Communications, Communications White Paper, 2000, available at <http://www.communicationswhitepaper.gov.uk/pdf/index.htm>, 83.

111 See ROBERT BALDWIN/MARTIN CAVE, Understanding Regulation, Theory, Strategy and Practice, Oxford 1999, 136.

112 For more details see WEBER, Selbstregulierung und Selbstorganisation, 22–25.

113 LANGHART, 116–118.

114 LANGHART, 118–124.

115 More details with graphic overviews are given by WEBER, Selbstregulierung und Selbstorganisation, 23, 25.

116 This notion of self-regulation comes close to the lex mercatoria (see also PERRITT, Threat, 433/34).

b) Legal Quality of Self-Regulation

Since provisions of a self-regulating nature are not enforceable through public action and usually do not address an unlimited number of people in a general and abstract way, such rules do not have the legal quality of laws. At best, self-regulation can result in moral pressure or lead to sanctions based on contract or association law.[117]

Contracts can be seen as "private laws or norms" enforceable with the support of government bodies.[118] Certain forms of self-regulation are quite close to the understanding of contracts, in particular gentleman's agreements. Nevertheless, even if this term contains the word "agreement", these legal relations do not fully correspond to contractual arrangements. Quite often, the participants in a gentleman's agreement consider this understanding a non-binding undertaking. The same principles apply in respect to codes of conduct.[119]

Self-regulation can also be understood as a social control model. Such a system of control consists of rules of normatively appropriate human behavior, similarly to the notion of a "social contract".[120] Socially accepted rules are enforced through reputational sanctions. The social control model uses the social constraints of a cohesive community; sanctions range from truthful negative gossip to excommunication from the community.[121] The problem with this theoretical approach is that the "participants" of the Internet world are not members of a community, or, in other words, citizens cannot be easily removed from the online community.[122]

During the last few years, the legal doctrine has developed a new notion of law, namely "soft law" for commitments in international relations expressing more than just policy statements, but less than law in its strict sense, although possessing a certain proximity to law and a certain legal relevance.[123] Nevertheless, the term "soft law" does not yet have a clear scope or reliable content. Particularly in respect to the enforceability of rules, law is either in force ("hard law") or not in force ("no law"), meaning that it is difficult to distinguish between various degrees of legal force. Generally, it can only be said that soft law is a social notion close to law and that it usually covers certain forms of expected and acceptable codes of conduct, such as resolutions of international organizations as well as non-binding agreements. Furthermore, the role of soft law for the development of

[117] See WEBER, Selbstregulierung und Selbstorganisation, 26.
[118] For more details see WEBER, Selbstregulierung und Selbstorganisation, 27.
[119] See PRICE/VERHULST, 190 ss.
[120] GIBBONS, 518 ss; ELLICKSON, 124 ss; for further details see below IV.A.
[121] GIBBONS, 520; ELLICKSON, 287.
[122] GIBBONS, 522.
[123] The term "soft law" was introduced by DUPUY, 252; see also THÜRER, Soft Law, 452.

good faith and customary rules and the need to establish rules to govern international relations should not be underestimated. Moreover, soft law may contribute essentially with respect to the interpretation of international law.[124]

2.3 Strengths and Weaknesses of Self-Regulation

a) Strengths of Self-Regulation

Self-regulation is often used by the participants of a specific community to enhance the image of the market segment and improve marketing possibilities. Furthermore, self-regulation tends to be used as a measure to induce government legislators not to pass any formal laws.[125] These tactical and psychological factors, however, do not mean that self-regulation would have no further advantages. The general benefits of self-regulation include the following:[126]

- Rules created by the participants of a specific community are efficient because they respond to real needs and mirror the technological aspects as they actually occur.
- Meaningful self-regulation provides the opportunity to adapt the legal framework to changing technology in a flexible way.
- Since rules are not imposed by a specific authority in cases of self-regulation, chances are good that the rules contain incentives for compliance.
- Self- regulation can usually be implemented at reduced costs (saving effect).
- Effective self-regulation induces the concerned people to be open to a permanent consultation process in respect to development and implementation of the rules. Their involvement is necessary to ensure that the self-regulatory mechanism accurately reflects real needs.

Apart from a self-regulatory stand-alone scheme, it is also possible that such "private norms" can help to interpret general legislative norms allowing for broad discretion in their scope of application.[127]

b) Weaknesses of Self-Regulation

Certain weaknesses of self-regulatory mechanisms cannot be overlooked. These mainly concern the processes of implementation of "private norms" as well as the

---

124 WEBER, Selbstregulierung und Selbstorganisation, 28; THÜRER, Soft Law, 439 ss; MALCOLM, Governance, 136 ss.

125 WEBER, Selbstregulierung und Selbstorganisation, 26.

126 See JOHNSON/POST, 1370; GREWLICH, Governance, 324/25; MICHAEL, 181 ss; PRICE/VERHULST, 157 ss.

127 WEBER, Selbstregulierung und Selbstorganisation, 26.

procedure for their enforcement.[128] In particular, the following should be taken into account:

- In the context of the creation of self-regulatory provisions the quality of the "legislative" process can hardly be judged. Often the process is not transparent. Furthermore, legitimacy concerns may arise in light of the fact that the establishment of self-regulatory provisions does not necessarily involve each and every relevant group.[129] Furthermore, self-regulation tends to concentrate on concrete rules applicable on a case-by-case basis, rather than on establishing general provisions. Finally, such voluntary rule-setting mechanisms may entail the risk that some participants spend significant resources on the development, monitoring, and implementation of codes and standards, while others simply profit from their existence ("free rider-problem").
- Self-regulatory mechanisms are not generally binding in legal terms. Regardless of their legal quality as such, "private norms" are only applicable to those parties who have accepted the regulatory framework.[130] The need for some kind of submission to self-regulation results in the problem of "outsiders" or "dark sheep"; if the number of outsiders is substantial, the self-regulatory regime loses its legitimacy.
- Since self-regulations are very much based upon their acceptance by the concerned market participants, standards could differ from sector to sector depending on the willingness of the concerned people to agree on the scope of the self-regulatory framework. Consequently, even on adjacent markets the level of protective measures may not be equivalent and can lead to unjustified discrepancies.
- Self-regulatory mechanisms are not always stable. At virtually any time, participants in a specific community can decide to abolish a self-regulatory structure without being forced to follow a specific procedure. The risk thus exists that a self-regulatory framework that has become too burdensome for the key players in the market will be weakened eventually.[131]
- Furthermore, a main problem of self-regulation concerns the lack of enforcement procedures; non-compliance with "private norms" does not necessarily lead to sanctions. Possibly and to the extent of which a contract has been concluded, the threat of being forced to pay a penalty can be a sanction; also, if market participants are organized in an association, "dark sheep" could be re-

[128] WEBER, Selbstregulierung und Selbstorganisation, 28, 30; CAMPBELL, 717/18; PERRITT, Internet, 923.

[129] WEBER, Selbstregulierung und Selbstorganisation, 28/29; on the unreviewable discretion also MICHAEL, 190/91.

[130] WEBER, Selbstregulierung und Selbstorganisation, 31/32.

[131] WEBER, Selbstregulierung und Selbstorganisation, 32.

moved as members of the association. Contrary to the norms of governmental regulation, real enforcement is not possible in case of self-regulation.[132]

Nevertheless, even considering the weaknesses of self-regulatory mechanisms described above, the advantages of having efficient and flexible rules in an area where government regulations are hard to establish should not be underestimated. Self-regulation is thus an adequate tool to tackle "legal" problems in the Internet world.

3. Concluding Remarks

The theoretical analysis of the mentioned regulatory models leads to the concluding remark that any approach on its own would probably fail in reality. A mix or mosaic of different concepts seems to be unavoidable.[133] Hereinafter, within the discussion of the substantive issues, the inherent limits of each theoretical approach must be kept in mind.

At any rate, however, the online world needs a governance scheme composed of policy rules which can exercise an umbrella function for members of the society in order for them to be able to co-exist harmoniously in these new spaces created under the notion of the Internet.[134] Furthermore, lawmakers need to understand (i) how spaces are created, (ii) why they are created, and (iii) what such spaces must do to prosper.[135]

132 WEBER, Selbstregulierung und Selbstorganisation, 30/31; PERRITT, Internet, 923.
133 WEBER, Regulatory Models, 100.
134 GREWLICH, Governance, 12; to the architecture of control in general see LESSIG, version 2.0, 38 ss.
135 WEBER, Regulatory Models, 100.

II. Historical Developments

The attempt at introducing principles of governance in respect to information services, now transmitted by way of the Internet, is insofar not completely new as the issue of the information flow has been a discussion topic for many decades. The Internet is a new online medium, but tradional media also exercise cross-border information services which have called for an applicable legal framework. Subsequently, the main aspects of the regulatory frameworks related to the flow of information are summarized, followed by a description of the organizational Internet regulations' developments.

A. From McBride to WSIS

Already in the seventies of the last century, a group of block-free countries discussed the idea of a "New World Information Order" (NWIO).[136] After its launch at the Summit of Algier in 1973, it soon became obvious that the NWIO would have to be incorporated into a broader concept of a third world development policy.

At the same time, the Soviet Union proposed to release a "Mass Media Declaration" under the auspices of the United Nations Educational, Scientific and Cultural Organization (UNESCO). This attempt provoked the opposition of Western and Northern countries which were afraid that the principle of the "free flow of information" could be jeopardized.[137] Subsequently, parallel to the negotiations on a possible Declaration, at the Nairobi Conference of the UNESCO in 1976, the idea prevailed that it would be wise to start inquiries about the factual background of the information and communication order.

In December 1977, an International Commission for the study of information and communication problems, appointed by the UNESCO, began its work. Within two years, the Commission, chaired by Nobel laureate Sean MacBride, compiled an impressive Report under the title "Many Voices One World". The purpose of the Report consisted in the description of a possible "new world information and communication order which was defined as a process, not actually as a given set of conditions and practices".[138] Already during the working processes of the

---

136 The text of this subchapter is a shortened version of Weber, McBride-Report, 97–104; additional references can be drawn from this article.

137 See Leonard R. Sussman, What the North Wants from UNESCO, Mediator and Catalyst, UNESCO Sources, October 1989, 13.

138 Foreword to the MacBride-Report by Director-General M'Bow, xviii.

Copyright © Schulthess Juristische Medien AG, Zurich – Basel – Geneva 2009.
Published by Springer-Verlag GmbH Berlin Heidelberg 2010. All Rights Reserved

MacBride-Commission, the participants of the UNESCO General Conference agreed in November 1978 on the "Declaration on the Fundamental Principles Concerning the Contribution of the Mass Media to Strengthening of Peace and International Understanding, the Promotion of Human Rights and to Encountering Racialism, Apartheid and Incitement to War".[139]

This agreement (which was reached within a relatively short period of time), based on the wording of the originally proposed Mass Media Declaration, was possible due to the fact that the developed countries offered infrastructural help and in return developing countries declined substantive requests. At the end of the negotiations the objective of the Mass Media Declaration only consisted of a "new equilibrium and greater reciprocity in the flow of information" in order to correct existing inequalities (Art. VI); the preamble of the Declaration acknowledged the efforts of the developing countries "for the establishment of a new, more just and more effective world information and communication order"; the developed countries accepted to contribute to the "promotion of a free flow and wider and better balanced dissemination of information".

The MacBride-Report contains much more substance than the Mass Media Declaration and addresses a large number of matters, in particular the following topics:[140]

- Strengthening independence and self-reliance;
- Social consequences of the NWIO and new tasks;
- Professional integrity and standards;
- Democratization of communication;
- Fostering international cooperation;
- Provision of more extensive financial resources in favor of less developed countries.

After the publication of the MacBride-Report, only a fairly limited discussion took place within the UNESCO; the General Conference of 1980 in Belgrad solely took note of the Report without initiating specific action, the only exception being the incorporation of the "International Programme for the Development of Communication" according to Recommendation 78 of the Report.[141] Moreover, the topic of the information and communication order became less relevant in the eighties of the previous century due to the fact that both the United States and the United Kingdom cancelled their membership between 1983 and 1985. This led to a vital financial crisis of the UNESCO and forced the UN-Organization to

[139] UNESCO Doc. 20C/Res. 4.9.3/2 of 28th November, 1978.
[140] MacBride-Report, 14 ss and 254 ss.
[141] UNESCO Doc. 21C/Res. 4/19.

concentrate on its "survival plans". Consequently, the UNESCO did not have the funds to subsidize the communication infrastructure of less developed countries and the project of a NWIO disappeared from the political agenda.

Some 10 to 15 years later, with the rise of the Internet, regulatory needs became apparent again. At first instance, the main topics—as will be discussed subsequently[142]—concerned the design and architecture of the technical infrastructure and the allocation of addresses. Apart from these apparent issues, the International Telecommunications Union (ITU) took up the discussion of a global information and communication order.[143] The major objectives of an information society which should serve the world-wide population became an important topic of the first World Summit on the Information Society (WSIS) held in Geneva in December 2003. Policy issues are contained in the Declaration of Principles, supplemented by an Action Plan outlining possible steps for the implementation of the key requirements of an inclusive society and by a Digital Solidarity Agenda listing co-operative measures.[144] The inclusion of public policy principles into the international agenda related to Internet governance was later strengthened at the second WSIS in Tunis not least thanks to the establishment of the Internet Governance Forum.[145]

In the aftermath of the publication of the MacBride-Report no specific political movement or follow-up action was taken. Even if such activities should have been exercised in a financially difficult period of the UNESCO, it cannot be overlooked that the approach chosen in the late seventies of the last century was too idealistic: The considerations of the MacBride-Report were based on the idea of common values and common aims of the countries in the field of communications and disregarded the commercial side of any information order.[146] Furthermore, expectations of goodwill in sponsoring, cost reduction and preferential tariffs for developing countries were expressed without getting into the details of the corresponding actions. It was also not clear whether the developing countries should have a primary responsibility to undertake the necessary changes to overcome their dependency on the information flow order. Assuming the existence of such a responsibility, appeared to be particularly problematic considering the fact that not all countries have equal rights or full access to available information.[147]

142 See below II.B.

143 For further details see Weber, Legal Framework, 26/27.

144 Available at <http://www.itu.int/wsis/docs/geneva/official/dop.html>.

145 See below III.D.

146 A typical example can be seen in the objective to grant priority to non-commercial forms of communications in expanding systems over commercial activities; even a reduction of the commercialization of communications is recommended (MacBride-Report, 260).

147 Weber, MacBride-Report, 102.

Therefore, lessons should be learnt from the experiences made subsequent to the presentation of the MacBride-Report: Idealistic goals and wishes can hardly be realized; moreover, it is imperative—in respect to the newly established principles of the WSIS—to focus on the actual implementation of the general objectives in reality. In other words, political declarations do not bring much actual progress if the implementation is not secured by an appropriate organizational approach and by the availability of financial funds.[148]

B. From ICANN to WSIS

1. First Steps towards the Internet's Institutionalization

In order to be present on the Internet for private or professional purposes, an individual or an enterprise needs to have a specific address. Comparable to a piece of land in the real world, the establishment of a domain name traces out a "territory in cyberspace", which enables e-business. Therefore, the management of domains as names in the online world is of utmost practical, commercial, and strategic importance.[149] Originally, the Internet address system was based on the unique Internet Protocol (IP) numbers which are assigned to every website and allow for their identification by the system. By 1984, these addresses had become very complicated to use, what lead to the translation of the numbers into words and their organization into the generic domains by the Domain Name System.[150]

The United States quickly identified the meaning of the DNS and developed a "soft Internet policy" by making an effort to institutionalize its management. At first, the domain names were managed by Network Solutions, a monopoly company in the United States. In 1989, the US Department of Commerce concluded a contract with the Department of Post and Telecommunications' Information Sciences Institute (ISI) at the University of Southern California, establishing the Internet Assigned Numbers Association (IANA). The organization assigned IP addresses, allocated domain names and monitored root services. Therewith, the United States' forerunner position in the global field of the Internet became evident. In contrast, international attempts to find a global framework for interna-

148 Weber, MacBride-Report, 102 and 104.

149 Kleinwächter, Internet Governance, 74.

150 Jonathan Postel, the Internet pioneer, coordinator of the DNS defined seven "generic top level domains" (gTLDs): three for universal use (".com" for commercial activities, ".org" for organizations and "net" for networks), three for use in the US (".gov" for governments, ".edu" for universities, "mil" for the military) and one for intergovernmental treaty organizations (".int"). Countries and territories were given their own last names with the so-called "country code top level domain" (ccTLDs).

tional communication in general did not expand to cyberspace for a long time. In particular, the discussion of a "New World Information Order" (NWIO) in the early 1970s did not mention the role of the Internet.[151] The political and economic dimensions of the Internet became only more apparent in the early 1990s, when the National Science Foundation (NSF) received the authority to commercialize the Internet and develop the World Wide Web (WWW). It was against this background that a world-wide structure of the DNS was called for.[152]

2. Internet Corporation for Assigned Names and Numbers (ICANN)

In the light of these developments the United States discussed possible changes of the DNS on the basis of a Green Paper and a subsequent White Paper brought forth by the government. In July 1997, the privatization of the DNS was suggested which led to the foundation of the "Internet Corporation for Assigned Names and Numbers" (ICANN) in November 1998, as the successor of IANA.[153]

ICANN is established as a private non-profit organization, governed by Californian law and domiciled in California. It used to operate based on a Memorandum of Understanding (MoU) with the US Department of Commerce.[154] The MoU expired on September 30, 2006, but was extended through the adoption of the three-year Joint Project Agreement between the two parties.

The organization is responsible (i) for allocating Internet Protocol (IP) addresses, (ii) for managing the root servers that enable devices on the network to identify

[151] See above II.A. and Kleinwächter, Beyond ICANN vs. ITU.

[152] Postel, director of the IANA, wanted to move IANA under the Internet Society (ISOC), a policy oriented network of Internet technicians. However, this plan was opposed to in particular by the US government, the private industry, and the European Commission. In order to avoid governmental and commercial control, Postel initiated the so-called "Interim Ad Hoc Committee" (IAHC) for the purpose of establishing a "Policy Oversight Committee" (POC), as the highest decision making body for the management of domain names. Furthermore, the plan was to move the "A Root Server" from Herndon, Virginia, to Geneva, Switzerland. Moreover, the "Memorandum of Understanding on generic Top Level Domains" was signed on 2nd May 1997, and deposited by the ITU. It was established as a legally non-binding recommendation signed by governmental and business institutions. However, both of the new initiatives were faced with opposition by the US government which particularly wanted to keep the "A Root Server" within the United States (for further information see Kleinwächter, Beyond ICANN vs. ITU, 234–240).

[153] On the establishment of ICANN see Weinberg, 192–212; Montes, 38–46; on the development of the White Paper as a partial solution see Liu, 600–604 and 615–618; Harvard Law School, 1671–1676; Malcolm, Governance, 33–50.

[154] For further details see below III.C.1.

and find each other and for information to travel from senders to recipients, finally, (iii) for managing the generic (gTLD) and country code (ccTLD) Top-Level Domain name systems. Hence, ICANN is responsible for deciding which devices can connect to the Internet and under which names.[155] New Top Level Domain names have to be approved by the US Government, which thus has a form of veto power over the Internet addressing system.[156]

The corporate organization of ICANN is based on the decision making capacity of the providers and users of Internet services, however, national governments can exercise an influential role through the "Governmental Advisory Committee" (GAC) within the organization.[157] Furthermore, a specific dispute resolution process has been established in the form of the Uniform Domain Name Dispute Resolution Policy (UDRP).[158] Institutionally, the organization is governed by fifteen voting directors, establishing the "Board of Directors". Originally five members of ICANN's Board were to represent users in specific geographic regions and were elected through Internetwide elections. However, due to the very small percentage of Internet users actually participating in the elections, these At-Large Board Members were reduced in number in 2002 by an internal selection process which took into consideration geographic diversity.[159] The critizism which arose as a result of this reduction was not appeased, but on the contrary, further irritated by ICANN's adoption of techniques from US administrative agencies aiming to enhance legitimacy.[160]

Although ICANN was constituted as a global organization, it has been materially influenced by and politically dependant on the United States. Over time, and in particular during the first phase of the WSIS, many objections were levied against this fact. The theoretical possibility that the US could limit the access to the root servers or hinder Internet communications by deleting country codes from the root has sufficed for culminating in a call for an internationalized organization, notwithstanding the fact that ICANN has not proven these concerns to be right. Particular objections have addressed ICANN's lack of an adequate democratic and legitimized background and have expressed misgivings sustaining that pri-

155 Mayer-Schönberger/Ziewitz, 192–193 with further references; see also <http://www.icann.org/general>.

156 See Mayer-Schönberger/Ziewitz, 194 with further references.

157 For further details see below III.C.3.

158 See Uniform Domain Name Dispute Resolution Policy, adopted on 26th August 1999, available at <http://www.icann.org/udrp/#udrp>.

159 Articles VI-X of the ICANN Bylaws 2002; see also Mayer-Schönberger/Ziewitz, 196; Weber, ICANN, IV.

160 Mayer-Schönberger/Ziewitz, 196; Weinberg, 235, 245, 249, 258; for further details see below III.C.4 c).

vately established rules supposedly erode the power of sovereign States.[161] As one of the most important actors in the present Internet governance system, ICANN is a prevailing issue on the international level dealing with the World's Information Society.

3. World Summit on the Information Society and Internet Governance Forum

In the light of the growing importance of information and communication, the International Telecommunication Union (ITU) passed a resolution in 1998 proposing the idea of a World Summit on the Information Society (WSIS) under the auspices of the United Nations.[162] In 2001, the ITU Council endorsed the approach of holding the Summit in two phases, the first one in Geneva in 2003, the second one in Tunis two years later.[163] This led to the adoption of the General Assembly Resolution 56/183,[164] which set as objective of the WSIS the development of an international "common vision and understanding of the information society" and the adoption of a declaration of fundamental principles for the creation of an information society which is truly global in participation and benefits. Internet governance was not yet explicitly mentioned in these resolutions, however, the ITU Plenipotentiary Conference did stipulate its consciousness "of the fact that the globalization of telecommunications ought to take account of a harmonious evolution in policies, regulations, networks and services in all Member States".[165]

3.1 First Phase: Geneva 2003

In the first phase, after two preparatory committee meetings (PrepComs) and various regional conferences had been held, the Geneva Conference in December 2003 finally enacted the Geneva Declaration of Principles and the Geneva Plan of Action, which define a framework for future actions.

---

161 On the criticisms on ICANN see the overview provided below III.C.4.2); see also WEBER, ICANN, VI; WEBER/GROSZ, Legitimate Governing of the Internet, 317–320; MAYER-SCHÖNBERGER/ZIEWITZ, 194–198; KLEINWÄCHTER, Beyond ICANN vs. ITU, 4; WEINBERG 192 ss; LIU, 616–618; on the distinction between public and private ordering in particular see PERRITT, 921–923; MALCOLM, Governance, 46–50.

162 Resolution 73 of the ITU Plenipotentiary Conference; for further details on the historical developments see MALCOLM, Governance, 324–329.

163 Resolution 1179, ITU Council 2001, available at <http://www.itu.int/wsis>.

164 UN General Assembly Resolution 56/183 (31st January 2002), UN Doc. A/RES/56/183.

165 See Resolution 73 of the ITU Plenipotentiary Conference.

During the series of regional conferences, Internet governance gained more and more attention, but none of the PrepComs managed to find an agreement on the emerging topic. Difficulties arose whilst trying to find a common notion of the term "Internet governance". Part of the difficulty in coming to an agreement at international level was due to the fact that depending on whether the focus is set on the technical management of the Internet's core resources in terms of a restrictive definition, or whether the Internet is understood more extensively including further issues arising such as e-commerce, spam, cybercrime etc., different notions of the concept exist.

What became clear during the discussions though, was that both approaches have considerable economic and political implications.[166] In particular, discussions on the responsibility for Internet governance were an issue, putting the activities of ICANN in the center of the debate. On the one hand, the US government—supported by the European Union, Canada, Australia and Japan—adopted the position that the principle of "private sector leadership" had stood the test of time concerning the management of the Internet under ICANN;[167] they referred to the narrower definition of Internet governance and held the view that the present system under ICANN worked, making changes needless. On the other hand, China, India, Brazil, and South Africa, supported by the majority of the developing countries, argued that Internet governance was related to national sovereignty, making it necessary to put governments in charge of the process, preferably under the supervision of the UN organization ITU.[168]

What started out as one topic amongst many, became one of the most conflict-laden issues at the conference; the first part of the World Summit almost collapsed under its weight.[169] Eventually, the Geneva Declaration of Principles explicitly acknowledged the evolved importance of the Internet and stipulated that Internet governance should constitute a core issue of the Information Society agenda. In terms of a general mandate, it was stated that "the international management of the Internet would have to be multilateral, transparent and democratic, with the full involvement of governments, the private sector, civil society and international organizations. It ought to ensure an equitable distribution of resources, facilitate access for all and guarantee a stable and secure functioning of the Internet, taking into account multilingualism".[170]

166 Kleinwächter, Internet Governance, 215/16; Hubbard/Bygrave, 215–217.

167 This approach was emphasized in the Joint Project Agreement between the US Department of Commerce and ICANN in 2006.

168 Peake, 5.

169 Kleinwächter, Internet Governance, 215; see also Malcolm, Governance, 329–334.

170 WSIS, Geneva Declaration of Principles, Article 48.

The emphasis on such a "multi-stakeholder" approach for Internet Governance was explained with the following words:

> "(a) Policy authority for Internet-related public policy issues is the sovereign right of States. They have rights and responsibilities for international Internet-related public policy issues; (b) The private sector has had and should continue to have an important role in the development of the Internet, both in the technical and economic fields; (c) Civil society has also played an important role on Internet matters, especially at community level, and should continue to play such a role; (d) Intergovernmental organizations have had and should continue to have a facilitating role in the coordination of Internet-related public policy issues; (e) International organizations have also had and should continue to have an important role in the development of Internet-related technical standards and relevant policies."[171]

This approach was maintained throughout the further discussions.[172] It stands out as an example of the previously mentioned model of "co-regulation" between different stakeholders, it overrides differences between the public and the private sectors and appears to be only consequent for the field of the Internet.

3.2 Working Group on Internet Governance (WGIG)

The WSIS Geneva Declaration of Principles asked the former UN Secretary General, Kofi Annan, "to set up a working group on Internet Governance [WGIG]" by 2005, which would ensure a mechanism for the full and active participation of all of the stakeholders involved and "investigate and make proposals for action, as appropriate, on the governance of the Internet".[173] The WGIG was established as a compromise between the governments that felt that the WSIS process was not open enough to the private sector and civil society, and the governments that wanted a process within the UN framework. Its implementation was borne by the hope to resolve the differences of opinion that had become apparent during the first phase of the WSIS.[174] The Swiss diplomat Markus Kummer was appointed Executive Co-ordinator of the WGIG's Secretariat.

In July 2005, the WGIG submitted its report to the UN Secretary General, in time for the second phase of the WSIS. Pursuing the mandate received, it had mainly

171 WSIS, Geneva Declaration of Principles, Article 49.

172 This approach was specially supported by Switzerland which organized particular Multistakeholder Summit Events; see Abriss über das Engagement der Schweiz als Gastland der ersten Phase des WSIS im Dezember 2003 in Genf, 9, available at <http://www.bakom.ch/org/international>; Compilation of Comments received on the Report of the Working Group on Internet Governance (WGIG), Doc. WSIS-II/PC-3/DT/7(Rev. 2)E, 23rd September 2005, 3, available at <http://www.itu.int/wsis/wgig/index.html>.

173 WSIS, Geneva Declaration of Principles, Article 50.

174 Peake, 5; in general see Hubbard/Bygrave, 217–221.

concentrated its attention on (i) developing a working definition of Internet governance; (ii) identifying the public policy issues which were relevant for Internet governance; and (iii) developing a common understanding of the respective roles and responsibilities of governments, existing international organizations and other fora as well as those of the private sector and civil society in both developing and developed countries.[175]

The working definition of Internet governance proposed was based on a broad notion and reinforced the concept of co-governance. As a result "Internet governance is the development and application by governments, the private sector and civil society, in their respective roles, of shared principles, norms, rules, decision-making procedures, and programs that shape the evolution and use of the Internet".[176] This definition was supplemented by the establishment of four key clusters of public policy issues[177] as well as the identification of 16 issues of highest priority.[178]

Last but not least, the Report of the WGIG recognized that the management of the Internet should not be inherited by a sole organization or a sole group of stakeholders, but rather by all of the stakeholders in mutual co-action such as the governments, the private sector, civil society, the academic and technical community, as well as the already existing intergovernmental and international organizations and similar fora. Thereby, the WGIG stressed the need for enhanced communication, coordination and cooperation between the different stakeholders, in a so-called "multilayer multiplayer mechanism", and particularly pointed out the importance of full participation of developing countries. The establishment of a "multilateral, transparent and democratic" multi-stakeholder forum, preferably linked to the United Nations, was recommended as a space for dialogue, involving

175 See WSIS, Geneva Plan of Action para. 13; for more details see Malcolm, Governance, 334–342.

176 Report of the WGIG, paras. 10, 29–48.

177 The public policy issues addressed were: (i) "issues relating to infrastructure and the management of critical Internet resources"; (ii) "issues relating to the use of the Internet, including spam, network security and cybercrime"; (iii) "issues that are relevant to the Internet but have an impact much wider than the Internet and for which existing organizations are responsible, such as intellectual property rights (IPRS) or international trade"; and (iv) "issues relating to the developmental aspects of Internet governance, in particular capacity-building in developing countries" (Report of the WGIG, para. 13).

178 These are: (i) administration of the root zone files and system; (ii) interconnection costs; (iii) Internet stability, security and cybercrime; (iv) spam; (v) meaningful participation in global policy development; (vi) capacity-building; (vii) allocation of domain names; (viii) IP addressing; (ix) intellectual property rights (IPR); (x) freedom of expression; (xi) data protection and privacy rights; (xii) consumer rights; (xiii) multilingualism; (xiv) convergence; (xv) next generation networks; (xvi) e-commerce (Report of the WGIG, paras. 15–28).

all stakeholders and relevant organizations, without allowing any government to have a pre-eminent role in international Internet governance.[179] Furthermore, the Report provided for recommendations to address Internet-related issues and for allocating specific and adequate governance mechanisms to the 16 issues of highest priority mentioned above.[180]

3.3 Second Phase: Tunis 2005

In the forefront of the second phase of the WSIS, taking place in Tunis in November 2005, the organization of the Internet remained a very controversial issue. The United States had opposed any internationalization of the process, arguing that the current DNS under the auspices of ICANN provided for security and stability, something an intergovernmental process could not guarantee. The European countries formally proposed a more international and intergovernmental framework for the Internet's naming and numbering, and therewith provoked high-tension with the US. Nevertheless, the mutual adoption of the Tunis Commitment and the Tunis Agenda succeeded on 18th November, 2005, not at least to their partly open wording.[181]

The Agenda outlines a medium-term future for global Internet governance.[182] The working definition of Internet governance, established by the WGIG, was adapted with special emphasis on the fact that Internet governance "includes more than Internet naming and addressing. It also includes other significant public policy issues such as, inter alia, critical Internet resources, the security and safety of the Internet, and developmental aspects and issues pertaining to the use of the Internet".[183] Moreover, it recognizes that social, economic and technical issues encompassing affordability, reliability and quality of service are further issues at hand.[184]

The establishment of the Internet Governance Forum (IGF) under the auspices of the United Nations was considered as being of particular importance. Its mandate was very carefully formulated: it stipulates the purpose of the forum to support

---

179 Report of the WGIG, paras. 29–48. This approach also corresponds to general tendencies in international law questioning the sole subjectivity of nation States and gradually acknowledging new actors at the international level; see also MALCOLM, Governance, 103–131.

180 KLEINWÄCHTER, Internet Governance, 219–220; for further information on the WGIG see KLEINWÄCHTER, Kontroverse des WSIS, 30–32; MALCOLM, Governance, 334–342; HUBBARD/BYGRAVE, 221–230.

181 For more details on the WSIS 2005 see MAYER-SCHÖNBERGER/ZIEWITZ, 190–191; MALCOLM, Governance, 342–349.

182 See WSIS, Tunis Agenda, paras. 29–82.

183 See WSIS, Tunis Agenda, para. 58.

184 See WSIS, Tunis Agenda, paras. 34, 58 and 59.

the United Nations Secretary General in convening a new forum for multi-stakeholder policy dialogue. The IGF was set up as a consequence of a compromise: In the light of the United States' reluctance, its mandate includes only soft powers, such as the discussion of public policy issues, the facilitation of discourse and exchange of information and best practices, the advising of all stakeholders, the contribution to capacity building for Internet governance in developing countries etc.[185] Thereby, it is made clear that the IGF has "no oversight function" and does "not replace existing arrangements, mechanisms, institutions or organizations", but involves them and takes advantage of their expertise. The forum is "constituted as a neutral, non-duplicative and non-binding process", having no involvement in day-to-day technical operations of the Internet, but featuring a "multilateral, multi-stakeholder, democratic and transparent" structure.[186]

Furthermore, the recognition of "enhanced cooperation in the future" was underlined as an important outcome.[187] The process towards enhanced cooperation was set out "to be started by the UN Secretary General, involving all relevant organizations by the end of the first quarter of 2006".[188] However, in practice the international attempts did not go beyond the installation of the Internet Governance Forum.[189]

3.4 IGF Meetings

The Inaugural Meeting of the Internet Governance Forum (IGF) took place in Athens from 30th October to 2nd November 2006.[190] There were six panel sessions taking place in a format of interactive multi-stakeholder panels with remote participants joining via blogs, chat rooms, e-mail and text messaging. Concerns voiced in the run-up to the meeting that controversial themes would not find a

185 See WSIS, Tunis Agenda, para. 72.

186 See WSIS, Tunis Agenda, paras. 73 and 77.

187 See WSIS, Tunis Agenda, para. 69 stating that: "We further recognize the need for enhanced cooperation in the future, to enable governments, on an equal footing, to carry out their roles and responsibilities in international public policy issues pertaining to the Internet, but not in the day-to-day technical and operational matters, that do not impact on international public policy issues".

188 See WSIS, Tunis Agenda, para. 71.

189 See Mayer-Schönberger/Ziewitz, 209; WSIS, Tunis Agenda, paras. 69 and 71 were affirmed anew in the tenth session of the UN Economic and Social Council (ECOSOC) Commission on Science and Technology for Development (CSTD) from 21st–25th May 2007, see Draft resolution for adoption by the Council, paragraph 2, in: CSTD Report on the tenth session, Doc. E/CN.16/2007/4, ECOSOC, Official Records 2007, Supplement No. 11, available at <http://www.unctad.org/en/docs//ecn162007d4_en.pdf>.

190 See also WSIS, Tunis Agenda, para. 82; on the preparatory works and the discussed topics see below III.D. and Doria/ Kleinwächter, 87 ss.

forum were not confirmed. The IGF brought together various stakeholders from civil society, private sector, governments and international organizations in an equal and voluntary platform. The openness as well as the absence of procedural rules and provisions in envisioning the adoption of resolutions enabled valuable open dialogues and non-binding approaches to current topics among actors who would otherwise barely have encountered one another. In fact, a very broad range of issues was addressed and their substantiation proceeded in dynamic coalitions. Alltogether, the test run of Internet governance was considered successful.[191]

The second meeting of the IGF took place in Rio de Janeiro from 12th to 15th November 2007. The preparatory process was based on the—in the meanwhile acknowledged—framing of the working definition of Internet governance as well as on the key principle of multi-stakeholder cooperation. Based on the consultations and the discussions held in Athens in 2006, the subjects which the meeting in Rio focused on, concerned enhanced communication, coordination and cooperation. It particularly tackled the broad themes of "critical Internet resources", "access", "diversity", "openness", "security", as well as the cross-cutting priorities of "development/capacity building" inter alia.[192]

The third meeting of the IGF, held in Hyderabad from 3rd to 6th December 2008, addressed the previously discussed broad themes and the participants deliberated in a wide variety of workshops. In particular, not strictly organized so-called dynamic coalitions tried to push forward the approach of a civil society forum. Since the IGF cannot render legally-binding decisions, the discussions' results are hard to measure; partly the impression exists that the progress is remote; nevertheless, IGF's contribution to the multi-stakeholder dialogues on Internet governance was reinstated.[193]

The fourth meeting of the IGF will take place in Sharm-el-Sheik from 15th to 18th November 2009; but the program's details are not yet known. Further important inputs are provided by the Global Internet Governance Academic Network (GigaNet), a scholarly community established in spring 2006.[194] It offers a platform for the exchange of academic research and for dialogue among interested parties. The research symposia organized by the GigaNet are held one day prior to the IGF meetings. These initiatives play an important role in the development of Internet governance, particularly by upholding moral and scientific pressure on the existing mechanisms to proceed.

---

191 Schneider, 8/9.

192 For further details see below III.D; Doria /Kleinwächter, 226 ss; Malcolm, Governance, 384–395; see also <http://www.intgovforum.org/cms/index.php/secondmeeting>.

193 See below III.D.

194 For further information see the GigaNet-homepage at <http://www.igloo.org/giganet>.

III. Organizational Framework in Internet Governance

A. Overview

Many international, intergovernmental and non-governmental organizations, as well as the private sector and civil society, play a role in the "structuring" of the Internet. Therefore, in order to frame a matrix which maps the roles of the various actors involved in the Internet, different possibilities exist. A good approach was chosen by DON MACLEAN, referring to the legal quality of the regulations (from "soft" to "hard" law) on the one hand, and to the scope of international governance (from "narrow" to "broad") on the other hand. The respective matrix looks like this:[195]

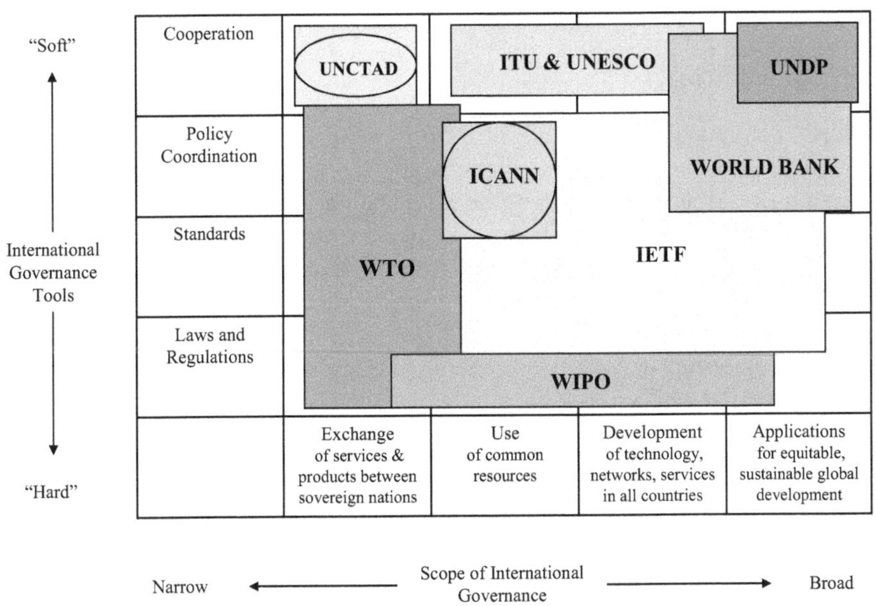

The best known organization is ICANN, which also stands at the center of attention within the Internet governance discussions. In the subsequent chapter, further organizations directly involved in the Internet structuring process will be addressed; these organizations exercise different functions, thereby focusing particularly on technical, policy, or administrative issues. Organizations being gener-

[195] MACLEAN, 15.

Copyright © Schulthess Juristische Medien AG, Zurich – Basel – Geneva 2009.
Published by Springer-Verlag GmbH Berlin Heidelberg 2010. All Rights Reserved

ally involved in global activities (such as UNCTAD, World Bank, WTO, WIPO) will not be discussed in detail.

B. Policy and Technology Organizations

1. International Telecommunication Union

The International Telecommunication Union (ITU) is the oldest international organization in the information and communication field. Its origin can be traced back to 17th May 1865, when, following relatively short negotiations (less than three months), 20 European founding members signed the International Telegraph Convention and established the International Telegraph Union in Paris.[196] The rapid expansion of telegraph networks after the year 1844, when SAMUEL MORSE sent his first public message over a telegraph line, made it necessary to develop a framework agreement covering international interconnection and harmonizing technical standards; the Convention was concluded only slightly over 20 years after MORSE's invention.[197]

Shortly before and after the turn of the 20th century, the International Telegraph Union adopted international regulations governing telephone and radiocommunication (the latter in the form of the International Radiotelegraph Convention). These were followed by broadcasting regulations in the twenties of the past century. At the Madrid Conference of 1932, the two existing Conventions were combined to form the International Telecommunication Convention.[198] The new name of "International *Telecommunication* Union" came into effect on 1st January 1934. ITU's membership includes governments joining as Member States and, since 1994, private organizations joining as Sector Members.[199]

After the Second World War the ITU became a UN spezialized agency (on 15th October 1947), and the headquarters of the organization were transferred from Berne to Geneva in 1948. The following years were mainly devoted to meeting the challenges posed by new space communication systems; in particular the allocation of frequencies to the various space services (satellite use of the radio-frequency

196 For a general overview see GEORGE A. CODDING, The International Telecommunication Union—An Experiment in International Cooperation, New York 1972 (reprint of 1952 edition).

197 See TEGGE, 27 ss.

198 TEGGE, 43 ss.

199 MALCOLM, Governance, 58; IRION, 90/91.

spectrum and associated orbital slots, including non-geostationary satellites) was tackled.[200]

In 1989, the Plenipotentiary Conference held in Nice recognized the importance of enhancing technical assistance to developing countries, with similar emphasis on the pursuit of ITU's traditional activities of standardization and spectrum management. Aiming to make the organization more flexible, interactive and competitive, the Additional Plenipotentiary Conference held in Geneva in 2002 substantially remodelled the internal structure of the ITU (encompassing three sectors, namely the Radiocommunication Sector, the Standardization Sector, and the Development Sector). This step forward was also based on the results of the Kyoto Plenipotentiary Conference (1994) which established the World Telecommunications Policy Forum (WTPF), an ad hoc meeting encouraging the free exchange of ideas and information on emerging policy issues.[201]

The Minneapolis Plenipotentiary Conference in 1998 enlarged the field of ITU activities to Internet matters and the Marrakesh Plenipotentiary Conference from 2002 addressed the problem of bridging the digital divide in particular and formulated objectives to be achieved in order to realize fully interconnected and interoperable networks on a global scale.[202] Consequently, the ITU assumed a leading role in the preparations and follow-up of the two World Summits on the Information Society (WSIS).[203]

The core of ITU's activities focuses on standard-setting: The use and operation of radiocommunication is standardized in ITU-R, all other standardization efforts are done through ITU-T.[204] According to the Geneva Declaration of Principles, "standardization is one of the essential building blocks of the Information Society."[205] The objective of standards must be to optimize the means of exploitation of technical resources. However, ITU's influence on the preparation process of rules which are to be introduced, has remained limited.[206] Criticism has also been expressed in respect to ITU's corporate culture. It has been argued that the organization does not properly include civil society in its goodwill activities and that the balancing test related to private/public interests does not always corre-

200 See also JAMES G. SAVAGE, The Politics of International Telecommunications Regulation, Boulder et al. 1989, 104 ss.

201 For further details see <http://www.itu.int/osg/csd/wtpf>.

202 See also PATRICIA McCORMICK, Private Sector Influence in the International Telecommunication Union, info, Vol. 9/4, 2007, 70, 74/75.

203 See above II.B.3.

204 For more details see IRION, 91 ss.

205 Geneva Declaration of Principles, Art. 44.

206 MALCOLM, Governance, 60/61.

spond to the actual existing interests, ultimately due to the fact that stakeholder participation is not a core issue of ITU.[207]

2. Internet Engineering Task Force and Internet Architecture Board

(1) The *Internet Engineering Task Force* (IETF) constitutes an "independent, unincorporated, international standards body of continually floating membership".[208] The IETF describes itself as "a large open international community of network designers, operators, vendors, and researchers concerned with the evolution of the Internet architecture and its smooth operation."[209] The IETF's de facto constitution is a detailed Internet Standards Process[210] aiming to achieve technical excellence, implementation and testing, clear, concise and easily understandable documentation, openness and fairness, and timeliness.[211] The funding which had originally been provided by the US Defense Advanced Research Projects Agency (DARPA) and the National Science Foundation (NSF) was later shifted to the Internet Society (ISOC),[212] which is now the major source of funding of the IETF and is responsible for its management.[213] ISOC also houses the IETF Administration Support Activity (IASA) which provides administrative structures for supporting the IETF standards process and its technical activities.[214]

IETF has a similar function to ITU in standard-setting,[215] but exclusively related to the Internet; however, the IETF members do not represent sovereign States. The standards developed by the IETF include the Transfer Control Protocol/Internet Protocol (TCP/IP) and the Simple Mail Transfer Protocol (SMTP). A few hundred individuals, mainly software engineers, are working on behalf of IETF and aim at improving the technical background of the Internet. The IETF is characterised by a lack of a formal hierarchy, a decision-making process based on con-

---

207 See also Irion, 96 ss and Drake, Implementation, 272/73.

208 Froomkin, Wrong turn in cyberspace, 17; Paul Hoffman/Scott Bradner, Defining the IETF, February 2002, RFC 3233; Harald Alvestrand, Mission Statement for the IETF, October 2004, RFC 3935; in general Alvestrand/Lie, 126 ss.

209 <http://www.ietf.org/home.html>.

210 RFC 2026, Internet Standards Process, October 1996, IETF.

211 Caral, 14; Malcolm, Governance, 52/53.

212 See hereinafter III.B.3.

213 Erik Huizer, IETF—ISOC Relationship, October 1996, RFC 2031.

214 Network Working Group, Structure of the IETF Administrative Support Activity (IASA), April 2005, RFC 4071.

215 See also Weber/Grosz, Vague Ideas, 119, 120; Harvard Law School, 1660–1662; Gibbons, 488; Malcolm, Governance, 53–55; Alvestrand/Lie, 133–138; Bygrave/Michaelsen, 97–99.

sensus, and an informal culture; therefore, the relations between ITU and IETF are rather loose which makes the coordination of standardization processes partly difficult.[216]

(2) The *Internet Architecture Board* (IAB), formerly known as the Internet Activities Board, was established as an independent committee of researchers and professionals coordinating Internet design, engineering and management.[217] The IAB is framed as a committee of the IETF and as an advisory body to the Board of Trustees and the Officers of the Internet Society.[218] Its responsibilities include the supervision of the architecture for the Internet protocols and procedures and the oversight over the Internet standard creation process; it also functions as board of appeals for complaints regarding standard processes and it manages the Request for Comments (RFC) document series.[219] Additionally, the IAB can act as representative of ISOC's interests in terms of so-called external liaisons.[220] These relationships embody the formalized efforts to communicate and coordinate activities in Internet-related issues among different organizations.[221]

3. Internet Society

The Internet was originally developed and managed by the relatively small community of its technical constructors as well as the providers and users of Internet services. Based on self-regulation in a bottom-up manner and on an ad hoc basis, measures were taken depending on the specific communication needs of the networks.[222] However, with the increased use of the Internet it became apparent, that some basic institutional structures would have to be established. Therefore, the Internet Society (ISOC) was founded in 1992 as a non-profit, non-governmental membership society (pursuant to the District of Columbia Non-Profit Corporation Act) with the aim to promote the development, the availability and the associated technologies of the Internet.[223] Consequently, ISOC does not issue any capital stock.[224]

216 CARAL, 14/15; MALCOLM, Governance, 59/60.

217 VINTON CERF, The Internet Activities Board, May 1990, RFC 1160; on CERF in general see GOLDSMITH/WU, 36 ss.

218 See hereinafter III.B.3.

219 GROSZ, ISOC, II.

220 Charter of the Internet Architecture Board, May 2000, RFC 2850.

221 GROSZ, ISOC, II.

222 WEBER, Regulatory Models, 25, 93; GIBBONS, 475; KLEINWÄCHTER, ICANN as the "United Nations", 454–456; WALKER/WALL/ARDENIZ, 6.

223 CERF, IETF and ISOC; LEINER/CERF/CLARK ET AL.; BYGRAVE/MICHAELSEN, 95–97.

224 On ISOC's financing sources see GROSZ, ISOC, V.

ISOC is the organizational home for entities responsible for Internet infrastructure standards, as mentioned inter alia for the Internet Engineering Task Force (IETF) and the Internet Architecture Board (IAB).[225] ISOC is estimated to encompass more than 100 Organizations and approx. 30 000 Individual Members in over 180 countries, with its principal offices in Washington D.C., USA, as well as in Geneva, Switzerland.[226] ISOC's efforts are amplified on a local and regional level by the Internet Society Chapters and the Regional Bureaus, which currently encompass an African, a Latin American and Caribbean as well as a newly established South and Southeast Asian Bureau. In 2005, ISOC, IETF, and the Corporation for National Research Initiatives created the IETF Trust, with the purpose of holding existing and future intellectual property used in connection with the Internet standards processes and their administration.[227]

Article 3 of ISOC's Articles of Incorporation phrase the purpose of the organization: ISOC operates exclusively for educational, charitable, and scientific purposes. These include activities (1) to facilitate and support the technical evolution of the Internet as a research and educational infrastructure, (2) to educate the scientific community, the industry and the public at large concerning the technology, use and application of the Internet, (3) to promote educational applications of Internet technology, and (4) to provide a forum for exploration of new Internet applications, as well as to stimulate collaboration among organizations. ISOC fosters "the voluntary interconnection of computer networks into a global research and development communications and information infrastructure".[228]

Membership of ISOC is open to both individuals and organizations, which are engaged in the evolution of the Internet.[229] Various types of organizations (corporations, non-profit organizations, trade and professional groups, foundations, educational institutions, government agencies, and other international entities) can become ISOC members. The Organization Members are categorized into six different levels of membership, depending on the organizations' specific needs and the annual funding they provide. Each Organization Member is allowed to designate two representatives to ISOC's Advisory Council, regardless of its membership level.[230]

---

225 See above III.B.2.

226 This subsection follows the more detailed desciption of ISOC given by Grosz, ISOC, III.

227 Network Working Group, RFC 3978 Update to Recognize the IETF Trust, October 2006, RFC 4748; Network Working Group, RFC 4181 Update to Recognize the IETF Trust, March 2007.

228 Cerf/Kahn/Chapin.

229 For further information see <http://www.isoc.org/membership>.

230 Article VI, Section 2 ISOC Bylaws; ISOC Advisory Council Charter.

Individuals (approx. 30 000), who support ISOC's mission and principles and who agree on ISOC's code of conduct, may join the Internet Society.[231] Two different membership levels exist for them: the Sustaining Members contribute to ISOC's funding, whilst the Global Members' membership is free of charge. Both member types are involved with the organizational activities, such as ISOC's surveys and discussion groups.

ISOC's Individual Members are often affiliated to ISOC Chapters. Such Chapters encompass at least twenty-five Individual Members from different geographical regions.[232] The Chapters manage to provide the Internet Society with information from a regional and local basis; active Chapters exist all over the world.[233]

ISOC's Board of Directors is known as the Board of Trustees, which directs the affairs of the Internet Society. The Trustees assemble individuals from the industry sector, from educational bodies, from non-profit organizations, and from governments.[234] They are elected by the Organization Members, the Chapters, the IETF standards organization through the IAB, and the Sustaining Individual Members. The Board consists of twenty Trustees at most, which generally hold office for a term of three years.[235]

The Board of Trustees may designate three or more Trustees to constitute an Executive Committee, by resolution adopted with the affirmative vote of at least two-thirds of the members of the Board of Trustees in office. The Executive Committee provides for a certain specialization and is generally permitted to exercise the Board's authority in the management of the affairs of the Society.[236] In order to facilitate the Society's activities, the Board of Trustees can appoint additional committees.[237]

ISOC Officers include the Chairman, the President, the Treasurer, and the Secretary. The Board of Trustees may appoint additional officers when necessary.[238] The Chairman of ISOC is selected from among the members of the Board of Trustees. The appointment of the President of ISOC requires the approval of at least a majority of the members of the Board of Trustees.[239]

---

231 ISOC, Annual Report 2007, 13.

232 ISOC, Policy for Establishing New Chapters, available at <http://www.isoc.org/isoc/chapters/policy>.

233 ISOC, Annual Report 2007, 13 ss; see also <http://www.isoc.org/isoc/chapters>.

234 Article II, Section 2 ISOC Bylaws.

235 Article II, Section 1 ISOC Bylaws.

236 Article II, Section 13 ISOC Bylaws.

237 For further details see GROSZ, ISOC, IV.

238 Article IV, Section 3 ISOC Bylaws.

239 For further details see GROSZ, ISOC, IV.

Since the establishment of ISOC in 1992, the Internet has grown to become a vast commercial network with a broad and increasing user community. The operation and the governance of the Internet as a whole is, by definition and design, a distributed task. Depending on the focus set, different players are in charge of the processes of the Web. ISOC positions itself against any one organization managing the Internet, stating that better use of technology and broad participation in today's Internet coordination processes are more effective to satisfy governance concerns.[240] ISOC's rather central role thereby focuses on supporting, facilitating and promoting different aspects of the Internet's development. ISOC's members, Chapters, and Regional Bureaus influence its fields of action and enable it to constitute a multi-stakeholder forum for the Internet.

Apart from its functions in the standard-setting processes as well as in education and training efforts[241] ISOC's main function concerns its participation in Internet public policy discussions in which it plays a major role—notwithstanding the fact that ISOC should not be perceived as an actual policy-making entity. In fact, ISOC has had an important leading role to play on the international stage in context of the two World Summits on the Information Society (WSIS) and particularly within the Internet Governance Forum (IGF) in Rio de Janeiro (2007) and Hyderabad (2008).

ISOC's guiding public policy principles include: open, unencumbered, and beneficial use of the Internet, self-regulated content providers, no prior censorship of on-line communication, open-forum for the development of standards and Internet technology, no discrimination in use of the Internet, privacy protection, and misuse prevention in cooperation among networks.[242] Consequently, ISOC is also a member of the Global Internet Liberty Campaign.[243] In light of the prevailing discussions on Internet governance, ISOC's Strategic Operation Plan 2006 proposed different tools for enhancing public policy attempts, such as the implementation of the so-called Policy Portal, providing for educational resources for policy-makers and influencing entities, and an advocational tool for ISOC and the Internet Community.[244]

ISOC is constantly challenged by new topics arising in the continuously developing field of the Internet. In this context, the improvement of technologies is of major importance for the functioning of cyberspace. Therefore, ISOC rather early adopted a supportive role regarding the global transition to the new technology

240 ISOC, Developing the Potential of the Internet through Coordination, not Governance, Bulletin no. 7, 9th December 2003, available at <http://www.isoc.org/news>.

241 On these aspects see SADOWSKY, Paving the Way.

242 See ISOC Principles and Goals, available at <http://www.isoc.org/isoc/mission/principles>.

243 See Global Internet Liberty Campaign (GILC) Homepage, <http://www.gilc.org>.

244 ISOC, Strategic Operating Plan, Part II, 15–17, 19.

of Internet Protocol version 6 (IPv6), which provides for a much larger address space than its predecessor IPv4.[245] Furthermore, ISOC addresses different issues challenging the common and open Internet. Particularly the technological solutions for multilingualism in the Internet remain an important issue.

A central point for realizing ISOC's core values and public policy goals is its regionalization on the one hand and (simultaneously) its globalization on the other. Consequently, the Regional Policy Advisory Groups (RPAGs) and the Global Policy Council (GPC) will be of increasing importance, as well as the fostering of the Chapter programs.[246] Regional Bureaus might expand further in order to deepen and strengthen ISOC's regional and global presence.[247]

4. World Wide Web Consortium

The World Wide Web Consortium (W3C) was founded as an industry consortium in 1994, five years after the invention of the World Wide Web.[248] The W3C's origins are tightly linked to Tim Berners-Lee's first attempts to connect devices in order to make knowledge more accessible (at that time working at the CERN, the European Organization for Nuclear Reasearch in Geneva), following the inventions of Vannevar Bush (who tried to link documents by a photo-electrical-mechanical device called Memex) and of Ted Nelson (who described "literary machines" that referred to a new, nonlinear, "nonsequential" text format of compuer writing called "hypertext").[249] The mission was "to lead the World Wide Web to its full potential".[250]

By the 1990s the Web was open to commercialization and more and more being used by the public, thereby spreading around the world. New browsers and servers appeared, threatening to question the consistency of a uniform Web. It was in light of these developments that the idea of installing an organization emerged. This entity was envisaged to be a body with oversight which could ensure, the Web stayed what it was originally intended to be, namely "a universal medium for sharing information".[251] It was based on the vision that all bits of information could

245 ISOC, Background briefing on IPv4 to IPv6 transition, available at <http://www.isoc.org/pubpolpillar/issues/ipv6transition.shtml>; for further details see below VII.B.2.

246 ISOC, Strategic Operating Plan, Part II, 18.

247 ISOC, Strategic Operating Plan, Part II, 18.

248 This subsection follows the more detailed description of the W3C, given by Grosz, W3C, II; in general see also Jon Bing, Building Cyberspace: A Brief History in Internet, in: Bygrave/Bing (eds), Internet Governance: Infrastructure and Institutions, Oxford 2009, 8, 40 ss; Alvestrand/Lie, 138 ss.

249 Bush; Berners-Lee, Weaving the Web, 5; see also Caral, 15.

250 W3C, Process Document, Abstract.

251 Berners-Lee, Weaving the Web, 84 (in general 75–102 for further information).

potentially be made available to everyone, within a type of globally connnected information space.[252]

After the first International WWW Conference in May 1994, the formal establishment of the World Wide Web Consortium followed on 1st October 1994, founded by Berners-Lee in collaboration with CERN at the Massachusetts Institute of Technology, Laboratory for Computer Science (MIT/LCS). It was further supported by the US Defense Advanced Research Project Agency (DARPA) and the European Commission.[253] Eventually, CERN transferred its position to INRIA (Institut national de Recherche en Informatique et Automatique), which became the first European W3C host. It was replaced by the European Research Consortium in Informatics and Mathematics (ERCIM) in 2003. In 1996, the Keio University became W3C's Asian host in Japan.[254]

The enhancement of interoperability among different technical means is particularly crucial for the functioning of the Web's information flow. Therefore, W3C is engaged in the development of common technical Web standards, referred to as the W3C Recommendations. Following the Internet's basic principle of openness, the consortium promotes the harmonization of the Web's technologies based on the consensus of its members, its staff, invited experts, as well as the public.[255]

W3C is not incorporated, but is based on contractual relationships with its hosts and its members. Its activities are administered by the MIT Computer Science and Artificial Intelligence Laboratory (CSAIL) in the USA, the European Research Consortium for Informatics and Mathematics (ERCIM) with headquarters in France, and the Keio University in Japan. Furthermore, W3C holds World Offices around the globe facilitating its collaboration with regional Web communities and promoting W3C's technologies, thereby encouraging international participation.[256]

Membership of the W3C is open to any entity capable of signing the Membership Agreement and agreeing to the terms of its Appendix 1. All types of organizations (commercial, educational, as well as governmental entities, irrespective of their structure as profit or non-profit entities) as well as individuals can become W3C members. However, W3C processes are primarily designed for organiza-

---

252 Berners-Lee, Information Management; Berners-Lee, Weaving the Web, 1–6, 28–51, 60–62; About W3C, History (last modified 2nd January 2008 by author Ian Jacobs), available at <http://www.w3.org/Consortium/history>.

253 Berners-Lee, Weaving the Web, 85–89.

254 About W3C, History (last modified 2nd January 2008 by author Ian Jacobs), available at <http://www.w3.org/Consortium/history>.

255 W3C, Process Document, 1.

256 About W3C, 1-page (last modified on 29th April 2008 by author Ian Jacobs), available at <http://www.w3.org/Consortium/Overview>.

tional participation.[257] Currently, W3C encompasses over 400 member organizations from various sectors and more than forty countries.[258] W3C members enjoy the right to elect a seat on the Advisory Committee.

The W3C was established as a consortium with the aim to hold the Web together as a universal medium for sharing information. Its legal form was chosen to enable a vendor-neutral viewpoint, which would have been more difficult to achieve, if framed as a corporation with commercial interests.[259] W3C is thus not a separate legal entity. It is based on its contractual relationships with different parties and formed as a voluntary association.[260]

The W3C Team consists of paid staff, unpaid interns, and W3C fellows, which also encompass the member's employees. The W3C Team is managed by the Consortium's Director and founder BERNERS-LEE, as well as the W3C Chair and the Chief Operating Officer.[261] The W3C Director has the role of a conciliator within the Consortium.[262] Furthermore, the W3C has an advisory body in the form of its Advisory Board, which is generally appointed by the W3C Team. It provides for guidance on issues of strategy, management, legal matters, process, as well as conflict resolution. Moreover, it is also responsible for hearing rejected member submission requests together with the Technical Architecture Group.[263]

Technical issues arising around the Web's architecture are handled by the W3C's Technical Architecture Group (TAG). Its responsibilities include the documentation and consensus-building concerning Web architectural principles, as well as their interpretation and clarification when necessary.[264] Furthermore, W3C possesses several specialized Groups (for example, Working Groups, Interest Groups, Coordination Group).[265]

As mentioned, W3C's work[266] mainly focuses on the standardization of Web technologies through its W3C Recommendations the Consortiums' equivalent to Web standards. They are defined as a specification or set of guidelines that, after extensive consensus-building, have received the endorsement of W3C Members and

257 About W3C Membership, Membership FAQ, (last modified on 2nd January 2008 by author IAN JACOBS), available at <http://www.w3.org/Consortium/membership-faq>, 1.
258 See the W3C Members at <http://www.w3.org/Consortium/Member/List>.
259 BERNERS-LEE, Weaving the Web, 83–85.
260 W3C, Member Agreement, 9; W3C Process Document, 2.2.
261 W3C Process Document, 2.2.
262 For further details see GROSZ, W3C, IV.
263 W3C, Process Document, 2.3; see also W3C Advisory Board, information available at <http://www.w3.org/2002/ab>.
264 W3C, Process Document, 2.4.
265 For further details see GROSZ, W3C, IV.
266 To the financing of the W3C see GROSZ, W3C, V.

the Director, and are recommended for wide application.[267] Since its establishment in 1994, more than ninety Recommendations have been produced, including HTML, XHTML, and XML.[268] They are developed in a consensual process, based on expressed interests and contributions from the members, the team, the different offices as well as the public.[269] This multi-stakeholder approach and the openness for inputs from different sectors abides to the Internet's architectural principles of openness, interoperability, connectivity, as well as the consideration of technological development.[270] The mentioned characteristics enable the Consortium to adopt a relatively neutral role, while different interests from various fields find their representation within the activities of the Consortium. Furthermore, the process making of the W3C enables the consortium to pick up and implement inputs from specialized parties.[271] In this manner, W3C provides for a very efficient and acknowledged standardization process, which enables it to play an important role in the field of Internet governance, regulation, and development.

A further challenge consists on the promotion of technologies, which render the Web independent of particular hardware platforms. Possible developments will include access to the Web through telephones, automotive telematics, home entertainment systems, etc. For example, the Mobile Web Initiative works on making Web access from any device as easy and convenient as from a computer desktop. In order to achieve this goal, W3C is building a database of device descriptions and is developing best practices for the creation of mobile-friendly web sites.[272] In addition, the W3C is engaged in the development and integration of the necessary frameworks. Furthermore, it is concerned with the development of a "Semantic Web" that provides information for both human and machine processing, with the aim to enable problem-solving that would otherwise possibly be too complex.[273]

---

267 W3C, Process Document, 7.1.1; see also MALCOLM, Governance, 56/57; ALVESTRAND/LIE, 141–143.

268 CARAL, 15/16; About W3C, Technology (last modified on 2nd January 2008 by author IAN JACOBS), available at <http://www.w3.org/Consortium/technology>.

269 W3C, Process Document.

270 IETF, Architectural Principles of the Internet, RFC 1958.

271 WEBER, Regulatory Models, 120/21.

272 Mobile Web Initiative Homepage available at <http://www.w3.org/Mobile>.

273 BERNERS-LEE, Weaving the Web, 157–175, 199–209; About W3C, Goals (last modified on 2nd January 2008 by author IAN JACOBS), available at <http://www.w3.org/Consortium/mission>; About W3C, Future (last modified on 2nd January 2008 by author IAN JACOBS), available at <http://www.w3.org/Consortium/future>.

C. Internet Corporation for Assigned Names and Numbers

1. Basic Framework and Development

The Internet Corporation for Assigned Names and Numbers (ICANN)[274] was created through a Memorandum of Understanding (MoU) between the US Department of Commerce and ICANN in 1998.[275] It is a non-profit public benefit organization with the legal status of a corporation, organized under the California Non-profit Public Benefit Corporation Law for charitable and public purposes. The organization is governed by Californian/US law and domiciled in Marina del Rey, State of California, where its principal office is situated. A further office in Brussels, presences in Africa, Latin America, Europe, and the Middle East, as well as the Pacific Rim, provide for its international outreach.[276]

The origins of ICANN can be traced back as far as the development of the Domain Name System (DNS):[277] The Internet originally emanated from ARPANET, a project established by the Department of Defense's Advanced Research Projects Agency (DARPA) in the 1960s. Every computer linked to the Internet needs a numeric address—an Internet Protocol (IP) address—in order to be identified and addressed by others. JONATHAN POSTEL, one of the founders of the Internet, had the idea of translating these numbers into names, the so-called domain names, which identify every user of the Internet and guarantee that each web and email address is unique. As part of this project, he maintained a list of host names and addresses, and therewith commenced with the DNS.

POSTEL defined seven "generic top level domains" (gTLDs), three of which were meant to be universal top level domains (".com" for commercial activities, ".org" for organzations and ".net" for networks); three further ones were designed for exclusive use in the USA (".gov" for governments, ".edu" for universities and ".mil" for the military); finally ".int" which was meant for intergovernmental treaty organzations. Eventually the list of gTLDs was enlarged. In particular, each country was given its own name according to the so-called "country code top level domain" (ccTLDs) such as ".de" for Germany, ".ch" for Switzerland, ".uk" for the United Kingdom and ".us" for the USA. Whilst the gTLDs were managed according to a contract between the US government and Network Solution Inc. (NSI), private or public national information centres were often linked to national

274 For further details on the historical development see above II.B.2.

275 This section is mainly based on the more detailed description, given by WEBER, ICANN, II.

276 ICANN Fact Sheet.

277 On the history see also MALCOLM, Governance, 31/32.

universities or academic research centres which supervised the ccTLDs. The Internet Assigned Numbers Authority (IANA), established in 1989 and chaired by POSTEL, was the responsible entity to coordinate this network. IANA was concerned with administrative issues, with the monitoring of the root servers as well as with the allocation of Internet Protocol addresses and corresponding domain names according to the "first come, first served" principle.[278]

With the invention of the World Wide Web in 1992,[279] the Internet expanded significantly. More and more private and commercial users world-wide went online and recognized the economic value of the web and email-addresses as "territories in cyberspace".[280] It was in light of these developments, that the reform of DNS governance was tackled.

In September 1996, the International Ad Hoc Committee (IAHC) was collectively established by different organizations involved with the Internet such as the IANA, the Internet Architecture Board (IAB), the Internet Society (ISOC), the International Telecommunication Union (ITU), the World Intellectual Property Organization (WIPO) and the International Trademark Association (INTA), with the prospective of examining the global domain name system. One year later the IAHC drafted a "Memorandum of Understanding for the gTLDs" (gTLD-MoU), which was signed in Geneva on 30nd April 1997. The gTLD-MoU proposed to introduce seven new gTLDs and to license twenty-eight new registrars around the world to manage them, thereby forming a Council of Registrars (CORE), a non-profit organization under Swiss law. A Policy Oversight Committee (POC) was established as the highest accounting body within the new system. Furthermore, the signataries of the gTLD-MoU formed a Policy Advisory Committee (PAC). ITU functioned as the depositary of the gTLD-MoU. However, due to the lack of support from the Internet community, the industry, and the governments, the project was finally deemed a failure and was not considered any further. Inter alia, it was criticized that the gTLD-MoU under the auspices of ITU would lead to a bureaucratic governmental organization. Moreover, its incorporation under Swiss law and its link to other international organizations threatened to reduce the United States' influence on the DNS.[281]

---

278 KLEINWÄCHTER, ICANN as the "United Nations", 456; HARVARD LAW SCHOOL, 1661; DE VEY MESTDAGH/RIJGERSBERG, 2; CHIK, 14; MALCOLM, Governance, 33–38; on the work of POSTEL in general see GOLDSMITH/WU, 29 ss, 43 ss.

279 See also above III.B.4.

280 KLEINWÄCHTER, ICANN as the "United Nations", 459–457; HARVARD LAW SCHOOL, 1663 with further references; CHIK, 9–16.

281 KLEINWÄCHTER, ICANN as the "United Nations", 458–459; HARVARD LAW SCHOOL, 1665–1666.

In July 1997, "A Framework for Global Electronic Commerce" was published by the US White House, containing a proposal for an alternative governance mechanism of the DNS, completely under the control of the private sector. The Department of Commerce released a "Request for Comment on the Registration and Administration of Internet Domain Names", which became the starting point for the establishment of ICANN. In February 1998, the US government published a Green Paper, which proposed the foundation of a "new private, non-commercial corporation" (NewCo) that should take over IANA's functions. Emphasis was put on transferring the DNS to private sector control, thus fully commercializing and opening it to competition. Furthermore, the DNS was to be incorporated under US law. Almost simultaneously, the US government unilaterally decided to terminate its contracts with NSI and IANA by the end of September 1998.[282]

The Green Paper was not accepted silently. Particularly the European Union criticized the US dominance in Internet governance, which was perceived as contrary to the international interests calling for a more global structure.[283] However, the idea of transferring the DNS to private, non-profit control remained. On 5th June 1998, the US government modified its proposal with the publication of the "DNS White Paper". According to this submission, the newly established organization should be based on the four principles of stability, competition, private bottom-up coordination and global representation. Furthermore, the World Intellectual Property Organization (WIPO) was invited to propose suggestions for a dispute resolution mechanism. Apart from the incorporation under US law, international interests were assessed by constituting the company's Board of Directors with members from different parts of the world. Nevertheless, official government representation was avoided.

Following the bottom-up, consensus-building tradition of the Internet, a so-called "International Forum on the White Paper" (IFWP) was organized with the objective of drafting a legal framework for NewCo. Furthermore, IANA and JAN POSTEL activated an online discussion for the governance of the DNS. On 17th July 1998, the first draft of a constitution for a new organization was published on the Internet, together with drafts and comments from all over the world. Yet in spite of these efforts, the global discussion was overshadowed by the time pressure emerging from the announced termination of the contracts between the US government and NSI as well as IANA by the end of September 1998.[284] On 2nd October 1998,

282 KLEINWÄCHTER, ICANN as the "United Nations", 459.

283 EU, Communication from the Commission to the Council, International Policy Issues Related to Internet Governance, 20th February 1998, COM (98)111 final; see also HARVARD LAW SCHOOL, 1666–1667; KLEINWÄCHTER, ICANN as the "United Nations", 460; WEBER, Regulatory Models, 104.

284 KLEINWÄCHTER, ICANN as the "United Nations", 461.

IANA sent the draft constitution of the newly conceived NewCo under the name "Internet Corporation for Assigned Names and Numbers" (ICANN) to the US Secretary of Trade. On 25th November 1998, ICANN was officially acknowledged by a Memorandum of Understanding (MoU) between the Department of Commerce and itself.[285]

To this day vital tasks for the functioning of the Internet are accomplished by ICANN. Its mission is to coordinate the unique technical identifiers' allocation and assignment, the operation and evolution of the DNS root name server system as well as the policy developments related to these technical functions.[286] ICANN's aim is the preservation of the operational stability of the Internet, the promotion of competition, the achievement of Board representation of global Internet communities, and the development of policies appropriate to its mission through bottom-up, consensus-based processes.[287]

2. Membership and Financing

According to Article XVII of ICANN's Bylaws, ICANN does not have members, as defined in the California Non-profit Public Benefit Corporation Law, notwithstanding the use of the term "member" in different ICANN documents. Participation within the organization is nevertheless open to all who have an interest in global Internet policy through online forums, mailing lists and public meetings.

At present, ICANN's primary sources of income are the domain name gTLD Registrar Fees. They are charged for each gTLD registrar-level transaction, as well as per gTLD registrar in general. In total, gTLD Registrar Fees amounted to approximately 50 percent of ICANN's revenue sources for the fiscal year 2008.[288]

Another important source of income derives from Registry Revenues that consist of gTLD Registries and IP Address Registries. Regarding gTLD Registries, ICANN has signed agreements with .net, .biz, .info, .org registries in particular, calling for per-transaction fees. The operation agreement for the .com registry contributes to ICANN's budget through an appointed fixed fee.[289]

Further contributions are received from the ccTLDs and the Regional Internet Registries.[290] ICANN also expects to receive investment income from the invest-

285 Kleinwächter, ICANN as the "United Nations", 462; for further details see Mueller, ICANN, 499 ss and Antonova, 33 ss.

286 Article I Section 1 ICANN Bylaws.

287 ICANN Fact Sheet; see also Mueller, ICANN, 516 ss.

288 ICANN, Adopted Budget 2009, 19–20.

289 ICANN, Adopted Budget 2009, 21–22.

290 ICANN, Adopted Budget 2009, 19.

ment of the rather recently established operating reserve fund.[291] An alternate source of revenue may be expected from different stakeholders and commercial entities, which profit from ICANN's functions and operations, according to the basic cost recovery principle. Furthermore, ICANN accepts voluntary contributions from governments, however, not making its budget dependent upon governmental contributions.[292]

3. Organizational Structure

3.1 Board of Directors

a) Composition

ICANN's organizational structure is built around its Board of Directors: ICANN's powers are generally exercised, its property controlled, and its business and affairs conducted by or under the direction of the Board of Directors ("Board").[293] ICANN's Board consists of fifteen voting members, referred to as "Directors". Annually, the Board elects a Chairman and a Vice-Chairman from among the Directors.[294]

According to Article VI Section 2 para. 1 ICANN Bylaws the Directors consist of:

(1) Eight voting members selected by the Nominating Committee;[295]

(2) Two voting members selected by the Address Supporting Organization;[296]

(3) Two voting members selected by the Country-Code Names Supporting Organization;[297]

(4) Two voting members selected by the Generic Names Supporting Organization;[298]

(5) The President, ex officio, as a voting member.

Furthermore, six non-voting liaisons are designated to attend Board meetings, participate in Board discussions and have access to materials provided to the Di-

291 ICANN, Adopted Budget 2009, 29.

292 See Task Force on Funding, Draft Final Report and Recommendations on ICANN Permanent Funding Arrangements, 30th October 1999, <http://www.icann.org/financials/general.htm>; ICANN, Adopted Budget 2009, 22.

293 Article II Section 1 ICANN Bylaws; see also Bygrave/Michaelsen, 107–113.

294 Article VI Section 2 para. 4 ICANN Bylaws.

295 Article VII ICANN Bylaws; <http://nomcom.icann.org>.

296 Article VIII ICANN Bylaws.

297 Article IX ICANN Bylaws.

298 Article X ICANN Bylaws.

rectors of the Board. However, they are not entitled to perform the other rights and privileges that the Directors possess.[299]

The ICANN Directors need to fulfil the criteria set forth in Article VI Section 3 of the ICANN Bylaws in order to be selected. The Nominating Committee and the Generic Names Supporting Organization particularly seek to ensure that the Board is composed of members who display diversity in geographical and cultural tems as well as in terms of skills, experience and perspective.[300] According to the multinational reach of the Internet and the aspired international representation, one intent of the diversity provisions of the Bylaws is to ensure that each geographic region have at least one Director; at no time may a region have more than five Directors on the Board.[301]

b) Meetings

ICANN's Bylaws provide for annual, regular, as well as special meetings of the Board. Special meetings may be called by or at the request of one-quarter of the members of the Board or by the Chairman of the Board or the President.[302] A progressive approach is taken by the Bylaws provisions in two respects: First by allowing for the meetings to take place by telephone or other means of communication such as electronic video screening;[303] second by taking into consideration rendering electronic mail equivalent to any communication otherwise required to be in writing.[304]

In general the Board may act by majority vote of those present at any meeting.[305] If all of the directors entitled to vote consent in writing, actions required can also be taken without a formal meeting.

c) Duties

Each Director has the duty to act in what he/she believes are the best interests of ICANN.[306] For this purpose, every Director has the right to inspect and copy all books, records and documents, as well as to inspect the physical properties of ICANN, within the constraints set up for protection against inappropriate disclo-

299 Article VI Section 9 ICANN Bylaws.
300 Article VI Section 2 paras. 2 and 3 ICANN Bylaws.
301 Article VI Section 5 ICANN Bylaws.
302 Article VI Sections 13–15 ICANN Bylaws.
303 Article VI Section 18 ICANN Bylaws.
304 Article VI Section 20 ICANN Bylaws.
305 Article II Section 1 and Article VI Section 17 ICANN Bylaws.
306 Article VI Section 7 ICANN Bylaws.

sure of confidential information.[307] On a case-by-case basis, the Board may allow the reimbursement of its member's expenses. However, the Directors are not entitled to receive a compensation for holding their office.[308]

Special attention is given to the avoidance of potential conflicts of interests.[309] In particular, no official of a national government or a multinational entity is permitted to serve as a Director on the Board.[310] Any person materially affected by a Board decision or action, insofar as inconsistent with the Articles of Incorporation or the Bylaws, can access a special third-party review process of Board actions. Requests for such independent review procedures are referred to an Independent Review Panel (IRP).[311]

d) Committees

The Board can establish committees out of two or more Directors. At present, eight Committees have been formed: (1) the Audit Committee, (2) the Board Governance Committee, (3) the Committee on Conflicts of Interest, (4) the Committee on Reconsideration, (5) the Compensation Committee, (6) the Executive Committee, (7) the Finance Committee and (8) the Meetings Committee.

Generally, each Committee possesses all legal authority of the Board, with certain exceptions listed in Section 2 of Article XII ICANN Bylaws.

3.2 Officers

ICANN's Officers consist of (1) a President, (2) a Secretary and (3) a Chief Financial Officer.[312] Furthermore, ICANN's Board may appoint additional officers if deemed appropriate.[313]

The President serves as the Chief Executive Officer (CEO) of ICANN, responsible for all of the organization's activities and business. In this function, all other officers and staff report to him or his delegate. Additionally, the President is empowered to call special meetings of the Board. Ex officio, the President also serves as a member of the Board.[314]

---

307 Article VI Section 21 ICANN Bylaws.
308 Article VI Section 22 ICANN Bylaws.
309 Article VI Section 6 ICANN Bylaws.
310 Article VI Section 4 ICANN Bylaws.
311 Article IV Section 3 ICANN Bylaws.
312 Article XIII Section 1 ICANN Bylaws.
313 Article XIII Section 7 ICANN Bylaws.
314 Article XIII Section 4 ICANN Bylaws.

The Secretary's duty is to keep the minutes of the Board, to supervise that all notices are duly given, and to perform further duties prescribed by the President or the Board.[315]

The Chief Financial Officer (CFO) is in charge of all of ICANN's funds and is generally responsible for all of the organization's matters relating to its financial operation. In its function, the CFO is particularly in charge of ICANN's financial planning and forecasting and assists the President in the preparation of the organization's annual budget.[316]

3.3 Ombudsman

The Ombudsman acts as a neutral and independent dispute resolution practitioner, with the function of providing an independent internal evaluation of complaints by ICANN members, who believe to have been subject to unfair or inappropriate treatment.[317]

The Ombudsman operates on a full-time basis, with an initial term of two years, that can be renewed by the Board.[318]

3.4 Advisory Mechanisms

The different advisory mechanisms provide for a certain degree of specialization and facilitate ICANN's mission to coordinate, at an overall level, the Internet's systems of unique identifiers, and to ensure the stable and secure operation of the corresponding systems.

a) Advisorory Committees

ICANN's Bylaws provide for at least four Specific Advisory Committees that report their findings and recommendations to ICANN's Board:

(i) The *Governmental Advisory Committee (GAC)* consists of all national governments involved with ICANN's activities as they relate to concerns of governments, particularly if there is an interaction between ICANN's policies and various laws, international agreements, or if public policy issues may be affected.[319]

315 Article XIII Section 5 ICANN Bylaws.
316 Article XIII Section 6 ICANN Bylaws.
317 Article V Section 2 ICANN Bylaws.
318 Article V Section 1 ICANN Bylaws; for further information see <http://www.icann.org/ombudsman>.
319 For further information see <http://gac.icann.org>.

(ii) The *Security and Stability Advisory Committee (SSAC)* advises ICANN on security and integrity matters of the Internet's naming and address allocation systems.[320]

(iii) The *Root Server System Advisory Committee (RSSAC)* brings together particularly the operators of an authoritative root name server; its function is to advise the Board about the operation of the root name servers of the DNS.[321]

(iv) The *At-Large Advisory Committee (ALAC)* consists of two members selected by the Regional At-Large Organizations (RALO's), and five members selected by the Nominating Committee. ALAC's members are elected to represent the different regions of the world, this in response to its function of providing advice regarding the activities on ICANN insofar as they relate to the interests of individual Internet users.[322]

(v) The Board is entitled to create additional Advisory Committees.[323]

b) External Expert Advice

In order to benefit from the knowledge of public or private expert entities outside the ICANN structures, the Bylaws expressly allow for the organization to seek advice from such bodies or individuals. In particular, the Board may appoint Expert Advisory Panels.[324]

c) Technical Supporting Group

The Technical Liaison Group (TLG) was established in order to connect the Board with sources of technical advice on matters pertinent to ICANN's activities. Since the Internet is rendered technically possible through Internet standards, the TLG is formed by four organizations of importance in this sector: the European Telecommunications Standards Institute (ETSI), the International Telecommunications Union's Telecommunication Standardization Sector (ITU-T), the World Wide Web Consortium (W3C), and the Internet Architecture Board (IAB).[325]

---

320 See <http://www.icann.org/committees/security>.

321 See <http://www.icann.org/committees/dns-root>.

322 One RALO is established for each Geographic Region, the five members selected by the Nominating Committee include one citizen of a country within each of the five Geographic Regions; see <http://alac.icann.org>.

323 See Article XI Sections 1 and 2 ICANN Bylaws.

324 Article XI-A Section 1 ICANN Bylaws.

325 Article XI-A Section 2 ICANN Bylaws.

3.5 Supporting Organizations

Policy making of ICANN is supposed to follow a "bottom-up" approach. ICANN's Bylaws differentiate between three different Supporting Organizations: the Address Supporting Organization, the Country-Code Names Supporting Organization and the Generic Names Supporting Organization:[326]

(i) The Address Supporting Organization (ASO) advises the Board and reviews or develops recommendations on policy issues relating to the operation, assignment, and management of Internet Protocol (IP) addresses.[327]

(ii) The Country-Code Names Supporting Organization (ccNSO) is responsible for the development and recommendation of global policies relating to country-code top-level domains to the Board. Furthermore, it fosters consensus within the ccNSO's community and coordinates itself with other ICANN Supporting Organizations.[328]

(iii) The Generic Names Supporting Organization (GNSO) is perceived as a policy-development body, responsible for substantive policy development and recommendation relating to country-code generic top-level domain issues (ccTLD).[329] The newest relevant group in this context is the very active Noncommercial Users Stakeholders Group (NCSG) representing views and interests of those who engage in noncommercial (academic) activity.[330]

4. Discussions about the Role of ICANN

4.1 ICANN's Significance for the Governance of the Internet

In order to ensure universal accessability, which allows the netizens from all over the world to find all valid addresses on the Internet, the so-called global Internet's system of unique identifiers needs to be coordinated and their stable and secure operation ensured.[331] The unique identifiers for the Internet are classified into three sets: the domain names, the Internet protocol (IP) addresses and the autonomous system (AS) numbers, finally the protocol port and the parameter

326 Articles VIII, IX, and X ICANN Bylaws.

327 See <http://aso.icann.org>.

328 See <http://ccnso.icann.org>; see also Annex B to the ICANN Bylaws, on ccNSO Policy-Development Process.

329 See <http://gnso.icann.org>; see also Annex A to the ICANN Bylaws, on GNSO Policy-Development Process and Annex C on the Scope of the ccNSO.

330 For further details see <http://gnso.icann.org/en/improvements/ncsg-petition-charter.pdf>

331 FROOMKIN, International and National Regulation, 3; DE VEY MESTDAGH/RIJGERSBERG, 5; CHIK, 66–71; ANTONOVA, 108 ss, 113 ss, 124 ss.

numbers. ICANN is responsible for the management and oversight of these specific functions.[332]

ICANN's importance for the governing of the Internet is connected to the significance of the Domain Name System (DNS), securing the functioning of today's cyberspace; the DNS can be considered as the lingua franca of the Internet. With the increasing commercialization, Domain Names constitute a particular form of property in the digital age. Moreover, their function can be compared to trademarks with corresponding economic values.[333] As the responsible organization for controlling the Internet's naming and numbering, ICANN is in the position to decide which devices can connect to the Internet and with which names.[334] However, ICANN has focused on the DNS and has not gained complete control over other aspects of Internet governance.[335] Furthermore, ICANN does not hold a complete monopoly; alternatives have been developed, these offer competitive TLDs, but increase the risk of becoming incoherent;[336] in view of such developments, a comprehensive, unified international regime for the DNS in general has been proposed.[337]

4.2 Points of International Criticism

a) Public Policy Set by a Private Entity

ICANN is neither an international organization with sovereign competencies nor a national legislator; it does not have a genuine authority to issue legal norms. In fact, ICANN has generally denied its engagement in the governance of the Internet. For a long time, the organization positioned itself as a standards setting and technical coordination entity. This perception has been subject to harsh criticism, since it seems clear that important public policy choices are made within the entity. For example, ICANN's adding of new TLD's to the root does not only have technical implications, but also requires value choices.[338]

It has been stated that ICANN's decisive role as a private entity could raise weighty legal questions such as constitutional review and accountability issues.[339] Furthermore, another argument issued against the privatization of the DNS was the risk

[332] Article I Section 1 ICANN Bylaws; for further details on the substantive policies see ANTONOVA, 229 ss.

[333] LEAFFER, 139–145; CHIK, 9–16; ANTONOVA, 113 ss.

[334] MAYER-SCHÖNBERGER/ZIEWITZ, 193.

[335] DRISSEL, 113.

[336] DE VEY MESTDAGH/RIJGERSBERG, 5; see also CHIK, 16–31.

[337] See for example CHIK, 66–71.

[338] FROOMKIN, Wrong turn in cyberspace, 94–105; KLEIN/MÜLLER, 2.

[339] For further details see below IV.B.4.

that privately-established rules could erode or undermine the power of sovereign States. Other voices, however, opined that a consensus-driven and bottom-up approach would lead to broader transparency and accountability of the private entity to the public, giving also non-State actors a voice in the rulemaking process. Furthermore, the fact that private organizations implicate more efficient functioning than governmental bureaucracy should not be underestimated.[340]

b) US Influence

Although ICANN was composed as a global organization, and incorporates both governments and individual users as stakeholders, as mentioned above, it has been materially influenced by and politically dependent on the US.[341] ICANN is legally governed by Californian Law and domiciled in California. It used to operate based on a Memorandum of Understanding (MoU) with the US Department of Commerce. On 30th September 2006, the MoU expired, but was extended through the adoption of the three-year Joint Project Agreement between the two parties which in turn will elapse in September 2009 (JPA). The influence US domestic concerns may have on ICANN's actions as well as on the debates regarding the organization's dispute-resolution process, particularly on the Uniform Domain Name Dispute Resolution Policy (UDRP), have levied many objections that have culminated in a call for a more internationalized organization.[342]

c) Democratic Legitimacy

Major objections have addressed a lack of an adequate democratic and legitimized background which would be required for an entity such as ICANN, that plays the sort of role more commonly adopted by public entities.[343] Questions on ICANN's democratic legitimacy arise in particular due to the fact that its techniques of representation are deemed to be unsatisfactory, since they do not actually reflect the heterogeneous Internet community within the organization's structures.[344]

340 Harvard Law School, 1670; Weber, Regulatory Models, 106–108; Malcolm, Governance, 46–50.

341 See Froomkin, Form and Substance, 94.

342 Mayer-Schönberger/Ziewitz, 194–197; Froomkin, Wrong turn in cyberspace, 95, Weinberg, 216–217, 250, Drissel, 115; Chik, 16–31, 31–71; see also Mueller, Ruling the Root, Chapter 11, and de Vey Mestdagh/Rijgersberg, 4–5 pointing out alternatives to US based root zone file and root zone servers systems.

343 Weber/Grosz, Vague Ideas, 123; Mayer-Schönberger/Ziewitz, 194; Antonova, 167, 191; Hunter, 1155; Kleinwächter, Global Governance, 4; Kleinwächter, Beyond ICANN vs. ITU, 248–249; Caral, 20; Weinberg, 216; Weber, Regulatory Models, 74, 105.

344 For further details see below IV.B.4.1 and V.B.

Initially, the individual Internet user's participation in ICANN's activities and particularly his/her role selecting ICANN's Board Members was endorsed: After strong political pressure in the aftermath of ICANN's incorporation and its assumption of the functions related to the Domain Name System, ICANN decided to have five out of nine members of ICANN's Board (so called "At-Large Directors") directly elected by the Internet community.[345] In theory, this proposal looked very promising, however, in practice the project failed: Of the estimated 375 million Internet users at the time, less than 0,01% actually voted. In light of this quite negative experience ICANN decided to abandon the idea of direct elections in 2002 and closed the experiment.[346] In exchange, ICANN provided for a selection process, which merely tries to enhance a certain geographic diversity amongst the Board Members. This was criticized and not appeased by ICANN's subsequent adoption of legitimizing techniques from US administrative agencies.[347] In particular, the representation of the governments through ICANN's General Advisory Committee (GAC) is not deemed satisfactory, since it is only based on ICANN's Bylaws and not on an intergovernmental treaty.[348] Furthermore, the GAC does not enable the governments' actual representation, since it merely possesses a consultative status.

Beside the general question whether the concept of democracy should really be applicable to ICANN,[349] further questions arise out of the formation of a representative and "fair" organizational basis; procedures enabling "real" consensus and rulemaking are called for, giving bargaining power to all of the participants including those with politically less powerful interests.[350] Legitimate validation of the institutional decisions could be fostered further by introducing a judicial review procedure for rendered decisions, as well as accountability provisions and criteria to protect third parties.[351]

345 Article II Section 1 & 2, Article V Section 6 ICANN Bylaws July 2000.

346 For further details see De Vey Mestdagh/Rijgersberg, 29.

347 Mayer-Schönberger/Ziewitz, 196; Weinberg, 235, 245, 249, 258; De Vey Mestdagh/Rijgersberg, 3; see also Article VI-X ICANN Bylaws.

348 Weinberg, 235, 249, 258.

349 Hunter; Weber/Grosz, Legitimate Governing of the Internet, 319 ss.

350 Weinberg, 256–257.

351 See also De Vey Mestdagh/Rijgersberg; Weber/Grosz, Legitimate Governing of the Internet, 324 ss on new approaches for enhancing legitimacy in the field of Internet governance.

4.3 Possible Adaptations

Originally, tackling Internet governance had not been the main objective of the World Summits on the Information Society (WSIS).[352] However, the issue gained more and more importance during the preparatory regional conferences for the first phase. Particularly, debates on the role of ICANN almost caused the collapse of the first part of the WSIS under the weight of the conflict-laden issue. Eventually, the WSIS Geneva Declaration of Principles, adopted at the end of the first WSIS, asked the UN Secretary General "to set up a working group on Internet Governance [WGIG]", which would be responsible for working out an action plan.[353]

Prior to the second phase of the World Summit, the WGIG submitted its Report to the UN Secretary General in July 2005,[354] which recommended the establishment of a "multilateral, transparent and democratic" multi-stakeholder forum, as a space for dialogue on Internet-related public policy issues.[355] Three of the four alternative models for Internet governance proposed in the Report called for changes in the status quo.[356] Referring to ICANN, the US government, together with the European Union, Canada, Australia, and Japan, adopted the position that the principle of "private sector leadership"[357] had stood the test of time proving that it worked for the management of the Internet and making changes such as any internationalization of its processes needless. In contrast, China, India, Brazil, and South Africa, supported by the majority of the developing countries, argued that Internet governance was related to national sovereignty, making it necessary to bring governments in charge of the process, preferably under the supervision of the UN organization ITU.[358] The European Union finally shifted their opinion and also proposed a more international and intergovernmental framework for the Internet's naming and numbering system.[359] Despite the relatively successful conclusion of the Summits, no agreement was achieved regarding the role of ICANN, thereby leaving its position untouched.[360]

---

352 See below III.D.

353 WSIS, Geneva Declaration of Principles, Article 50.

354 See above III.B.3.2

355 Report of the WGIG, paras. 29–48.

356 Drissel, 116.

357 On the advantages of self-regulation in this field see also Weber, Regulatory Models, 107–109; Mueller, ICANN, 516–520; Caral, 5–6.

358 Peake, 5; Mayer-Schönberger/Ziewitz, 190; Kleinwächter, Beyond ICANN vs. ITU, 241.

359 Mayer-Schönberger/Ziewitz, 190–191, 198–203.

360 Weber/Grosz, Vague Ideas, 123–125 with further references; Mayer-Schönberger/Ziewitz, 198.

Based on the Tunis Agenda the Internet Governance Forum (IGF) was established under the auspices of the United Nations.[361] Its mandate was very carefully formulated, since it was set up as a consequence of compromise: The IGF's mandate only includes soft powers, i.e. the forum has "no oversight function" and does "not replace existing arrangements, mechanisms, institutions or organizations", but involves them and takes advantage of their expertise. The forum is "constituted as a neutral, non-duplicative and non-binding process", having no involvement in day-to-day technical operations of the Internet, but featuring a "multilateral, multi-stakeholder, democratic and transparent" structure.[362]

5. Outlook

Unveiling ICANN's role in policy making and Internet governance together with the clear presentation of the US government's influence on the DNS, as well as the communication of represented interests within the Board, could provide for a step towards the appeasement of criticism of the organization and the strengthening of public confidence.[363] For example, ICANN has realized the potential of transparency enhancement.[364] ICANN also stresses the need to uphold and improve high standards on accountability;[365] amongst other undertakings, ICANN endorses the translation of important documents and meeting proceedings.[366] Furthermore, the organization has developed a set of Management Operating Principles related to accountability and transparency topics supporting the approach towards a multi-stakeholder community as a key area to be addressed for structural improvements.[367] Different reform steps within ICANN, for example related to governmental representation and the organization's global policy role, have been taken at hand.[368]

The rapid growth and expansion of the Internet provide for constant challenges for organizations concerned with the Internet such as ICANN. The ability to absorb technologies such as television, radio and telephone is a prominent model of the Internet's potential applications that may only be at the beginning of exploration. The development of the Internet, its ongoing access speeds and its growing user population will—in the future—continue to challenge the preservation of acces-

361 See above II.B.3.3 and below III.D.
362 WSIS, Tunis Agenda, paras. 73 and 77.
363 WEBER, Enhancement of Transparency, 315–316.
364 See below V.C.
365 ICANN, Annual Report 2008, see in particular 104–127.
366 See below V.E.
367 ICANN, Improving Institutional Confidence in ICANN, 3–4.
368 See CARAL, 22–24; on the reform campaign see also ANTONOVA, 257 ss.

sibility, renderability, and interpretability of increasing amounts of information on the Internet. Furthermore, maintaining the ability of users to find registered domain names unambiguously, calls for constant technological improvements.

New challenges will emerge with the accommodation of Internationalized Domain Names (IDN), adopting different alphabets that are not based on the Latin script, such as the Chinese, Japanese, Arabic, or Cyrillic alphabets; such developments will need to be tackled to secure global communication and prevent the fragmentation of the Internet. Moreover, the expansion of new gTLD's towards allowing applicants to self-select their domain names, as decided at ICANN's 32nd International Public Meeting in Paris in June 2008, will demand further policy responses.[369] Securing access to the Internet at the highest speed is another major issue that needs to be addressed, especially in the light of new numbering systems, such as the next-generation of IPv6 addresses; furthermore, the smooth transition from the IPv4 to the IPv6 platform also merits the attention of ICANN and its policy makers.[370]

D. World Summits of the Information Society and Internet Governance Forum

As mentioned,[371] Internet governance topics originally mainly concentrated on the spheres of technical coordination and standards development rather than public policy governance issues.[372] In other words, the transnational law on the Internet principally comprised the technical coordination regime of ICANN and its constituent bodies.[373] This situation has only started to change in the beginning of the 21st century and was particularly addressed at the two World Summits of the Information Society (WSIS) as well as at the meetings of the Internet Governance Forum (IGF), where Internet governance debates continue.

The first phase of the World Summit on the Information Society (WSIS) took place in Geneva form 10th to 12th December 2003, bringing together over 11 000 participants from 175 countries, including nearly 50 heads of States and govern-

---

[369] ICANN, Annual Report 2008, 62–63; Announcement, Biggest Expansion in gTLDs Approved for Implementation, 26th June 2008, available at <http://www.icann.org/en/announcements/announcement-4-26jun08-en.htm>; Announcement, ICANN Concludes Successful 32nd Meeting in Paris, 26th June 2008, available at <http://www.icann.org/en/announcements/announcement-3-26jun08-en.htm>.

[370] See below VI.B.2.

[371] See above III.B.3.

[372] See also MALCOLM, Governance, 68–69.

[373] MALCOLM, The Space Law Analogy, 7.

ments. The WSIS was the first gathering of global leaders addressing the issues of the information society. The Conference was concluded with the release of key principles for building an inclusive information society, the so-called "Geneva Declaration of Principles" (2003).[374]

The second phase of the WSIS was held in Tunis from 16th to 18th November 2005, with the participation of over 19000 participants from 174 contries and again nearly 50 heads of States and governments. This Conference resulted in four outcome documents addressing the issues of the information society, including the use of ICT for development,[375] cybersecurity, Internet governance, affordable access to communications, infrastructure, capacity building, and cultural diversity.

The dialogue and debate initiated after the WSIS in the Internet Governance Forum (IGF) is based on the Tunis Agenda and encompasses the following main objectives (para. 72):[376]

"a. Discuss public policy issues related to key elements of Internet governance in order to foster the sustainability, robustness, security, stability and development of the Internet.

b. Facilitate discourse between bodies dealing with different cross-cutting international public policies regarding the Internet and discuss issues that do not fall within the scope of any existing body.

c. Interface with appropriate intergovernmental organizations and other institutions on matters under their purview.

d. Facilitate the exchange of information and best practices, and in this regard make full use of the expertise of the academic, scientific and technical communities.

e. Advise all stakeholders in proposing ways and means to accelerate the availability and affordability of the Internet in the developing world.

f. Strengthen and enhance the engagement of stakeholders in existing and/or future Internet governance mechanisms, particularly those from developing countries.

g. Identify emerging issues, bring them to the attention of the relevant bodies and the general public, and, where appropriate, make recommendations.

h. Contribute to capacity building for Internet governance in developing countries, drawing fully on local sources of knowledge and expertise.

i. Promote and assess, on an ongoing basis, the embodiment of WSIS principles in Internet governance processes.

j. Discuss, inter alia, issues relating to critical Internet resources.

---

374 Available at <http://www.itu.int/wsis/docs/geneva/official/dop.html>; see also above II.B.3.4.

375 See Weber/Menoud, 11 ss.

376 Available at <http://www.itu.int/wsis/docs2/tunis/off/6rev1.html>.

k. Help to find solutions to the issues arising from the use and misuse of the Internet, of particular concern to everyday users.
l. Publish its proceedings."

According to para. 73 of the Tunis Agenda, the IGF had to be established as a multilateral, multi-stakeholder, democratic and transparent forum. Insofar, the IGF marks a significant development and progress as it is open to all stakeholders, including not affiliated individuals, a characteristic unique for a UN body.[377] Being democratic and transparent implies a lightweight and decentralized structure subject to periodic review.[378] The delegates of the Internet governing organizations such as ICANN, IETF or ISOC do not have an official voice at the meetings of the IGF.[379] Furthermore, the text of the output documents was allowed in the WSIS-context only on an ad hoc basis making it more difficult for governmental representatives to influence the process.[380] Such kind of approach has been chosen in order to allow civil society (including the technical community) to take advantage of equal opportunities to participate in policy discussions.

The IGF's inaugural meeting took place in Athens (Greece) in October/November 2006. Its second meeting was held in Rio de Janeiro (Brazil) in November 2007, its third meeting in Hyderabad (India) in December 2008. The fourth meeting is scheduled in Sharm el Sheikh (Egypt), for November 2009.[381]

The proceedings of the IGF's meetings are well recorded and also made public: Summaries of the deliberations of the Athens and Rio de Janeiro IGF meetings can be found in the volume edited by DORIA/KLEINWÄCHTER, mainly composed of the following sections:

(i) Introductory part, containing messages from SHA ZUKANG (United Nations Department of Economic and Social Affairs/UNDESA), HAMADOUN I. TOURÉ (ITU), KOICHIRO MATSUURA (UNESCO), MARKUS KUMMER (Executive Coordinator of the IGF-Secretariat). NITIN DESAI (Chairman of IGF) as well as from the three host country representatives (Greece, Brazil and India);[382]

(ii) Background papers from involved politicians, scholars, representatives of industry and civil society, namely TAREK KAMEL, FRANCIS GURRY, MAUD DE BOER-BUQUICCHIO, CATHERINE TRAUTMANN, LYNN ST. AMOUR, SUBRAMANIAM RAMADO-

377 See also DE LA CHAPELLE, Governance Paradigm, 19 ss.
378 MALCOLM, The Space Law Analogy, 8.
379 During a preparatory conference of the WSIS, ICANN president PAUL TWOMEY was even expelled from the negotiation room (see KLEINWÄCHTER, New Diplomacy, 112).
380 BLOEM, 99; MALCOLM, The Space Law Analogy, 21.
381 For further details see above II.B.3.3.
382 See DORIA/KLEINWÄCHTER, 2 ss.

RAI, NAOYUKI AKIKUSA, ANRIETTE ESTERHUYSEN, QIHENG HU, JEAN REVEILLON/ RICHARD SAMBROOK, DON MACLEAN AND VINCENT G. CERF;[383]

(iii) Excerpts from the discussions in the preparatory process including a general description given by CHENGETAI MASANGO;[384]

(iv) Excerpts from the proceedings during the Athens Meeting 2006,[385] and the Rio de Janeiro Meeting 2007;[386]

(v) Summary of the workshops organized during the Athens Meeting 2006, and the Rio de Janeiro Meeting 2007.[387]

The four broad themes of the IGF meeting in Athens were:[388]

- Openness,
- Security,
- Diversity,
- Access.

Notwithstanding the fact that these four themes cover the main topics of the Internet governance discussions[389], it was already recognized in the preparation of the agenda of the Rio de Janeiro Meeting 2007, that the number of themes should be extended by two other issues, namely,

- Critical Internet resources,[390]
- Further emerging issues.[391]

This enlargement of the agenda reflects the new discussion topics and also shows the flexibility being applied by the IGF in choosing the themes for deliberation. For the participants of the Rio de Janeiro Meeting 2007, KLEINWÄCHTER collected expert contributions in a book (The Power of Ideas: Internet Governance in a Global Mulit-Stakeholder Environment), in which he addressed the six men-

383 See DORIA/KLEINWÄCHTER, 13 ss.
384 See DORIA/KLEINWÄCHTER, 57 ss; see also MALCOLM, Governance, 355–366.
385 See DORIA/KLEINWÄCHTER, 87 ss; see also MALCOLM, Governance, 366–384.
386 See DORIA/KLEINWÄCHTER, 226 ss; see also MALCOLM, Governance, 384–395.
387 See DORIA/KLEINWÄCHTER, 370 ss.
388 See DORIA/KLEINWÄCHTER, 70, 72 ss, 82 ss, 88 ss, 124 ss, 228 ss, 237 ss, 277 ss.
389 See also below VI.A.
390 On this topic see below VI.B.1.
391 See DORIA/KLEINWÄCHTER, 80 ss, 93 s, 210 ss, 227/28, 237, 259 ss, 346 ss.

tioned topics, namely access,[392] openness,[393] diversity,[394] security,[395] critical Internet resources,[396] and emerging issues.[397]

Since the IGF was not created with the objective to supervise or replace existing institutions or organizations, the openness of the forum can induce all stakeholders to actively participate in the discussions. In particular it is noteworthy that the number of participants at the previous three IGF annual symposia continually increased. Therefore, issues like access to the technical infrastructures and diminution of the geographical gaps are gaining priority.

An important consequence of the establishment of the IGF should also be seen in the fact that stakeholders with similar interests have had and still have the opportunity to gather in so-called "Dynamic Coalitions". In the meantime, more than a dozen such dynamic coalitions exist, such as the Dynamic Coalition on Internet and Climate Change, the Dynamic Coalition on Accessibility and Disability, the Dynamic Coalition on Child Online Safety, the Framework of Principles for the Internet, the Gender and Internet Governance, the Online Collaboration Dynamic Coalition, the Freedom of Expression and Freedom of the Media on the Internet, the A2K@IGF Dynamic Coalition, the Coalition Dynamique pour la Diversité Linguistique, the Dynamic Coalition on the Internet Bill of Rights, the Dynamic Coalition on Access and Connectivity for Remote, Rural and Dispersed Communities, the Dynamic Coalition on Open Standards, the Dynamic Coalition on Privacy, and the Stop Spam Alliance.

The advantage of these dynamic coalitions consists not only in the possibility to channel and more strongly express the voices regarding a specific topic, but also

392 With contributions of Titi Akinsanmi, Fatimata Seye Sylla, Olga Cavalli, Veronica Cretu, Anriette Esterhuysen/Willie Currie, George Sadowsky (see Kleinwächter, Power of Ideas, 26 ss).

393 With contributions of Christian Möller, Ronald Koven, Peng Hwa Ang, Seiiti Arata Jr., Claudia Padovani/Elena Pavan, Dirk Cordel (see Kleinwächter, Power of Ideas, 76 ss).

394 With contributions of Koichiro Matsuura, Guy Sebban, Michael Yakushev, Kaili Kan, Jean Réveillon, David Maher/Ram Mohan/Philipp Grabensee, Sarbuland Khan (see Kleinwächter, Power of Ideas, 116 ss).

395 With contributions of Hamadoun Touré, Pier Carlo Padoan, Steve Crocker/David Piscitello, John Carr, Avri Doria (see Kleinwächter, Power of Ideas, 168 ss).

396 With contributions of Vint Cerf, Milton Mueller, Adiel A. Akplogan, Latid Latif, Elmar Knipp, Annette Mühlberg (see Kleinwächter, Power of Ideas, 208 ss).

397 With contributions of Bertrand de la Chapelle, William J. Drake, Louis Pouzin, Kenneth Neil Cukier (see Kleinwächter, Power of Ideas, 256 ss).

to continue particular discussions during the annual conference of the IGF; some coalitions now play important roles that should not be underestimated.[398]

During the more than three years since its establishment, the IGF has been appraised as an innovative experiment in global governance, but has also been subjected to criticism.[399] Generally speaking, the IGF can be perceived as a success to the extent that it provides a new venue which allows for discussions among all the stakeholders concerned and thereby manages to fill an institutional vacuum. However, the fact that the IGF tends to avoid confrontation in critical areas such as censorship or copyright protection should not be overlooked. This position can probably be traced back to and exlained by the fact that the founders of the IGF never intended to incorporate a strong policy-making body.[400] Indeed, the IGF tries to achieve its objectives in a more subtle way than would be possible if it were endowed with formal authority, i.e. with soft powers in the absence of decision-making competences. Nonetheless, more transparent and accountable mechanisms for linking the deliberations of the IGF to other institutions should be enhanced and the limitation of the IGF to an annual conference should be overcome.[401] In principle, a healthy eco-system of competitive governance institutional bodies helps to promote their mutual accountability, however, the effective disparities between the powers of the different IGF stakeholders must be more thoroughly addressed. Furthermore, the political and economic realities of the IGF should be taken into account more seriously.[402] Thereby, the existing discussions could lead to a more deliberative democratic process for the IGF.[403]

E. European Dialogue on Internet Governance

The discussions held in the context of the Internet Governance Forum have also shown that a number of topics merit to be deliberated on at a regional level. Therefore, the Council of Europe gathered some 200 government, industry and civil society representatives in a pan-European meeting on 20th–21st October 2008 in Strasbourg.

This European Dialogue on Internet Governance (EuroDig) put particular emphasis on a participatory approach for dealing with Internet governance, examining

398 On the Dynamic Coalition on the Internet Bill of Rights see below VI.C.4.2 b) and on the Dynamic Coalition on Privacy see below VI.D.2.1 d).

399 For a more extensive analysis see Malcolm, Success, 1 ss.

400 For more details see Malcolm, Success, 3–5.

401 Malcolm, Success, 7.

402 See also Malcolm, Success, 14.

403 For more details see Malcolm, Success, 10/11.

among others, the interplay between security, privacy and freedom on the Internet. Participants stressed the importance to make discussions "bottom-up", with a primary focus on European users, and advocated a human rights-based approach to Internet governance.[404] In particular, EuroDig illustrated the benefits of open and direct interaction among all stakeholders since there was a real momentum and willingness for such a dialogue to be nurtured by representative actors from civil society as well as from the private and governmental sectors.

A second EuroDig meeting is scheduled to take place from 14th-15th September 2009, under the auspices of the Council of Europe and the Swiss Office for Communications, in Geneva (Switzerland).

404 See Council of Europe, Press Release "Landmark European conference stresses "bottom-up" course of action for Internet governance", No. 183(2008), available at <http://www.coe.int/press>.

IV. Philosophical and Sociological Environment

As main parts of this publication, the discussion topics and regulatory issues in the Internet governance context shall not be directly liaised with the deliberations related to the organizational framework, but be generally introduced by a more theoretical description of the philosophical and sociological environment. Therefore, two intensively addressed concepts, namely the concept of a social contract and the concept of multi-stakeholderism, are subsequently elaborated and appraised in respect to their applicability within the Internet governance context.

A. Philosophical Concepts of a Social Contract for the Internet Community

1. Introduction

The heterogeneity of Internet users originating from different geographical zones, linguistic areas, and cultural backgrounds leads to very different conceptions related to the organization of the Internet.[405] However, the structuring of the online world needs to be supported by a large part of the Internet community in order to ensure its effective functioning. With the introduction of participation possibilities for civil society which enhance accountability, stability, and sustainability of the Internet community, the integration and harmonization of netizens will be increased. By realizing transparency regarding decision-making processes with the provision of adequate information by the governing bodies in order to effectively bridge information asymmetries,[406] by increasing the observance of the accountability framework by the Internet governing bodies,[407] and by letting the public participate in the decision making processes,[408] active involvement of civil society can be encouraged.[409]

Apart from such kind of topic-related improvements, general efforts should also be undertaken to find a method of consensus-building which includes all interested parties and creates the opportunity to make decisions acceptable for as large a part of the civil community as possible. Notwithstanding the fact that the Inter-

---

405 This chapter follows the deliberations given in WEBER/WEBER, Social Contract, 92 ss.

406 See below V.C.

407 See below V.D.

408 See below V.E.

409 See also STEFFEN/NANZ, 7; in general to the concept of civil society see MALCOLM, Governance, 122 ss and 152 ss.

Copyright © Schulthess Juristische Medien AG, Zurich – Basel – Geneva 2009.
Published by Springer-Verlag GmbH Berlin Heidelberg 2010. All Rights Reserved

net society is a newly emerging civil society, considerations taken into account in earlier contexts can lead to valuable insights. In this respect, a theory which seems to offer a feasible approach encompasses the concept of a so-called "social contract" which, from a historical and philosophical perspective, addresses issues of civil society's participation. The concept of a social contract is widely referred to by Internet research scholars, such JOHN PERRY BARLOW in his famous and early manifesto[410], however, an established definition of a social contract, going further than the understanding that members of the society agree to a certain form of collectivity, does not yet exist.[411] Therefore, it seems justified to shed light on the respective philosophical approaches.

2. Philosophical Concept of the Social Contract

2.1 Form of Integration

JEAN-JACQUES ROUSSEAU departed from the idea that individuals transform into members of the society. He proceeded on the assumption that it is only with the emergence of personal property that social structures develop and a need for regulation can be recognized. ROUSSEAU herewith followed the ideas of JOHN LOCKE, who argued that inequalities start to exist with the emergence of personal properties which can then lead from disagreements to actual war, where individuals join together in order to protect their properties.[412]

According to ROUSSEAU, a contract has to be concluded among all members of society due to the fact that individuals by themselves are unable to originate new forces; therefore, they have no other choice than to unify under a so-called social contract[413]. The purpose of this social contract is the accumulation of forces within a community which can protect each individual.[414] Although each member of the society stays as free as before and only obeys to himself, the individual merges completely and utterly with the collectivity.[415] Similarly, IMMANUEL KANT argues that individuals do not naturally live in communities and create law, but do so for rational reasons.[416] In other words, individuals rationally weigh and bal-

410 See above I.A.1.

411 See the description in Wikipedia, available at <http://en.wikipedia.org/wiki/social_contract>.

412 LOCKE, 71.

413 JEAN-JACQUES ROUSSEAU wrote his Social Contract in 1754/62.

414 ROUSSEAU, Livre I, Chapitre VI, para. 2.

415 ROUSSEAU, Livre I, Chapitre VI, para. 5.

416 KANT, Metaphysics of Moral, 1797, XIX 99/100 ; however, it cannot be overlooked that KANT does not remain with the contract principle, but develops it further to the concept of a categorical imperative.

ance the advantages of living in a society against its disadvantages, and will thus draw the conclusion that they profit more from the establishment of a community.

Even though the social contract may never have been pronounced aloud, its validity is implicitly accepted and approved on the whole territory of a community because it is perceived as mirroring everyone's personal will.[417] Each individual is transformed from a solitary human being into a part of a greater communitarian whole.[418]

The social contract itself does not constitute an authoritative power which would legitimize the governing of some individuals by others. Rather, the individuals responsible for the leadership of the community are appointed by the entire community, however, only after the establishment of the social contract. Therefore, it is the population that is the sovereign of the State; the government is established only to carry out the will of the sovereign and to act as an arbitrator.[419]

In "A Theory of Justice",[420] JOHN RAWLS advanced these theoretical approaches on the social contract to a higher level of abstraction. By departing from the hypothetical situation that people live in an original position of equality (which corresponds to the state of nature in the traditional theory of the social contract) and that a "veil of ignorance" blinds out the indiviuals' knowledge about their place in society, their class, position or social status, fortune and abilities, intelligence, strength and the like, RAWLS assumes that choices would be made by the individuals based on principles of justice and would thus result in a fair agreement or bargain. Therefore, in decision-making processes, individuals—oblivious of their position—would opt for the most favorable solution, regardless of their own personal interests. Individual and selfish interests thus non-existent or blinded out, only the common interest of civil society would be implemented.[421]

2.2 Necessity of Overall Approval

The social contract includes every single member of the community. If someone does not agree to the terms stated in the social contract, such a person is considered a foreigner.[422] ROUSSEAU sees the reason for the necessity of a consensus of all individuals to be bound by the social contract, in the fact that the civic mem-

417 ROUSSEAU, Livre I, Chapitre VI, para. 5.
418 ROUSSEAU, Livre I, Chapitre VI, para. 5.
419 ROUSSEAU, Livre III, Chapitre I, para. 18; ROUSSEAU disagrees with THOMAS HOBBES, who argued that individuals confer their right to self-determination and self-protection to the sovereign; in response, the sovereign protects all parties to the contract (see HOBBES, 1651).
420 Published in 1971.
421 RAWLS, para. 3, 10 ss; see also KERSTING, 142–143.
422 ROUSSEAU, Livre IV, Chapitre II, para. 6.

bership is the most voluntary action of all. Only the free will of all members justifies the institution of a common society.[423] Insofar the social contract constitutes an understanding according to which the participants of the arrangement morally commit themselves to follow the agreed provisions notwithstanding their lack of legal force.[424] Therefore, the social contract is an agreement among people which obliges each and every one to comply with certain duties in consideration of the benefits gained when all members fulfil similar duties, the overall objective thereby being to preserve both social order and property.[425]

3. Adaptability of the Social Contract Concept

Regarding other decisions aside from the social contract itself, two basic principles apply and shall be further examined in view of the adaptability of the social contract's approach to the governance of the Internet:

(i) The ratio between degree of approval and importance of a decision increases proportionally, so that the more important the decision, the higher the approval needs be. Consequently, ROUSSEAU does not propose a simple majority rule, but a proportional majority rule depending on the importance of the particular matter.[426] With a society as large as the Internet community, a proportional majority would be necessary in order for the decision to be supported and effectively carried out. If a decision has extensive consequences for civil society, it needs to be supported by a large part of it. At this stage, only a minority of active netizens controls the functioning of the Internet and takes decisions relating to Internet governance. More netizens need to be included in these processes in order to achieve legitimacy of taken decisions. Otherwise, as awareness and activeness of netizens increases, they will have the power to boycott the respective decisions taken by a minority if they have not thus been included in the decision-making processes.

(ii) According to ROUSSEAU, the faster a decision has to be taken, the fewer agreeing voices are necessary.[427] If a decision needs to be taken within a short period of time, it may not be possible to consult the entire Internet community. Therefore, a smaller number of agreeing voices should be sufficient to take the necessary

423 ROUSSEAU, Livre IV, Chapitre II, para. 5.

424 See WEBER, Regulatory Models, 82; BIEGEL, 101/02; see also GIBBONS, 518 ss and ANITA M. ALLEN, Social Contract Theory in American Case Law, Florida Law Review, Vol 51, 1999, 1 ss.

425 WEBER, Regulatory Models, 82.

426 See also WEIRICH, 11 ss.

427 ROUSSEAU, Livre IV, Chapitre II, para. 11.

actions.[428] With respect to the Internet, such an incident could for example be, the emergence of an aggressive virus threatening the sound functioning of the framework.

3.1 Inclusion of Civil Society in All Areas

a) Bottom-up Approach

All aspects of the Internet can have an impact on its daily use by civil society. Without any doubts, civil society is the most active user of the Internet and therefore the most significant player. Individuals not only have to be able to contribute to the decision-making matters, but they are also charged with carrying out the respective decisions in practice. Therefore, the understanding of civil society members as well as their specific requests have to be taken into account, regardless of whether the organization of the Internet, its governance, access or other topics are concerned.

The inclusion of civil society calls for a bottom-up process. Even if the various actors of civil society are independently organized, common strategies and goals can be developed and new networks created. The bottom-up approach also facilitates the enlargement of the foundation for active participation of Internet users.

This bottom-up approach may be implemented in practice by establishing a hierarchical framework, within which representatives from all regions are elected by the population. These representatives may have to, in a second phase, elect individuals among themselves who then are legitimate representatives of the whole population and receive a democratically based mandate to govern the Internet.

Already ARISTOTLE explained the best governance regime to be a combination of various features for the sake of the common good, however, he did not perceive democracy as the mandatory best regime, but rather aristocracy.[429] In aristocratic regimes, only a few are able to act as representatives for the benefit of the communal good. In order for this regime to fulfil the expectations of the whole community, the best ruling people should act "with a view to what is best for the city and for those who participate in it".[430]

In deciding who should be admitted as a representative and whether specific requirements need to be applied, valuable inputs could be derived from supranational organizations such as the EU, which also has to balance the interests of

428 See also PUTTERMAN, 459 ss.

429 ARISTOTLE, Book III, Chapter 7, 1279b.

430 ARISTOTLE, Book III, Chapter 7, 1279a36.

the organization against the interests of the individual States.[431] The consensus-making processes need to come under scrutiny, as representation only has a legitimizing effect if the outcome of decision-making processes reflects the values of the represented stakeholders. In particular, attention has to be paid to equal bargaining powers, fair proceedings, as well as enhanced transparency and review mechanisms.[432]

While the initial participation of civil society in the Internet is important, the follow-up processes also should be considered. Informing the public about ongoing issues, as well as about possibilities for active involvement in decision-making processes, has to be guaranteed.[433] Insofar, transparency and accountability are important pillars of an adequate structure.

Transparent procedures allow for a certain level of democratic legitimization and credibility through the active involvement of citizens as well as through certain controls over the decision-making processes.[434] Accountability is a pervasive concept, according to which the rulemaking body explains and justifies its actions or decisions as well as take responsibility for any committed fault. However, accountability of Internet governing bodies is not only important for the public to oversee the organizations' activities, but also serves the self-interest of the respective entities. A clear definition of the authority of each governing body and a justification for actions taken contributes to their respective effectiveness and credibility.[435]

The inclusion of civil society also means that responsiveness is a decisive criterion. Responsiveness of the concerned actors improves democratic quality, particularly in the context of "negotiations", since it best captures the legitimacy of the policy output.[436] In a deliberative approach to democracy, a rational discourse based on the actors' responsiveness would be an indicator of justification for the viability of the chosen system.[437]

b) Realization of an Open Society

In 1945, Karl Popper postulated the necessity of an "open society" which evolves in a perpetual process of attempting to ameliorate and correct errors.[438] Aims of

431 Komaitis, 69–75, with reference to "enhanced cooperation" as a particular approach.
432 Weber/Grosz, Legitimate Governing of the Internet, 326; Antonova, 8/9, 14–21, 97, 187–226.
433 See also Weber/Weber, Civil Society, 11 ss.
434 Weber, Enhancement of Transparency, 318.
435 Weber, Accountability, 146/147.
436 Dany, 54.
437 See also Dany, 54.
438 Popper, 462.

this openness are the preservation of individual freedom as well as the ideal of a political-ideological pluralism. Openness and acceptance of other approaches and solutions for problem-solving should be available; this would lead to a comparative environment and allow it the best approach to establish itself.[439]

This theory of an "open society" is particularly applicable to the Internet. As technical progress is enormous, new possibilities for participation may be discovered and former involvement processes could be ameliorated. The acceptance of other individuals' opinions is also extremely important considering the fact that people from all over the world participate in negotiations, despite their having different backgrounds and manifold ideas.

This "openness" presupposes that public fora remain accessible for a certain period of time so that members of civil society have the opportunity to make several statements, as well as respond to the inputs given by other actors. Furthermore, all people interested in Internet matters should be able to ask for information on particular subjects without having to prove a specific interest; a distinction between directly involved individuals and third parties does not need to be made. At the same time, special attention has to be given to include under-represented groups (e.g. indigenous people, disabled people, individuals from developing countries, etc.). As a consequence, the removal of access and linguistic barriers from negotiations is a necessary action, since it is particularly important to include these minorities, as they are the ones most affected by the digital divide.[440]

Time will show which proposals are effective. But in order to find out which methods should be pursued, several theoretical approaches need to be tested in practice.

3.2 No Authority of one Individual through the Creation of a Social Contract

The Internet is accessible from everywhere by everyone. At least theoretically, every member of civil society has the same opportunities and chances to benefit from this framework. However, this assumption can only be made if access to and active participation in the decision-making processes are open to all interested individuals.

Consequently, every user of the Internet should have the same opportunity to be heard and to influence the decision-making processes. Ideas and recommendations are to be considered on equal terms, irrespective of their source. In this

439 See also SALAMUN, 65/66 and SUNSTEIN, 105 ss, 169.

440 DANY, 60.

respect, members of civil society have alleged that the internationalization of Internet governance would be a first step towards overcoming the digital divide.[441]

Since the Internet needs to be governed and due to the fact that it may be difficult to establish a framework within which it is possible for the entire community to fulfil such a task together, a body (or bodies) performing this function needs to be appointed. Indeed, the technicalities of certain aspects of the Internet might not be easily manageable by a large part of civil society. Thus, not only a solution acceptable for all members needs to be found, but also a recourse system for the community to remonstrate in cases of disaccord concerning the actions of such an appointed body.

In order to prevent disagreement, the established body should consist of individuals with different backgrounds, bringing in diverse approaches and perceptions so that the debates among the different members of the body resemble discussions of all members of society. The body has the task to take care of day-to-day activities. However, if important questions regarding the Internet have to be addressed, civil society needs to be involved.

The Working Group on Internet Governance (WGIG), rather than having one body governing the Internet, proposes governance by different organizations and stakeholder groups, which communicate, coordinate and cooperate when managing their tasks.[442] On the one hand, this approach has the advantage of providing a more balanced governance regime, as there would be no organization in such a dominant position as to be allowed to take decisions by itself and, for example, to decide which suggestions should be submitted to civil society for evaluation. On the other hand, coordination of the different organizations involved may be difficult to achieve. Furthermore, an additional dispute mechanism would have to be established for deciding cases of dispute between the different organizations involved.

3.3 Application of the General Will (Volonté Générale)

a) Derived from Everyone

The "volonté générale", the general will of all individuals in a society, is the core of the social contract, originally applied to State theories. Finding a consensus amongst the entirety of civil society and merging its members into a moral and political collectivity is the main problem in the context of establishing a State. The better a consensus can be found, the less additional regulation is necessary, as all

441 WEBER/MENOUD, 3–20.

442 KLEINWÄCHTER, Multi-Stakeholder, 20/21.

members of the society agree on the appropriate rules of behavior.[443] The will of the ruler of a country should be identical with the will of the entire population, since State authority emerges from all individuals. In case of a diverging opinion related to an important issue, the social reunion and the entire political body would have to be dissolved.[444]

When applying ROUSSEAU's ideas to the Internet, the establishment of a public forum to which all interested parties have access should be addressed in a first step. Over a certain period of time, the public would have the possibility to submit ideas, contradict others and generally express its opinion. Based on this active involvement of civil society, groups with representatives having a voice on their behalf, would need to be formed. These representatives would have to meet regularly to find a common understanding for arising questions and to bring in the different points of view of the manifold parts of the society they represent. The governing body could consist of a number of such representatives. By narrowing down the number of participants through an actual vote in the end phase of the decision-making process, chances of finding a solution acceptable to all members of civil society (i.e. a solution that reflects the general will of all individuals), would be increased.

In 2001, LAWRENCE LESSIG described the Internet as "commons of knowledge" and compared it to an "Allmend", a medieval collective pasture land.[445] According to this perception, the Internet is open to all interested people. However, it also has to be used by the individuals in consideration of all other users. Such an open forum for communication should not be withdrawn from the population by privatization, for example.[446] Rather, this "openness" calls to be preserved within the established Internet framework enabling all netizens to participate in the regulation of the Internet.

In the field of Internet governance, it might be difficult to realize this idea in a way that all actors or stakeholders of civil society participate and express their voices in the relevant decision-making processes. Potentially, marginalized groups are faced with barriers to be heard; within civil society, some groups are likely to be under-represented, for example people from developing countries, indigenous people, disabled people, etc.[447] This fact is a particular concern since those groups may be the ones most affected by the digital divide.[448] Opportunities and mea-

443 ROUSSEAU, Livre IV, Chapitre I, para. 3; for Rousseau's concept of general will see also SREENIVASAN, 545 ss.

444 ROUSSEAU, Livre III, Chapitre I, para. 17.

445 LESSIG, Future of Ideas, 22.

446 LESSIG, Future of Ideas, 17–99.

447 DANY, 60.

448 WEBER/MENOUD, 4–7.

sures need to be worked out in order to increase the likelihood of participation by these stakeholders, as well as to remove the obstacles to participation and inclusion of these voices in the democratic process. Technical assistance by developed countries seems indispensable to achieve this goal. The cooperation among governments, contributing with financial aid, and non-governmental organizations (NGOs), providing knowledge and workforce, can help to distribute the various efforts among different actors and to increase the participation of inhabitants from developing countries, thereby enhancing democratic and legitimate processes.[449]

The commitment to establish participation by civil society based on equal rights in the given legal framework can be considered as an expression of the intention to realize participatory democracy. A major role must be played by the citizens, including the possibility of popular discourses and social actions.[450] Individuals can create their own communities of common concern and contribute to the opinion-building process of civil society. The advantage of this participatory model as compared to professional politicians and bureaucrats is to be seen in the fact that civil society knows its own preferences and is therefore better able to express them politically.

Direct elections are seen as a mechanism to improve participation of civil society and reduce the accountability and legitimacy deficit of the Internet. However, as the failed attempt to establish such open-access Internet-wide elections by ICANN showed, such an attempt poses major challenges.[451]

However, it may be questionable whether the termination of ICANN's experiment was in fact the right decision or whether other means to encourage the public to vote could have been found, thus enabling proper elections and therewith actually contributing to accountability enhancement. Information about the possibility to vote should have been disseminated through the Internet itself, but also through other channels such as newspapers, radio and television. That way, a broader public might have been approached. If individuals only use the Internet for specific purposes, or very infrequently, they most probably do not visit ICANN's webpage and therefore may not have known about the elections. However, these individuals could have been interested in the subject and likely to vote if they had been informed about the voting possibility.[452]

[449] For the importance of access to the Internet see also ESTERHUYSEN/CURRIE, 60 ss; SADOWSKY, Importance of Access, 68 ss.

[450] CHARNOVITZ, 312.

[451] Of the estimated 375 million Internet users at the time, less than 0.01% actually voted; WEBER/GROSZ, Legitimate Governing of the Internet, 318/19; WEBER/WEBER, Civil Society, 14 fn. 52; DE VEY MESTAGH/RIJGERSBERG, 29; see also above III.C.4.2 c).

[452] WEBER, Accountability, 154/55.

Even if a method for participation of netizens can be found which effectively includes all interested people in decision-making processes, it should not be overlooked that multi-stakeholderism (as the term suggests) cannot circumvent the big differences which exist among the manifold entities involved; therefore, influential States (mostly, developed ones) will remain very powerful actors within the Internet framework. Unlike developing States or individual representatives of civil society, these States will have the necessary power to implement their ideas of good governance.[453]

b) Aimed at Everyone's Welfare

According to ROUSSEAU, through the establishment of a society, each individual is protected by the whole of the community. As a single person, the individual may not have the necessary force to protect himself against attacks from outside, but the entire society together is strong enough to resist such incidents.[454]

The efforts to find a consensus can also contribute to the development of an individual's character. During negotiations, others have to be respected, their views and ideas need to become subjects of deliberations and compromises have to be made. It is indispensable to define standard rules of behavior expected to be followed by the individuals participating in a forum which allows the exchange of different views. These rules, too, must take into account the cultural diversity of the Internet society.

Through the Internet, the exchange of views and ideas is facilitated. Online forums accessible to everyone can be established. By way of these forums, individuals from all over the world can communicate, however, Internet access is needed. The Internet is suited to serve as a framework for innovations and help civil society to progress in its development. Cross-cultural dialogues broaden individuals' horizons and help to create a common understanding.

Furthermore, by enhancing access to and participation in the Internet, better use can be made of the public service value of the Internet. No other medium is able to spread information in such a short period of time, making it possible for netizens all around the world to communicate on current topics. In addition, organizing events and helping people in need, is facilitated because information flow is faster and details about what is needed can be transmitted more easily.

A problem related to responsiveness and participation concerns the question of whether input actually and effectively leads to impact. Obviously, the multi-stakeholder approach is not accomplished by merely providing the preconditions for

453 KOMAITIS, 57.

454 ROUSSEAU, Livre I, Chapitre VI, para. 2.

the participation of civil society; it also requires the provision of a real opportunity to shape policy output.[455] In so far, an evaluation should be conducted regarding the influence which the voices of the various stakeholders have on the decision-making process. The listening to the voices of the members of civil society should not become a mere delusion since in such case the outcome of the deliberations would not result in everyone's welfare according to the social contract theory.

The governing body has to effectively take into account inputs made by civil society and be able to justify specific cases in which it might depart from a particular request stemming from the community. Only if reasons have to be given for the performance of the governing body, can civil participation in fact be democratic and have a legitimizing effect.

Online deliberations are realizable at a much lower cost than offline deliberative democracy processes, they are more synchronous and less limited in practice. Group discussions, collaborative authorships as well as decision-making can be improved within an online framework. Audio and video conferencing software already exists (e.g. Skype); further technical improvements are scheduled and should be supported in order to allow large groups of netizens to access debates synchronously.[456]

4. Enshrinement of Fundamental Rights

4.1 Right to Freedom

a) Continuing Freedom for Everyone

ROUSSEAU, with his concept of a social contract, envisaged overcoming all inequalities and bondages, by establishing a system in which everyone had the same rights and obligations so that individuals could feel as free as they would in their natural state. For each part of liberty that the individual had to give up when a society was established, it received a corresponding part of another individual's liberty, so that in the end, after the society had been established, each member had received adequate compensation or even additional forces and strengths to preserve what he or she owned.[457] Therefore, the social contract helped to secure the self-determination of all individuals.[458] KANT followed the same ideal by arguing that individuals remained free because they only had to submit their will to the

[455] DANY, 61.

[456] MALCOLM, Governance, 277–278; see also ZITTRAIN, 162–163 and SUNSTEIN, 38/39, 153 (deliberative democracy).

[457] ROUSSEAU, Livre I, Chapitre VI, para. 8.

[458] HERB, 146/7.

law which represented the public will. Only if they had to obey to another person, would individuals have to give up their freedom.[459]

Deductions for the Internet community can be made by analogy from ROUSSEAU's social contract theory. On the one hand, the members of civil society may have to give up a part of their decision-making powers to a specialized governing body (for example ICANN); this fact may limit their freedom inasmuchas direct influence on certain decisions may no longer be possible, even though the individual may be affected by them. On the other hand, such a body also supervises and guarantees the permanent functioning of the Internet to the advantage of the individual, who would not manage the respective tasks on his/her own.

b) Socialization and Right to Freedom

Each individual, according to ROUSSEAU, dissolves completely and with him all his rights into the collectivity, without any reservation whatsoever.[460] The group of individuals concluding the social contract is replaced by a collective body.[461] Only if power, freedom and rules coalesce in one authority, can a "republic"—the ideal constitution according to IMMANUEL KANT—be guaranteed.[462]

However, concerning personal rights, each individual stays as free as before and only obeys to himself. In particular, all property rights are preserved. Unlike the socialist doctrine, ROUSSEAU protects the institution of personal property and does not intend to abolish it.

The same conclusions can be drawn for participation in the Internet. Obviously, certain compromises are inevitable and decisions of the majority have to be accepted by the minority. However, personal self-determination as well as all other fundamental rights are preserved. Contrary to the social contract, the Internet touches only on a part of an individual's rights, such as the fundamental aspects of dignity, integrity and equality of individuals, as well as the right to freedom of expression and information and privacy rights. Therefore, its effect is also less far-reaching than the establishment of a society. Nevertheless, a social contract could be perceived as a basis for the tendencies towards increased humanization of Internet governance and towards a comprehensive human rights architecture for the Internet.[463]

459 KANT, III 492; see also NIEBLING, 51–61.
460 ROUSSEAU, Livre I, Chapitre VI, paras. 5 and 6.
461 ROUSSEAU, Livre I, Chapitre VI, para. 10.
462 IMMANUEL KANT, Anthropologie in programmatischer Hinsicht, Königsberg, 1798, 330/31.
463 BENEDEK, Human Rights, 31 ss.

4.2 Equity and Equality

ROUSSEAU departs from the idea that every individual has a natural dignity, a right to self-determination and a demand for equality. By equality, ROUSSEAU does not necessarily mean material equity, but rather the same chance of development for everyone.[464]

In Internet matters, too, each interested party has the same rights and obligations. All inputs and opinions have the same weight and are considered by the rest of the Internet community, whatever their source may be. Discriminatory treatment of individuals' comments by the governing body, regarding origin, religion or any other individual characteristic, may not be tolerated.

This theoretical concept, of course, implies that a possibility to access the Internet in all geographical areas exists; since this is not actually the case for the time being, access needs to be increased. For a large part of the world's population, technical and financial barriers impede effective use of the proposed fora. Practical and monetary support needs to be given to developing countries in order to increase their access to the Internet. Experienced and skilled countries, international organizations and civil society have to share their knowledge with less-developed countries.[465] Official development assistance programs, the International Monetary Fund, the World Bank Group, public-private partnerships or the Global Digital Solidarity Fund could contribute to the financial means needed for spurring world-wide access to the Internet.[466]

4.3 Fairness

Apart from equity and equality, a further principle needs to be introduced in the discussion, namely the notion of fairness. Decision-making processes are by far not always fair. For example, in the present international landscape, two principles are compromising the fairness of decision-making processes, namely (i) the fact that the general rule according to which each State possesses one vote does not consider the size of the population and (ii) the fact that only governments, not stakeholders of civil society have a vote in the relevant processes. Such kinds of fairness deficit—coming close to the perception of clientelism—create problems for humanized structure of the international system, in particular due to the discrepancies between the claimed values (such as equity, justice, protection of weak people) and the vehicles of practical actions and programs.

464 ROUSSEAU, Livre I, Chapitre VI, para. 8.
465 WEBER/MENOUD, 179.
466 WEBER/MENOUD, 63–177; see also below VI.B.3 and VI.E.

In order to overcome this "fairness deficit", a new forum should be created "in which people rather than governments are directly represented".[467] Such a new forum could help to establish an adequate correlation between population and representation. This objective would "provide an opportunity for institutionalizing the democratic entitlement and certifying the authenticity of the link between people and their representatives".[468] If the multi-stakeholders concerned express their voices, the concept of a general will (volonté générale) is more likely to be achieved than in a system with a strict political structure in the traditional sense.

An example for such a public discussion forum is the Internet Governance Forum (IGF),[469] which has the objective of collecting the voices of civil society and bringing forward proposals for the improvement of Internet governance.[470] Participatory processes and regular, democratic elections enhance accountability within the IGF.[471]

5. Outlook

In the historical and philosophical discussion, the model of a social contract has been developed (mainly according to Rousseau), encompassing all individuals of a society voluntarily unifying themselves in order to originate new forces. According to this theory, a positive outcome of societal processes calls for implementation of common interests.

Similarly, civil society as the most active user of the Internet needs to be included in the participatory and decision-making processes of its governance. Relevant aspects to be properly tackled encompass transparency, accountability, stability, and sustainability of participants' activities. The inclusion of civil society requires the implementation of a bottom-up process allowing responsiveness of the concerned actors in a rational discourse which improves democratic quality of the structures. In practice, e-inclusion must be enhanced on all levels; this means, among other things, that approaches with e-voting should be revitalized again in an improved way, that discussion fora need to be implemented, and that the building of new coalitions merits to be tested. Thereby, policy and legal decisions are to be accompanied by empirical investigations based on a solid research methodology.

467 Franck, Fairness, 482.
468 Franck, Fairness, 482.
469 For the establishment process of the IGF see above III.D. and Masango, 63–77.
470 Weber/Grosz, Vague Ideas, 125–127.
471 Malcolm, Governance, 498.

With the establishment of civil society, each individual is protected by the whole of the community, receiving the same rights and obligations which enable equal opportunities of development for everyone, in particular, with respect to ensuring the individual freedoms—which secure the self-determination of all individuals. Furthermore, a new forum should be created to realize appropriate fairness in all decision-making matters.

All these ideas related to the creation of a sound civil society in the Internet world are not completely new. Historical and philosophical theories have already laid down many valuable thoughts, mainly related to the creation of a social contract, which could be revitalized and further developed in the context of the discourse on Internet governance. Insofar, much room is left for further interdisciplinary academic research.

B. Multi-Stakeholderism in Internet Governance

1. Introduction

As outlined, several steps have been taken towards an international conciliation in the field of Internet governance.[472] However, so far, the attempts to reach a common understanding of Internet governance have not really been successful,[473] i.e. some major issues remain controversial and are of predominant relevance in view of the ongoing discussions.

Fresh thinking is needed, taking into account that a new global infrastructure calls for different forms of governance in order to be appropriate and efficient.[474] On the one hand, when addressing the Internet and its governance in general, a consensus should be found on the key principles at issue with regard to the particularities of this specific field of action. On the other hand, the strengths and weaknesses of the present architectural frameworks, and ICANN in particular, need to be identified, before daring to frame ideas for possible future Internet governance institutional mechanisms.

Several aspects merit to be discussed; in particular the question of, who governs the Internet (in international politics), needs to be addressed. Many answers can be given, partly based on theories already developed for the real world, which seem adaptable to the virtual world. At any rate, shared power among several

472 This chapter partly follows the deliberations in WEBER/GROSZ, Vague Ideas, 127 ss.

473 PARÉ, 58.

474 From a sociological angle see CRAMPTON, 94 ss; see also SINGH, 32 ss and 276 ss to the power configuration in the context of governance.

social participants of the online world seems to be unavoidable, i.e. multi-stakeholderism must become the underlying concept for the development of the Internet regulatory environment.[475] Hereinafter, subsequent to a description of the architectural and constitutional principles applicable in the Internet environment, light will be shed mainly on the theories of an international regime formation and on government networks.

2. Architectural and Constitutional Principles

The Internet was established mainly by the private sector which mostly followed a bottom-up approach in self-regulation, taking special account of the technical issues raised by this new network system. In the meantime, the development of Internet regulation by State law has become an undisputed fact. The legal doctrine has realized that a fitting of the legal framework needs to consider the principles of the subject it addresses and hence pay special attention to the technological environment of the Internet.[476] Subsequently, some initiatives which are suited to lead to a new regulatory environment will be discussed.

The European Union proposal, submitted to the WSIS process during the third preparatory conference for the Tunis meeting (PrepCom 3) on 30th September 2005, explicitly addressed "the architectural principles of the Internet, including the interoperability, openness and the end-to-end principle", however, without providing for a definition of these concepts.[477] A certain definition can be found in the RFC 1958, a document of the Internet Architecture Board's (IAB) Network Working Group entitled "Architectural Principles of the Internet"[478] which also mentions technological change and development in the information technology industry. Furthermore, this document states that the Internet community's belief is "that the goal is connectivity, the tool is the Internet Protocol, and the intelligence is end-to-end rather than hidden in the network".[479] The end-to-end principle (e2e) in particular is referred to as one of the most fundamental architectural principles of the Internet. It stipulates that the network should merely transmit data pack-

---

475 ANTONOVA, 8; MALCOLM, Governance, 319/320; FELIX DODDS, in: HEMMATI, 26 ss; whether ICANN is really the pioneer of global multi-stakeholderism (in this sense ANTONOVA, 9 and 14/15) seems to be doubtful.

476 First theoretical attempts to develop a legal framework were undertaken by JOEL REIDENBERG in 1998 with the "lex informatica" and by LAWRENCE LESSIG a year later with the concept of a "code based regulation". For further information on the standard-setting model of coordination see LIU, 587–590, 595–604; see also WEBER, Regulatory Models, 89–100; SOLUM, 61–68.

477 § 63, fourth bullet point of the European Proposal.

478 See IETF, Architectural Principles of the Internet, RFC 1958.

479 See IETF, Architectural Principles of the Internet, RFC 1958, 2.1.

ages, without performing further functions such as authentication, processing or filtering based on the contents of the data, etc., therewith taking due account of the principle of net neutrality.[480]

Perspectives for the development of Internet governance could also be drawn from the experience made in other segments of the economy with similar characteristics as the Internet. In particular, areas of international resources that should be open to all people could allow for potential analogies.[481] However, in contrast to the finite key resources of the Industrial Age such as natural resources, energy, satellite positions etc., the virtual resources of the Internet, i.e. IP addresses in particular, especially after the adoption of the Internet Protocol version 6 (IPv6), will be comparably unlimited and geographically non-locatable.[482] Therefore, regulation priority in Internet governance should not be given to equal distribution, but moreso to unhindered access.[483]

However, the flexibility and openness aspired should not disregard a minimum of predictability required for an adequate legal framework in order to establish reliable relations between natural or legal persons. The sole regard of the technical aspect of a rule setting framework would leave several problems—in terms of governance issues—unsolved,[484] not least because each civil society must be based on a minimal "constitutional" framework.

In this sense, it is interesting to note that the European Proposal attaches values to the technical principles mentioned, by referring to them as "architectural" and therewith situating them on a higher, "constitutional" level together with the Geneva Principles and further guidelines as well as general legal principles. The latter are accepted by most States and play an important role in international law.[485] They may encompass behavior in good faith, principles of equal treatment and fairness in trade etc., i.e. fundamental rules that can be found in every legal system and are recognized by the entities concerned.[486] The Geneva Principles in

---

480 See Mayer-Schönberger/Ziewitz, 22 with further references; for additional information on characteristics of global networks see Weber, Regulatory Models, 41–43; to the net neutrality principle see below VI.3.2.

481 See Weber, Regulatory Models, 75–77.

482 Whilst the Internet Protocol version 4 (IPv4) provided for just over four billion unique addresses on the network, IPv6 will expand the number of Internet addresses considerably (see ICANN, Factsheet, IPv6—The Internet's vital expansion, October 2007, available at <http://www.icann.org/en/announcements/factsheet-ipv6-26oct07.pdf>; see also below VI.B.1.

483 Kleinwächter, Internet Governance, 221–222. For further details on the transition from IPv4 to IPv6 see VI.B.2.

484 Weber, Regulatory Models, 89–100 and 99 in particular.

485 See above I.C.1.1 d).

486 See Weber, Regulatory Models, 66–67.

particular include efforts for an inclusive information society with access to information and knowledge, the respect for cultural identity, cultural and linguistic diversity, as well as the right to freedom of expression and opinion.

For example, censorship of the Internet should not be tolerated; diversity and pluralism of the contents of the Internet have become a common objective.[487] Furthermore, specific aims can be drawn from the communication rights perspective, chosen by the various civil society coalition campaigns, for example on Communication Rights in the Information Society (CRIS) or on the Internet Bill of Rights,[488] aiming at the democratization of access to and the strengthening of communications in favor of sustainable development. This approach lays its focus on building a more people-centred communications landscape based on human rights and social justice.[489] The final objective should be the more sophisticated use of the Internet, and thereby greater global participation by an increasing number of citizens from diverse linguistic and cultural backgrounds.[490]

The key principles have to be considered as a source for legislation and respected as guidelines when referring to Internet governance in general.[491] Furthermore, they have to provide for substantive self-constraints in the policy-making of the governing institutions themselves.[492] The establishment of consensus on their content should be a main issue in the future rounds of negotiations. In the process, due attention should be paid to the attempts taken and the principles chosen by the European Proposal as well as to the CRIS. Unlike ICANN's legitimacy, which is founded on the selection process of its Board Members, the mandate to follow the principles of the Internet community, at least to an extent, addresses legitimacy issues more effectively, by referring to a level of principles which exists independently of the actual policies of individual representatives. By adhering to fundamental principles of cyberspace, the Internet community experiences a form of representation on the international level.[493]

---

487 § 63 of the European Proposal; see Mayer-Schönberger/Ziewitz, 204–205; see also UNESCO Position Paper on Internet Governance available at <http://portal.unesco.org> and Schmidt/Coudray, 221–229.

488 See above III.D and below VI.C.4.2 b).

489 Buckley; for further information on CRIS see <http://www.crisinfo.org>.

490 See UNESCO Position Statement on Internet Governance, available at <http://portal.unesco.org>.

491 See The Recipes, Recommendations of the OSCE, Representative on Freedom of the Media from the 2004 Amsterdam Internet Conference, first bullet point under "A. Legislation & Jurisdiction", available at <http://www.osce.org/publications/rfm/2004/12/12239_91_en.pdf> and printed in: Möller/Amouroux (eds), 15–27.

492 Mayer-Schönberger/Ziewitz, 205–207.

493 Mayer-Schönberger/Ziewitz, 206–207; Weber/Grosz, Legitimate Governing of the Internet, 324/25.

3. Theories of Global Rulemaking

3.1 Processes of International Regime Formation

Already in 1975, JOHN GERARD RUGGIE described the processes of international regime formation and of international organizations' establishment as products resulting from the interactions between science and politics on the one hand, and collective response and national control on the other hand.[494] Based on the assumption that high levels of cognitive interdepence (defined as "the recognition that a collective situation exists and that continued national isolation would be mutually inefficient, whereas collective awareness and attention may be mutually beneficial"[495]) do exist, the logical international response can be given in three different ways: through epistemic communities, international regimes and/or international organizations.[496] Epistemic communities are created when "no State goes out of its way to construct international collective arrangements".[497]

In the light of the important technological developments, RUGGIE[498] proposed that international organizations should become leading players in the development and implementation of policies; power of States was seen as lacking, and the level of interaction required between States made other responses rather inappropriate. The weakness of this approach seems to consist in the unilateral determination of the successful model; in view of the numerous stakeholders playing a role in Internet governance, it might be unavoidable to rely on different models of governance. So far, the following types have been acknowledged in practice:[499]

- Top-down, hierachical: Governments and international organizations;
- Non-governmental, self-regulatory: Commercial actors, ICANN, TRUSTe[500];
- Bottom-up (decentralised), but lightly coordinated: IETF, ISOC;
- Bottom-up, disperse (decentralised self-governance[501]): Civil society, users.

Furthermore, civil society might have general interests which are not taken into account by "technology". If regulation is left to code-based techniques[502] collective values such as public order and morals will be left out of consideration; full

494 RUGGIE, Concepts, 559 ss.
495 RUGGIE, Concepts, 562.
496 RUGGIE, Concepts, 569–574.
497 RUGGIE, Concepts, 570.
498 RUGGIE, Concepts, 573/74.
499 See also PARÉ, 58.
500 On TRUSTe see ESTHER DYSON, Release 2.0, A Design for Living in the Digital Age, New York 1997, 28.
501 See PARÉ, 47.
502 See LESSIG, Code, 25 ss, 43/44, 67, 87–89, 126 ss, 206.

disintermediation and private rulemaking could Balkanize public discourse and leave civil society without reasonable possibilities to assess the reliability of Internet information and expressions.[503]

In elaborating on the process of international regime formation, the reality that the call for globalization is not unanimous in the scholarly literature should not be disregarded. Apart from the fact that no single universally agreed definition of globalization exists,[504] skeptical voices cannot be overlooked, as they come from economic and ideological points of view.[505] The discussions can be summarized in the following chart:[506]

	Globalists	**Skeptics**
Concepts	– One world, shaped by extensive, intensive and rapid flow of goods/services/data	– Internationalization, not globalization – Regionalization
Power	– Rise of multilateralism – Decline of nation State – Erosion of State sovereignty, autonomy and legitimacy	– National State rules – Intergovernmentalism
Culture	– Emergence of global popular culture	– Resurgence of nationalism and national identity
Economy	– Transnational economy – Global informational capitalism	– Development of regional blocs – New imperialism
Inequality	– Growing inequality within and across societies – Erosion of old hierarchies	– Growing North-South divide – Irreconcilable conflicts of interests
Order	– Global civil society – Multilayered global governance – Cosmopolitanism	– International society of States – Political conflicts among States – Communitarianism

The financial and economic crisis which has been spreading around the world since 2008, seems to have weakened the promoters of a globalist approach. Nevertheless, the difficulties in the real world should not lead to the assumption that global governance could lose grounds within the context of the information soci-

503 See WEBER, Regulatory Models, 99.

504 See ANTONOVA, 66 ss with further references.

505 On the sceptical, particularly neo-Marxist view see HELD/MCGREW, 5.

506 Partly adopted from ANTONOVA, 67/68.

ety; moreover, the need to come to generally applicable non-discriminatory rules for the governance of the Internet is not impaired.[507]

3.2 Creation of Government Networks

Cyberspace significantly differs from nation States according to the Westphalian perception of international law and its subjects. Therefore, the need to substitute national regulatory approaches with globally standardized actions is undisputed and leads to the emergence of intensified global responsibilities and possibly shared sovereignty.[508]

In connection with the need for establishing global rules and institutions in terms of global governance, the so-called "governance dilemma"[509] or "globalization paradox"[510] arises according to which, institutions essential to human life, nevertheless, bear certain threats for the society's liberty. When referring to the Internet, "liberty" is contained within the key values such as freedom of expression, cultural diversity and openness. Governance of the Internet should not hinder the free flow of ideas and knowledge or complicate technical innovation.[511]

The legal doctrine has addressed this "governance dilemma" and proposed new concepts of looking at international law; subsequently, light will be shed on the work of KAL RAUSTIALA and ANNE-MARIE SLAUGHTER in particular:

RAUSTIALA assesses the viability of transgovernmental networks and evaluates their relationship to liberal internationalism.[512] The transgovernmental cooperation is exemplified in the fields of securities regulation, competition policy and environmental regulation.[513] A special focus on the "informal" information exchanges among the competent authorities for the sectoral legal rules is based on sets of direct interactions among sub-units of different governments which are not controlled by the decision-making bodies of the respective States. This kind of cooperation leads to a disaggregation of States in favor of the established networks, i.e. to a "disaggregated sovereignty";[514] thereby, actual cooperation and solution achievement could be improved.[515] Even treaty compliance might gain bet-

507 On the global governance theories see also ANTONOVA, 74–77.

508 KLEINWÄCHTER, Internet Governance, 221; see also WEBER, Regulatory Models, 77.

509 KEOHANE, 1.

510 SLAUGHTER, 8–11.

511 See UNESCO Position Statement.

512 RAUSTIALA, 17 ss.

513 RAUSTIALA, 26 ss.

514 RAUSTIALA, 10.

515 RAUSTIALA, 23/24, 55/56.

ter attention in a system of transgovernmentalism.[516] Nevertheless, the weakness of this approach consists on the lack of political control and on the democratic deficit as well as on the normative concerns regarding the missing (formal) legal framework.[517]

In "A New World Order", SLAUGHTER attempts to offer a solution for the "governance dilemma" by referring to "government networks". These are set out as "relatively loose, cooperative arrangements across borders between and among like agencies that seek to respond to global issues"[518] and that manage to close gaps through coordination among governments from different States, "creating a new sort of power, authority, and legitimacy".[519] This model presupposes disaggregated States, in other words, it sees governments as a decomposed collection of disparate institutions, each with its own powers, mandates, incentives, motivations, abilities etc. similar to the term "government" which can be understood as the various activities of the courts, the parliaments, the regulatory agencies and the executive itself.[520] This approach is contrary to the perception of unitary States according to traditional international law. In SLAUGHTER's view, national governments cannot effectively address every problem in a networked world and should therefore delegate their responsibilities and "actual sovereign power to a limited number of supranational government officials"[521] which then should engage in intensive interaction and in the elaboration and adoption of codes of best practice and agreements on coordinated solutions to common problems.[522]

Translated into terms of Internet governance, this theory leads to a model of a governance body, formed by the networks achieved through negotiations at international level. This forum for government officials specialized on Internet issues would permit coordination on a global level and create a new authority responsible and accountable for Internet governance. The focus would not be set on unitary sovereign nation States' governments, but on a limited number of supranational government officials within the Internet governance body. Their networks would, thereby, take due account of already existing international organizations, corporations, NGOs and other actors in the transnational society.[523]

---

516 RAUSTIALA, 76 ss.

517 RAUSTIALA does not address the democratic elements of a liberal State; on this aspect see below V.B.

518 ANDERSON, 1257; see also SLAUGHTER, 14.

519 ANDERSON, 1257.

520 SLAUGHTER, 12–13.

521 SLAUGHTER, 263.

522 SLAUGHTER, 263.

523 SLAUGHTER, 262–263.

However, the concept of government networks has not been spared from criticism. Although governments are specifically legitimized through democratic elections, it has been objected that, over time, this proposed new world order could fail to preserve democracy and democratic accountability; last but not least, due to its top-down approach, it could finally lead to a form of liberal internationalism.[524]

4. Milestones for Multi-Stakeholderism in Internet Governance

With respect to the developments at an international level, it seems probable that ICANN will not be able to continue as it is constituted at present. The call for a more legitimate organizational structure will not fade away; therefore, a more satisfactory governance system has to be worked out for the appeasement of all involved parties. As a first step, the need for better transparency should be tackled. Second, attempts of governing the Internet at an international level need to address the basic question of whether a new international governance body replacing ICANN should be established at all. If this question is answered affirmatively, solutions have to be found for its set-up and, additionally, for the issues it should deal with and regulate. Some of them will be outlined in the following.

4.1 Improvement of ICANN's Democratic Legitimacy

As a non-profit organization and at first glance, ICANN seems to correspond to the model of government networks. Nation States are not in a position to mutually govern the technical regulation of the Internet, therefore, the corresponding responsibilities are delegated to the specialized Californian organization. However, even if ICANN should establish a network, in terms of an internationally active organization, the delegation to "supranational government officials" seems questionable, in particular because ICANN's role as a political representative is ambivalent. On the one hand, ICANN has repeatedly insisted on being percepted as a merely technical organization, not as a political policy-making entity; on the other hand, the organization's legitimacy is questioned and its techniques of representation are deemed to be unsatisfactory, since the heterogeneous Internet community is not actually reflected throughout the organization's structures, despite the fact that ICANN emphasizes the representative component within its Board.[525] The GAC cannot officially claim to represent the governments in their

[524] ANDERSON, 1301–1310.

[525] ICANN Management Operating Principles, Accountability & Transparency, Framework and Principles, 21–22.

entirety, since it is established based only on ICANN's Bylaws, not on an intergovernmental treaty.[526]

Legitimacy can be described as "the aspect of governance that validates institutional decisions as emanating from right process. What constitutes right process is described in a society's adjectival constitution or rules of order, or is pedigreed by tradition and historic custom".[527] Democratic processes are not mandatory for the constitution of legitimate decision-making; however, they play a major role in fairness and legitimacy debates in the West and in the foreign policy of the US in particular. "Democracy" generally addresses the role of people in governance. In order to facilitate governing, the people holding actual political power transfer their control over the nation's validation process to another level, which encompasses national electoral commissions, parliaments etc. Legitimate validation is achieved by these entities that decide whether democratic guidelines have been met by those claiming the right to govern.[528]

As outlined above,[529] the lack of an adequate democratic and legitimized background of ICANN was repeatedly brought forward during the discussions of Internet governance on the international stage. Originally, the US pointed out that the At-Large Board Members election was a specific form of a democratically legitimated, bottom-up decision-making process, five of the members of ICANN's Board were selected through Internet-wide elections to represent users in various geographic regions. However, in 2002 ICANN's reorganization abolished these At-Large Board Members and introduced an almost entirely internal selection process, subject to certain rules requiring geographic diversity. This lack of transparency was criticized[530] and was not appeased by ICANN's subsequent adoption of legitimizing techniques from US administrative agencies.[531]

An additional aspect must also be taken into account: The private sector has an influence on the architecture of the Internet and on ICANN in various respects. Not only do representatives of global companies participate in discussion fora and in particular, in the opinion-building within the IGF framework, but these companies (like Google, Yahoo, Microsoft, Cisco) have also participated in actions of some national governments, for example in China, to limit freedom of expression on the Internet.[532] After some critical motions were made at IGF's meeting in

---

526 Weinberg, 235–249, 258–259.

527 Franck, Democracy, Legitimacy and the Rule of Law, 1.

528 See Franck, Fairness, 83–91; Weber/Grosz, Legitimate Governing of the Internet, 322/323 on different perceptions of democracy.

529 See above III.C.4.2 c).

530 Mayer-Schönberger/Ziewitz, 196 with further references.

531 Mayer-Schönberger/Ziewitz, 196; Weinberg, 235–249, 258–259.

532 See Goldsmith/Wu, 10, 93–96; Malcolm, The Space Law Analogy, 19.

Rio de Janeiro, the concerned companies announced that they would build a new multi-stakeholder network aiming to produce a code of conduct on the private sector involvement in national Internet regulation.[533] In the meantime, the respective code, called Global Network Initiative was published.[534] Insofar, legitimizing efforts are also made outside of the framework of the institutionalized fora such as ICANN and IGF.

Legitimacy crises are well-known to many international organizations, such as the European Union, the World Trade Organization or the United Nations.[535] In debates concerning this situation, the question may arise as to whether the traditional perception of democratic legitimacy is appropriate for these specific fora. Even if the election of an international organization's council, for example, pays due regard to the need of equitable distribution of council seats among the five world regions, the democratic legitimacy of the individual functionary—after all in charge of specific policy decisions—may remain rather questionable and not much more favorable than the direct election of board members via the Internet.[536] Therefore, if the legitimacy of the international entities is deduced from the legitimacy of national regimes, without taking due account of the national situation,[537] even the most democratic process at international level, may not suffice to meet the desired standards. As a consequence, in Internet governance, legitimacy based on democratic entitlement solely, should not be overestimated.[538]

4.2 Need for Better Transparency and Accountability

Transparency is a recognized significant norm and principle for regulatory systems. Its importance stems from its relevance in the achievement of other necessary tenets of regulation, such as independence and accountability of regulators or providing sufficient information to enable informed decisions.[539] Accessibility, clarity, logic and rationality, truthfulness and accuracy, as well as openness are further major characteristics associated with the notion of transparency. Modern legal jurisprudence asserts that the validity of legal rules depends in part, on whether those obliged by the rules can ascertain in advance what behavior or re-

533 Press release available at <http://www.cdt.org/press/20070118press-humanrights.php>.
534 See below VI.C.4.1 b).
535 See the discussions following the rejection of a European Constitution and the ideas to reform the United Nations. For more information on the general debates see amongst many others: Kluth, 30 ss; Elsig, 80; Clark, 11–30, 173–189.
536 See also Kleinsteuber, 73.
537 See Franck, Fairness, 91.
538 See also Weber/Grosz, Legitimate Governing of the Internet, 320–324 and Hunter, 1181 ss.
539 Amtenbrink, 2.

straint is required.[540] Since a transparent methodology for rulemaking processes based on revisable procedures reduces mistrust and can have a legitimizing effect, transparency should be a persistent objective of any governance mechanism.

Elements of transparency[541] have become significant aspects of good regulatory governance and have been increasingly acknowledged as important in many areas of public policy. In fact, transparency and accountability issues were mentioned both in ICANN's Bylaws[542] as well as in the Joint Project Agreement between the US Department of Commerce and ICANN which replaced the MoU in 2006.[543] Their importance was further underlined within ICANN itself by an independent review of its accountability and transparency as well as by its recent posting of the Draft Management Operating Principles for Community Consultation.[544]

Correspondingly, accountability merits further examination.[545] Indeed, in order to achieve transparency in the regulation process, the Internet could be used to improve open access to negotiations, to collect proposals and statements from the various stakeholders concerned, to present the decisions and results, and thereby to enhance and facilitate communication and dialogue.[546]

4.3 Creation of an International Internet Governance Body

To date, several players are concerned by the governing of the online world. The major stakeholders involved are governments, Internet Services Providers (ISPs), local telephone companies, builders and custodians of Internet backbone, hardware and software companies, as well as numerous Internet organizations.[547] In view of the complexities entailed by the involvement of such different players with diverging points of view and varying approaches regarding the same field of interest, the question of whether it would be more appropriate to establish a uniform international Internet governance body must be addressed.

a) Appropriateness and Framework

The European Proposal brought forward the suggestion to build on the existing mechanisms and structures of Internet governance, adding special emphasis to

540 See also KLEINSTEUBER, 73; HART, 10.
541 For further details see below V.C.
542 ICANN Bylaws, Article III Section 1 and Article I Section 2.
543 Section V.B.1 of the Joint Project Agreement.
544 See Announcement of 23rd June 2007, available at <http://www.icann.org/announcements>.
545 For further details see below V.D.
546 See KLEINSTEUBER, 73; MALCOLM, Governance, 260–266; WEBER, Transparency, 348; WEBER, Accountability, 153/54.
547 WEBER, Regulatory Models, 51–52.

the complementarity among all the actors already involved in the process. Switzerland supported this approach.[548] The idea makes sense in terms of efficiency—since the existing bodies concerned with the Internet are experienced and possess a high level of specialization—and should not be completely replaced by new mechanisms.

At international level, expert bodies are a familiar instrument. The Financial Stability Board (FSB) (until April 2009, known as the Financial Stability Forum [FSF]), for example, brings together representatives of national financial authorities, international financial institutions, international regulatory and supervisory groupings, committees of central bank experts and the European Central Bank with the objective of promoting international financial stability, by means of exchanging information and of cooperating in financial supervision and surveillance.[549] Both the International Monetary Fund (IMF)[550] and the World Bank[551] provide for representation of their shareholders in the Board of Governors, which convenes one governor and one alternate governor for each member country. Generally these governors are government officials who meet once a year and constitute the highest decision-making bodies of these entities.

The establishment of an international forum of governments confirms the constitutional approach mentioned above[552]. Thereby, the fields of action of the States on the one hand, and the private sector on the other hand, need to be distinguished: The States remain responsible for addressing public policy issues related to key elements of Internet governance as well as typical sovereignty issues, such as the execution of criminal proceedings. However, the technical management of the Internet core-resources should be regulated only when necessary and be left in the hands of private entities composed of technicians, service providers, users, etc. The feared blockage of the Internet's operational functioning by dissenting government policies could be avoided with this approach. By separating technical from political aspects in governance, yet at the same time respecting both in their achievement, a kind of division of powers could be realized, which would enable a positive balance between the different interests involved.[553]

Such an approach would provide for a compromise in addressing issues about legality and constitutionality of a governance body, it also would encounter the risk

548 § 63 of the European Proposal, fourth bullet point; see also Switzerland's position in the Compilation of Comments received on the Report of the WGIG.

549 For further information see <http://www.fsforum.org/home/home.html>.

550 For further information see <http://www.imf.org>.

551 For further information see <http://www.worldbank.org>.

552 See V.B.3.

553 See § 63 of the European Proposal, second and third bullet point; see also para. 29–34 of the Report of the WGIG; Kleinwächter, Internet Governance, 219.

of privately-established rules eroding or undermining the power of the sovereign States.[554] Furthermore, the United States could be propitiated by the fact that an international body would not be involved in technical day-to-day operations and functions of the Internet. However, the concern, whereby nations which do not appreciate the freedom of ideas and open communication, may have a say in Internet policy-settings, would not be met.[555] This issue could only be solved by stating that the existing influence of nations with different perceptions of freedom of expression, such as China, Cuba, Iran, etc. should remain unchallenged with or without an Internet governance body. The set-up of a forum would not confirm these countries' attitudes, but rather provide a space where the necessary discussions about the different perceptions could take place, similar to the IGF at present, but with further participation mechanisms, binding procedures, decision-making processes, etc.

In political science the public choice theory is drawn on to analyze political decision making economically: The theory assumes that human beings generally act rationally, driven by the desire to maximize their gains. As a consequence, the opposition of the United States to the European Proposal can be interpreted as the reflection of domestic political dynamics, since none of the interested stakeholders had the incentive to accept an accordant model.[556]

However, perhaps too much focus has thus far been set on short-term deliberations. As outlined above, it seems clear that ICANN cannot carry on without taking into account the criticisms expressed. Moreover, the long-lasting discussions on an international Internet governance body hinder the creation of a stable legal Internet governance framework which is necessary in the light of the increased economic relevance of cyberspace. The existing debates cannot be avoided. But by providing a specialized forum, they could be concentrated and therefore kept out of other important Internet governance negotiations. The creation of an Internet governance body would provide for a global compromise incorporating all of the States' interests and enabling communication and dialogue among the different stakeholders involved. The States' gains could particularly be maximized by ensuring their Internet access and the fair distribution of domain names. Furthermore, a coordinated approach to issues such as cybersecurity, for example, would probably prove more effective and could reinforce counter-terrorism measures globally. In the long term, the importance of a consistent Internet should particularly not be underestimated in the light of the theoretically possible establishment

---

554 Weber, Regulatory Models, 106–109.

555 See Mayer-Schönberger/Ziewitz, 204.

556 See Mayer-Schönberger/Ziewitz, 217–220, 227–228. Furthermore, the US' rejection of an international Internet governance body has to be considered in the context of the rather reluctant US position regarding international law in general.

of alternative roots by new Internet markets which could construct "Internets of their own". New challenges will arise by the accommodation of Internationalized Domain Names (IDN) in characters other than the Latin script and by the expansion of new gTLDs which will allow applicants to self-select their domain names.[557] Consequences of a fragmentation of the Internet would be devastating and contradictory to the perception of the World Information Society. Thus, a consistent framework guaranteeing a unique Internet should undoubtedly be aspired to.

b) Governing Structures within a New Entity

Generally speaking, "for a system of rules to be fair, it must be firmly rooted in a framework of formal requirements about how rules are made, interpreted and applied".[558] When referring to governance, legitimacy and fairness issues need to be considered.[559]

The specialized field of Internet regulation requires a high level of competence and expertise. Joint involvement of all stakeholders having the necessary know-how is desirable.[560] Additionally, the multi-stakeholder approach, which was already set out on the international stage thanks to the Geneva Declaration of Principles and the WGIG, provides for valuable inputs. Including all stakeholders concerned with the Internet in one way or the other, generally ensures a form of representation at international level. This is an important aspect when considering the legitimacy of governance; the stakeholders' co-action, enhanced communication, coordination and cooperation in a kind of forum, frame a central governance point for Internet issues, allowing for participation and dialogue. As a model of "co-regulation", this overarching concept is rather new in governance doctrine. It appears to be only consequent for Internet governance in the light of the special nature of the Internet as a public sphere, generally open to everyone and accessible from everywhere, crossing national borders.

However, the question does arise, of how these multi-stakeholder representatives should be appointed, since their legitimacy cannot be achieved by adopting one-to-one democratic elections, like the governments can. It has been put forth, that the best way would be to base their legitimacy on net-based votes and elections, as it has already been practiced by ICANN in the past.[561] Yet then, if legitimate Inter-

557 See above III.C.5.

558 Franck, Fairness, 7–8.

559 On enhancing legitimacy aspects of Internet governance in general see Weber/Grosz, Legitimate Governing of the Internet, 316 ss.

560 Kleinsteuber, 72–73.

561 Kleinsteuber, 73–74.

net governance should include all of the world regions and developing countries' interests in particular, global Internet access would have to be achieved. Since the bridging of the digital divide is a complex and ambitious undertaking which will not be achieved any time soon, net-based votes alone cannot be a viable solution: Indeed, the dialogue with all of the stakeholders should not be interrupted. The actual formation of a forum should be established in a "fair" procedure.[562] As a general principle, the forum needs to be open and accessible for all of the interested parties. Therefore, the fact that the initial status of the stakeholders differs to a large extent, has to be addressed: Due account must be given to the fact, that developing countries in particular, do not have the same technical know-how or infrastructure so as to possess equal opportunities in the information society and to engage in significant participation on Internet governance negotiations. A forum legitimately referred to as international would have to be accessible by both developed and developing countries and provide for specific solutions to address these delicate issues of inequality.

In addition, procedures enabling "real" consensus and rulemaking would have to be established. In order to have a legitimizing effect, bargaining power should be given to all of the participants including those with politically less powerful interests. Since ICANN cannot afford to antagonize its powerful members and is, therefore, especially dependant on the US government, it has been criticized for not providing corresponding procedures.[563] Furthermore, the GAC lacks—at present—a sufficiently autonomous status and plays a merely consultative role.

A further important issue would be the introduction of judicial review procedures for rendered decisions. ICANN lacks a meaningful constraint mechanism in this respect.[564] The Uniform Domain Name Dispute Resolution Policy (UDRP) of ICANN has been subjected to complaints, stating that disputes among US-based claimants and domain names registered in the US by non-State parties are to be treated differently to those disputes dealing with domain names between two non-US claimants before a non-US registrar.[565] Hence, the establishment of an independent dispute resolution process, on the basis of international law, would be invaluable. Additionally, accountability provisions as well as criteria to protect third parties should be specially addressed.[566]

562 See Franck, Fairness, 25–29.

563 Weinberg, 252–257.

564 Weinberg, 231–235.

565 See Mayer-Schönberger/Ziewitz, 194–195.

566 See also the list of aspects which should be considered when referring to self-regulatory approaches in Weber, Regulatory Models, 109.

V. Discussion Topics of Internet Governance

A. Introduction

Although the term "Internet governance" has only existed for about five years, literature addressing themes related to Internet governance has substantially increased in that period of time and conferences in this field have become numerous.

Obviously, many aspects of Internet governance merit being discussed in detail. Nevertheless, four main topics have crystallized to be of particular importance, namely legitimacy, transparency, accountability, and participation. Subsequently, these four topics will be dealt with at some length and embedded in the general framework outlined previously, which already provided for some cross-references to specific regulatory issues of Internet governance.

B. Legitimacy

1. Introduction

Internet governance tackles central questions such as: who rules the Internet, in whose interest, by which mechanisms and for which purposes?[567] Particularly with the growing influence which some Internet organizations have achieved, questions on their legitimacy have arisen. The envisaged realization of a concept of "multi-stakeholder governance", perceived as the new way ahead in favor of the inclusion of the whole of society, goes beyond the scope of traditional governance theories, which generally pursue an approach strictly distinguishing the State (public law) from the society (civil law).[568]

Such a development challenges the traditional international legal and political understanding of legitimacy as a concept primarily relevant to sovereign States—subjects of international law according to traditional doctrine. Can the same criteria for assessing States' legitimacy be applied to international entities in the field of the Internet? Furthermore, looking at the multi-stakeholder approaches in Internet governance, the general question of who could be a legitimate stakeholder, needs to be addressed. Or, to put it differently: Should legitimacy issues actu-

567 This chapter is based on the contribution of WEBER/GROSZ, Legitimate Governing of the Internet.

568 WEBER/GROSZ, Vague Ideas, 119/120.

Copyright © Schulthess Juristische Medien AG, Zurich – Basel – Geneva 2009.
Published by Springer-Verlag GmbH Berlin Heidelberg 2010. All Rights Reserved

ally be addressed in this field? Is not multi-stakeholderism as such, legitimizing enough? Are specific values to be met at all? What could such values be?

2. Present Problems with Legitimacy

The development of the World Wide Web has generally led to an increased influence of organizations and entities engaged with the Internet. However, with the gradual extension of their operational sphere beyond merely technical questions and towards addressing policy issues, the legitimacy of their actions has been questioned, with the debates on ICANN as a conspicuous example.

2.1 Criticism on Internet Governance Organizations' Legitimacy

ICANN is neither an international organization nor a national legislator, but a privately organized entity, established as a private non-profit organization, governed by Californian law and domiciled in California.[569] ICANN is in charge of running the Domain Name System (DNS); this makes it the responsible entity to decide which devices can connect to the Internet and under which names.[570] ICANN's organizational structure, however, does not grant it the authority to issue legal norms; the chosen structure places the DNS outside the scope of sovereign legislative powers, i.e. beyond constitutional review and without the public having any legitimizing influence.[571] This organization of the DNS has been subject to various objections.[572]

Critiques can also be expressed against other organizations governing aspects of the Internet, namely the World Wide Web Consortium (W3C) and the Internet Engineering Task Force (IETF), for example. Both organizations have the mandate to develop standards for the World Wide Web, thus, fulfiling a predominantly technical task.[573] Neither W3C nor IETF has the mandate to develop policy; they both lack the consensus of the broad community which could endorse such decisions. However, the boundaries between standards setting and public policy decisions are rather blurred as the example of the Platform for Internet Content Selection (PIC) tool illustrates. This instrument was developed by the W3C and enables Web publishers to mark their pages with computer-readable tags rating the con-

---

569 For more details see above III.C.1.

570 MAYER-SCHÖNBERGER/ZIEWITZ, 192–193; WEBER, Looking ahead. More harmonization in the DNS, 75–76; WEINBERG, 209–212; KLEINWÄCHTER, ICANN as the "United Nations", 456–462.

571 WEBER, Regulatory Models, 106–107.

572 For more details see above III.C.4.

573 See above III.B.2 and 3; MALCOLM, Governance, 52–57; GROSZ, W3C, VII.

tent of the page, thus, enabling the restriction of access to such pages. What was designed for parents or teachers to protect their children, however, also facilitates the establishment of filter-mechanisms for repressive governments.[574]

As outlined above,[575] another objection against ICANN's structure is related to the substantial influence that the US possesses within the organization.[576] Based on the standing other countries have within the organizational structure, much of the expressed criticism is based on the finding that ICANN lacks a democratic basis, which culminated in the challenge of ICANN's legitimacy to regulate the DNS.[577] ICANN has responded to such confrontations by initiating different reforms, which particularly tackle the enhancement of democratic processes within the corporation, by supporting the individual Internet users' participation within ICANN's activities and particularly their role as an electing body of ICANN's Board Members.[578] Nevertheless, the claim that ICANN lacks democratic legitimacy has persisted, making ICANN a rather controversial entity in Internet governance.

2.2 Adherence to Democracy as a Remedy?

What attracts attention in ICANN's case is the resort to democracy and democratic processes in order to enhance the organization's political legitimacy, an approach stemming from modern political science theories of the Western hemisphere.[579] Indeed, the Internet, as a medium generally open to everyone and accessible from everywhere, crossing national borders, seems to provide for the perfect premise for a democratic governance approach. This was also recognized in the Geneva Declaration of Principles, adopted by the World Summit on the Information Society (WSIS) in 2003, which stated that "the international management

574 MALCOLM, Governance, 68–69.

575 See above III.C.4.2.

576 See above III.B.4.2 b).

577 WEINBERG, 224–257; HUNTER, 1154–1159; WEBER, Regulatory Models, 74, 105; FROOMKIN, Wrong turn in cyberspace, 93–165; MALCOLM, Governance, 46–50; DRISSEL, 113–116.

578 For example, the Bylaws dated 16th July 2000, stipulated the election of five At-Large Members from different geographic regions through Internet-wide elections (See Article II Section 1 and 2, Article V Section 6 ICANN Bylaws March 2000). However, this reform failed to provide for the legitimizing basis expected, particularly because of the very small percentage of actual participating voters in the Internet-wide election process (HUNTER, 1156). As a consequence, ICANN abolished these At-Large Members in 2002, and established internal selection processes instead, which comply with certain rules on geographic diversity (see Articles VI-X and Article VI Section 5 ICANN Bylaws on geographic diversity; DE VEY MESTDAGH/RIJGERSBERG, 29; HUNTER, 1177–1179).

579 HUNTER, 1159.

of the Internet should be multilateral, transparent and democratic, with the full involvement of governments, the private sector, civil society and international organizations"[580] and thereby advocated in favor of a multi-stakeholder approach, which has coined the discussions over the participating Internet governance actors to this day.[581] In particular, the Internet Governance Forum (IGF) was established as a forum for multi-stakeholder policy dialogue based on a "neutral, non-duplicative and non-binding process".[582]

However, precisely the example of ICANN's At-Large Members initiative[583] reveals some particular problems in adhering to democracy in the vast field of the Internet: The practicability of Internet-wide elections with the aim of leading to a representative result by reflecting the shared will of the Internet-users world-wide is questioned by the low number of participating electors. Although participation may have been increased through improved information of the potential Internet-users via additional communication channels on the Internet as well as through newspapers, broadcasts, etc.—since not all interested and potential electors can be reached merely by corresponding announcements on the elections on ICANN's website –[584] the question as to how world-wide representation can be achieved, remains to be answered.

As long as the digital divide persists, global participation is a very ambitious objective, due to the fact that particularly developing countries do not have the same technical know-how or infrastructure which provides them with the same opportunities to engage in the information society.[585] An election legitimately referred to as international would have to be accessed by both developed and developing countries.[586] Furthermore, in the specific field of the Internet, the question of how the election of specialized board members can be secured and populist, symbolic results avoided, remains paramount. Does democracy mean that the candidature should be open to everyone or should the candidates meet particular criteria? If criteria are required, who will devise them and how will such an authority in turn be legitimized? Indeed, rather similar questions on democratic legitimization are raised as in the case of administrative agencies within States, which make public policy decisions, but are generally neither directly accountable to nor elected by the public.[587] The specific field of the Internet, however, also entails difficulties

580 See WSIS, Geneva Declaration of Principles, Art. 48.
581 Weber/Grosz, Vague Ideas, 123–127; Malcolm, Governance, 330.
582 WSIS, Tunis Agenda, paras. 72, 73 and 77.
583 See fn. 578 with further references.
584 Weber, Accountability, 154/55.
585 To the framing of the digital divide see Weber/Menoud, 1–20 and below VI.E.
586 Weber/Grosz, Vague Ideas, 134.
587 Weinberg, 218.

when attempting to frame its "demos". In particular, global participation among like-minded stakeholders can be questioned with regard to developments of the Internet which suggest a tendency to fragmentation of communication through specialized websites and rather "privatized information" that lead to increased self-isolation instead of the desired confrontation with different views and global deliberation and cooperation within a public forum.[588]

Apart from that, several counterarguments have been made concerning the objections to the ICANN-system which are also applicable to other Internet governing organizations: Private entities generally work efficiently and quickly, a vital asset in the fast-changing world of cyberspace and a possible legitimizing factor for private authorities in international governance.[589] Furthermore, private rulemaking in the Internet can enhance participation of non-State actors in terms of a multi-stakeholder approach. Consensus-driven regulation might help to impose multilateral action and to monitor regulatory deficiencies. Moreover, a self-regulating concept will ensure flexibility which in turn will help develop new forms of cooperation, for example, facilitating the exchange of know-how which is a very important aspect in the technical field of the Internet.[590]

In light of such considerations, it seems appropriate to question the link between legitimacy and democracy more generally.

3. Linking Legitimacy and Democracy?

3.1 Attempts towards framing Legitimacy

Legitimacy can be perceived as a justification of authority. In broad terms, the concept is to be framed as giving the governed the feeling that their own values are represented in a decision-making context,[591] i.e. as establishing an authority's "right to rule".[592] This interpretation can also be traced back to a translation of the Latin word "legitimus" as meaning "lawful, according to law". Particularly after the French revolution in 1789, different theories attempted to explain legitimacy as a general concept regarding State authority in particular, thereby aiming at filling the notion with more contents.[593]

---

588 SUNSTEIN, 5–10, 51–88, 192.

589 MALCOLM, Governance, 151.

590 WEBER, Regulatory Models, 83–87, 107–108.

591 WEBER, Regulatory Models, 46–47.

592 BUCHANAN/KEOHANE, 25–26.

593 CLARK, 17.

Legitimacy can also be perceived as a factual, sociological phenomenon. The sociological doctrine on States' legitimacy goes back to MAX WEBER. By analyzing the general reasons why State authority is factually accepted, WEBER distinguished three ideal types of governance: the rational or legal, the traditional and the charismatic authority.[594] Legitimacy may further be understood in a wider sense, encompassing an ethical-philosophical dimension, which heaves legitimacy above positive law.[595] A similar differentiation has been adopted by scholars distinguishing between "normative theories" on legitimacy, which set out general criteria for evaluating the right to rule, and "empirical theories", which focus on belief systems of those subject to government.[596] In other words, legitimacy can either be justified by formal ideas as the rule of law rationale (legality) or by substantial value rationality based on morality and justice.[597]

Theories on democracy, differentiating source- and procedure- or result-oriented types of legitimacy provide for further valuable approaches and indicate a rather promising basis to tackle legitimacy in Internet governance:[598] According to a source-oriented perception of legitimacy, for example, an authority may be qualified as legitimate when referring to democratic States which base their authority on the "demos", the public.[599] Constructing such a legitimizing source from the various stakeholders involved in the governance of the Internet, however, implies particular difficulties which will be outlined subsequently.

The legitimacy of policy-making decisions on the Internet may also be enhanced by procedural aspects within the different governing entities. This comprehension of legitimacy can be traced back to NIKLAS LUHMANN who founded the doctrine whereby legitimization can be effected by adequate procedures.[600] In his tradition THOMAS M. FRANCK described legitimacy as "the aspect of governance that validates institutional decisions as emanating from a right process. What constitutes right process is described in a society's adjectival constitution or rules of order, or is pedigreed by tradition and historic custom".[601]

The procedural approach is complemented by a result-oriented type of legitimacy, i.e. a substantive conception which looks at the outcome of the legitimizing procedures. This result-oriented approach will depend, not least, on the values deemed as "right" by the stakeholders concerned, thus, in part leading us back to questions

594 MAX WEBER, 122–142.
595 HALLER/KÖLZ/GÄCHTER, 17.
596 CLARK, 18.
597 CLARK, 19.
598 SCHARPF, 16–28; WOLFRUM, 6.
599 HABERMAS, 117.
600 LUHMANN, 9–53.
601 FRANCK, Fairness, 1.

on legitimizing sources. Such a perception reveals a particular difficulty, because it relies on subjective perceptions of legitimate values which depend on cultural and societal differences and evolve over time.[602] For such reasons, result-oriented legitimacy is rather difficult to operationalize.[603] JÜRGEN HABERMAS tried to link the procedural aspects with specific notions of contents with the "discourse principle"; in this context HABERMAS assumes that just those norms can claim validity which receive the approval of all potentially affected people, insofar as they participate in a free rational discourse.[604] For the open medium of the World Wide Web, such an approach might seem rather tailored for Internet governance at first glance. However, the discourse principle is challenged by particular aspects of fair processes of consensus-making that will be addressed subsequently.

State conduct is further measured in light of constitutional values and principles. Such a constitutional approach to the governing of the Internet, based on particular architectural principles, could provide for important inputs and will be addressed as a new approach hereinafter. Indeed, IAN CLARK specifies "three cognate concepts—legality, morality, and constitutionality", which are said to "mark out the terrain within which the practice of legitimacy tends to take place".[605] Legitimacy is thereby perceived as a reconciling norm, enabling consensus on how these three elements can be accommodated amongst each other.[606]

Such perceptions of legitimacy emphasize the concepts' origin in the political sciences, i.e. the concept's primary applicability to nation States. The governance of the Internet—for historical reasons—has not focused specifically on States. As a "virtual province" of cyberspace, the Internet has mainly been managed by a rather small community of technical constructors and has based its self-regulation on private entities in a bottom-up manner, with technical issues standing in the limelight. Legitimacy in Internet governance as a particular field of international policies is being further challenged by the role it plays in international law; with international law gaining importance, legitimacy questions become weightier not only for the international society in general, but also for the stability of international order.[607]

602 CLARK, 13.
603 ASHFORTH/GIBBS, 177 with further references.
604 HABERMAS, 161.
605 CLARK, 19.
606 CLARK, 20.
607 CLARK, 12–17.

3.2 Perceptions of Democracy

In general, "democracy" is understood as a term which refers to politically liberal States whose authority is traced back to the people as a legitimizing basis. Hence, the parliament, i.e. the legislative power, which is elected by the public is deemed as a reflection of the people's will and thus as their representative. The executive, for its part, also receives legitimate power through public (direct elections) or through the mandate given (indirectly) by the parliament. This seemingly clear and common understanding of democracy at a first glance, however, appears to be a quite complex concept when taking a closer look.

Democracy, throughout history, has been differently shaped and framed. Its origins can be traced back to the Greek word "demos", meaning "people", and "kratos", referring to "rule, strength", thus "the rule of the people", also called "politeia" by ARISTOTELE, i.e. the "rule of the many". Suggested by its name, first theories of democracy primarily focused on questions of representation. The first significant democratic State in history was Athens in 508 BC, which assigned the highest authority within the Athenian State to all at least 18 years old male citizens, forming a political forum. Interestingly enough, however, the representation of the "people" as a cooperative basis was restrained to the "citizens", therewith excluding women, the underaged, foreigners and slaves from any political participation.[608] In ARISTOTLE's view, democracy as such was not necessarily the best regime; rather, the best regime was considered to be the result of a combination of various features for the sake of the common good.[609]

The perceptions of democracy during the Age of Enlightenment were characterized by a more individualistic conception, concentrating more on the primacy of the value of human autonomy.[610] One of the most fundamental theories on democracy was proposed by JEAN-JACQUES ROUSSEAU in 1762 in his opus "Du contrat social."The social contract was established amongst the individuals within a society, independently of their status, stand, sex, possessions, or education. The social contract served as a legitimizing source for State power, thereby protecting freedom and equality among all people. As a consequence, sovereignty was granted to the society as a whole, making sovereignty inalienable and indivisible, thus excluding the possibility of appointing sovereign representatives, since the sovereign basis for action was acknowledged only for the assembly of the people, making direct democracy the only legitimate form of government.[611] ROUSSEAU himself acknowledged the limited practicability of his theoretical model. Indeed,

608 MALCOLM, Governance, 229.

609 ARISTOTLE, Book III, Chapter 7, 1279b.

610 MALCOLM, Governance, 227.

611 ROUSSEAU, Livre II, Chapitre I et II, Livre III, Chapitre XV; for more details see above IV.A.

only a few States adopt a direct democratic approach today; representative democratic State structures are currently the more dominant form of government. In representative democracies, the "demos" receives the power and responsibility to delegate representatives to rule on its behalf.[612] MONTESQUIEU perceived the insertion of an intermediary representative as a more feasible option to enable democracy in larger States.[613]

Switzerland stands out as an example that combines both characteristic types of democracy. Although Switzerland has a parliament exerting the functions of the legislative State power, and hence, features a representative democratic basis as a form of government, direct democratic instruments are implemented additionally, namely the initiative (which allows civil society to suggest amendments to the constitution by effecting a plebiscite) and the referendum (which allows the electorate to vote over particular issues after or before adoption by the parliament).[614]

Scholars have also addressed questions on whether democracy entails particular values and principles. For example, democracy can be interpreted as the form of government which acknowledges individual civil and political rights, which in turn emphasize the fundamental assumption that citizens' freedom of self-determination is the basis of the democratic State per se; this interpretation is also referred to as "the democratic principle".[615] Indeed, the social contract can be perceived as implementing such constitutional principles as a society would consensually adopt if framing a State originally; or in accordance with JOHN RAWLS: as such basic structures of society that would be adopted collectively by representatives behind a fictive "veil of ignorance" which blinds out all possible personal and selfish interests and instead creates an obligation to evaluate principles only on the basis of general considerations in order to establish a fair new order for all members of society.[616] Further theories which deal with substantive democracy focus rather on the compliance with such fundamental values, insofar as consent regarding higher-ranking criteria needs to be reached by the citizens.[617] Consent is achieved in appropriate procedures of consensus-making; "deliberative democracy" focuses on the existence of "free, inclusive, rational debates" among citizens, which determine the underlying point of public policy. As a consequence, democracy is perceived as hinging on the open exchange of views and informed debates as a basis for consensus.[618] Accountability to the people, coupled with

612 MALCOLM, Governance, 231; HUNTER, 1161.
613 MONTESQUIEU, Livre XI, Chapitre VI, 166.
614 See also MALCOLM, Governance, 230; KOBACH, 56–69.
615 MALCOLM, Governance, 227.
616 RAWLS, paras 24 and 118 ss; see also IV.A.
617 MALCOLM, Governance, 234–236.
618 HUNTER, 1161–1162.

transparency requirements, are conceived as further democratic elements with a legitimizing effect.[619]

Such a brief overview reveals particular difficulties in crystallizing a generally acknowledged content common to the different understandings and characteristics inherent to the rather heterogeneous concept of democracy. Generally speaking, democracy is not a normative standard as such, guaranteeing legitimate government structures. Therefore, the application of such State-based principles to the multi-stakeholder actors in Internet governance, encompassing both State and non-State actors, is not a panacea but a rather complicated venture. In the specific context of international governance, it has been argued that if globalization has lead to the shaping of national procedures by international processes, democracy can no longer focus solely on nation States; as a consequence, democracy has been framed as an international legal standard for legitimate authority.[620] Indeed, several international organizations, such as the UN or the WTO, have been criticized for a lack of democratic structures. At the same time, globalizing processes have brought about consequences for the States' position in the international arena; in particular, the acknowledgment of new players has shifted the State's status as main subject of international law and thus reduced its power.[621] What seems clear is that the role of democracy for the international world generally needs further elaboration.[622]

3.3 Assessment

Both democracy and legitimacy are very ample terms. In general, skepticism is appropriate if addressing the question of whether democracy and legitimacy mean the same for a liberal democratic nation State as they do for international and multi-stakeholder governance networks, each in turn, with distinctive features.[623] In a nutshell, relying on democracy and democratic principles in order to enhance legitimacy in Internet governance increases the risk that one very complex and vague generic word could merely be replaced by another, without much contribution having been made to the actual content of the terms. Furthermore, dependence on individual theories alone, e.g. the source-based approach to legitimacy, for the enhancement of the legitimate governing of the Internet as a whole, holds the risk of adopting a too narrow perception and thus of not corresponding to the

619 Marks, 47–68, 50; Malcolm, Governance, 228, 240–291.
620 Marks, 49–54, 65.
621 Marks, 48–49; Slaughter, 262; Franck, Fairness, 477.
622 Marks, 55.
623 Malcolm, Governance, 228; Marks, 50–52, 66.

broad and manifold notion legitimacy implicates. In light of such considerations, new approaches are welcome and deserve further examination.

4. New Approaches

4.1 Conceptual Shifts in addressing Democracy and Legitimacy in International Governance

Adopting democracy as a legitimizing concept for international governance, thus expanding its scope beyond national States, raises several questions; therefore, scholars have addressed international democracy rather differently. For example, one approach envisions the gradual disappearance of the States' system and its replacement by a world-wide democratic government, another one pictures the achievement of global democracy through democratization at the level of each State, also referred to as "pan-national democracy".[624] Furthermore, the concept of "cosmopolitan democratic law" has been developed; it encompasses the establishment of "a democratic public law entrenched within and across borders"[625] and makes democracy within States and democracy in international affairs mutually supportive developments.[626] Democracy would thus become a transnational affair, without a territorial base.[627] Although State-based democracy should not be applied one-to-one to Internet governing entities, such an approach endorses the idea of adopting particular elements—commonly perceived as "democratic"—that provide for valuable inputs. Such constituents could include transparency issues, the establishment of accountability mechanisms, as well as procedures enabling consensus making.

As outlined[628], a recent approach outlining a "new world order" is provided by ANNE-MARIE SLAUGHTER and her theory on "transnationalism". According to SLAUGHTER, the perception of States as unitary entities is misleading and requires a conceptual shift towards the acknowledgment of "disaggregated States".[629] Accordingly, States can be classified into their separate parts (such as courts, regulatory agencies, executives, and legislatures), as disparate institutions with their own powers, mandates, incentives etc. Coordination among these different entities across borders, between and among like agencies creates a new web of relations,

624 MARKS, 52.
625 HELD, 227; see also MALCOLM, Governance, 236 ss and 243 ss.
626 MARKS, 53.
627 MARKS, 54 with further references.
628 See IV.B.
629 SLAUGHTER, 12–15.

and thus, a new transgovernmental (horizontal) order.[630] A vertical dimension is implemented alongside, based on the fact that national governments cannot effectively address every problem in a networked world and should therefore delegate their responsibilities and sovereign power "to a limited number of supranational government officials, such as judges and arbitrators in the WTO, NAFTA, and the ICC".[631]

Besides the fact that such government networks are deemed more flexible and efficient in contrast to centralized, hierarchical procedures of international institutions, this form of transnationalism is also regarded as enjoying greater legitimacy than international institutions, due to the fact that the government networks are not disconnected entities, but are based on national processes, thus enforcing the law made at the national level.[632] The States' power could thus be bolstered as the primary actor in the international system[633] and accountability of the disaggregated State functions could be secured for the people.[634] For Internet governance, such an approach would be suitable to be interpreted as leading to a model of a new governance body and different governing bodies respectively, formed by the cross-border networks achieved through negotiations on Internet issues between the different competent players within the States. However, different uncertainties persist. For example, it remains unclear, how legitimacy deficiencies on a national level should be balanced in the international sphere if legitimacy is generally traced back to the States.

4.2 Framing the Stakeholders

In order to give the governed the feeling that their own values are being represented in the decisions made, a fundamental question needs to be answered: Who are the governed stakeholders of the Internet governing organizations? i.e. Who encompasses the "demos"? Only clarity over the different actors involved can be the starting point for enhancing legitimacy.

The heterogeneity of the different actors in the field of the Internet has been addressed by the concept of "multi-stakeholderism",[635] which encompasses governments, the private sector, civil society and international organizations, thus, overriding differences between public and private actors[636] and building up global

630 Slaughter, 135–144.
631 Slaughter, 263.
632 Marks, 56.
633 Slaughter, 269.
634 Marks, 58.
635 See above IV.B; see also Hemmati, 40 ss.
636 WSIS, Geneva Declaration of Principles, Art. 48.

participation.[637] The sources of the different stakeholders' legitimacy deserve particular analysis: Whilst democratic entitlement may suffice for State government, the private sector might generally derive its legitimacy from superior efficiency characteristics. Civil society could be perceived a stakeholder due to the mere fact of being particularly affected by decisions on the governance of the Internet or by the substantive values it promotes. The question will arise as to whether this suffices to make civil society a legitimate actor or whether particular experience and expertise can be demanded, in which case, however, only a limited number of civil society members—such as non-governmental organizations (NGOs)—would be enabled to participate. How can the fact that civil society generally lacks accountability, accounted for?[638] Or does the legitimacy of the multi-stakeholder basis consist of the entity as a collaborating whole? Indeed, the comprehension of a unitary stakeholder foundation may be questioned, in particular in view of perceptions of a rather fragmented and polarized Internet.[639]

Shifting the focus to the different organizational bodies involved in the manifold aspects of the Internet helps channelling the very broad stakeholder-basis into an intermediate level of representatives within the organizational structures. For example, standard setting organizations such as the IETF probably involve more technically specialized stakeholders than the IGF which was established as a public policy forum. In deciding who should be admitted as a representative within such organizational structures and whether specific prerequisites should be met, valuable inputs could be derived from the EU as a supranational organization, that has had to balance the objectives of the Union as a whole with the interests of the individual Member States.[640] Furthermore, an interesting approach can be drawn from the governmental networks outlined in SLAUGHTER's view of a new world order.

In a nutshell, legitimate "representatives" would result from responsible entities on a national level, such as particular magistrates, establishing a specialized network amongst themselves across borders. This reveals a very different approach to perceptions of multi-stakeholderism, a concept that is not primarily based on national States' actors but was created to explicitly encompass private players and individual Internet users. Tracing the multi-stakeholder representatives' role back to their national origins, i.e. their citizenship or country of domicile, would be a shift of conceptualization and could provide for a valuable input towards enhancing legitimacy. As consequence, the question of how such a national foundation should be structured, proves the inevitable. In terms of a multi-stakeholder ap-

637 WSIS, Geneva Declaration of Principles, Articles 33, 40, 48, inter alia; see also above IV.B.

638 MALCOLM, Governance, 147–157.

639 SUNSTEIN, 51–88.

640 KOMAITIS, 69–75 with reference to "enhanced cooperation" as a particular approach.

proach, the national civil society, i.e. the citizens alone would not form a legitimate basis, but would have to be complemented by all of the people affected by the governance of the Internet, in order to provide for an appropriate "demos".

4.3 Legitimacy through Fair Processes of Consensus-Making

Effective techniques of consensus-building could improve the organizations' legitimacy in terms of LUHMANN's approach to legitimacy through process. In order to enable "real" consensus among the very different stakeholders, procedures would have to be established which give bargaining power to all of the participants and thus ensure equal opportunities, also for stakeholders with less powerful interests.[641] Multi-stakeholderism as a general concept should not conceal the fact—inherent in the term—that rather big differences among the players remain; in terms of "Realpolitik", influential States will remain very powerful players in a multi-stakeholder setting as compared to developing States or individual representatives of civil society, for example.[642]

Due to such rather unequal starting positions of the different stakeholders involved, a particular difficulty for a free discourse to develop in terms of HABERMAS is revealed. Mechanisms are necessary to enable participation and interaction to take place in fair terms, so as to give different stakeholders a real voice. FRANCK frames "fairness" as embracing both legitimacy and justice, and establishes the term "fairness discourse" as a way forward in enhancing legitimacy of international law and its institutions.[643] Thereby, transparency—access to information—is deemed to be, on the one hand, a major prerequisite for enabling "real" consensus in terms of informed decisions and, on the other hand, a constituting element for effective participation in terms of facilitating deliberative processes.[644] It is thus crucial that organizations governing the Internet inform their stakeholders and make effective use of the often bespoken facilitated information flow on the Internet. As a consequence, the involvement in decision-making processes should strengthen public confidence in the decisions taken and enhance their legitimacy.[645]

641 WEINBERG, 255–256.
642 KOMAITIS, 57.
643 FRANCK, Fairness, 477–484.
644 WEBER/WEBER, Civil Society, 13.
645 WEBER/WEBER, Civil Society, 9.

4.4 Architectural Principles

With the affected stakeholders delineated, legitimacy could be improved by adhering to particular architectural principles.[646] Key principles need to be considered as a source for legislation and a guideline for governing different aspects of the Internet. Similarly to a Magna Charta or a constitutional approach, substantive principles should call for self-constraint to bind the governing authorities: by existing independently of the actual policies and the decision-making entities, such principles foster the establishment of a sort of "checks and balances" regime, they provide for a basis for the assessment of the governing outcome and could thus facilitate accountability.[647] Indeed, adherence to fundamental principles common to the different stakeholders could ensure a form of representation of the Internet community at international level,[648] thus a source of representation, on a value-rational ground.[649] Furthermore, consensus on architectural values would help establish a particular form of stability.[650]

However, the question of which elements such principles encompass, remains open. A proposal submitted by the European Union to the WSIS in Tunis stands out in this context: it requests that decision-making on Internet governance should adhere to the general principles set out in the Geneva Principles on the one hand and additional specific principles on the other hand. The latter would encompass principles on the mechanisms of governance as well as substantive values, so-called "architectural principles, including the interoperability, openness and the end-to-end principle".[651] Such core liberal values could be seen as common beliefs of the community of Internet users.[652] Further values can be derived from a human rights approach, particularly requiring respect for the freedom of expression, data security and data protection, etc. Indeed, human rights have been perceived as fundamental principles in the present world order, in addition to democracy and legitimacy, for implementing good governance.[653] The establishment of consensus on such core values—either for the Internet as a whole or for the governance of specific sectors of the Internet—should be a main issue in the field of Internet governance. Such architectural principles could be compiled in an international legal framework on the Internet as a general statement with soft law implications.

646 See also above IV.B.2.
647 Weber, Accountability, 36; on governance and constitutionalization Grewlich, Konstitutionalisierung des "Cyberspace"; see also Komaitis, 71.
648 Mayer-Schönberger/Ziewitz, 206–207; Weber/Grosz, Vague Ideas, 128.
649 Malcolm, Governance, 153.
650 Clark, 15–17.
651 European Proposal, § 63 bullet point 4; see also Mayer-Schönberger/Ziewitz, 198–203; Komaitis, 70–71.
652 See IETF, Architectural Principles of the Internet, RFC 1958.
653 Sano, 125–127.

Additionally, key values should also be established in the articles of corporation or the bylaws of the particular entities involved in the governing of the Internet.

5. Outlook

In order to respond to existing calls for enhanced legitimacy of the international players involved with the governance of the Internet and to prevent new ones in the fast developing sphere of the World Wide Web, innovative thinking is necessary. Different approaches to advance legitimacy in this particular field should be scrutinized. Whether concepts such as "social contract" or "transnationalism" are applied or other approaches to international governance endorsed, the fundamental "democratic" question—as inherent in any approach to legitimacy—needs to be answered; it reads: Which governed "demos" forms the basis that is in the position to decide on legitimacy?[654] Based upon this first appreciation, consensus should be secured as to how the players can effectively receive a legitimizing background in order to represent the multi-stakeholders within the different organizational structures. In order to ensure legitimate decision-making, the processes of consensus-making need to come under scrutiny. Representation only has a legitimizing effect, if the outcome reflects the values of the represented stakeholders.[655] In particular, such a comprehension calls for procedures that establish equal bargaining powers and fair proceedings, as well as enhanced transparency and review mechanisms which enable the allocation of accountability. In this regard, the elaboration of architectural principles can have a legitimizing effect by providing for certain criteria needed for the assessment of Internet governing decisions.

By way of conclusion and in terms of an outlook, it can be summarized that blind adherence to the made-believe panacea of "democracy" or to the concept of "multi-stakeholderism" as such will not provide for the tailor-made solutions desirable for such a specific field as Internet governance. Rather, differentiation is needed: Whilst valuable inputs deriving from such prominent concepts should be adopted, new approaches that challenge existing international Internet governing entities and actors and at the same time freshly address aspects of legitimacy, are not to be eschewed.

654 See also above IV.A.

655 See also below V.E.

C. Transparency

1. Introduction

One hundred years ago the Supreme Court Justice Louis Brandeis said: "Sunlight is said to be the best of all disinfectants."[656] This statement is still true and even particularly relevant in the context of Internet governance. In the meantime, it seems to be generally acknowledged that an enhancement of transparency is needed, in order to establish a satisfactory governance system for all of the different stakeholders involved.[657]

2. Assessing Guiding Principles of Transparency

Transparency is central, both as a goal of regulation and as an attribute of the regulatory system.[658] Moreover, the importance of transparency stems from its relevance for the achievement of other important tenets, such as independence and accountability of regulators.[659]

Transparency is often defined as "easily seen through or understood."[660] It is usually perceived and understood as encompassing characteristics such as clarity, accountability, accuracy, accessibility and truthfulness.[661] Transparency is an important topic in many market segments. On the one hand, transparency enables access to the information necessary for the evaluation of opportunities and costs of operation in a specific market.[662] As stated in a judgment of the English Court of Appeal (Civil Division), the principle of transparency is affected if "uncertainty as to the nature or effect of the amendments that might be made deterred, or was liable to deter" a potential party to a contract from concluding an agreement.[663] On the other hand, transparency has been addressed most notably in the discussions

---

656 BRANDEIS, 92.

657 The following subchapter is a shortened version from WEBER, Transparency; for a similar approach see also WEBER, Enhancement of Transparency.

658 FAWCETT, 49.

659 WEBER/GROSZ, Vague Ideas, 131; AMTENBRINK, 7, in general see also MALCOLM, Governance, 260 ss and 493 ss.

660 See Oxford Dictionary under the keyword "transparency".

661 WEBER/GROSZ, Vague Ideas, 131.

662 See US Proposal for Transparency Disciplines in Domestic Regulation: Building on Existing International Disciplines and Proposals (JOB(04)/128), dated 15th September 2004, para. 1.

663 R (Law Society) v. Legal Services Commission; Dexter Montague and Partners (a firm) v. Same [2007] EWCA Civ 1264, para. 80.

on governance, in particular, regarding financial markets.[664] With the increasing importance of international players, governance has become more complex, encompassing local, regional and global zones, which in fact, do not operate independently from one another. Under the term of global governance, processes of integration and harmonization can be detected within governance discussions.[665] Thereby, transparency is seen as an important component of good governance.

Transparency can be differentiated into three main aspects:[666]

- *Procedural transparency* encompasses rules and procedures in the operation of organizations; such rules must be clearly stated, have an unambiguous character, and be publicly disclosed. In addition, they should make processes of governance and lawmaking accessible and comprehensible for the public. An important aspect is the due process principle.
- *Decision-making transparency* is based on the acknowledgement of access to political mechanisms; reasoned explanations for decisions, together with public scrutiny, strengthen the institutional credibility and legitimacy of governmental decisions.
- *Substantive transparency* is directed at the establishment of rules containing the desired substance of revelations, standards and provisions which avoid arbitrary or discriminatory decisions; additionally, substantive rules often include requirements of rationality and fairness.

Furthermore, various "directions" of transparency can be summarized as follows:[667]

- Transparency *upwards* means that the hierarchical superior/principal is in a position to observe the conduct, behavior, and/or "results" of the hierarchical subordinate/agent, usually in a principal-agent relation.
- Transparency *downwards* means that the "ruled" are in a position to observe the conduct, behavior, and/or "results" of their "rulers"; this relationship figures prominently in democratic theory and practice often under the umbrella of "accountability".
- Transparency *outwards* means that the hierarchical subordinate or agent is in a position to observe what is happening "outside" the organization; this ability is important to monitor the behavior of an organization's peers and/or competitors.

---

664 Lastra/Shams, 170; Mock, 1082.

665 Brownsword/Lewis, vii.

666 See Weber, Transparency, 344.

667 See Heald, 27–28.

- Transparency *inwards* means that those outside are in a position to observe what is going on inside the organization; the topic insofar addresses the freedom of information.

To the extent to which upward and downward transparency co-exist, there is symmetrical vertical transparency. As far as outward and inward transparency exist parallel to one another, there is symmetrical horizontal transparency. Otherwise, transparency (both vertical and horizontal) is either completely absent or asymmetrical.[668]

"Transparency facilitates compliance, effectiveness and the ability to assess both."[669] In light of these findings, transparency has become a key issue within private enterprises and governmental organizations, both at national and international levels. Discussions under the notion of corporate governance have addressed transparency in particular and have carved out important aspects on the subject. Both theory and practice attempt to limit information asymmetries or to specify information flow among the central players of an entity. This facet of accounting and disclosure was developed substantially—along with the corporate institutional developments—in the 19th century, when the obligation to post publicly accessible accounts became a condition of limited liability status and the stock market listing.[670] In the 20th century, the corporations' obligation to disclose and publish internal information was extended steadily; together with advanced regulations, as well as audit and accounting reforms, "reassurance" in the economy—in the aftermath of a financial "crash"—was ostensibly intended.[671] The extension of disclosure obligations is also partly a reflection of the development of ideas about "information asymmetry" by institutional economists working on transaction costs and principal-agent theories.[672] Furthermore, legal thinkers started to "look inside" institutions and devise doctrines and systems of regulation that focused on their information flow, thus examining the kinds of information that had to be reported to the board of directors, for instance, or looking at the kind of expertise that was to be represented in such fora.[673]

The emerging appreciation of the right to access information can be linked to these developments. It is of importance because it introduces a human right's aspect known as freedom of information.[674]

---

668 HEALD, 27 and 29.
669 MITCHELL, 111.
670 HOOD, Transparency, 17 and 20.
671 HOOD, Transparency, 17.
672 BERLE/MEANS, passim.
673 HOOD, Transparency, 18.
674 BIRKINSHAW, 204 and 216.

Transparency has also been acknowledged to be a crucial issue when addressing the effectiveness of international regimes. The promotion of transparency is often enough one of the most important functions, for instance when referring to the submission of reports to the Human Rights Committee according to Article 40 ICCPR. However, the methods with which a regime can actually promote transparency have remained rather unexplored so far. Generally speaking, transparency enhancement depends on the purposes for which information is sought, on the capacity and incentives of actors to provide that information, and on the strategies adopted to encourage transparency.[675]

3. Addressing Transparency in Other Markets

The issue of transparency is becoming an increasingly important issue in different international markets. Improving transparency is perceived as a decision on management style and a stance of good governance. Standing out, due to their explicit referral to transparency issues, are the WTO, the IMF/World Bank, as well as the EU. Valuable inputs for Internet governance can be deduced from these regulatory frameworks and merit further examination.

3.1 Transparency in the WTO Framework

The fact, that transparency is addressed in many provisions within the WTO framework leads to the generally accepted acknowledgement that this principle is at the core of virtually all trade agreements.[676] Article X of the GATS addresses the issue of transparency in a dual manner: On the one hand it delivers a definition of transparency as a general obligation; on the other hand it defines the area of its application in connection with the publication and administration of trade regulations—for this purpose it specifies the need for prompt publication of laws, regulations, judicial decisions and the like.[677] Similar obligations of transparency are contained in Articles III, VI and VII (indirectly) of the GATS. The purpose of the transparency provisions can be seen in the objective to achieve a greater degree of clarity, predictability and information about regulations. As far as services are concerned, transparency deals with categories such as the establishment of contact points, the development of domestic regulation, the application and

[675] See MITCHELL, 109–110.

[676] Due to the fact that in the field of Internet governance trade in services stands at the centre of attention rather than trade in goods, the following outline shall focus solely on the GATS provisions on transparency.

[677] VAN DEN BOSSCHE, 467–471.

enforcement of regulatory measures and finally the procedures for licensing and qualification.[678]

The achieved transparency facilitates the Member States of the WTO to enter into the cross border trade of goods and services thanks to the fact that the regulations of the trading partner countries are foreseeable. In other words, the predictability of international "relations" increases with the degree of transparency. Therefore, transparent regulation is a core requirement for attracting investment and promoting economic growth. Furthermore, inequalities can be tackled that may arise due to the fact that large firms generally have resources to compensate for the absence of transparency disciplines, while smaller enterprises, more often stemming from developing countries, lack such resources; the establishment of transparency principles may endorse market access disciplines according to Article XVI GATS by granting fair opportunities for market participants and thus encountering possible inequalities effectively.[679]

As a general observation from the experiences within the WTO, the conclusion can be drawn that the importance given to transparency issues by WTO law helps to overcome uncertainties in business processes and to improve the general basis for cooperation. This fact should also be thoroughly considered within the different Internet organizations' frameworks.

3.2 Transparency in the IMF/World Bank Framework

Elements of transparency have become a significant aspect of good regulatory governance and have gained increasing importance in many areas of public policy, in particular in the banking sector.[680] An international approach in this direction can be found in the "Code of Good Practices on Transparency in Monetary and Financial Policies", developed by the International Monetary Fund in cooperation with the Bank for International Settlements and in consultancy with several other actors in 1999. Assessments of the Code have highlighted the main benefits of transparency within the monetary and financial policies: (1) greater transparency enhances accountability of policymakers; (2) it fosters the effectiveness of monetary policy by making it more predictable; (3) it benefits the operation of financial markets, which are based on information, and it improves monetary and fiscal policy coordination; (4) furthermore, the publication of analyses and fore-

678 Van den Bossche, 496–497.

679 US Proposal for Transparency Disciplines in Domestic Regulation: Building on Existing International Disciplines and Proposals (JOB(04)/128), dated 15th September 2004, para. 2.

680 See Goodhart, 159–162.

casts by central banks and financial agencies provides impetus for the staff to maintain a high quality of work.[681]

Additionally, starting in the 1990s, the World Bank has sponsored the establishment of a world-wide database containing regulatory provisions and practices relevant to banking activities. The survey is very thorough and encompasses the banking regulations of more than 150 countries; relevant aspects are the accounting practices, the external auditing, the financial statement transparency as well as the external ratings and the creditor monitoring. The details are expressed in form of variables that measure the extent of effectiveness or strength of a given entity in the different practices and enable comparisons across the countries.

Lessons to be learned from the IMF/World Bank legal framework mainly concern the accounting practices (in a large sense); actions taken by ICANN representatives should always encompass the accountability principles leading to the result that recipients of such actions are in a position to follow the line of thinking.[682]

3.3 Transparency in the EU Framework

Transparency has always been an important aspect in the single European market's legal framework, particularly in the context of financial markets. The so-called "Transparency Directive" 2004/109/EC[683] envisages introducing regulatory instruments for transparency in the EU. Its preamble states:

> "Efficient, transparent and integrated securities markets contribute to a genuine single market in the Community and foster growth and job creation by better allocation of capital and by reducing costs. The disclosure of accurate, comprehensive and timely information about security issues builds sustained investor confidence and allows an informed assessment of their business performance assets. This enhances both investor protection and market efficiency".

Consequently, transparency as an objective to be achieved is intended to support an effective integration of national markets, thereby increasing economic growth and generating employment. Furthermore, accuracy, comprehensiveness, and timing are perceived as a powerful tool for the improvement of market conditions.

---

681 International Monetary Fund, Assessments of the IMF Code of Good Practices on Transparency in Monetary and Financial Policies—Review of Experience, December 2003, available at <http://www.imf.org/external/np/mae/mft/assess/122303.htm>; Weber/Grosz, Vague Ideas, 131.

682 Barth/Caprio/Levine, 145–146.

683 EC Directive 2004/109/EC of the European Parliament and of the Council of 15th December 2004 on the harmonization of transparency requirements in relation to information about issuers whose securities are admitted to trading on a regulated market and amending Directive 2001/34/EC, OJ 2004 L 390/38.

In particular, the Transparency Directive builds a framework which establishes minimum standards for data quality. Even if the fact that the EU constitutes an integrated European market cannot be overlooked, ICANN developments should also consider the key elements of the EU legal framework in transparency matters.

4. Enhancing Transparency for the Future of Internet Governance

Aspects of fostered transparency in other markets should flow into Internet governance discussions. Nevertheless, the particularities of the governance of the Internet merit further specific examination.

4.1 Tackling Controversies over ICANN

In order to address the controversies over ICANN and to build confidence in this entity, enhancing transparency could be a viable approach. The disclosure of ICANN's effective role in policy making and Internet governance could provide for a first step towards the appeasement of critics against the organization. Furthermore, the clear presentation of the US government's influence on the DNS, as well as the open communication of represented interests within the Board would strengthen public confidence. Together with more transparent election-processes and decision-making procedures both within the organization as well as within its Uniform Domain Name Dispute Resolution Policy (UDRP), ICANN's legitimacy could also be improved. Generally, a consensus-driven and bottom-up approach leads to broader transparency and additionally makes the private entity accountable to the public, also giving non-State agents a voice in the rulemaking process.

ICANN has realized its potential and the possible dimension transparency enhancement could promise. It presently acknowledges the following transparency provisions:[684]

- Art. III Section 1 of the ICANN Bylaws states that the corporation "shall operate to the maximum extent feasible in an open and transparent manner and consistent with procedures designed to ensure fairness". Furthermore, Art. I Section 2 includes several objectives such as "employing open and transparent policy development mechanisms that (i) promote well-informed decisions based on expert advise, and (ii) ensure that those entities most affected can assist in the policy development process" (No. 7), "making decisions by applying documented policies neutrally and objectively with integrity and fairness"

684 See also ICANN, Management Operating Principles, Accountability & Transparency.

(No. 8), "acting with a speed that is responsive to the needs of the Internet while, as part of the decision-making process, obtaining informed input from those entities most affected" (No. 9) and "remaining accountable to the Internet community through mechanisms that enhance ICANN's effectiveness" (No. 10).

- If ICANN's Board considers policies for adoption that substantially affect the Internet's operation or third parties, ICANN is held to (i) provide public notice on its website explaining the considered policies and the reasons for their adoption, at least 21 days prior to any action by the Board; (ii) provide a reasonable opportunity for the parties to comment on such proposed policies, to access the comments of others, and to reply to such comments prior to any Board action; (iii) request the opinion of the Governmental Advisory Committee (GAC) and to take into account any advice presented by the GAC in cases where the policy affects public policy concerns; (iv) hold an in-person public forum for discussions of any proposed policies prior to final Board action where practically feasible and in accordance with the relevant policy development process; and (v) guarantee the transparency after having taken such action; for that purpose the Board is obliged to publish the meeting minutes including the reasons for any action taken, the vote of each Director, and the separate statement of any Director.[685]
- No. 7 of the so-called "Core Values" of ICANN reads as follows (corresponding to Art. I Sect. 2 No. 7 of the Bylaws): "Employing open and transparent policy development mechanisms that (i) promote well informed decisions based on expert advice and (ii) ensure that those entities most affected can assist in the policy development process" should guide each of the decisions and actions of ICANN, respectively.[686]
- The Joint Project Agreement between the US Department of Commerce and ICANN contains a specific provision on transparency:

  > "The Department reaffirms its policy goal of transitioning the technical coordination of the DNS to the private sector in a manner that promotes stability and security, competition, bottom-up coordination, and representation. Consistent with this objective, the Department agrees to perform the following activities: 1. Transparency and Accountability: Continue to provide expertise and advice on methods and administrative procedures to encourage greater transparency, accountability, and openness in the consideration and adoption of policies related to the technical coordination of the Internet DNS (…)." [687]

685 ICANN, Management Operating Principles, Accountability & Transparency, 8.

686 ICANN, Annual Report 2008, 16.

687 ICANN, Joint Project Agreement, I.B.1.

- In the Annual Report of 2008, ICANN endorses the translation of important documents and meeting proceedings, thereby stressing the need to uphold and improve high standards of accountability.[688]

In the meantime, ICANN started to review its responsibilities with the support of an expert group. Thereby, transparency is being addressed in connection with five major duties:[689]

- Established consultation should be enhanced to develop Transparency and Accountability Management Operating Principles;
- Commenced work on the website should continue to improve accessibility and transparency;
- Established subscriber news alerts and newsletter services should be maintained;
- Project plans should be linked to the Operating Plan and published so that work progress can be clearly monitored;
- Policy for considering new registry services should be fully implemented.

According to ICANN's Management Operating Principles on accountability and transparency of January 2008, the elements of transparency and thus accountability which are to be improved are the following:[690]

- ICANN's Accountability in the Public Sphere (encompassing commitments to transparency, ICANN's documentary information disclosure policy, ICANN's dispute resolution mechanism, financial transparency and accountability, as well as a general commitment to the highest transparency standards);
- ICANN's Legal and Corporate Accountability; and
- ICANN's Accountability to the participating community (entailing obligations to a representative composition of ICANN's Board, review of the corporation's structures, consultation principles, translation principles and codes of conduct).

In a nutshell, it can be said that ICANN has become aware of the importance of transparency issues and is working on their improvement.

4.2 Further Developments

Obviously, the governing of the Internet encompasses more aspects than are controlled by ICANN and involves additional players. Furthermore, several country

688 ICANN, Annual Report 2008, 104–127.
689 ICANN, Annual Report 2005–2006, 33.
690 ICANN, Management Operating Principles, Accountability & Transparency.

code top-level domain (ccTLD) registries and regional Internet registries (RIFs) have refused to relinquish their autonomy in favor of ICANN's oversight.[691] Due to the development of alternatives offering competing TLDs, ICANN does not hold a complete monopoly.[692] The market for Internet governance related commodities can be described as encompassing the registration of domain names and Internet protocol addresses (IP addresses), the administration of the root server system, technical standards, infrastructure, as well as further issues.

The reflections on Internet transparency made by ICANN-related organizations and working groups (for example the IETF Trust) highlight the fact that new technical developments might jeopardize the transparency objective. On the one hand, because the Internet has greatly expanded both in size and in application diversity, its degree of transparency has diminished.[693] On the other hand, recent inventions preserve the illusion of transparency while actually interfering with it; in particular the decline of transparency is having a severe effect on the deployment of end-to-end Internet protocol security; furthermore, private addresses and Network Address Translators affect the degree of transparency.[694] Filtering, intended to block or restrict application usage, also has a negative impact.

Another aspect concerns the problem that transparency, although it might provide great flexibility, also makes it easier for unwanted as well as wanted traffic to pass. Indeed, unwanted traffic (for example spam) is increasingly referred to as a specific justification for limiting transparency.[695] Probably even more complex transparency barriers will have to be developed in order to counter increasingly sophisticated security threats. Transparency, once lost, will be hard to regain, so that such an unsuccessful approach would lead to an Internet that is more insecure and lacks transparency.[696] The elaboration of highly developed host-based security mechanisms is less likely to sacrifice transparency in the process.

The principle of transparency must be seen as an important aspect of good regulatory governance, since it allows the exercise of authority to be publicly accessible and the public stakeholders to monitor the decision making processes. This development could be explained in view of the rise of an egalitarian culture, which generally demands transparency for everyone. However, this perception contradicts the emergence of more individualist approaches in the new century, which suggest the rise of privacy-protection policies and further security concerns. A more functional strain of explanation sees the increased transparency as a necessary

[691] Drissel, 113.
[692] De Vey Mestdagh/Rijgersberg, 5; see also above III.C.4.1.
[693] Network Working Group, Reflections on Internet Transparency, RFC 4924, 2.
[694] Network Working Group, Internet Transparency, RFC 2775, 10.
[695] Network Working Group, Reflections on Internet Transparency, RFC 4924, 2.
[696] Network Working Group, Reflections on Internet Transparency, RFC 4924, 2.

kind of adaptation to prevailing technological and social changing conditions for governments and many other kinds of organizations.[697] In light of this perception, a certain limitation of the vast information flow could in fact promote transparency in the long-term, due to an enhanced overlook of the material available.

5. Outlook

The current concern for transparent political and economic structures suggests the need to reach a common understanding regarding transparency. This can be achieved by observing the following five elements:[698]

- Availability of an organization or an institution with sufficient power to influence the management of resources in the society, i.e. with a role in governance;
- Existence of publicly reliable information, i.e. substantive quality standards related to information, supported by an adequate legal framework which influences the people's choices since a rational person would arguably organize his or her conduct in accordance to the law;
- Definition of the recipient as an essential component for the perception of both information and transparency;
- Availability of information, for example by establishing disclosure procedures, reporting requirements, granting the recipient investigative powers or a general right of access to information;
- Observance of the time element, i.e. transparency implies constant visibility of information.

The medium of the Internet itself offers valuable opportunities for transparent communication. In fact, in order to achieve transparency in the regulatory process, the Internet could be used to achieve open access to negotiations, to collect proposals and statements from the various stakeholders concerned, to present the decisions and results, and thereby enhance and facilitate communication and dialogue between the different Internet governance-regulated institutions and the interested parties. Open access to negotiations and information can also promote the mobilization of new actors and help them play their part in Internet governance. The IGF is a prominent and valuable example for such enhancement of dialogue. Indeed, transparency reflects the architectural and constitutional principles of the Internet, such as flexibility and openness.[699]

697 Hood, 216–217.

698 Lastra/Shams, 171.

699 Weber, Transparency, 348.

Modern legal jurisprudence asserts that the validity of legal rules partly depends on whether those obliged by the rules can ascertain, in advance, what behavior or restraint is required,[700] meaning that the postulated level of details of information can be deduced. Applied to the field of the Internet, the achievement of a greater degree of clarity and predictability also fosters the stability of the legal framework applicable to the Internet and consequently fosters e-trade. Furthermore, the open communication of its governing bodies improves the stakeholders' confidence in the cross-border nature of the Internet. Transparent minimum quality standards also enhance the Internet's conditions and the assessment of performance and accountability, as well as facilitate the coordination of Internet governance related regulations.

Another important issue concerns the participation of civil society. Transparent procedures allow for a certain level of "democratic" legitimization and credibility through active involvement of citizens as well as through certain control over the decision-making processes. However, democratic participation in the Internet is dependent on Internet access, which from a global perspective, is still a very ambitious goal.[701] Furthermore, the question should be generally addressed, as to whether democratic theories are suitable to be applied in the field of the Internet.[702] Nevertheless, since a transparent methodology for rulemaking processes based on revisable procedures reduces mistrust and can have a legitimizing side effect, transparency should become a persistent objective of governance mechanisms.[703]

D. Accountability

1. Introduction

Since a fundamental change of the present system with ICANN—as main body in the Internet Governance content—cannot be expected in the near future, means of improvement become important. Apart from the already discussed transparency issues, the topic of accountability, being closely related, merits further attention.[704]

700 See also R (Law Society) v. Legal Services Commission; Dexter Montague and Partners (a firm) v. Same [2007] EWCA Civ 1264, para. 80, regarding contracts.

701 See WEBER/MENOUD, 11/12.

702 See HUNTER, 1149 ss.

703 WEBER/GROSZ, Vague Ideas, 123, 131; KLEINSTEUBER, 73; MAYER-SCHÖNBERGER/ZIEWITZ, 193.

704 This subchapter is adopted from WEBER, Accountability; see also MALCOLM, Governance, 260 ss and 493 ss.

2. Notion and Importance of Accountability

"Accountability" stems from the Latin word *accomptare* (to account), a prefixed form of *computare* (to calculate), used in the money lending system developed in Ancient Greece and Rome. Accountability is the acknowledgement and assumption of responsibility for actions, products, decisions, and policies within the scope of the designated role. Various types of accountability can be distinguished, namely moral, administrative, political, managerial, market, legal/judicial, constituency related and professional accountability.[705] The key elements are political accountability binding the government, civil servants and politicians, administrative accountability addressed to civil servants and governmental commissions, market accountability requesting the services providers to act in a "customer-driven" way and constituency relations making the public agency accountable for voices expressed outside the established channels.

In the meantime, accountability has become an important topic in the discussion about the legitimacy of international institutions. Due to the lack of a "global democracy" to which organizations must abide, global administrative bodies are confronted with requests to overcome accountability gaps. Even non-government agencies are beginning to prepare and sign "accountability charters".[706]

Accountability is a pervasive concept, encompassing political, legal, philosophical and other aspects; each context casts a different shade on the meaning of accountability. Nevertheless, a general definition incorporating basic elements remains recognizable in the sense that accountability consists in the obligation of a person (the accountable) to another (the accountee), according to which the former must give account of, explain and justify his actions or decisions against criteria of the same kind, as well as take responsibility for any fault or damage.[707]

Accountability of Internet governing bodies is not only important for the public to oversee the organizations' activities, but also serves the self-interest of the respective entities. A clear definition of the authority of each governing body and a justification for actions taken contributes to their respective effectiveness and credibility.[708]

705 See DWIVEDI/JABBRA, 5–8.
706 See for example HAPI (Human Accountability Partnership International).
707 LASTRA/SHAMS, 167; MALCOLM, Governance, 262.
708 BAIRD, 18.

3. Accountability in Internet Governance at Present

3.1 Accountability in ICANN's Documentation

Up to now, debates about accountability have particularly focused on ICANN's role in Internet governance. However, it should not be overlooked that similar issues are bound to arise with regard to other Internet organizations, often in relation to ICANN (for example, ISOC, IETF, W3C).[709]

The tasks to be fulfilled by ICANN are described in the Joint Project Agreement between ICANN and the US Department of Commerce, as well as ICANN's corporate organization.[710] Nevertheless, the self-regulatory legal framework is quite meager. For many years, topics such as the accountability of the Internet governing bodies have not, or at least only vaguely, been addressed.[711] Therefore, civil society has been pushing towards more accountability, even if it cannot be overlooked that ICANN's accountability structures do not easily fit into any traditional definition.

The fact that ICANN has realized the importance of transparency and accountability provisions is—at least indirectly—reflected in the following documents:[712]

- In Art. III Sect. 1, the Bylaws of ICANN state that the corporation "shall operate to the maximum extent feasible in an open and transparent manner and consistent with procedures designed to ensure fairness". Furthermore, Art. I Sect. 2 includes several objectives such as "remaining accountable to the Internet community through mechanisms that enhance ICANN's effectiveness" (no. 10).[713]
- The Joint Project Agreement with the US Department of Commerce contains the following provision (no. 2): "The Department agrees to (...) continue to provide expertise and advice on methods and administrative procedures to encourage greater transparency, accountability, and openness in the consideration and adoption of policies related to the technical coordination of the Internet DNS." Furthermore ICANN agreed to "take action on the Responsibilities set out in the Affirmation of Responsibilities [regarding accountability]

709 See Grosz, ISOC; Grosz, W3C.

710 See Weber, ICANN, IV; and Schweighofer, Review of the UDRP, 96–97.

711 See also Weber, Transparency, 347.

712 See also ICANN, Management Operating Principles, Accountability & Transparency; ICANN, Annual Report 2005–2006, 6, 34–35; ICANN, Annual Report 2008, 106–127. Since ICANN has addressed accountability together with transparency, the two issues should be tackled together; for further information on transparency see above V.C.

713 See Article I Section 2 (10) ICANN Bylaws; see also Schweighofer, Role and Perspectives of ICANN, 85.

established by the ICANN Board in ICANN Board Resolution 06.71, dated September 25, 2006".[714]

- In the Annual Report of 2008, ICANN emphasizes the need to uphold and improve the accountability standards.[715]
- The President's Strategy Committee (PSC) paper, "Improving Institutional Confidence in ICANN" names ICANN's accountability responsibility towards its multi-stakeholder community as a key area to be addressed for structural improvements. A proposal for discussion included the establishment of "additional accountability mechanisms that allow the community to request reconsideration of a decision from the Board, and, as an ultimate sanction, to remove the Board collectively and reconstitute it".[716]

Consequently, ICANN and other Internet governing bodies are in the process of improving transparency and accountability. ICANN has introduced two new mechanisms, namely:[717]

- an independent review of ICANN's accountability and transparency principles (related to structures and practices) and
- the execution of management operating principles for consultation of civil society enabling its members to participate in responsive procedures.

ICANN's Management Operating Principles of January 2008, refer to "accountability" and "transparency" as the foundations that support the elements of the corporation's operating model.[718]

3.2 Relevant Accountability Types

In its own documentation, ICANN distinguishes three types of accountability which encompass three ways of action, thereby addressing some of the major, already mentioned, accountability elements:[719]

- *Public sphere accountability* deals with mechanisms for assuring stakeholders that ICANN has behaved responsibly;

714 See II. C.1. of the Joint Project Agreement between the U.S. Departmen of Commerce and the Internet Corporation for Assigned Names und Numbers, available at <http://www.icann.org/en/general/JPA-29sept09.pdf>

715 ICANN, Annual Report 2005–2006.

716 ICANN, Improving Institutional Confidence in ICANN, 3–4.

717 See also ICANN, Annual Report 2005–2006, 25–27.

718 See ICANN, Management Operating Principles, Accountability & Transparency, 3.

719 ICANN, Management Operating Principles, Accountability & Transparency, 4; ICANN, Annual Report 2008, 106; see also above V.D.2.

- *Corporate and legal accountability* covers ICANN's obligations under the legal system and its Bylaws;
- *Participating community accountability* ensures that the Board and the executive perform functions in line with the wishes and expectations of the ICANN community.

ICANN is aware of the fact that inherent tensions exist among the three types of accountability, making it necessary to establish effective navigation mechanisms which allow for a careful weighing and balancing of the diverging interests involved:[720]

(i) Tensions between corporate/legal accountability and accountability to the participating community: ICANN is accountable to the global community, however, the governing bodies are of the opinion that its unique mission does not permit "members" of the organization to exert undue influence and control over its activities, meaning that ICANN is accountable to the public at-large rather than to any specific "member" or group of "members".[721] Furthermore, ICANN may collaborate and not really compete with other constituents of the Internet community. In addition, Board Members are responsible to the community at-large for the due fulfillment of their obligations (duty of care, loyalty and prudence), however not necessarily to the members or groups having elected them. Consequently, the decision-making bodies can advance views which run counter to the interests of individuals or groups as long as the interests of the whole community are met.[722]

(ii) Tensions between public trust accountability and corporate/legal accountability: This tension is quite obvious in the area of information disclosure; the decision-making bodies are accountable to the public at-large, but at the same time, just as in other organizations, a director generally has a legal and fiduciary obligation to hold some types of information confidential.[723]

These attempts towards establishing improved accountability may be considered as first steps in the realization of a new structural framework. Accessibility of information and accuracy of available data are now recognized as significant issues of good regulatory governance and have become increasingly important in public policies. The explicit reference to accountability in the Joint Project Agreement[724]

---

720 ICANN, Management Operating Principles, Accountability & Transparency, 5–6.

721 "Membership" is not the formally correct term, since ICANN does not have members, according to Article XVII ICANN Bylaws and as defined in the California Non-profit Public Benefit Corporation Law, notwithstanding the use of the word in different ICANN documents.

722 ICANN, Management Operating Principles, Accountability & Transparency, 5.

723 ICANN, Management Operating Principles, Accountability & Transparency, 6.

724 See Articles V.B.1. and V.C.1. Joint Project Agreement.

makes it clear that the Internet governing bodies, and ICANN in particular, need to concentrate more on this issue.[725] However, further progress must be made in a broader context; therefore, in view of the ongoing developments, it appears to be worthwhile to shed light on the general discussions related to accountability in regulated markets.

4. Evaluation of Accountability Elements

The given accountability elements related to ICANN need to be improved along the lines of the general discussion in respect to holding international organizations more accountable. Thereby, inspiration cannot only be drawn from the accountancy segment as such, but also from the attempts undertaken by other globally active organizations being the target of respective discussions.

4.1 Organization Level Aspects

As far as the "organization" of the Internet is concerned, accountability problems can arise at different levels. In terms of a democratic governance understanding, the most important elements of the decision-making processes should lie in the hands of the "body" establishing the constitutional level or international agreements, respectively, which can traditionally be traced back to the States' citizens. In the Internet world, a certain democratic deficit cannot be avoided.[726] Civil society only has a restricted influence on the highest bodies of the Internet's "organization"; furthermore, so far, possibilities for direct influence of civil society on the rulemaking processes are virtually non-existent.

Addressing the roots of a voting system, the extent of adequacy of the traditional one-person = one-vote principle in Internet governance can be questioned. Other international organizations, such as the International Monetary Fund (IMF) and the World Bank, allocate votes in a structured process according to the economic strength of a country; major critics have pointed out the disadvantages of this disproportionate allocation of voting shares, which put developing countries in a bad situation and cause a moral hazard problem.[727] Therefore, a middle way between the two mentioned systems should be envisaged.

Accountability is further affected by the partial lack of transparency with respect to deliberations of the decision making bodies in Internet governance. Obviously,

[725] A specific issue is the financial accountability; see ICANN, Management Operating Principles, Accountability & Transparency, 14.

[726] See WEBER/GROSZ, Vague Ideas, 133–134 with further references.

[727] EBRAHIM/HERZ, 13–14.

secrecy provisions for statements made by individuals in established bodies of an organization play a certain role. Such secrecy clauses, however, should not be used as pretext for not revealing how decisions were made, i.e. on what grounds and with which objectives. Transparency in this sense is an important part of overall accountability.[728]

In democratic nation States, governments typically bolster public accountability through measures of institutional checks and balances in which certain branches or agencies of the government are empowered to oversee and sanction others. No such "horizontal" mechanism exists in relation to Internet governance. In particular, review bodies are not available and traditional control does not exist in respect to "governmental" decisions by the highest bodies of the Internet.[729] Furthermore, virtually no judicial review is available in Internet governance matters; governance rules do not fall under courts' judicial competences.[730]

Finally, no strict structures have been established on the staff level. Due to the weak structuring of the Internet "organizations", the staff members' independency is relatively large; furthermore, many volunteers who are not tied to specific organizational structures are involved. In addition, on the staff level, the knowledge available is mainly of a technical nature due to the emphasis laid on technical skills and experience; therefore, the main focus of the staff is not directed towards cooperation with citizen groups. In other words, the staff does not have incentives to spend scarce time and resources on the development of mechanisms enhancing downward accountability to the netizens. For obvious reasons, such a concept does not meet the normal accountability criteria, even if the degree of efficiency achieved may be quite high.[731]

4.2 Project Level Aspects

The technological changes and business needs in the use of the Internet require substantial project work to be performed by the Internet governing bodies. Many working groups exist, each of them engaged in the elaboration of techniques and technological models.

In principle, it would be possible to design specific information disclosure or other safeguard policies, which could contribute to the information of the public

---

728 See also ICANN, Management Operating Principles, Accountability & Transparency, 9–11.

729 Ebrahim/Herz, 16 related to the World Bank Group.

730 Generally to this problem see Page, 144–145.

731 Ebrahim/Herz, 5–8 (generally to international financial institutions).

on such developments and thereby increase accountability.[732] However, such a compliance regime does not exist for the time being. For example, the Board of ICANN has not yet established quality assurance bodies to address the manifold aspects of accountability. Insofar, it is quite difficult for civil society to evaluate conduct (and misconduct) of the project working groups and to hold account on the respective bodies.

An additional problem consists in the fact that civil society plays a role in the context of the IGF, whereas the framework of ICANN for example (as well as IETF, ISOC, W3C, etc.), is mainly determined by technical expertise. Consequently, civil society does not have a direct influence on such technical expertise. As a result, cooperation between the institutionalized "technical" bodies and civil society is not encouraged and also not seen as a reasonable option, instead perceived as investments of time and capacity.[733]

4.3 Policy Level Aspects

The policies chosen by the competent bodies of the Internet have a major input on the future of infrastructural networks. Therefore, such policies should be checked in view of the needs and wishes of the netizens. Practically, this objective could be achieved through feedback mechanisms designed to play an important role, also regarding accountability. Policy processes need to be consultative in the sense that civil society is invited to comment on policy proposals.[734] In substance, mainly the respective processes need to be improved accordingly, not necessarily the outcomes.[735]

A first possibility to observe the feedback approach could consist in the distribution of iteractive drafts of policy provisions prior to their release for comments stemming from civil society. Comments from many different sources in various regions of the world should be facilitated over the Internet. According to its own documentation, the Board of ICANN is indeed asked to look for comments from civil society: Art. I Sect. 2 of the Bylaws provides for consultation processes in order to achieve the aim of "seeking and supporting broad, informed participation reflecting the functional, geographic, and cultural diversity of the internet at all levels of policy development and decision-making" (no. 4) as well as "employing open and transparent policy development mechanisms that (i) promote well-informed decisions based on expert advice, and (ii) ensure that those entities most affected can assist in the policy development process" (no. 7).

732 EBRAHIM/HERZ, 9–10 and 18–27.
733 See also WEBER/WEBER, Civil Society, 9.
734 EBRAHIM/HERZ, 11.
735 See also GOODHART, 162–163.

Another mechanism could consist in the publication of a matrix which compiles all comments and explains how each input was addressed within the policy review, or why it was not approved of. Thereby, civil society would become aware of its input's potential effect on the reasoning of the competent bodies in accepting or rejecting comments. Such an approach would establish a high level of accountability.

5. Approaches for Improving Accountability

As mentioned,[736] ICANN and other Internet governing bodies have become aware of the need to shed light on accountability issues and to deepen inquiries concerned with the question of, to what extent their accountability—in respect of exercised activities—could be ameliorated and their constituents (particularly the netizens) be motivated to augment their participation in the manifold decision-making processes. Generally, any form of accountability is based on the assumption that objectives and standards exist against which an action or decision may be assessed.[737] Such improved accountability, be it ex ante (a priori), or ex post (a posteriori),[738] would also help to overcome the intensively discussed problem of legitimacy of Internet governing bodies and to increase the effectiveness of activities. Therefore, experiences made in other market segments should be taken into account, for example more transparent structures need to be introduced at the organizational level, more cooperative technical expertise is needed at the policy level, additionally, more extended inclusion of all the involved "netizens" seems desirable.[739]

5.1 Extended Consultation of Civil Society

In democratic nation States, governments typically bolster public accountability through institutional checks and balances based on transparent information; supervisory authorities have the capacity to oversee certain activities which have been undertaken by lower-ranked bodies and may sanction misleading activities.[740]

In the field of the Internet, according procedures do not yet exist. There is no entity with the power to oversee the activities of other bodies. In order to avoid movements in undesirable directions, new developments should be examined in

[736] See above V.D.3.

[737] LASTRA/SHAMS, 168.

[738] For further details see LASTRA/SHAMS, 169–170.

[739] See above V.D.4.

[740] In general see GRANT/KEOHANE, 29–33; SINGH, 298–301.

advance and consultation processes should be put into effect to help streamline the establishment and the implementation of policies. Consultation with civil society allows addressing potential disputes at an early stage and looking for solutions within due time.[741]

The design of consultation processes depends on the matters involved and on the availability of active netizens' groups. However, netizens should not only be consulted in the preparational phase of projects, but also be informed after the project's launch. Feedback mechanisms concerning reviewing processes need to be consistently utilized—an aspect which would also allow the participants in the process to understand how their insights and expertise have influenced the policy outcomes.[742] Final decisions of the governing bodies, together with the considerations that led to them, are to be published. Only in a corresponding framework, can the public exercise a certain control over the decision-making process. Indeed, by presenting the results of negotiations, communication and dialogue to civil society, accountability would be enhanced and facilitated.[743]

Consultation processes require the disclosure of information. Concerns of civil society regarding accountability, in particular at the project level, usually address transparency issues. Several means can be considered in order to tackle the lack of transparency.[744] ICANN has realized the importance of transparency and has initiated certain measures to improve the situation.[745] For example, according to the framework of ICANN's Documentary Information Disclosure Policy (DIDP), ICANN makes information concerning its operational activities available on its website, unless there is a compelling reason for confidentiality. Furthermore, ICANN responds, to the extent feasible, within thirty days to information requests from the public.[746]

5.2 Improved Inclusion of Civil Society

Making activities and achieved results accountable to the "public" is particularly important in respect to participation of civil society.[747] The Internet governing bodies can only be held to account if their activities are visible and subject to

---

741 Ebrahim/Herz, 23.

742 See Ebrahim/Herz, 25–26; Saul, 134.

743 Weber/Weber, Civil Society, 15.

744 See above V.C.4.

745 On the aspects of transparency see Weber, Transparency, 346–348.

746 See also ICANN, Management Operating Principles, Accountability & Transparency, 9–11.

747 See also ICANN, Management Operating Principles, Accountability & Transparency, 20–24.

evaluation. Therefore, accountability should also extend to the monitoring stages of a project's realization and empower the development of effectiveness through citizen participation.[748]

In light of the technical improvements which allow large groups of netizens to access debates synchronously,[749] different kinds of capacities need to be made available in order to meaningfully improve participation during a decision-making process, namely (i) the ability to understand and criticize technical issues, (ii) sufficient knowledge on the given structures and potentials, and (iii) the skills necessary to negotiate with more powerful actors.[750] Therefore, respective assistance to civil society has to be provided by the competent body. This could be achieved in one of two ways: States could inform their citizens through channels already in use for other (domestic) information, or instead of States, an internationally active organization could establish contact points interested people would be able to access. The first method would have the advantage that governments are able to inform their citizens in their own language as opposed to an international organization, which most likely would publish information only in a few languages, as extensive translations would be too excessive to afford. As a consequence, the exclusion of certain groups could probably not be avoided should the second method be adopted.

If the participatory processes are considered to be insufficient or if concerns and comments by the public have not been adequately addressed by the competent Internet bodies, civil society should also be able to get redress. A means for redress could help facilitate the implementation of projects at a later stage.[751]

According to its Management Operating Principles on Accountability and Transparency Frameworks and Principles, ICANN aims at maximizing participation in any consultation by:[752]

- Providing information on upcoming issues as far in advance as possible to give the Internet community time to respond;
- Maintaining a calendar of current consultations and, where practicable, forthcoming consultations;
- Using online fora as the basic mechanism for conducting consultation;
- Providing sufficient context and background material to enable participants to understand the issues on which they are being asked to comment;

748 SAUL, 5.
749 MALCOLM, Governance, 277–278; see also ZITTRAIN, 162–163.
750 EBRAHIM/HERZ, 26.
751 EBRAHIM/HERZ, 27 refer to "social accountability".
752 ICANN, Management Operating Principles, Accountability & Transparency, 25–26.

- Making clear the purpose of the consultation and the way in which comments will be used;
- Using developments in technology to enhance the consultation process;
- Maintaining a public participation site that encourages the community to discuss particular issues ahead of time and to clarify arguments and positions in advance.

A specific approach adopted from national-democratic frameworks consists on the implementation of direct elections. Generally, direct elections are seen as a mechanism to reduce the accountability deficit and the legitimacy problem. However, ICANN's original attempt to integrate direct elections of (a part of) its Board of Directors into its organizational structure, was deemed a failure and consequently stopped, particularly due to the very small percentage of voting Internet users who actually participated in the elections.[753]

However, whether the decision to terminate the experiment was in fact the right one, remains doubtful. Especially due to the fact, that the other option of encouraging the public to vote was not even given a chance. The untried option would admittedly have contributed to an improvement of accountability. Information about the possibility to vote could have been disseminated through the Internet itself, but also through other channels such as newspapers, radio and television. Therewith, a broader public might have been approached. If individuals only use the Internet for specific purposes, or very infrequently, they most probably do not visit ICANN's webpage and therefore may not have known about the elections. However, these individuals might still be interested in the subject and likely to vote if they were informed of the respective possibility.

5.3 Intergovernmental Supervision

Another possibility to increase the accountability of the Internet governing bodies and to tackle the apparent legitimacy problem consists in the introduction of some kind of intergovernmental supervision (treaty-related model of governance). Thereby, in theory, organizations such as ICANN would become accountable to the international community.[754] A cluster of proposals has been presented by the UN Working Group on Internet Governance (WGIG); the roots of this type of proposals can be seen in the concern regarding the (alleged unilateral) US power in the Internet field. Furthermore, members of civil society believe that the

[753] For further details see De Vey Mestdagh/Rijgersberg, 29.
[754] See De Vey Mestdagh/Rijgersberg, 29.

internationalization of Internet governance is a first step in overcoming the digital divide.[755]

The aspect of an intergovernmental supervision of ICANN was a heatedly debated topic during the UN World Summit on the Information Society (WSIS) in November 2005, in Tunis.[756] Pressure to internationalize ICANN came from countries such as Russia, China and Brazil, but at the end of the summit an agreement was reached to not fundamentally change the status quo. However, the establishment of the Internet Governance Forum (IGF)[757] should facilitate the collection of the voices of civil society and bring forward proposals for the improvement of Internet governance.[758] Participatory processes and regular, democratic elections enhance accountability within the IGF.[759]

Nevertheless, certain limitations to the mechanisms of the IGF are not to be overlooked: First, reports should be prepared better and contributions synthesized in order to give the public the chance to understand the content of consultations. Second, more detailed documents and precise reasons leading to a particular decision should be provided to the public. Third, ways for the public to object to decisions of the Secretariat or Advisory Group which are not in accordance with the consensus of the plenary body need to be established.[760]

The Secretariat of the IGF should also enhance transparency concerning its activities in order to be more accountable. The (up to now) very limited transparency combined with the appointment of the Secretariat solely by the UN Secretary-General restricts the possibilities of netizens to oversee the actions of the Secretariat.[761] The installation of internal hierarchies within the IGF introducing a structure for accountability would be desirable and could improve today's oversight executed by the Secretary-General.[762] Accountability can be provided for best if independence between the decision-making body and the body reviewing its decisions is guaranteed.[763]

Intergovernmental supervision has to be distinguished from democratic supervision processes, which were originally designed to avoid governmental power abuse by letting the public participate in policy matters. However, intergovernmental supervision does not encompass civil society, but rather consists of State

755 See also WEBER/MENOUD, 3–20.
756 DE VEY MESTDAGH/RIJGERSBERG, 29; see also above III.D.
757 For the establishment process of the IGF see MASANGO, 63 ss.
758 See above III.D.
759 MALCOLM, Governance, 498; WEBER/GROSZ, Vague Ideas, 124–127.
760 MALCOLM, Governance, 498–499.
761 MALCOLM, Governance, 451–452.
762 MALCOLM, Governance, 499.
763 MALCOLM, Governance, 502.

officials speaking on behalf of international organizations, which, regularly, are not elected by the community, but by the concerned government. Looking at this fact, such international supervision would not enhance participation of civil society in Internet governance matters.[764]

5.4 Market-Oriented Accountability

In view of the fact that normative State-oriented models of accountability cannot easily overcome the problems of the present situation, alternatives have to be considered. Market-oriented aspects of accountability might shed light on specific accountability requirements of Internet organizations and their hybrid organizational structure.[765]

Contrary to traditional political accountability, market accountability is based on informal economic mechanisms rather than on highly formal hierarchical control types. A private enterprise principally focuses on its role with regard to the aspect of demand; its ability to attract and maintain customers is a central indicator of its accountability to the public in the market place, i.e. the main accountability mechanism is reflected in the responsiveness to the customer needs; insofar, choices of the concerned market players are the key constituents for the enterprises.[766] Applying this concept to the Internet would imply that the Internet governing bodies would assume the role of private enterprises, and the Internet users the role of the customers, i.e. the demand side. Internet governing bodies should then focus on the wishes and desires of the Internet users if they want the Internet to continue being an important framework for the actual communication needs, inter alia by being responsive to netizens due to the fact that primarily their choices influence the smooth functioning of the Internet.

Since the needs of the market participants might not always be easily understandable and the definition of the relevant markets difficult to achieve in a global framework such as the Internet, participation of civil society and the "customer-side" in the decision-making bodies should be increased to help crystallize the different market participants' needs and interests. In view of ICANN in particular, its At-Large Advisory Committee (ALAC) stands out as a suitable body to collect the ideas and inputs of the Internet community, since it is the ALAC's primary role to consider and provide advice on the activities of ICANN, insofar as the advice relates to the interests of individual Internet users.[767] Consequently, membership in the ALAC reflects different world regions: the ALAC consists of

---

764 De Vey Mestdagh/Rijgersberg, 29.
765 De Vey Mestdagh/Rijgersberg, 32.
766 De Vey Mestdagh/Rijgersberg, 32.
767 See Article XI, Section 2 para. 4a ICANN Bylaws.

two members selected by the Regional At-Large Organizations (RALO's), which are established for the different geographic regions, and five members selected by the Nominating Committee originating from the five geographic regions. Indeed, the Internet users are also represented in the Nominating Committee, and in this position they are involved in the appointment of ICANN's directors and of the Country Code Name Supporting Organization's (ccNSO) Council responsible for developing ccTLD policies. Furthermore, they are represented by the voting members in the Generic Names Supporting Organization (GNSO).[768] Insofar, the Internet users influence the appointment of the majority of ICANN's directors and the development of the organization's policies.[769] ICANN's organizational structures also include State representatives in addition to Internet users, thereby effectively implementing a multi-stakeholder approach. Both representative categories are domain name customers and, thus, affected by ICANN's policies. For these reasons, ICANN's market oriented accountability mechanisms attract positive attention;[770] nevertheless, the task remains to make the different procedural aspects fully transparent and to encompass them into an accountability framework.

The market oriented accountability model could also benefit from the potential availability of alternative root server systems and competing TLD provisions, however, rules need to be established in this context to avoid the occurrence of market abuses in case a few providers of the technical infrastructure take control of access to the network without regard to the basic "checks and balances" principles. Even if the traditional State based mechanisms cannot be the only means to ensure accountability for ICANN's governance, market "regulations" alone might not heed the needs of political accountability, which are anything but superfluous as the financial and capital markets have shown in the past few years.

6. Outlook

Accountability is regularly called for to improve the governance regimes of organizations in the field of the Internet in terms of enhancing their legitimacy. Accountability has been principally addressed and developed within ICANN as the pre-eminent organization in the field of Internet governance. However, the difficulties in establishing accountability principles as part of an adequate Internet governance model for the virtual sphere should not be underestimated. Improvements of the accountability elements are possible, but the details need thorough discussion.

[768] See Article X Section 3 para. 1 and Section 5 ICANN Bylaws.
[769] See also De Vey Mestdagh/Rijgersberg, 33–34.
[770] See De Vey Mestdagh/Rijgersberg, 34.

One difficulty that needs to be tackled, particularly in the context of accountability as a seemingly uniform standard, arises from the vast and transnational nature of the Internet, a feature which intrinsically implies a struggle with myriad complexities very similar to those already known in the physical world. This heterogeneity is reflected in the existence of various organizations addressing different subject areas. Additionally, the predominant multi-stakeholder governance approaches highlight the diverse constitutions of the accountees, or in terms of market oriented accountability, the customers, who have different interests and needs that all play a role in the framing of accountability. Consequently, accountability mechanisms should reflect the different particularities in the various segments of civil society on a case-by-case basis.

For the enhancement of accountability in Internet governance, it is helpful to frame accountability to include the following three elements:[771]

- Standards need to be introduced which hold governing bodies accountable, at least on the organizational level; such standards help to improve accountability.[772]
- Information should be made more easily available to accountability-holders, enabling them to apply the standards in question to the performance of those who are held to account;[773] in order to make information flow rather active than passive (seen from a recipient's point of view) consultation procedures are to be established.[774]
- Accountability-holders must be able to impose some sort of sanction, thus, attaching costs to the failure to meet the standards; such kind of "sanctioning" is only possible if adequate participation schemes are realized through direct voting channels[775] and indirect representation schemes.[776]

In particular the establishment of standards in terms of specific values that lay the foundation of accountability could provide for a viable way forward. Similarly to a Magna Charta or a constitutional approach, such standards could help implement a legitimizing structure and a guideline for Internet governance in general. Furthermore, they would be suitable to entail significant self-constraints for the policy-making institutions, and hence, move towards substantiating the realistic implementation of accountability.[777] Nevertheless, the strengthening of the legal

771 See BUCHANAN/KEOHANE, 51.
772 See above V.D.4.1.
773 See above V.D.4.2.
774 See above V.D.5.1.
775 The application of the voting procedures has arguably been given up at a too early stage (see above V.D.5.2).
776 See above V.D.4.3 and V.D.5.2.
777 See also WEBER/GROSZ, Vague Ideas, 128.

framework by a treaty-related model of governance, encompassing some kind of intergovernmental supervision, would have supplemental merits since pressure on privately introduced structures has the tendency to improve compliance by the "market players".[778] Consequently, private initiatives are to be complemented by functional surveillance, for example under the auspices of the Internet Governance Forum (IGF) or a newly established intergovernmental body.

E. Participation

1. Introduction

1.1 Desirability of Public Participation in the Internet

Public participation in the Internet enhances accountability, stability, and sustainability of the structural framework governing the growing information society.[779] For obvious reasons, activities of Internet organizations necessarily have an influence on the respective developments, and consequently, these organizations are too important so as to remain non-responsive. However, concerns about the lack of adequate democratic legitimization of Internet organizations have often been expressed, particularly regarding ICANN.[780] Acceptance of decisions can only be achieved if the members of civil society have the possibility to express their opinion and if their considerations are taken into account.

By introducing fora of discussion in which all actors can participate, integration and harmonization of netizens will be increased. Information asymmetries among the central players of the Internet need to be avoided;[781] thereby, the effectiveness of information flow among different players should be enhanced. By providing information on decision-making processes and letting the public participate in respective procedures, arbitrary or discriminatory decisions can more likely be avoided, considering the possibilities of the public to brand such behavior.

---

778 See above V.D.5.3.

779 This chapter is an extended version of a shorter contribution published by WEBER/WEBER, Civil Society, 9 ss; in general also see MALCOLM, Governance, 229 ss, 266 ss and 504 ss; KLEIN, 186 ss; SINGH, 301 ss.

780 For an overview see SCHWEIGHOFER, Role and Perspectives of ICANN, 79 ss.

781 On the transparency aspects see above V.C.

1.2 Comparable Developments in Environmental Law

a) Justification for Comparison

The lack of transparency and public participation in various policy matters has been the topic of many discussions in the past few years. As civil society is concerned by decisions taken, it should also be able to participate if interested. Participation means, to express one's voice. The right to freedom of expression is relevant in all policy matters; it can, however, only be fully enforced if opportunities are created for civil society to express its view. In order to effectively participate in the discussions, full information is a requirement. By giving place to the interests of civil society, public participation as well as the mobilization of new actors can be enhanced.

A few years ago, questions related to information rights and public participation were intensively addressed in the environmental field. Obviously, environmental matters affect civil society. After two years of discussions and negotiations, the below described Aarhus Convention was signed and thereafter put into force. In the meantime, the respective legal framework governs the informational and participatory relations between the authorities and civil society.

The interest of civil society to participate in the Internet is very similar to its interest to participate in environmental matters; the public is affected by both topics and should therefore be able to express its view. This is confirmed by the fact that basic rights (i.e. right to information,[782] freedom of expression[783]) are protected with respect to both topics.

Subsequently, a comparison between developments in international environmental law and in the Internet will be made. In view of many similarities to be discussed, such a comparison seems to be fruitful eventhough several discrepancies between the two legal frameworks should not be overlooked: The Aarhus Convention is a multilateral treaty, signed by sovereign States, whereas the "structuring" of the Internet is based on a self-regulatory regime, making it necessary to balance different interests of stakeholders (e.g. Internet as an advertising and connecting platform vs. State's sovereign rights and control).[784] Another difference between the two legal frameworks concerns the fact that the Aarhus Convention is

782 Stated for example, in Article 19 of the European Convention on Human Rights, signed by the Council of Europe on 4th November 1950; entry into force on 3rd September 1953.

783 Stated for example, in Article 10 of the European Convention on Human Rights; for further reading on Internet governance and human rights see below VI.C.

784 For a general overview see WEBER/GROSZ, Vague Ideas, 119 ss.

mostly concerned with the role of the public on a national level,[785] whereas the Internet is an international platform allowing access to everyone from everywhere.

b) Aarhus Convention—Background and Contents

The Convention on Access to Information, Public Participation in Decision-Making and Access to Justice in Environmental Matters (Aarhus Convention) has been developed based on the non-binding UN/ECE Guidelines on Access to Environmental Information and Public Participation in Environmental Decision-Making ("Sofia Guidelines"),[786] postulated in 1995, at the Ministerial Conference "Environment for Europe".

Hereafter, an ad hoc group was formed in January 1996 by the Committee on Environmental Policy; its task was the preparation of a Convention reflecting the scope of the "Sofia Guidelines". The main features of the "Sofia Guidelines" were the starting point for the negotiations among countries and NGOs.[787] After ten negotiating sessions held from June 1996 to March 1998, the Convention was adopted at the fourth Ministerial Conference on 25th June 1998, in Aarhus, Denmark. The Convention was signed by 35 States and the European Community and became effective on 31st October 2001.[788]

The Aarhus Convention is an environmental agreement, linking environmental and human rights (i.e. freedom of information). It acknowledges that the environment has to be preserved in order to enable future generations to live in a healthy atmosphere.[789] The aim of the Aarhus Convention is to establish an "environmental democracy".[790] In accordance with Principle 10 of the Rio Declaration,[791] the public should be given the opportunity to participate in environmental matters.

Before the actual adoption of the Aarhus Convention, obligations of States to inform other States already existed under international law. Information had to be provided on particular behavior, projects or events with a likely environmental impact on other States. Furthermore, environmental impact assessments had to be carried out, particularly with respect to projects possibly affecting the environ-

785 Holder/Lee, 131.

786 UN/ECE Guidelines on Access to Environmental Information and Public Participation in Environmental Decision-Making, signed in Sofia on 25th October 1996.

787 Economic Commission for Europe, Aarhus Convention Implementation Guide, 1–4.

788 Brady, New Convention, 69; Thurnherr, 62–63; Zschiesche, 177–178.

789 Economic Commission for Europe, Aarhus Convention Implementation Guide, 1.

790 Hughes/Jewell/Lowther/Parpworth/de Prez, 157.

791 Rio Declaration on Environment and Development, Report of the United Nations Conference on Environment and Development, UN Doc. A/CONF.151/6/Rev.1, (1992), 31 ILM 874 (1992).

ment across national borders.[792] Information of the public, however, was not guaranteed. As a consequence, the obligations of States existing already before the adoption of the Aarhus Convention were complemented with the possibility given to individuals to bring specific claims against the State and with the enforcement of environmental information of the public.[793]

The Aarhus Convention consists of three interconnected pillars: (1) Access to information, (2) public participation in decision-making, and (3) access to justice. The first and second pillar and their analogue application in the Internet will be discussed subsequently. The third pillar related to the access to justice is not suitable to be addressed in the context of Internet governance since the corresponding legally established rights depend on the character of the Aarhus Convention as multilateral treaty; a self-regulatory framework cannot offer access to justice in a similar way, it only has the possibility to install alternative dispute resolution procedures.

The general provision of Art. 3 of the Aarhus Convention contains the obligation of States to take the necessary measures to implement the information, public participation and access-to-justice principles and to provide for appropriate enforcement mechanisms. Awareness of the public should be raised as well as education in environmental matters. Therefore, training of authorities as well as support of groups promoting environmental protection is necessary. Of special importance is the prohibition of discrimination of people requesting information, participating in decision-making processes and seeking justice. Authorities also have to ensure that people making use of their rights as stated in the Convention are not persecuted or harassed in any way.

2. Access to Information

Access to information should provide civil society with the necessary means to understand ongoing processes in the Internet. Supply with information is necessary for the public to be able to participate in decision-making procedures. It is only on the basis of adequate information that individuals can build an opinion and participate in negotiations.[794] Subsequently, with respect to each substantive topic, the solutions as agreed on in the Aarhus Convention will be described and analyzed (1), followed by the discussion of a potential analogous application of such a solution in the field of Internet governance (2).

792 Epiney/Scheyli, Aarhus-Konvention, 18.
793 Epiney/Scheyli, Umweltvölkerrecht, 145–146.
794 Steffek/Nanz, 7.

2.1 Modalities of Publication of Information

(1) Art. 4 of the Aarhus Convention states the right of the public to seek information from public authorities and the obligation of public authorities to provide information in response to such a request.

Art. 5 specifies the right of the public to receive appropriate information and the obligation of authorities to collect and disseminate information of public interest without preliminary request. If the authority does not have the solicited information, it must transfer the request to the authority that does hold it or inform the applicant of the existence and competence of that authority.[795]

In principle, information has to be provided in the manner requested (paper, electronic media, videotape, recording etc.[796]), unless it is already available in another form. The authority is also allowed to publish the information by different means if the form requested is not reasonable or charged with disproportionate inconveniences. In that scenario, the authority has to state its reasons for choosing another form,[797] which must however be equivalent and easily accessible.[798]

The form in which information is transmitted is important because time and cost of transmission depend on it. It also influences access to information for people with special needs, such as disabilities, different languages or lack of certain equipment.[799]

(2) The Internet itself can offer valuable opportunities for the flow of information and communication between Internet organizations and netizens. Indeed, information is easily receivable, in the light of the fact that the Internet offers the advantage of being accessible from everywhere to everyone. It is highly available, near-to-instantaneous and inexpensive.[800] Online deliberations can be realized at a much lower cost (than offline deliberative democracy) and are more synchronous and less limited in practice. Group discussion, collaborative authoring as well as decision-making can be improved in an online framework. Audio and video conferencing software already exists (e.g. Skype), further technical improvements have to be made in order to allow large groups of netizens to access deliberations simultaneously.[801] The creation of a website containing information is an effective way to keep the public up to date. Regular publication of relevant data on the Internet would also enhance active information of the public, rather than having

795 Article 4 para. 5 of the Aarhus Convention; for the timing issue see below V.E.2.2.
796 Economic Commission for Europe, Aarhus Convention Implementation Guide, 54.
797 Article 4 para. 1 of the Aarhus Convention.
798 Economic Commission for Europe, Aarhus Convention Implementation Guide, 55.
799 Economic Commission for Europe, Aarhus Convention Implementation Guide, 55.
800 Malcolm, Governance, 269.
801 Malcolm, Governance, 277–278.

Internet organizations wait passively for requests.[802] In the Aarhus Convention, too, it is stated that the availability of information in electronic databases through telecommunication networks should be introduced progressively.[803]

An alternative is to regularly send e-mails to interested parties. Within ICANN, interested people can subscribe to newsletters in order to be individually informed by the organization. If further information is needed, ICANN may be asked specific questions through a contact link on the webpage. A special access to informational documents also exists for the press.[804] Furthermore, ICANN provides for a monthly magazine containing all the latest news and developments. Individuals can sign up to receive the magazine and unsubscribe at any time. ICANN also invites the public to make comments on the magazine.[805] Moreover, a blog is supported by ICANN where news are published periodically.[806]

This method of informing civil society, however, makes Internet access necessary for all interested parties in order to be comprehensive. This aspect is still a very ambitious goal, especially in developing countries. Internet access has a technical and personal dimension. On the one hand, technical means to have physical access, on the other hand, digital literacy of individuals is necessary to make use of the technical access provided.[807] Another problem inherent to this approach arises from the fact that the interested public grows continuously; therefore, it may be difficult to reach every person individually, as not all of them may be known to the concerned Internet organization.

2.2 Passive Authentication

(1) According to the Aarhus Convention, requests for information should be addressed to "public authorities". This term is concretized in Art. 2 para. 2: Governments (at any level), natural or legal persons performing public administrative functions, having public responsibilities or providing public services as well as institutions of any regional economic integration organization which is party to the Aarhus Convention fall under this category. Judicial or legislative bodies, however, are not considered to be "public authorities". Privately owned companies also fall under the scope of application of the Aarhus Convention if they exercise public functions in order not to create the possibility of evading the ob-

802 Brady, Aarhus Convention, 174.
803 Article 5 para. 3 of the Aarhus Convention.
804 See <http://www.icann.org/press>.
805 See <http://www.icann.org/magazine>.
806 See <http://blog.icann.org>.
807 Kettemann, 53.

ligation to comply with the Convention by attributing public functions to private corporations.[808]

Authorities are responsible for providing information if they act in relation to the environment. Attempts to explicitly exclude "non-environmental" governmental authorities in the definition, however, were unsuccessful; as a consequence, the definition refers to the "government at national, regional and other level".[809]

(2) There is no central governing body of the Internet.[810] The Internet is self-regulated by its users in a cooperative approach of governments and civil society.[811] There are, however, governance-related institutions (such as ICANN for example) which could serve as a transmitter of information. Their task should consist in publishing information on their own initiative as well as in responding to requests for information from the public.

Responsiveness of an authority is necessary for the public to obtain the necessary information. It is the basis for any exchange of opinions among different stakeholders and has therefore to be considered as a "must" if the inclusion of civil society in Internet matters should be achieved. Only when a responsive body—accessible to individuals—is provided, can decision-making processes be democratic.[812]

One of the most important bodies in the Internet framework is ICANN. So far, ICANN's task has been to coordinate the global Internet's systems of unique technical identifiers. ICANN particularly coordinates allocation and assignment of the three sets of unique identifiers for the Internet, operation and evolution of the DNS root name server system as well as of policy developments related to these technical functions.[813] An Advisory Committee, especially established for this purpose, has the task of providing for the information flow. This Committee is constructed similarly to the four already existing Advisory Committees.[814] As the obligation to inform substantially consumes time and efforts, it might prove wise to install a specific unit within the organization which is only responsible for providing civil society with information. The established Advisory Commit-

808 See also HUGHES/JEWELL/LOWTHER/PARPWORTH/DE PREZ, 157; KISS/SHELTON, 157.

809 BRADY, New Convention, 70.

810 WEBER, ICANN, VI.

811 WEBER/GROSZ, Vague Ideas, 120.

812 DANY, 54.

813 Article 1 Section 1 of the ICANN Bylaws; on ICANN see above III.C.

814 Governmental Advisory Committee (GAC), Security and Stability Advisory Committee (SSAC), Root Server System Advisory Committee (RSSAC) and At-Large Advisory Committee (ALAC).

tee responsible for public information could then report to ICANN's Board of Directors.[815]

2.3 People Entitled to Be Informed

(1) For a request of information, no specific interest has to be demonstrated according to Art. 4 para. 1 (a) of the Aarhus Convention. Individuals as well as associations, organizations and other groups have the right to be informed.[816]

Third parties may be included in the procedure; national laws have to provide for and regulate this possibility.[817]

(2) As far as public participation in the Internet is concerned, all people who have an interest in global Internet policy[818] are to be informed as well as entitled to ask for specific information. Similar to the environmental legal framework, the information holder may not ask the information searcher for proof of a specific interest. A distinction between directly involved people and third persons does not need to be made except, for example, in case of dispute resolution procedures.

Special attention needs be given to ensure the inclusion of under-represented groups (e.g. indigenous people, disabled persons, people from developing countries). The removal of access and linguistic barriers to negotiations is necessary. It is particularly important to include such minorities as they are the ones most affected by the digital divide.[819]

2.4 Extent of the Obligation to Inform

(1) According to the Aarhus Convention, all information related to environmental matters may be requested.[820]

The information may be stored in every technically possible form (written, oral or other forms). The only requirement is that the information be recorded on some kind of data carrier; information within the "brain" of a person does not qualify for disclosure[821]. Once recorded, assumptions, errors, incomplete knowledge,

815 For the structure of ICANN see Weber, ICANN, IV.

816 Reference is made to the definition of "the public" in Article 2 para. 4 of the Aarhus Convention.

817 Thurnherr, 137.

818 Weber, ICANN, VI.

819 Dany, 60.

820 Article 2 para. 3 of the Aarhus Convention.

821 Epiney/Scheyli, Aarhus-Konvention, 32.

false information and unfinished documents also qualify as information open to request.[822]

(2) Likewise, all information related to the Internet can be of interest to civil society and should therefore be provided to the requesting information searcher. However, the information must be requested in a detailed way, i.e. the searching person needs to specify his/her request as the amount of information could otherwise be overwhelming (considering the extensive spread of information that the Internet encompasses).

As a general rule, most information is stored in digital form. If this is not the case, measures to digitalize the respective information may have to be examined in order to facilitate civil society's access to the relevant information.

2.5 Exceptions to the Obligation to Inform

(1) Requests for information can be refused in the circumstances provided for by Art. 4 paras. 3 and 4 of the Aarhus Convention.

According to Art. 4 para. 3, a request for information can be refused:

- If the authority does not hold the information requested: This provision is related to Art. 5 para. 1(a) which requires authorities to possess and maintain information; if another authority holds the information, the contacted body must refer the applicant to that authority according to Art. 4 para. 5.
- If the request is manifestly unreasonable or formulated in a too general manner; the term "manifestly unreasonable" is not expressly defined by the Convention. However, it is held as a higher standard than the volume and complexity referred to in Art. 4 para. 2 which does not permit a refusal of the request, but only an extension of the time frame in which information has to be provided.[823]
- If the request concerns information in the course of completion or internal communication, as long as national law or customary practice provide for such an exemption; even if a respective exemption does exist, the public interest served by disclosure needs to be taken into account before a definitive decision is taken.

---

822 THURNHERR, 108.

823 ECONOMIC COMMISSION FOR EUROPE, Aarhus Convention Implementation Guide, 57.

According to Art. 4 para. 4, information can also be refused if the disclosure would:

- Adversely affect the confidentiality of the proceedings of authorities, there where national law provides for such confidentiality; internal operations of an authority are addressed by this clause;[824]
- Interfere with international relations, national defense or public security; national law has to specify these terms;[825]
- Impair the course of justice, fair trials or the execution of enquiries;
- Affect the confidentiality of commercial and industrial information as protected by the law; information can be justifiably withheld, if it protects a "legitimate economic interest";
- Interfere with intellectual property rights;
- Encroach the confidentiality of personal data relating to a natural person if consent has not been given and if domestic law provides for such confidentiality; this exception does not apply to legal persons;[826]
- Interfere with the interests of a third party which has supplied the information without being under an obligation to do so; this exception is meant to encourage the voluntary flow of information from private persons to the government, by ensuring the informing third party that his/her information will be withheld if its disclosure would adversely affect his/her interests;[827]
- Impair the environment.

The grounds for refusal mentioned in Art. 4 para. 4 are to be interpreted in a restrictive manner. Public interest served by disclosure has to be weighed against the desire of authorities to keep the information confidential.

If a part of the information can be disclosed without prejudice to the confidentiality of the information exempted, that part has to be released.[828]

According to Art. 4 para. 7, the refusal has to be forwarded to the requesting person if the request itself was in writing. If the request was made verbally, the applicant can ask for a written refusal. Refusals have to include the reasons and make reference to the possibility of access to the review procedure according to Art. 9.[829]

---

824 Economic Commission for Europe, Aarhus Convention Implementation Guide, 59.
825 Economic Commission for Europe, Aarhus Convention Implementation Guide, 59.
826 Economic Commission for Europe, Aarhus Convention Implementation Guide, 61.
827 Economic Commission for Europe, Aarhus Convention Implementation Guide, 61.
828 Article 4 para. 6 of the Aarhus Convention.
829 For the time limit of the refusal see below V.E.2.6; see also Holder/Lee, 103–104.

(2) Concerning Internet matters, most of the conditions for exemption mentioned in the Aarhus Convention regarding environmental information can also be applied. Only the Aarhus Convention provision through which information is exempt from publication for reasons related to national States cannot be applied as far as Internet issues are concerned, due to the fact that national States have not signed a corresponding treaty and no according trials are held before national courts.

The other exemptions are principally also valid in the context of Internet governance. Exceptions to the obligation of providing the requested information to civil society can be made if:

- The competent body does not hold the information; in such a case it has to be examined, whether the body is obliged to procure the requested information;[830]
- The request for information is manifestly unreasonable or formulated in a too general way, or the volume of the information would exceed the capacity of the information holder;
- The information requested has not yet been completed or concerns an internal communication (especially considering the fact that Internet organizations are private institutions);
- The disclosure would adversely interfere with the confidentiality of the proceedings within the concerned Internet organization;
- The disclosure would affect the confidentiality of commercial and industrial information and a general understanding that the according kind of information is protected, exists;
- The publication of the requested information interferes with intellectual property rights;
- The confidential data of a natural person would be encroached if the information was released and the respective data is protected according to international consensus;
- Publication of the requested information interferes with the information supplier's interests if this person was not obliged to supply the information and has not consented to its publication.[831]

Wherever the Aarhus Convention requires national law to provide for a respective exemption, though, customary practice or international law have to be invoked in

830 See below V.E.2.9.

831 On the conditions for nondisclosure within ICANN see ICANN, Management Operating Principles, Accountability & Transparency, 10–11.

order to justify the exemption. International rules exist, for example, in the fields of intellectual property rights[832] and personal privacy.[833]

2.6 Time Limit

(1) As a general rule, information has to be made available as soon as possible, in principle, within one month after submission of the request; this duration can be extended to two months if the volume or complexity of the request requires such an extension.

The term "as soon as possible" means a few days or longer, depending on the extent of information requested and on the body handling the request. Parties are entitled to specify this period of time, as long as the maximum time limit of one month is not exceeded.[834]

Parties can establish specific criteria to define the circumstances under which an extension of the maximum time limit is necessary. In any case, people requiring information have to be informed of the extension and of the reasons why such extensions are necessary.[835]

The Aarhus Convention does not specify the exact point in time at which a request is deemed submitted; the administrative law of each State has to provide for such a regulation.[836]

The maximum time periods are also applicable in case of dismissal of a request or, if the public authority does not hold the information, in case the applicant is referred to another body according to Art. 4 para. 5.[837]

(2) If information is available to the concerned Internet organization, only very little time is necessary to make it available to the public. However, collecting the requested information also requires a certain amount of time, even if it is available within the institutional body responsible for handling the requests.

Still, the expression "as soon as possible" used in the Aarhus Convention can be applied by analogy to Internet matters. For example, ICANN envisages the response to a request within 30 days, in so far as an extension is not justified for specific reasons.[838] An extension of the time limit has to be justified.

---

832 See e.g. Agreement on Trade-Related Aspects of Intellectual Property Rights (TRIPS).

833 See e.g. Article 8 of the European Convention on Human Rights.

834 Economic Commission for Europe, Aarhus Convention Implementation Guide, 56.

835 Economic Commission for Europe, Aarhus Convention Implementation Guide, 56.

836 Economic Commission for Europe, Aarhus Convention Implementation Guide, 55.

837 Article 4 para. 5 of the Aarhus Convention uses the term "as promptly as possible".

838 ICANN, Management Operating Principles, Accountability & Transparency, 10.

As in the Aarhus Convention, these time limits should also be applicable in the Internet context if a request for information is dismissed.

2.7 Language (Translating Efforts)

(1) Information should be provided primarily in English in order to make it understandable for as many people as possible.[839] However, translating efforts should be undertaken so that information may be disseminated in at least the six United Nations languages (English, French, Spanish, Arabic, Chinese and Russian).[840]

(2) Internet users have diverse linguistic backgrounds. Therefore, also for Internet matters, translations of the relevant documents at least into English are necessary. Whether or not data should be translated into other languages (primarily the six UN languages) depends on the importance of the information and on the frequency of information releases. If the intervals between the different releases of data are short, translating all documents into several languages may not be possible.

The ICANN homepage is upheld in English, its brochure, however, can be downloaded in Arabic, Chinese, English, French, German, Indonesian, Italian, Japanese, Korean, Malaysian, Polish, Portuguese, Russian, Spanish, Swahili, Thai and Vietnamese. Work is in progress to translate the documents into Arabic, English, Spanish, French, Portuguese, Russian and Chinese.[841] Furthermore, with the authorization of Internationalized Domain Names (IDN) by ICANN, as decided at ICANN's 32nd International Public Meeting in Paris in Summer 2008, a noteworthy development can be observed and will provide for new challenges at international level.[842]

Languages in which requests can be made also have to be limited because the body responding to the request cannot be expected to translate the respective request from every possible language into a working language. An extensive concept would assume that the body has a staff of translators at hand; however, this would exceed both time and budget of most information holders. Admitting only requests in English might be too restrictive. If requests in the six UN languages are considered, the possibility for civil society to request information is adequate. The information holder should then respond to the request in the same language as the request has been submitted.

---

839 For the time being, English is assumed to be the language that reaches most people.

840 This is, for example, the standard for publication of CDM projects; see Eddy, 81.

841 ICANN, Annual Report 2008, 84; for the status of the translations see <http://www.icann.org/translations>.

842 See above III.C.5.

2.8 Charges for Supplying Information

(1) For information to be effectively accessible, it has to be affordable[843]. Therefore, any charges levied should be reasonable. Schedules of fees have to be made available defining the circumstances under which a fee can be levied or waived and establishing criteria for the cases in which the supply of information can be made conditional to the advance of a payment.[844]

Schedules help the public to know in advance how much the information requested will cost and thus contribute to the transparency and consistency of fees.[845] Fees cannot be charged at all if the request of information is refused.[846]

Fees have the purpose of covering costs arising from a specific request. General operating costs and costs for the collection of information, however, do not justify levying a fee since such a claim would contradict the principle of reasonable charges.[847]

(2) As the publication of information on the Internet is free of charge, no costs arise from the making available of information in response to specific requests.[848] However, expenses could accrue in cases in which the requested information needs to be searched. Considering that the body responsible for providing the information should have an easy access to all relevant information, a charge should usually not be levied on the individual.

However, expenses emerging from the general dissemination of information have to be covered in the end. If—based on an individual request—information of interest to the entire public community is made available, the information searcher should not be held to pay for the effort of the Internet organization to search the respective information. Such costs should rather be covered by the corresponding organization, such as ICANN for example. ICANN, in return, could raise generic top level domains (gTLD) registrar fees. Another scenario would consist in the approach that all countries have to contribute to the coverage of the expenses, possibly according to their economic capacity.[849]

843 Economic Commission for Europe, Aarhus Convention Implementation Guide, 65.

844 Article 4 para. 8 of the Aarhus Convention.

845 Economic Commission for Europe, Aarhus Convention Implementation Guide, 65.

846 Epiney/Scheyli, Aarhus-Konvention, 34; Holder/Lee, 105–106.

847 Epiney/Scheyli, Aarhus-Konvention, 33–34.

848 Considering that the unit responsible for disseminating information is obliged to possess all relevant data.

849 Since, in general, a country's economic capacity is also linked to the number of persons making use of the Internet in that country.

However, if a request is ascribed to a specific person and the information provided by the Internet organization is of interest only to the information searcher, costs should also be covered by this person.

2.9 Establishment of the Necessary Requirements for the Requested Information

(1) The provision of information according to Art. 4 of the Aarhus Convention presupposes that the information is available to the concerned authority. Therefore, Art. 5 para. 1 lists obligations of the authority:

- Authorities have to possess and update information; therewith, an actual obligation to search for information is stated, which, as a consequence, asks for binding structures encompassing the flow of information.
- Obligations concerning specific forms of information delivery are based on the principle that information has to be made available in a transparent manner in order to ensure the public's effective access.[850]

(2) The organization obliged to disseminate information could also be charged with the mandate to collect information. For Internet matters, too, the possession of the relevant information by the publishing organ is a prerequisite for civil society to be informed.

3. Participation and Involvement of Civil Society

Participation and involvement of civil society can have a legitimizing side effect and allow for better credibility of actions taken by the competent institutions. Public scrutiny—as an indispensable instrument to civil society—based on adequate information mechanisms, allows for public intervention in decision-making processes.

The involvement of civil society in decision-making processes strengthens public confidence[851] in decisions taken, as the public knows what reasons led to the respective "results". Furthermore, public participation increases transparency and accountability of the governing bodies.[852]

The inclusion of new issues, interests and concerns communicated by civil society also encourages the body responsible for making the decision to look at the

[850] EPINEY/SCHEYLI, Aarhus-Konvention, 36.

[851] WEBER, Transparency, 346; CERF, Looking Towards the Future.

[852] See also WEBER, Accountability, 154; MALCOLM, Governance, 272 ss and 504 ss.

specific question from different angles. Therewith, a more adaptable solution may be found.[853]

Considering that the Internet community is very heterogeneous, dialogues created on decision-making platforms can also have the side effect of integration and harmonization among different actors.[854] However, for the public to participate effectively in decision-making processes, it has to be able to (i) understand and criticize technical issues, (ii) possess sufficient knowledge of the given structures and potentials, and (iii) have the skills necessary to negotiate with more powerful actors.[855]

3.1 Participation Procedures

a) Overview

(1) The public has to be allowed to participate in decision-making matters (Art. 6), in the development of plans, programs and policies (Art. 7) as well as in the preparation of laws, rules and legally binding norms (Art. 8).

In order for the public to effectively take part in procedures, civil society has to be able to inform itself regarding the subjects of discussion. Art. 6 para. 2 states a respective obligation; the information is to be disseminated by public notice or individually as deemed appropriate. The obligation to publish the necessary information is reiterated: Once Art. 7 reminds of this obligation in regard to public participation concerning plans, programs and policies; Art. 8 (b) also states that the draft rules need to be provided. Parties have to describe the modalities for furnishing with information; the minimal standard stated in Art. 6 para. 2, however, has to be adhered to under all circumstances: Information must be released in an adequate, timely and effective manner.[856] In order to fulfil this criterion, the provided information needs to be updated when necessary; this may require more than a single notification at one point in time.[857]

(2) In respect to Internet matters, too, effective participation of civil society depends on its ability to inform itself in advance. Like in case of the Aarhus Convention, this information has to be provided in a timely manner in order to allow civil society to effectively take part in the participatory process with full knowledge of the topic. This aim also demands the information to be adequate. The term "adequate" implies that the information provided (i) has to be of value to

853 STEFFEK/NANZ, 3.
854 WEBER, Transparency, 344.
855 WEBER, Accountability, 153 ss.
856 See below V.E.3.5.
857 ECONOMIC COMMISSION FOR EUROPE, Aarhus Convention Implementation Guide, 96–97.

the recipient, (ii) improves his/her knowledge and (iii) enables him/her to use the respective information without being dependent on additional help.[858] All aspects of the topic have to be described in such a manner that the individual can make an informed choice.

As the circle of interested people is very large and located all over the world, it is more effective to inform by public notice announcement than by individual messages. The topic and time of the discussions could, for example, be posted on the same website where the information is provided. Of course, individual invitations to the discussions are also possible. They do not, however, replace a public notice since they would most likely not reach all interested people.

Besides the processes open to public participation mentioned in the Aarhus Convention, the organization of seminars and public fora may also enhance public awareness and raise people's interest.[859] Such events could specially increase the participation of individuals from developing countries if they are held in their areas.

b) Decision-Making Processes

(1) The possibility of public participation in decision-making processes has to be established according to Art. 6 of the Aarhus Convention. Access to decision-making processes must be foreseen particularly for activities that may have a significant impact. Even before the decision-making process starts, the public concerned should, if appropriate, be identified. By involving the public before the start of the negotiations, its involvement may be increased and potential conflicts minimized.[860] If conditions of a decision made are reconsidered or updated, the public once again has to be able to participate in the revision process.[861] If it is necessary to achieve an adequate information level, access to physical examination must be granted to the public concerned. This access has to be free of charge, in order for the public to be able to make use of it.[862]

Different levels of participation in decision-making can be distinguished: Participation of the public in decision-making processes includes consultation of the public,[863] the right of the public to render statements and its right to be heard.[864]

858 Weber, Governance of Information Quality, 165–186.
859 Steffek/Nanz, 15.
860 Article 6 para. 5 of the Aarhus Convention; Economic Commission for Europe, Aarhus Convention Implementation Guide, 103.
861 Article 6 para. 10 of the Aarhus Convention.
862 Article 6 para. 6 of the Aarhus Convention.
863 Consultation processes could help to streamline the establishment and implementation of policies; see also Weber, Accountability, 31.
864 See also Stookes, 2.54.

All these factors have to be borne in mind when deciding on an appropriate framework for public participation.

(2) In Internet matters, decisions including inputs from civil society could be made by means of online fora. This method allows making decisions faster without having to include time periods for sending out invitations, meetings, etc.

In 2000, ICANN introduced the idea of an online voting system. The operation of the e-voting-system was outsourced to an experienced vendor. Such a web-based system is localized (in terms of date, time and address formats) in major areas of the world and supports multiple major languages. It can handle 25 000 voters within a period of 10 days. In order to be as accessible as possible, the system interoperates with a wide variety of client-side platforms.[865] A voter needs to identify himself with a member number, password and PIN number. In case of suspected attempted fraud, the system automatically alerts ICANN. Ballots are implemented secretly, while allowing independent third-party monitors to verify that the ballots counted are the same number as the ballots cast. The personal data of voters is treated confidentially and the system ideally ensures that it cannot be determined how an individual voter has voted.[866] Direct elections have taken place for a part of the ICANN's Board of Directors. Even though this approach seems promising in theory, the project failed due to very low participation from the public and the experiment was closed in 2002.[867]

If the establishment of an e-voting system is not desired, however, civil society may also be included in the decision-making process by letting it send in written statements or public meetings can be set up.

Public fora should have open access for a certain period of time so that members of civil society have the opportunity to make several statements, also responding to inputs by other actors.

The three levels of decision-making participation mentioned in connection with the Aarhus Convention can be applied in connection with governance issues of the Internet, too. Effective participation in the Internet also comprises consultations, motion filings and hearings. Physical inspections, however, are unlikely in the context of Internet. Discussions will concern immaterial topics (as the Internet itself is immaterial), which makes physical inspections rather impossible.

---

865 For example Microsoft Windows, MacOS, Internet Explorer.

866 See <http://www.icann.org/committees/elcom/spec-13jun00.htm>.

867 See above V.D.5.2 and De Vey Mestdagh/Rijgersberg, 29.

c) Development of Plans, Programs and Policies

(1) According to Art. 7 of the Aarhus Convention, parties are to make available appropriate practical and/or other provisions for public participation during the preparation of plans and programs. In the preparation of policies, the public only has to be able to participate to the extent appropriate; a statutory duty is not stated.

The terms "programs" and "plans" are not described in detail in the Aarhus Convention. Concrete decisions are covered by Art. 6, normative efforts fall under Art. 8; Art. 7 can thus still be applied to cases of political planning instruments which usually only affect internal administration.[868]

Whether or not a party has fulfilled this obligation is not measured in terms of a specific result, but in view of the efforts undertaken.[869] To be examined yet is, whether the public authority has explored all possibilities for public participation in the concrete case and verified the impossibility of public participation under the given circumstances. As long as the public authority makes a real and sufficient effort not to violate the Aarhus Convention, that is, it considers every possible scenario and still does not discover a possibility to let the public participate in the development of plans, programs and policies, it can be said that the public authority complied with the established rules even if the public could not participate in the respective discussion.

(2) The structure of the Internet makes plans, programs and policies—even if effective only within the internal administration—very important. As the Internet is not governed by nation States, its structure depends on the regulations established by the private sector. The input of netizens as part of the private sector is therefore essential. The fact that binding laws do not exist, attributes even further importance to public participation in the establishment of plans, programs and policies.

These considerations lead to the conclusion that Internet providers must be obliged to make discussion fora accessible to civil society. Usually, private persons cannot be charged with a respective obligation. Considering that the Internet is a system based on private initiative, public authorities are not responsible for providing the public with information, either.

The classical understanding of human rights addresses the individual's protection mechanisms in the case of undue interference by State actors. Within the context of Internet, however, the relationship between non-State actors and individuals needs to be addressed. Specifically, in regard to the freedom of expression, the inevitable question arises as to whether the relationship between State and individual can analogously be applied (and thus expanded) to the relationship between

[868] EPINEY/SCHEYLI, Umweltvölkerrecht, 44.

[869] ECONOMIC COMMISSION FOR EUROPE, Aarhus Convention Implementation Guide, 119.

non-State actors and individuals. Two possibilities exist under the international legal framework to oblige private actors to respect human rights: (i) Either non-State actors can be directly bound by human rights, this possibility is sometimes known as "direct horizontal effect", or (ii) States can be obliged to protect human rights from violations committed by non-State actors.[870]

The duty of private persons to fulfil the task of making discussion fora accessible to the public has to be seen in view of the third-party effect of constitutional rights (in this case the right to information). Such a requirement, within the context of Internet, would go beyond the scope of the Aarhus Convention concerning policies, due to the fact that the public authority (in the sense of the Aarhus Convention) is only committed to include the public to the extent appropriate. However, as Internet governance is concerned, private actors have an enormous impact on its functioning. Mostly private entities, and not public agencies, govern the Internet. Therefore, imposing the duty to make discussion fora accessible to civil society is indispensable for the public to effectively be able to realize its right to free expression and information.

d) Preparation of Law, Rules and Legally Binding Norms

(1) According to Art. 8 of the Aarhus Convention, parties should promote effective public participation during the preparation of executive regulations and other generally applicable and legally binding rules which are likely to have a significant impact.

The public should be given the opportunity to comment on the respective rules. This is possible directly or by means of intermediaries. The Convention speaks of "representative consultative bodies". As the wording of Art. 8 indicates, this provision has only limited legal importance. The words used ("shall", "should", "strive to") cannot be read as stipulating specific obligations. Therefore, Art. 8 is interpreted as a non-binding behavior postulate.[871]

(2) As mentioned, the Internet is, unlike States, self-regulated, i.e. independent from any form of governmental rulemaking. At the same time, a self-regulatory regime has the advantage of being able to respond to real needs and mirror changing technology within a short lapse of time. However, standards established in the framework of a self-regulatory system cannot be enforced by an official authority. A superior governing body empowered to decree binding rules does not exist.[872]

---

870 See CHEUNG/WEBER, 419; for further details see below VI.C.3.2.

871 EPINEY/SCHEYLI, Aarhus-Konvention, 46.

872 WEBER, Regulatory Models, 79–89.

Public participation is possible in the framework of internal regulations of Internet organizations. ICANN supports a webpage inviting the public to submit comments on specific subjects before these are forwarded for final approval. The webpage gives an overview on subjects open to comments as well as on recently closed comment fora and on upcoming fora and recent changes.[873]

3.2 Exceptions to the Right of Participation

(1) The right to participate in decision-making processes can, according to Art. 6 para. 1 (c) of the Aarhus Convention, be denied if the proposed activity serves national defense purposes and such an exception is provided under national law.

The grounds of refusal to information according to Art. 4 paras. 3 and 4 may also be applied in the case of public participation in decision-making matters. Limitations to the use of such exceptions (such as the separation of uncritical information) are also applicable in this case.[874]

(2) As national States are not affected in their sovereignty by decisions taken related to the subjects of the Internet, the first exception to the right of participation mentioned in the Aarhus Convention cannot be directly relevant. National defense purposes only play a role as far as the technological infrastructure of a State is endangered by cyber-attacks and similar measures.

As for the other exceptions, the same reasons for denial of public participation apply as in the case of refusal of public information.[875] It is imaginable that specific areas are important enough to oblige Internet providers to publish information even though they would, under normal circumstances, be liberated from such an obligation (e.g. according to the obligation to always inform about specific environmental topics under the Aarhus Convention); for example, information is necessary if a danger is impending on the public.

3.3 People Entitled to Participate

(1) As far as public participation in decision-making matters is concerned, only the "public concerned" as specified in Art. 2 para. 5 of the Aarhus Convention, is legitimized to participate in the process.[876] This includes people affected directly

[873] See <http://www.icann.org/public_comment>.

[874] Economic Commission for Europe, Aarhus Convention Implementation Guide, 105.

[875] See above V.E.2.5.

[876] Article 6 para. 2 of the Aarhus Convention.

by the decision, people who could be affected and other people with an interest in the decision-making regarding a specific activity.[877]

For participation in the preparation of plans and programs, the authority can identify the public that may participate. The purpose and goals of the Convention, however, have to be kept in mind.[878]

(2) Decisions taken in respect to Internet matters can affect every netizen. Therefore, all people having an interest in Internet related issues should be entitled to participate in decision-making processes. Their proposals and statements are to be considered in order to achieve a widely supported decision.

No specific interest has to be demonstrated by the person willing to participate. Except for dispute resolution procedures, a distinction between people affected directly by the decision and third persons does not have to be made.

3.4 Form of Participation

(1) Art. 7 of the Aarhus Convention requires participation to take place within a transparent and fair framework. Therewith, effective participation is emphasized.[879]

According to Art. 6 para. 7, the public has to be allowed to submit to the applicant any comment, information, analysis or opinion it considers relevant with respect to the proposed activity. Thereby, the public as a whole is addressed. It is the public itself that measures whether its contribution is relevant; the weight given to it, however, depends on its objective relevance.[880]

(2) In Internet matters, according to the freedom of expression, any kind of input or comment has to be admitted.

The possibility of the public to submit discussion proposals should also be examined as it is possible that members of civil society—as users of the Internet—may come across unsolved problems when using the Internet.

Like for environmental matters, the participation procedure has to be executed in a transparent and fair framework. Only if these requirements are met, can a democratic decision be ensured.

877 Epiney/Scheyli, Aarhus-Konvention, 39.

878 Article 7 of the Aarhus Convention.

879 Economic Commission for Europe, Aarhus Convention Implementation Guide, 116.

880 Economic Commission for Europe, Aarhus Convention Implementation Guide, 108.

3.5 Time Frame for Participation

(1) According to the Aarhus Convention, public participation procedures should be established which are effectively and easily accessible and give recourse to the way in which information is made available.

The public has to be able to participate in the decision-making process at an early stage so that all options are still open and comments of the public can be widely considered.[881] For particular stages of the process, adequate time frames have to be established in order to allow the public sufficient time to become informed and prepared to participate effectively.[882]

(2) The same main features as mentioned in the Aarhus Convention can be applied regarding the Internet. For netizens, too, it is important to be informed of the discussions at an early stage in order to make sure that their inputs can be effectively considered. Accordingly, netizens also need time to prepare themselves for discussions.

3.6 Taking Account of the Results of Public Participation

(1) The results of public participation should be taken into account when making decisions.[883] Art. 7 of the Aarhus Convention specifically includes this accountability aspect. According to Art. 8, the outcome of the public participation has to be taken into account "as far as possible". This slightly different wording indicates that the requirements are less rigid than those for decision-making procedures. Even so, public input has to be considered seriously. A legal basis in domestic law for the authority is required to enable it to incorporate the inputs of the public.[884]

After a decision has been taken, the public must be informed of its contents in accordance with the appropriate procedures. The text of the decision along with the reasons and considerations has to be made accessible to the public.[885] These reasons should demonstrate why a particular public opinion was rejected.[886]

(2) Concerning Internet matters, too, final decisions, together with the considerations that led to them, should be published. Only if this is the case, a certain amount of control over the decision-making process can be exercised. By present-

881 Article 6 para. 4 of the Aarhus Convention.
882 Article 6 para. 3 of the Aarhus Convention.
883 Article 6 para. 8 of the Aarhus Convention.
884 Economic Commission for Europe, Aarhus Convention Implementation Guide, 109.
885 Article 6 para. 9 of the Aarhus Convention.
886 Economic Commission for Europe, Aarhus Convention Implementation Guide, 109.

ing the results of public participation, communication and dialogue within civil society can be enhanced and facilitated.

4. Recognition and Support of the Bodies Promoting Internet Governance

It is important for the Internet organizations, in particular the Internet Governance Forum (IGF),[887] to provide for appropriate recognition and support of institutions, associations or groups promoting Internet governance. The IGF is a discussion body and has the objective of gathering views from stakeholders about Internet governance. Participatory processes and regular, democratic elections enhance accountability within the IGF.[888]

These groups need recognition, because they are also obliged to provide information and possibilities for public participation and are in turn dependent on support by bigger, more experienced institutions. Such Internet organizations have more means to install adequate platforms and procedures and, as they probably use the according procedures more often (considering their size and the number of decisions taken) are more experienced in carrying them out. Concentrating all information in one single platform also reduces the cost of publication. Additionally, information research efforts can be combined and the resulting synergies can be used in the effective transmission of information to the public.

Internet organizations might include information released by bodies promoting Internet governance as well as their decision-making procedures on their own platform. Information on related topics made available by different Internet providers could be combined in order to facilitate the overview for individual information searchers. Such an approach would also enable interested people to compare different information sources. Furthermore, the combination of all information could serve civil society by centralizing all relevant information. The public cannot be expected to regularly check dozens of information sources in order to be up to date.

5. Access to Jurisdiction

(1) Art. 9 of the Aarhus Convention introduces a possibility for the public to directly enforce legal provisions. It strengthens the first two pillars (access to information and public participation) in the sense that violations can be reprehended.

887 For further details on IGF see above III.D.

888 Zittrain, 242–243; Malcolm, Governance, 498.

Complaints may be filed concerning the inappropriate handling of information requests, violations of the right of the public to participate as well as other violations of the Convention if the domestic law provides for respective procedures.

(2) In Internet matters, civil society cannot go to court in order to challenge the potential violation of rights similar to a violation of the Aarhus Convention. Whereas sovereign States have signed the Aarhus Convention and thereby committed themselves to establish the respective procedures and standards, corresponding obligations do not exist in the self-regulated Internet environment. Obligations concerning information of civil society and public participation cannot be enforced in court based on the self-regulatory framework, but only on possible national commitments.

However, independent dispute resolution processes on the basis of international law could be established.[889] The respective decisions, though, would not be enforceable through sovereign enforcement procedures. Their effectiveness would largely depend on the willingness of the dispute parties to engage in a dialogue and look for an amicable solution.

ICANN provides for a three-part dispute resolution process. The first formal appeal is directed to the Reconsideration Committee (for reconsideration of decisions made by the Board or the organization); the second dispute resolution channel takes place before the Independent Review Panel (for review of actions, decisions and inactions of the Board); the last possibility for appeal is the ICANN Ombudsman (dealing with decisions, actions, or inactions of ICANN which are perceived unfair).[890]

6. Outlook

The inclusion of civil society in the governing of the Internet has a legitimizing effect and enhances transparency, accountability and stability of the framework. The question of information rights and public participation has also arisen in the environmental field, ending in the establishment of the Aarhus Convention. Most basic ideas stated in that Convention can be taken into account for having civil society participating in the Internet.

Information has to be provided to the public in order to enable it to participate in discussions. The Internet itself offers valuable opportunities for the dissemination of information. However, the effectiveness of this information channel depends on

---

[889] WEBER/GROSZ, Vague Ideas, 134.

[890] See ICANN, Management Operating Principles, Accountability & Transparency, 12/13; see also SCHWEIGHOFER, Review of the UDRP, 91 ss.

access to the Internet for all interested parties, which is still a very ambitious goal and presupposes technical and financial aid to developing countries in particular. The publishing of information also requires the governing bodies to search for the requested information. Private bodies promoting Internet governance gain more and more importance and should be recognized and supported. They bear the primary responsibility of informing the public and allowing it to participate.

The informed public should then be included in decision-making processes. Online deliberations and e-voting systems seem most adequate within the Internet framework and allow for effective public participation. Inputs from civil society have to be taken into account in decision-making processes and reasons need to be given if the governing bodies diverge from the opinion of the public. Only in such cases, can transparency be ensured and the respective bodies be held to account.

Based on a Memorandum of Understanding (MoU) among the most relevant Internet organizations concerned with the participation of civil society in decision-making processes with respect to Internet governance (such as the ICANN, ISOC, IGF, IETF, IAB), general rules for the participation of civil society in the field of the Internet could be established. Such an understanding would allow the incorporation of basic standards regarding public participation within the Internet framework and enable the voluntary observation of the respective organizations. The proposed MoU should encompass all relevant Internet organizations in order to achieve the desired standardization of participation processes. The beneficiaries of the MoU would be the members of civil society; hence, the undertakings of the organizations should be phrased in favor of the netizens interested in participating in Internet governance.

One of the primary goals of the MoU should consist in the improvement of cooperation among institutions involved in Internet governance. These organizations should be obliged by the MoU to establish standardized processes for public participation, due to the relatively substantial number of entities engaged in Internet governance.[891] Cooperation among agencies with respect to specific issues (such as spam or cybercrime) as well as decision-making agencies may also help stakeholders to coordinate their search for information and their input in the decision-making processes.[892]

Such a MoU would not have the quality of an international treaty, moreover, it would have to be considered as a self-regulatory mechanism in terms of “soft

[891] A mapping of different entities involved in Internet governance can be found in the UN Exploratory report on the concept and possible scope of a code of good practice on participation, 12 ss.

[892] UN Exploratory report on the concept and possible scope of a code of good practice on participation, 13.

law". According to the traditional conception,[893] soft law is not enforceable and does not create duties of liability. Soft law is often used as a catchphrase for particular forms of social rules close to public international law. Although soft law is not legally binding, it nevertheless has a certain legal significance. For example, soft law may provide for a first step towards the creation of according customary law and its codification. Furthermore, courts can use soft law in the interpretation of formal legal sources.[894]

The non-binding character of such a MoU is suited to fit the self-regulatory and non-enforceable nature of the Internet's regulatory framework. Nevertheless, Internet organizations themselves or particular bodies within the organizations need to be appointed responsible for the introduction of the provisions of self-regulation, as well as for their implementation and enforcement. Thereby, the inclusiveness and quality of Internet governance could be improved and the effective participation of more stakeholders would be facilitated by more transparent decision-making processes.

The United Nations Economic Commission for Europe (UNECE), the Council of Europe and the Association for Progressive Communications (APC) are apparently considering the establishment of a "Code of Good Practice on Participation, Access to Information and Transparency in Internet Governance".[895] This code is drawn from the WSIS principles and the Aarhus Convention. The respective voluntary code is intended, on the one hand, to serve as a benchmark for public participation, access to information and transparency in Internet governance, on the other hand, to build a common understanding of the respective principles and their practice. According to the Exploratory Report, the respective code needs to be expressed in broad and general terms so as to not exclude particular decision-making areas. Nevertheless, sufficient substance should be given to its principles.[896]

The mentioned MoU could serve as a basis for the introduction of such a code, by outlining the general principles in more detail. The MoU, which encompasses fewer members, may be more easily realized since consensus within such a confined forum is more likely to be reached. Content-wise the MoU should concentrate on *process*, not on substance; procedural rules should provide for a framework which allows the active participation of civil society in Internet matters.

---

893 IPSEN, § 19 N 20; for more details see WEBER, Regulatory Models, 79–85 and above I.C.2.

894 WEBER, Selbstregulierung und Selbstorganisation, 28; IPSEN, § 19 N 20/21; THÜRER, Soft Law, 439 ss.

895 See UN Exploratory report on the concept and possible scope of a code of good practice on participation, 3.

896 UN Exploratory report on the concept and possible scope of a code of good practice on participation, 20.

VI. Regulatory Issues

A. Introduction

The Tunis Agenda mentions numerous public policy issues that should be considered by the Internet Governance Forum (IGF), however, without establishing a clear order or priority setting.[897] A preparatory document, namely the WGIG-Report, identified thirteen Internet-related public policy issues in more concrete terms which were partly adopted by the Tunis Agenda. In particular, the following issues are mentioned:[898]

- Administration of the root zone files and system (WGIG-Report, para. 15);
- Interconnection costs (WGIG-Report, para. 16; Tunis Agenda, paras. 49 and 50);
- Internet stability, security and cybercrime (WGIG-Report, para. 17; Tunis Agenda, paras. 40, 43, 44 and 45);
- Spam (WGIG-Report, para. 18; Tunis Agenda, para. 41);
- Meaningful participation in global policy development (WGIG-Report, para. 19; Tunis Agenda, para. 52);
- Capacity-building (WGIG-Report, para. 20; Tunis Agenda, para. 51);
- Allocation of domain names (WGIG-Report, para. 21; Tunis Agenda, paras. 63 and 64);
- IP addressing (WGIG-Report, para. 22; Tunis Agenda, para. 38);
- Intellectual property rights (WGIG-Report, para. 23);
- Freedom of expression (WGIG-Report, para. 24; Tunis Agenda, para. 42);
- Data protection and privacy rights (WGIG-Report, para. 25; Tunis Agenda, paras. 39 and 46);
- Consumer rights (WGIG-Report, para. 26; Tunis Agenda, para. 47);
- Multilingualism (WGIG-Report, para. 27; Tunis Agenda, para. 53).

As the list shows, the Tunis Agenda incorporated neither the issues of the root zone files or system nor the intellectual property rights from the WGIG-Report. Partly, these issues could be covered by the term "critical Internet resources" as used in para. 72 j) of the Tunis Agenda,[899] however, the notions do not fully correspond. Subsequently, the transition of the technical platform IPv4 to IPv6 will

---

897 MALCOLM, The Space Law Analogy, 26.

898 See also MALCOLM, The Space Law Analogy, 26–27.

899 On this aspect see below VII.B.5.1.

Copyright © Schulthess Juristische Medien AG, Zurich – Basel – Geneva 2009.

Published by Springer-Verlag GmbH Berlin Heidelberg 2010. All Rights Reserved

be discussed as a regulatory issue in the context of scarce (critical) resources' allocation.[900]

The Internet Governance Forum (IGF) narrowed the number of the discussed issues even further, by focusing on openness, security, diversity, and access; in a second step the IGF added critical Internet resources and emerging issues.[901] The deliberations during the IGF annual meetings generally touch upon the four to six themes, however, manifold extensions and enlargements, based on aspects of the Tunis Agenda (for example security, human rights, content issues, multilingualism), cannot be overlooked.[902] The following chapter does not intend to cover all regulatory issues at stake, but concentrates on a few key issues, namely the allocation of critical resources and the related access problems, the yardstick for a humanization of Internet governance (in particular through the acknowledgement of fundamental rights), security issues related to safety, trust, and reliability, as well as the important development issue of the digital divide.

B. Critical Resources and Access

The allocation of "critical resources" is a noteworthy theme in general and has not lost its importance for the specific field of the online world. Since access to infrastructure can also be considered an aspect of "critical resources", the two issues are discussed in the same subchapter hereinafter.[903]

1. Internet Governance and Critical Resources

The allocation of critical resources necessarily plays an important role and must certainly be considered in addressing the issue of Internet governance. In particular, an equitable and non-discriminatory use should be achieved by the allocation of such resources which are limited due to technical restrictions. The law is called upon to establish a framework allowing to implement a fair resources allocation management.

900 See below VI.B.2; as far as the critical resource "Internet Domain Names" is concerned, the problems of their allocation is addressed in the context of the organizational framework (see above III.C. regarding to ICANN).

901 See above III.D.

902 See DORIA/KLEINWÄCHTER, 94 ss, 240 ss.

903 See below VI.B.1 and 3.

1.1 Notion of "Critical Resources"

Voices in civil society as well as in the legal doctrine often address the problem of "critical resources" of the Internet without delineating a clear definition of this notion. For example, para. 72 j) of the Tunis Agenda[904]—which became the mandate of the IGF—stresses on the importance of being able to "discuss inter alia issues related to critical Internet resources" without providing for any further explanation.[905] Indeed, "critical resources" in the context of the Internet can have a very broad meaning: Over time, electricity may become a critical resource for a mobile computer; similarly, a wireless or fixed Internet access is needed if electronic communications are to be exchanged.[906]

In the context of the disussions within the IGF, the topic of critical Internet resources was not deeply addressed at the Athens Meeting in 2006.[907] However, some interventions during the deliberations referred to the respective problems and thus led to the inclusion of critical Internet resources into the agenda of the Rio de Janeiro Meeting in 2007.[908] The actual discussions were lively and intensive, but not always coherent or fully focused, as the excerpts from the transcripts show.[909]

In view of the concrete problems that "critical resources" cause, it appears obvious that the term does not only describe a technical access topic,[910] but also the administration of the Internet's naming and addressing of domains.[911] Theoretically, the routing slots could be a finite capacity; if routing would not work, the address would consequently not be available in the routing system. However, as the development of IPv6 shows, the technical industry provides for solutions in order to overcome such shortages.

Therefore, critical Internet resources should be understood in a way encompassing both the institutional as well as the human elements which are critical to the functioning of the Internet, such as organizations, regulatory frameworks and users. Viewed in this light, it is evident that the management of critical Internet resources has significant public policy implications. Insofar, the basic structure

904 See above III.D.
905 See <http://www.intgovforum.org/mandate.ttm>.
906 HUSTON, 1.
907 See DORIA/KLEINWÄCHTER, 72 ss (the preparatory process) and 94 ss (excerpts from the transcripts).
908 See DORIA/KLEINWÄCHTER, 80/81, 227/28, 237.
909 See DORIA/KLEINWÄCHTER, 259 ss; similarly, the expert contributions collected by KLEINWÄCHTER, Power of Ideas, 208 ss prior to the Rio de Janeiro Meeting address various topics without defining a clear concept of "criticality".
910 On this aspect see hereinafter VI.B 2.5 b).
911 On this aspect see hereinafter VI.B 2.5 c).

supporting corresponding decision-making processes must be internationally recognized and clearly mandated.[912]

In general, the role which the following regulatory issues play in easing access to scarce resources, is an important one: (i) open access, (ii) open standards, (iii) open source software as well as (iv) widespread availability of access points.[913] Within the Internet context, however, this approach needs adaptation since technical aspects are not the only relevant issue and administrative topics are gaining importance. In sum, the allocation of communication possibilities over the Internet must thus be realized within the framework of an emerging, global spontaneous and people-oriented environment.

1.2 Technical Occurrence of Critical Resources

a) Overview

In the past few years, several issues related to critical Internet resources, which have cross-border implications, have been discussed within the framework of international organizations. In its Recommendation 2007/16 the Committee of Ministers of the Council of Europe underlined the public service value of the Internet, by referring to the "legitimate expectation (of people) that Internet services be accessible and affordable, secure, reliable and ongoing".[914]

The most important resources which are referred to as "critical" in connection with Internet services are the following:[915]

- *Broadband access for everyone*: Broadband access is an important element for avoiding "info-exclusion" and for ensuring the participation of civil society.
- *Transition to IPv6*: The implementation of IPv6 is essential for the connectivity of networks and thereby for granting civil society adequate access to the Internet.

912 This objective is jeopardized by the fact that the influence on the actual activities in this field is not evenly distributed among all nations of the world; some nations feel that in particular the United States have a privileged position of control and influence, mainly due to their relationship to ICANN.

913 WEBER, Towards a Legal Framework, 96; see now also DENARDIS, Open Standards, 72 ss.

914 Adopted on 7th November 2007; text from the Recitals.

915 The Council of Europe addresses the problems of critical Internet resources in the context of its Steering Committee on the Media and New Communication Services (CDMC); in April 2009, the report of Council of Europe, Internet governance, was published (see p. 3 to the following list).

- *Internationalized domain names*: Multilingualism in cyberspace is a key concept to ensure cultural diversity and the participation of all linguistic groups in Internet information exchanges.
- *Equal distribution of Internet Exchange Points*: Ensuring local access on Internet Exchange Points is an important element in making the Internet affordable and sustainable, thereby avoiding high costs and latency in respect to international links.

Several technical components of the Internet play a crucial role in the smooth execution of Internet communications and information exchanges. In particular, the following components must be taken in to account:

b) Root Servers

Effective root server operations are an important component for providing a stable and secure, globally interoperable Internet. Currently, 12 operators running 13 root servers execute the necessary functions to establish the domain name system infrastructure of the Internet. The root servers are controlled by a not very clear "mix" consisting of governments, academic institutions and private/business entities. The coordination and evolution of the domain name system root server framework is operated by ICANN,[916] particularly by its Root Server System Advisory Committee (RSSAC) which advises the Board of ICANN about the operation of the root name servers of the domain name system. Further, "the RSSAC shall review the number, location, and distribution of root name servers considering the total system performance, robustness, and reliability".[917] Membership in the RSSAC consists of each operator of an authoritative root name server and such other people as are appointed by the ICANN Board.

Several problems in connection with the operation of the root server system merit careful attention:[918] (i) The operation of root servers functions without any formal relationship with any authority; even if the operators are not involved in policy making and data modifications, the exact accountability and responsibility, in particular related to the stability and the secure functioning of the Internet, is not clear. (ii) The geographical distribution of root servers is highly uneven, ten root servers are located in the United States, two in Europe and one in Japan. This geographical mapping does not correspond to the demand side, in particular in view of the growing Internet penetration in the thus less developed countries.

---

916 See Article I, Section 1.2 ICANN Bylaws.

917 See Article XI, Section 2.3 ICANN Bylaws.

918 See also Council of Europe, Internet governance, 10/11.

c) Backbone Structures

The Internet backbone consists of many different networks. The backbone providers usually offer connection facilities; furthermore, they themselves connect with other backbone providers at Internet Exchange Points (IXP). Backbone structures are effective mechanisms to accomplish cost efficiency and service quality. IXP are usually governed by the connected Internet service providers.[919]

So far, only 79 countries around the world have operational IXP. The lack of an IXP in many countries has an impact on the connectivity among Internet service providers; either the connectivity is relatively poor or local traffic must use expensive international links including costly outbound and inbound traffic (which could also cause lower quality). Furthermore, local content is less likely to be offered if no IXP is available since the content would otherwise have to be hosted outside of the country.[920]

Problems could also arise if two Internet service providers are not willing to enter into a direct traffic exchange relationship. Backbone Internet service providers may fail to interconnect either by peering or transit. This situation occurred regarding the Swedish network provider Telia in March 2008, subsequent to a decision of a private provider to stop routing packets from Sweden.[921]

d) Broadband Access

Broadband access is an essential element for ensuring the transmission of information in a speedy and efficient manner. Advanced applications and services can improve many sectors of civil society (business, administration, education, etc.).

In light of the fact that the establishment of Information and Communication Technologies (ICT) and in particular of broadband access causes substantial costs, remarkable differences in broadband access remain among different countries. Only in a few countries, such as Switzerland, a right to broadband access is legally stated.[922] In 2006, the European Commission started its strategy "Broadband for all" attempting to induce the member countries to speed up the civil engineering works necessary to build the ducts for the new fibre-rich networks.[923]

919 See IGF Rio de Janeiro (2007), Best Practices Forum, Internet Traffic Exchange in Less Developed Internet Markets and the Role of Internet Exchange Points (IXP), available at <http://www.isoc.org/educpillar/resources/igf-ixp-report-2007.html>.

920 See also Council of Europe, Internet governance, 11–13.

921 See <http://www.forbes.com/forbes/2008/1013/064_print.html>.

922 See Article 15 of the Swiss Telecommunications Services Ordinance of 7th March 2007 (SR 784.101.1).

923 See below VI.B.3.

In this connection, the principle of net neutrality is at stake. Since new network management techniques enable traffic prioritization, such possibilities could be used to apply anti-competitive practices such as unfair discrimination of certain traffic.[924] Furthermore, issues such as security and interoperability could be affected, in particular regarding possible changes of the technical platforms.[925]

e) Internet System of Names and Numbers

The Internet system of names and numbers is governed by ICANN. Domain names can become a scarce resource; therefore, governance issues are of importance.[926]

The Internet protocol is used to send data from one computer to another; therefore, each computer needs at least one Internet protocol address that uniquely identifies and demarcates it from all other computers. The respective address space will expire soon; therefore, the transition from the present IPv4 to IPv6 is of utmost importance.[927]

1.3 Protection of Scarce Resources in International Law

As mentioned, certain elements of the information and communication infrastructure of the Internet are scarce resources; the phenomenon of scarce resources is not completely new in the international legal order and did not only come up at the beginning of the Internet age. In many other societal areas, encompassing aspects of resource allocation, the establishment of an equitable resource management is also of importance. Therefore, inspiration can be drawn from international law relating to certain common resources.[928]

The principles laid down in international treaties are so far not coherent, but the question can be raised as to what extent basic guidelines establishing a legal framework could constitute a form of ordre public, representing the fundamental elements underlying and unifying every legal system.[929]

---

924 See Council of Europe, Internet governance, 13–15.

925 As far as the transition from IPv4 to IPv6 is concerned, see below VI.B.2.

926 Governance issues, in particular the legitimicy question, are addressed in detail in the preceding parts of the book (see above III.C.4.2 c) and V.B.).

927 See below VI.B.2.

928 Detailed comments to some of the below mentioned international treatise can be found in Council of Europe, Internet governance, 23–26; in particular, the first four treaties discussed are also referred to in this report.

929 WEBER/WEBER, ordre public, 61.

a) Allocation of Water Resources

As far as the allocation of water resources is concerned, associated State responsibilities are governed by international law. In particular, the UN Convention on the Law on the non-navigational Uses of International Watercourses of 1997[930] provides for rules which should lead to a reasonable use of international waterways for all States concerned. In particular, Article 5, related to the equitable and reasonable utilization and participation stipulates the following:

> "1. Watercourse States shall in their respective territories utilize an international watercourse in an equitable and reasonable manner. In particular, an international watercourse shall be used and developed by watercourse States with a view to attaining optimal and sustainable utilization thereof and benefits therefrom, taking into account the interests of the watercourse States concerned, consistent with adequate protection of the watercourse.
>
> 2. Watercourse States shall participate in the use, development and protection of an international watercourse in an equitable and reasonable manner. Such participation includes both the right to utilize the watercourse and the duty to cooperate in the protection and development thereof, as provided in the present Convention."

In the meantime, more than 20 States signed this Convention, however, it is not yet in force.[931] Nevertheless the underyling concept is clear and centers around the word "equitable", being a notion which governs legal systems in general.

Similar principles also apply in other matters related to environmental protection, for example air pollution. The Kyoto Protocol to the United Nations Framework Convention on Climate Change[932] refers—in connection with the financial resources—to the importance of appropriate burden sharing among developed countries (Art. 11 para. 2 [b]).

Furthermore, as already described in detail, the Aarhus Convention entitles civil society generally to receive information and to actively participate in environmental matters[933].

---

930 UN Convention on the Law of the Non-navigational Uses of International Watercourses, adopted by the UN General Assembly Resolution 51/229 (21st May 1997), 36 ILM 700 (1997), UN Doc. A/RES/51/229 (1997).

931 According to Article 36 para. 1 of the Convention, it shall enter into force "on the ninetieth day following the date of deposit of the thirty-fifth instrument of ratification, acceptance, approval or accession with the Secretary-General of the United Nations".

932 See FCCP/CP/1997/L.7/Add. 1; 1771 UNTS 107 (reprinted in 37 International Legal Materials, 1998); available at <http://unfccc.int/kyoto_protocol>; see also Rolf H. Weber, Emissions Trading, in Liber Amicorum Rolf Watter, Zurich 2008, 475, 477/478.

933 See above V.E.

b) Avoidance of Technical Risks

The problems related to technical risks, in particular hazardous activities, are addressed in the Convention on the Transboundary Effects of Industrial Accidents of 1992.[934] According to Art. 2, the Convention should "apply to the prevention of, preparedness for and response to industrial accidents capable of causing transboundary effects, including the effects of such accidents caused by natural disasters, and to international cooperation concerning mutual assistance, research and development, exchange of information and exchange of technology in the area of prevention of, preparedness for and response to industrial accidents".

As far as the responsibility of the States is concerned, in regard to protecting human beings and the environment against industrial accidents (hazardous activities) in general, Art. 3 of the Convention stipulates:

> "3.1 The parties shall, taking into account efforts already made at national and international levels, take appropriate measures and cooperate within the framework of this Convention, to protect human beings and the environment against industrial accidents by preventing such accidents as far as possible, by reducing their frequency and severity and by mitigating their effects. To this end, preventive, preparedness and response measure, including restoration measures, shall be applied.
>
> 3.2. The parties shall, by means of exchange of information, consultation and other cooperative measures and without undue delay, develop and implement policies and strategies for reducing the risks of industrial accidents and improving preventive, preparedness and response measures, including restoration measure, taking into account, in order to avoid unnecessary duplication, efforts already made at national and international levels."

Even if this Convention applies to activities involving hazardous substances, some analogies with critical Internet resources can be drawn: citizens in one State should be protected from effects that actions or accidents in another State could have on their Internet access.

c) Protection against Cyber-Attacks

Cyber-attacks have become a major problem at the global and cross-border level; even if a specific country is attacked, the consequences usually also affect other countries. Insofar, the protection against cyber-attacks merits the development of a common, cross-border approach.

934 UNECE Convention on the Transboundary Effects of Industrial Accidents (1992), available at <http://www.unece.org/env/teia/welcome.htm>.

The problems related to cyber-attacks are addressed by the Council of Europe in its Convention on Cybercrime.[935] The Convention includes general principles relating to mutual assistance and measures for common protection against cyber-attacks; most of the provisions have a procedural character. The Convention on Cybercrime is supplemented by the Convention on the Prevention of Terrorism, released by the Council of Europe in 2005.[936]

d) Resolution of Interstate Conflicts

The protection of fundamental rights is not yet expressly enshrined in international law related to the Internet; however, certain international law principles are applicable and can particularly be derived from the Helsinki Final Act of 1975, released under the auspices of the OSCE. The Declaration on Principles Guiding Relations between Participating States covers the following objectives:[937]

> "The participating States recognize the universal significance of human rights and fundamental freedoms, respect for which is an essential factor for the peace, justice and wellbeing necessary to ensure the development of friendly relations and cooperation among themselves as among all States.
>
> They will constantly respect these rights and freedoms in their mutual relations and will endeavour jointly and separately, including in cooperation with the United Nations, to promote universal and effective respect for them."

Furthermore, some general principles can be drawn from the text on "Responsibility of States for Internationally Wrongful Acts"[938] adopted by the International Law Commission in 2001. In particular, this document contains provisions related to international wrongful acts of a governmental body, and addresses for example preparations, objects and limits of countermeasures. The similarity with the problem of critical Internet resources can be seen in the fact that the promotion of universal respect leads to a reasonable and equitable behavior in cross-border relations.

---

935 Council of Europe, Convention on Cybercrime, Budapest, 23rd November 2001, CETS No. 185; for further details see below VI.D.1.2.

936 Council of Europe, Convention on the Prevention of Terrorism, Warsaw, 16th May 2005, CETS No. 196.

937 See Conference on Security and Co-operation in Europe, Final Act, Helsinki 1975, Declaration on Principles Guiding Relations between Participating States, VII, available at <http://www.osce.org/documents/mcs/1975/08/4044_en.pdf>.

938 ILC Draft Articles on the Responsibility of States for Internationally Wrongful Acts, U.N.Doc. A/RES/56/83 (2001).

e) Prohibition of Child Labor

Resources, which are theoretically available yet considered invaluable for mankind, can exist under the reservation that their use should be absolutely forbidden or at least restricted. This can be particularly illustrated with the example of child labor. Children in (bonded) labor situations are exposed to conditions affecting their health and moral integrity. Therefore, international conventions attempt to eliminate child labor. The International Covenant on Civil and Political Rights states the prohibition of forced labor in its Article 8. The United Nations Convention on the Rights of the Child of 20th November 1989 includes the right of the children to be protected from economic exploitation and any work that is likely to be hazardous (Art. 32).[939] The key document, however, is the ILO Forced Labor Convention of June 1930,[940] its Art. 25 obliges States to punish the use of forced or compulsory child labor as an illegal offence and to ensure that the penalities are adequate and strictly enforced. The ILO Convention is concretized by several ILO Recommendations.[941]

Even if the enforcement of these international rules is still unsatisfactory, the efforts to protect children from being exploited as cheap labor forces show that restricting rules can have an influence on the use and implementation of such "resources".

f) Access to Cultural Expressions

On 20th October 2005, the 33rd General Conference of UNESCO adopted the Convention on the Protection and Promotion of the Diversity of Cultural Expressions.[942] Cultural expressions are obviously related to human rights, but access to culture is also an important topic.[943] Insofar, Art. 2.7 of the Diversity Convention reads as follows:

> "Equitable access to a rich and diversified range of cultural expressions from all over the world and access of cultures to the means of expressions and dissemination

---

939 UN Convention on the Rights of the Child, adopted by the UN General Assembly Resolution 44/25 (20th November 1989), 1577 UNTS 3, 28 ILM 1456 (1989), UN Doc. A/44/49 (1989).

940 ILO Convention concerning Forced or Compulsory Labor, No. 29, 28th June 1930, 39 UNTS 55.

941 For further details see ROMANA WEBER, Child Bonded Labor, in: Mühlemann/Mannhart (eds), Freiheit ohne Grenzen—Grenzen der Freiheit, Zurich/St. Gallen 2008, 21 ss, 30.

942 See UNESCO DOC. 33 C/84 Prov, 20th October 2005, also available at <http://unesdoc.unesco.org/images/0014/001416/141610e.pdf>

943 For further details see ROLF H. WEBER, Cultural Diversity and International Trade—Taking Stock and Looking Ahead, in: Alexander/Andenas (eds), The World Trade Organization and Trade in Services, Leiden/Boston 2008, 823 ss.

constitute important elements for enhancing cultural diversity and encouraging mutual understanding."

The Diversity Convention does not directly address "resources" in an economic sense, but the access to culture generally spoken; it also concerns imminent interests of civil society. Therefore, an analogous perception of the term "equitable" does not seem to be unfounded.

g) Preliminary Evaluation

An overview over already existing international treaties dealing with the management of scarce resources shows that the notion of an equitable and reasonable use of critical resources is crucial. Only if the resources are allocated in accordance with principles which can be legally and socially justified, a common acceptance of the allocation is likely to grow in civil society.

The principle of equitable and reasonable use of resources could become a part of an international ordre public based on a normative understanding of its contents, representing common interest of the entire society based on a cultural and moral foundation of such society.[944] Recently, at the occasion of the 1st Council of Europe Conference of Ministers responsible for Media and Communication Services a specific resolution has been adopted related to the fair exploitation of critical Internet resources.[945]

2. Transition from IPv4 to IPv6 in Particular

2.1 Introduction

The details of an appropriate regulatory regime, taking into account the principles of an adequate allocation of scarce resources and thereby realizing "good" Internet governance, are subsequently discussed with respect to the example of the transition from Internet Protocol version 4 (IPv4) to Internet Protocol version 6 (IPv6).[946]

The Internet's technical environment is based on standardization attempts. In this respect it is commonly understood that technical standards should be open and promote interoperability.[947] In the online world, the regulatory approach is code-based. As governmental regulation is territorially limited, international organi-

[944] See also WEBER/WEBER, ordre public, 61.
[945] Reykjavik, 28th/29th May 2009, Resolution MCM (2009) 011.
[946] This section is based on a briefing note, delivered by the author to the European Parliament's Committee on Economic and Scientific Policy on 20th November 2008.
[947] WEBER, Towards a Legal Framework, 122.

zations are better suited for developing and implementing standard-setting processes and applicable standards.

The linkage between technical and public policy issues is of particular importance in the governing of the Internet. The transition from a specific Internet Protocol to another Internet Protocol is not only a technical matter, but it also includes policy issues and legal questions. Therefore, the Internet Corporation for Assigned Names and Numbers (ICANN) should not position itself as merely a standard setting and technical coordination entity,[948] since it seems clear that important public policy choices are made within the corporation, which accomplishes vital tasks for the functioning of the Internet, specifically with its operation of the Domain Names System (DNS) and of the Internet Protocol Addresses.

Technically, every Internet host wishing to be directly accessible for another Internet host must be assigned to a public IP address which serves as a unique identifier. The current IP addressing system, IPv4, however, is at risk of not being able to satisfy all Internet Protocol (IP) address requests made by the present and future Internet hosts. Therefore, a new version, IPv6, has been developed which has much bigger capacity. The ongoing adoption of IPv6 highlights the linkage between technical and public policy issues like a red thread, and its deployment shall therefore be examined in the light of widely accepted principles of Internet governance.

2.2 Transition from IPv4 to IPv6

The discussion topics in the context of the transition from IPv4 to IPv6 particularly relate to aspects of technical coordination and architecture. IP addresses function as unique identifiers of the technical backbone for the Internet hosts connecting them to the Internet, and as a consequence, they enable the interconnectivity among different Internet hosts.[949] The transition from the fourth to the sixth version of IP addresses entails several challenges not least in the field of Internet governance.

---

948 See to the respective discussion WEBER, Regulatory Models, 106–108.

949 ZITTRAIN, 28–29.

The following chart allows an overview and the framing of the IPv4/IPv6 allocation:[950]

	Technical coordination	Standards development	Public policy
Rules	ICANN/NTIA JPA	ITRs	Cybercrime Act
Norms	IAB oversight	RFCs	Spam blocklists
Markets	gTLD registries	S/MIME	Content regulation
Architecture	IPv4/IPv6 allocation	DNSSEC	CA/Browser forum
Networks	ICANN SOs and ACs	P3P	LAP

The technical coordination of IPv4 and its architecture need to be embedded in the legal framework in order to give some guidance on how to achieve an inclusive information society.[951] Manifold questions can be raised in this context: (i) How long will enough IPv4 addresses be available? (ii) How can a better allocation of the remaining IPv4 address space and better re-use allocated address space be achieved? (iii) What are drivers and challenges in IPv6 deployment? (iv) What are drivers and challenges in the transition towards IPv6 through a dual IPv4/IPv6 environment? (v) What is the role of the different stakeholders in the transition to IPv6? (vi) Are Internet-poor countries ready to upgrade to IPv6?

In the meantime, global and regional organizations are reacting to the technical developments and are tackling the consequences for civil society. At the forefront and as a good example, the EU Commission is dealing with the respective questions within the context of the Lisbon Strategy.[952] Besides its active involvement in the establishment of "IPv6 Task Forces" in different regions (European Task Force, African Task Force, Asia Pacific Task Force, Latin American Task Force, Middle East Task Force, and North American Task Force),[953] the European Commission adopted two noteworthy communications, namely:

- Communication from the Commission of the European Communities, Next Generation Internet—priorities for action in migrating to the new Internet protocol IPv6, Brussels, 21st February 2002, COM(2002) 96.[954]
- Communication from the Commission of the European Communities, Advancing the Internet, Action Plan for the deployment of Internet Protocol version (IPv6) in Europe, Brussels, 27th May 2008, COM(2008) 313.

950 See also Malcolm, Governance, 92.

951 See also the summary of the discussion of the respective Rio de Janeiro workshop in Doria/Kleinwächter, 398/99.

952 EU Commission, Advancing the Internet, 2/3.

953 Available at <http://www.ipv6tf.org>.

954 Available at <ftp://ftp.cordis.europa.eu/pub/fp7/ict/docs/ipv6-communication_en.pdf>.

In the following subchapter, the success and challenges caused by the transition from IPv4 to IPv6 with a view to Internet governance will be addressed.

2.3 Technical Framework

a) Problem of Restricted Capacity

The current IP addressing system, IPv4, is at risk to be unable to satisfy all IP address requests made by the present and future Internet hosts, since the architecture of addresses, constituted according to IPv4, is a limited resource.[955] As a consequence, a capacity shortage is anticipated; in early 2008, 16% of the capacity was still available in the pool, i.e. approximately 700 million IPv4 addresses. Scholars have not yet agreed on the specific point in time, at which the shortage will become an actual problem, however, assumptions count on slightly less than 1000 days.[956]

The problem of shortage could be mitigated by various techniques such as "Network Address Translation" (NAT), which hides multiple Internet hosts behind a single IP address by connecting private networks to the public Internet. However, such a procedure would have the disadvantage of breaking end-to-end connectivity. As a result, Internet interactivity would no longer be fully granted, making it difficult to establish Internet telephone calls directly between two hosts using standard voice over IP (VoIP) protocols. Furthermore, the method would increase complexity as there are two classes of computers (some with a public address and some with a private address) and increase costs for design and maintenance of networks as well as for the development of applications.[957]

Another measure could consist in establishing a market to enable a trade of IPv4 addresses; further alternatives could envisage offering incentives to sell unused addresses and reclaiming those already-allocated address blocks that are underutilized. However, these methods also have drawbacks, as IP addresses are not property in the strict sense, and mechanisms for enforcing the return of addresses do not exist.[958] Nevertheless, despite such technical and administrative means, sooner or later the demand for IP addresses can no longer be satisfied by the IPv4 version.

The impact a shortage will have on the Internet's interactivity underlines the difficulty in establishing architectural change. Already more than ten years ago (in

955 MALCOLM, Governance, 10.

956 See <http://www.potaroo.net/tools/ipv4/index.html>; EU Commission, Advancing the Internet, 3/4.

957 EU Commission, Advancing the Internet, 4.

958 EU Commission, Advancing the Internet, 4.

1998), the substitute for IPv4, namely IPv6, was recommended as the next generation IP addressing scheme for implementation.[959] The design of IPv6 aims at providing quantitative and qualitative advantages compared to the current IPv4. Originally, it was assumed that IPv6 would be adopted by the year 2005; however, the process has been delayed. In any case, it remains certain that the Internet's technical architecture must be re-engineered in order to cope with the future addressing needs.

IPv6 is deemed the best way forward, as it provides for a long term solution to address space problem, with a huge number of addresses which can be managed more easily than within the framework of IPv4. Furthermore, IPv6 includes issues such as service, auto-configuration, security, and mobility. Developing and deploying services and applications promises to be less complicated and less costly than under the IPv4, thereby providing a basis for innovation and for allowing users to have their own network connected to the Internet.[960]

b) Technical Standards

Both IPv6 and IPv4 define the network layer protocol, i.e. how data are sent from one computer to another over packet switched networks.[961] However, IPv6 contains specific addressing and control information to route packets for the next Internet generation. IPv6 has a very large address space and consists of 128 bits as compared to 32 bits in IPv4; the 128-bit system also provides for multiple levels of hierarchy and flexibility in addressing and routing. Therefore, the present shortage or even exhaustion of addresses in IPv4 can be overcome with IPv6, supporting 3.4 times 10^{38} unique IP addresses. In addition, this addressing scheme will also eliminate the need for network address translation that causes several networking problems (such as hiding multiple hosts behind a pool of IP addresses) and maintain the end-to-end nature of the Internet.[962]

The rules and packet sizes for the transportation of IPv6 datagrams differ depending on their topology; there is a Request for Comment (RFC), i.e. a technical standard on a particular aspect of the Internet, covering each topology in detail. For stateless auto-configuration, the Media Access Control (MAC) address is used to build the IPv6 address; the rules that govern how IPv6 multicast destination addresses are converted to MAC addresses are the same as those used on Ethernet. IPv6 address negotiation is different from IPv4 in that it is done through ICMPv6

959 MALCOLM, Governance, 13.

960 EU Commission, Advancing the Internet, 5; see also LATIF, 228 and 240–242.

961 Technical information is available at <http://www.ipv6.com/articles/general/ipv6-the-next-generation-internet.htm>.

962 See also LATIF, 229 ss.

neighbor discovery and not through Point-to-Point Protocol (PPP); this technical approach also allows using static addresses. The IPv6 functionality for address auto-configuration supports easy administration and customer configuration with minimal costs and enables peer-to-peer services, push services as well as VoIP.[963]

Mobile IPv6 is an IETF (Internet Engineering Task Force) standard that has augmented the roaming capacities of mobile nodes in the IPv6 network. The major benefit of this standard is that the mobile nodes change their point-of-attachment to the IPv6 Internet without changing their IP address, allowing mobile devices to move from one network to another and still maintain their existing connections. IPv6 uses both types of auto-configuration, such as stateless (network prefix and interface ID) and state-full auto-configuration (DHCPv6). The neighbor discovery feature enables (i) the finding of routers, (ii) the determination of link layer addresses and (iii) the maintenance of information accessibility. In comparison with the existing IPv4 situation, the advanced features of IPv6 make mobile IP easier to implement since the needed functionality, in particular the route optimization, is built into the program and ingress filtering problems do not occur.[964]

IPv6 addresses are denoted by eight groups of hexa-decimal quartets separated by colons in between them. The addresses are broadly classified into three categories, namely (i) unicast addresses acting as identifiers for a single interface, (ii) multicast addresses acting as an identifier for a group/set of interfaces that may belong to different nodes and (iii) anycast addresses acting as identifiers for a set of interfaces that may belong to different nodes. Multicast and anycast are an integral part of the protocol and available on all IPv6 nodes.[965]

c) Interoperability and Security

A major merit of IPv6 can be seen in its more efficient routing and its reduced management requirements facilitating the interoperability with existing protocols. However, IPv6 is not directly interoperable with IPv4: communication between the different devices is only possible by using application specific gateways.[966] Nevertheless, a good interoperability is necessary for the netizens to undertake a smooth transition from one standard to another without having to face any significant disruptions of the services. This is of importance, particularly since IPv4 will most likely still be used for a significant time to come. But any change from

963 Hagen, chapter 7.1; <http://www.ipv6.com/articles/general/ipv6-the-next-generation-internet.htm>.

964 Hagen, chapter 7.2; <http://www.ipv6.com/articles/general/IPv6-Addressing.htm>.

965 Hagen, chapter 7.2; <http://www.ipv6.com/articles/general/IPv6-Addressing.htm>.

966 EU Commission, Advancing the Internet, 5.

one protocol to the other requires resources—both in terms of money as well as in terms of time—in view of the fact that the processes need to be newly attuned.

Since ICANN modified the DNS route servers on 20th July 2004, the IPv6 adoption and its development have been stimulated. A number of transition mechanisms allow IPv6-only compatible hosts to access services offered by the IPv4 protocol; this forms the backbone of the interoperability ingrained in the IPv6 protocol.[967] Consequently, IPv6 can be enabled to run in parallel with IPv4 on the same device and on the same physical network. This co-existence is expected to last for 10, 20, or even more years.[968]

Recognizing the importance of IPv6 compatibility with the existing IT infrastructure, prominent research groups are conducting studies to test the interoperability parameters of the new protocol—both at the hardware and the software levels, including firewalls, voice, wireless and application layer interface testing. At the hardware level, such research comprises testing the performance of different system configurations in an IPv6 framework; at the software level testing involves an assessment of the coordination of various applications at different levels of protocol transition processes.[969]

IPv6 also improves the built-in security: Compliance with security concerns includes a facilitated implementation of encryption, authentication, and Virtual Private Networks (VPN) through header extension. The security elements are to be used within IPv6 itself or by applications on top of IP without imposing organizational or legal settings that may render the basic services unusable for the worldwide Internet. The security framework is standardized by the IETF IP Security Protocol Working Group (PSEC), encompassing specific security elements for encryption and authentification as well as definitions for using concrete cryptographic algorithms and specific security policies.[970] Notwithstanding the fact that the European Court of Justice recognized that IP addresses may be considered as personal data, thereby falling under the scope of application of the Data Protection Directives[971] and that concerns have been expressed about the IPv6 privacy,[972] technical experts assume an improvement of the security level in the IPv6 environment.

967 <http://www.ipv6.com/articles/hardware/IPv6-Interoperability.htm>.

968 EU Commission, Advancing the Internet, 4/5.

969 See <http://www.ipv6.com/articles/hardware/IPv6-Interoperability.htm>.

970 Hagen, chapter 5; <http://www.ipv6.com/articles/security/IPsec.htm>.

971 ECJ, Case C-275/06, Promusicae vs. Telefonica, judgment of 29th January 2008, para. 45.

972 Article 29 Data Protection Working Party, Opinion 2/2002 on the use of unique identifiers in telecommunication terminal equipments: the example of IPv6, available at <http://ec.europa.eu/justice_home/fsj/privacy/docs/wpdocs/2002wp58_en.pdf>.

2.4 Specific Issues Regarding the Transition Period

a) Time Factor

The transition from IPv4 to IPv6 is advancing and cannot be stopped, for both technical reasons as well as consumer needs; consequently, IPv6 will co-exist with IPv4. As experience with the introduction of new techniques regularly shows, however, the process is always slower than anticipated. Insofar, it is possible, if not to say probable, that the transition period will last for a few years. Since a better re-use of IPv4 only helps temporarily, however, the problems of the deployment of a new technical architecture cannot be avoided in the long term, but must be tackled and solved. Insofar the EU-Commission is consequent in advocating for a 25% penetration of IPv6 in Europe by the end of 2010.[973]

IPv6 deployment is gaining speed as IPv6 infrastructure is being installed throughout the Internet backbone and the major wide-area networks. In particular, the networks of many large telecommunications enterprises as well as the most important Research and Development (R&D) networks have already tested and introduced IPv6. The simplest way to start using IPv6 has proven to be the implementation of single IPv6 hosts in IPv4 networks; they will auto-configure for a link-local IPv6 address and will be able to communicate with one another over IPv6, by using ICMPv6 neighbor discovery messages.[974]

A further important issue concerns the question of how the remaining IPv4 capacity will be allocated during the next few years. As mentioned,[975] the shortage problem is not immediate and can be mitigated. However, measures need to be introduced to avoid the remaining capacity to be hoarded by a few market participants on the basis of a first come first served mechanism; so far, the respective efforts of the Regional Industry Registries still seem to be quite hesitant.[976] Moreover, less developed countries, having limited financial resources for the transition from IPv4 to IPv6, should receive special attention and therefore a priority allocation of capacity to such regions should be taken into account.

---

973 EU Commission, Advancing the Internet, 8; <http://www.ipv6.com/articles/general/timeline-of-ipv6.htm>.

974 Hagen, chapter 7.4; <http://www.ipv6.com/articles/secure-neighbor-discovery.htm>.

975 See above VI.B.2.3 a).

976 See the newest version of RIPE NCC (Réseaux IP Européens), IPv4 Address Allocation and Assignment Policies for the RIPE NCC Service Region, available at <http://www.ripe.net/ripe/docs/ipv4-policies.html>.

b) Compatibility

From a technical point of view, the risks related to the existence of two technical architectures and consequently two address systems functioning parallel to one another, do not seem to be very substantial. Most likely, the industry will gradually improve the technical environment and thereby facilitate the switch between the two architectures. Nevertheless, in the long run, it is not deemed efficient to have two systems. Their maintenance costs are relatively high and the handling for the users quite uncomfortable; therefore, a certain "pressure" will exist to completely adopt the IPv6 architecture over time. In addition, since technologies are in fact socio-technical systems, the characteristics of the systems are to be shaped by the economic and political incentives of the corporate and individual actors as well as by laws and social norms within the design and capabilities of the technologies deployed.

In light of such considerations, the transition period should be used to analyze and test initiatives capable of ensuring the interoperability of IPv4 and IPv6 during a period of smooth coexistence and transition.

Since the Internet is a global framework, many actors world-wide need to be considered. The relevant stakeholders and their responsibilities are listed subsequently:[977]

- Internet organizations (including the Regional Internet Address Registries) need to manage common IPv6 resources and services and continue to develop needed standards and specifications.
- Internet service providers need to offer IPv6 connectivity and IPv6 based services to custumers.
- Infrastructure vendors need to integrate IPv6 capability into their products.
- Content and service providers need to be reachable by enabling IPv6 on their servers.
- Business and consumer application vendors need to ensure that their soluations are IPv6 compatible; they increasingly have to develop products and offer services that take advantage of IPv6 features.
- End-users need to purchase IPv6 capable products and services and enable IPv6 on their own networks or home Internet access.

977 EU Commission, Advancing the Internet, 6/7.

The business sector in particular should be motivated to better promote the deployment of IPv6 and take into account the following actions:[978]

- The business sector should take advantage of scheduled equipment and software upgrades and develop a timeline, a program as well as procedures to upgrade Internet servers and relevant devices to IPv6, recognizing that the upgrade will require costs and entail further burdens. Such a demonstration of leadership by business will encourage other Internet stakeholders and underline the value that IPv6 brings to the Internet.
- The business sector must recognize that the security and stability of the existing network is an essential requirement in the transition period in which IPv4 and IPv6 will coexist.
- The business sector should continue its efforts to improve government and consumer appreciation of the importance and benefits of IPv6, for example, through initiatives such as the IPv6 Forum,[979] a consortium of vendors, which organizes information events around the world to increase awareness and promote the adoption of IPv6.
- The business sector should continue to provide expert input into the technical coordination bodies responsible for developing and overseeing IP and its related protocols, particularly the Internet Engineering Task Force (IETF). This input will help ensure that as new technologies develop, they are compatible with and take advantage of IPv6.

Since there is "no such thing as a free lunch", the introduction of the new IPv6 architecture will cause costs not only for the industry, but also for the registries and the users. This fact allows the assumption that the establishment and utilization of IPv6 is more likely to happen in developed countries in which civil society is less cost-sensitive. For the same reason, a slower transition process enlarges the risk of the "digital divide" becoming deeper, if fewer developed countries are not in the economic position to speed up the transition process on their own.

A major effort should be made in respect to encouraging the progressive compatibility between IPv4 and IPv6. Corresponding pressure could be introduced by governments, for example, in public procurement procedures if criteria such as compatibility and early migration are requested, as introduced in the "plan numérique" in France (October 2008). Governmental support should also attempt to elaborate a policy setting framework, outlining a long term vision for IPv6 and considering the users' expectations.

---

978 International Chamber of Commerce (ICC), An Inventory of Policy Positions and Practical Guidance, 1st edition Paris 2007, 35/36.

979 See <http://www.ipv6forum.org>.

2.5 Challenges for IPv6 Deployment

a) Allocation of "Critical Resources"

In the context of IPv4 and IPv6, address elements seem to be the major issue regarding the criticality of resources. From the angle of the informational context, access to valuable contents could also be regarded as a scarce resource. In view of the concrete problems that critical resources cause, it is obvious that the term does not only describe a technical access topic,[980] but also the administration of the Internet's naming and addressing of domains.[981] Theoretically, the routing slots could be a finite capacity; as a consequence, if routing would not work, the address would not be available in the routing system. However, as the development of IPv6 shows, the technical industry provides for solutions in order to overcome such shortages.

Since the management of critical Internet resources has significant public policy implications, the basic structure supporting decision-making must be internationally recognized and clearly mandated. This objective is jeopardized by the fact that the influence on the actual activities in this field is not evenly distributed among all nations of the world; some nations feel that in particular the United States have a privileged position of control and influence, mainly due to their relationship to ICANN. Consequently, since technical aspects are not the only relevant issues, light must also be shed on administrative topics, i.e. the allocation of IP communication possibilities needs to be realized in the framework of an emerging, global, spontaneous and people-oriented environment.

b) Open Technical Access

The issue regarding technical access is a well known regulatory problem in the telecommunications industry, usually dealt with under the headings of "interconnection" and "unbundling". For several years now, legal doctrine[982] and court decisions have recognized that in the case of a monopolistically controlled infrastructure in a specific market, legal intervention is justified if such enterprises misuse their position by not granting open access. This concept has come to be known as the "essential facilities doctrine".[983] A right to access to the essential

---

[980] On this aspect see hereinafter VI.B.2.5 b).

[981] On this aspect see hereinafter VI.B.2.5 c).

[982] WEBER/DÖRR, 76–84 with further references.

[983] See MCI Communications Corp. v. AT&T, 708 F. 2d 1081, 1132 (7th Cir. 1983), cert. den. 464 US 891 (1983); ECJ, Case C-251/91 P and C-242/91 P, Radio Telefis Eireann and Independent Television Publications Ltd. vs. Commission of the European Communities, judgment of 6th April 1995; ECJ, Case C-418/01, IMS Health GmbH & Co. OHG vs. NDC Health GmbH & Co. KG, judgment of 29th April 2004.

facility by a competing market participant can be justified on the basis of competition law[984] and of specific regulatory frameworks.[985] In the context of the Internet, however, experience has shown that open technical access has, so far, not become a problem.

c) Administration of Scarce Resources

As mentioned, an important body in the Internet governance field is the Internet Society (ISOC)[986] that was founded as a non-profit, non-governmental membership society with the aim of promoting the development as well as the availability and the associated technologies of the Internet. ISOC is strongly linked to the entities responsible for Internet infrastructure standards, including the Internet Engineering Task Force (IETF) and the Internet Architecture Board (IAB).[987] Since the establishment of ISOC in 1992, its central role has been to support, facilitate, and promote different aspects of Internet development; therefore, ISOC is engaged in the global transition to the new technology of IPv6. Its guiding public policy principles include open, unencumbered, and beneficial use of the Internet. However, ISOC does not have any decision-making power and can therefore not be seen as the "critical" body responsible for an adequate deployment of IPv6.

The present central governing entity of the Internet is ICANN.[988] In order to ensure universal resolvability, which allows the netizens from all over the world to find all valid addresses on the Internet, a global system of unique identifiers needs to be coordinated and must ensure stable and secure operations. The unique identifiers encompass three functional sets, namely the domain names, the Internet Protocol addresses and autonomous system numbers, as well as the protocol port and parameter numbers. ICANN is responsible for the management and oversight of these specific functions; thereby, its main values envisage the preservation and enhancement of the operational stability, reliability, security, and global interoperability of the Internet.

As already discussed,[989] an obvious risk of the present ICANN system concerns the fact that privately-established rules may erode or undermine the power of sovereign States. Moreover, the actual participation of the Internet users in the

---

984 Article 82 ECT.

985 See e.g. para. 6 of the EC Directive 2000/31 of the European Parliament and of the Council of 8th June 2000 on certain legal aspects of information society services, in particular electronic commerce, in the Internal Market, OJ 2000 L 178.

986 See above III.B.3.

987 See above III.B.2.

988 See above III.C.

989 See above III.C.4.2 a).

discussions is rather limited[990] and representatives of organizations do not always have a democratic legitimization.[991] Furthermore, the US influence might be considered as an undue privilege by other nations. Nevertheless, the fact that social norms in the form of self-regulation often create efficient rules in non-hierarchical communities should not be overlooked. With social norms, participants usually access problems more directly and generate fewer transaction costs compared to administrative legal frameworks. Furthermore, social norms signify a decentralized form of social control; experience in the online world shows that participants maintain a continuing commitment to the principle of open process developed in the field of the Internet.

The intensive discussions held in relation to ICANN's administration of the DNS equally apply to the allocation of IP parameters and the deployment of IPv6. The relatively young, but maturing institutions apart from ICANN, such as the IETF and the Regional Internet Address Registries provide a new locus of authority over governance processes affecting Internet standards and causing governments to begin figuring out how to react to the these newly established institutions. Consequently, adequate solutions are to be looked for in order to improve the legitimacy in Internet governance. Generally, a self-regulatory approach must fulfil certain basic conditions, particularly in respect to Internet Protocols:[992] (i) The administration of scarce resources needs to be transparent; (ii) a private organization should also be obligated to account for its actions; (iii) the rule making process and any dispute resolution system must provide due process; (iv) acceptable criteria are necessary to protect third parties. In a nutshell, satisfying democratic needs requires truly people-centred responses.

Notwithstanding the importance of these principles, it remains a fact, not to be overlooked, that the main actors allocating the mentioned critical resources are still the Internet Services Providers (ISPs). Substantive principles can "only" be promoted by governments in view of the fact that IPv6 has elements of a public good which are to be allocated to individuals based on reasonable and proportionate standards. Known approaches such as "first come, first served" or "auction procedures" can be too radical if the interests of the weaker parts of civil society are not properly taken into account. In addition, another aspect should not be underestimated: The transition from IPv4 to IPv6 could be taken as a pretense for changing the address allocation process from the present system—including ICANN, the Regional Internet Address Registries, and the Internet Service Providers—to a new system which would "insert" National Registries into the downwards procedure. Such a development could increase the risk of a strictly national

990 See above V.E.

991 See above V.B.

992 WEBER, Regulatory Models, 109.

control of Internet traffic, something that does not seem to be in the interest of civil society.

As outlined above, the heterogeneity of the different actors in the field of the Internet is addressed by the concept of "multi-stakeholderism". [993] The comprehension of a unitary stakeholder basis may be questioned, in particular in view of perceptions of a rather fragmented and polarized Internet. Shifting the focus to the different organizational bodies involved in the numerous aspects of the Internet helps channelling a very manifold stakeholder-basis into an intermediate level of representatives within the organizational structures. Thereby, valuable inputs could be derived from the EU as a supranational organization, which has to balance the objectives of the Union as a whole with the interests of the individual Member States.[994]

Furthermore, with the affected stakeholders delineated, legitimacy could be enhanced by adhering to particular architectural principles that need to be considered as a source for legislation and a guideline for governing different aspects of the Internet thus, for providing particular self-constraints by the governing authorities; such principles can help provide an assessment basis for the governing outcomes, and facilitate transparency and accountability.[995]

d) Availability of Resources—Financing Mechanisms

Another important topic concerns financing and knowledge-sharing aspects. The introduction and deployment of IPv6 causes costs and increases the need to support technologically less developed countries in building appropriate IT infrastructures in order to achieve an inclusive information society and bridge the digital divide. The Internet as a global framework asks for people of all regions to be involved. The fact that private persons can be involved in the deployment of IPv6 makes assistance to and support of developing countries important in order to include all interested parties in the process. This aspect merits further elaboration in two directions, namely the support available from the developed countries and the financing needs of the less developed countries:

(1) As a noteworthy example, the EU Commission has provided and will continue to provide financial aid through standardization support actions to improve interoperability of networks. In this context the Commission is supporting standardization actions on protocols running over IPv6 networks. In a public consulta-

993 See IV.B.

994 Komaitis, 69–75.

995 Komaitis, 71; Weber/Grosz, Legitimate Governing of the Internet, 327.

tion, the use of public procurement was identified as an efficient way of speeding up the transition to IPv6.[996]

Furthermore, the EU Commission is encouraging research projects funded by Framework Programme 7;[997] thereby, new IT hardware and software should be developed which can increase the possibilitiy of choosing computer network protocols and facilitate the utilization of IPv6.[998] The EU Commission is also looking into bringing together IT managers from Member States to exchange their experiences and to monitor the progress of IPv6 deployment; the EU Commission will also specify IPv6 capabilities as well as carry out timely and appropriate internal trials and projects to prepare for IPv6.[999]

In addition, the EU Commission intends to undertake awareness campaigns and support actions to disseminate practical deployment knowledge, it will also plan standardization actions in relation to IPv6 interoperability. Furthermore, Member States are invited to support the inclusion of IPv6 technology knowledge in relevant retraining curricula and in computer and network engineering courses of universities etc. The launch of accompanying studies as well as the organization of conferences is expected within the following year.[1000]

The efforts of the EU Commission in raising awareness for the challenges related to the transition from IPv4 to IPv6 merit positive appreciation. Indeed it is important to achieve compatibility and interoperability of standards at an early stage in order to allow the users of the Internet to easily adapt their requirements to the new protocol. The standards supporting actions are also valuable, but attention needs to be paid to the risk of eventual anticompetitive distortions by governmental interventions aimed at privileging certain suppliers of goods and/or services. Therefore, supporting actions should be supplier-neutral. As long as financial aid is mainly directed towards encouraging research projects of independent facilities, the respective risks can be mitigated. If properly applied, the actions designed by the EU Commission might contribute to the establishment of an inclusive society within a reasonable time frame.

(2) With regard to developing countries and although politicians and academics generally favor a market-based approach, it must be emphasized that investments are expected to be so high, that the private sector is unlikely to be able to meet the financial needs of the developing world alone, moreso, some support from the public sector may be inevitable. As the Recommendation (2007)16 of the Council

996 EU Commission, Advancing the Internet, 9.
997 See <http://www.nerc.ac.uk/funding/framework>.
998 EU Commission, Advancing the Internet, 9.
999 EU Commission, Advancing the Internet, 10.
1000 EU Commission, Advancing the Internet, 10.

of Europe[1001] requests, Member States should develop strategies which promote technical interoperability and open standards in ICT. It is therefore paramount, on the one hand, that governments strive to provide the enabling environment and basic conditions for the private sector to play its growth-driving role by spending more funds on development and, on the other hand, that the international community commits to increased payments. As the Commission for Africa Report underlines, "the promotion of growth is not a question of the State versus the private sector but a question of how they combine to generate growth".[1002]

Already large varieties of financing mechanisms are in place and could be taken into account when considering possibilities of financing ICT development:[1003]

- The Official Development Assistance (ODA) provided by national States has not yet received the 0.7% of the gross national product as foreseen in the commitment made in the Monterrey Consensus. This contribution is meant to improve governance aspects, notably by making more coordination disclosure efforts, as well as streamlining national ODA strategies in order to pay more attention to the Millennium Development Goals.
- The financial support given by the International Monetary Fund (IMF) and the World Bank Group should be coordinated better and designed in a more concrete way so as to improve country specific needs and to allow the provision of quick advisory support related to a country's agenda.
- Public-private partnership schemes are a valuable alternative if the public and private sectors cannot easily act individually, detached from each other, and if governance principles, transparency requirements and accountability disciplines are to be nailed down.
- A promising new financing mechanism is the 1% digital solidarity principle enabling a State authority (at a national, regional or local level) to levy a 1% charge on the value of public procurement contracts in the ICT field; such amounts are to be made available to ICT projects in less developed countries.

The costs of upgrading IPv4 to IPv6 should not be overestimated; however, apart from the actual financial needs, many less developed countries may also require technical assistance.

1001 Recommendation CM/Rec(2007)16 of the Committee of Ministers to Member States on the measures to promote the public service value of the Internet, adopted on 7th November 2007.

1002 Commission of Africa, Our Common Interest: Report of the Commission for Africa, March 2005, available at <http://www.commissionafrica.org>, chapter 7 para. 31.

1003 Weber/Menoud, 63–177; see also below VI.E.3.

2.6 Outlook

In a nutshell, the transition from IPv4 to IPv6 mainly concerns issues of technical coordination and architecture. Notwithstanding the fact that the capacity shortage of IPv4—as a limited resource—does not seem to materialize as early as previously assumed, political and social actors need to recognize the importance of interoperability conditions of the new protocol, both at the hardware and the software levels. Insofar, the critical aspects of the transition from IPv4 to IPv6 do not concern the openness of the technical access which can be secured by acknowledged mechanisms such as the essential facilities doctrine. Moreover, the allocation of IP communication possibilities must be realized within the framework of a developing, world-wide spontaneous and people-centred environment, i.e. the administration of scarce resources is the main feature. Since the introduction and deployment of IPv6 may be cost-intensive, the establishment and utilization of IPv6 will probably be realized particularly in developed countries. Consequently, increased support of less developed countries in building appropriate IT infrastructures is necessary in order to achieve an inclusive information society and to bridge the digital divide.

3. Access

3.1 Introduction

"Access" has been a key issue within the framework of the Internet Governance Forum (IGF) from the beginning.[1004] Access, as one of the four main themes dealt with, was later complemented by the issue of critical Internet resources. As already mentioned, access and critical Internet resource issues partly overlap.[1005] Generally speaking, the degree of openness in respect to access and interconnection substantially influences the participation possibilities of civil society.[1006] Insofar, "access and governance are inextricably connected".[1007]

The discussions within the context of the IGF justifiably stressed upon the fact that the issue of access could not sufficiently be addressed by a specific and narrow focus regarding the reform of the telecommunications sector. However, it was recognized that such a reform would be a necessary condition to establish

[1004] See above III.D.
[1005] See above VI.B. (Introduction).
[1006] WEBER, Regulatory Models, 111.
[1007] ANITA GURUMURTHY, in: DORIA/KLEINWÄCHTER, 284.

the appropriate framework for increasing access, in particular by addressing the following key issues:[1008]

- Independence and transparency;
- Removal of monopolies and licensing of new players;
- Competition and avoidance of competition barriers;
- Establishment of interconnection regimes that reinforce the competitive markets;
- Development of innovative policy measures such as universal access regimes.

Beyond the telecommunications aspects, increasing access remains a major challenge which has to be faced by the Internet community. Access is needed at different levels, for example related to networks, informational infrastructures, Internet search facilities, integrated products, electronic programming guides, and online services.[1009] In particular, access is also a prevailing question in digital divide concerns and insofar a multi-faceted and focal point in public policy responses.[1010] Furthermore, the need for enhanced capacity building cannot be overlooked as it is a key item that allows civil society to take advantage of the ongoing convergence of communications possibilities.

Subsequently, the discussion of the access issue will be limited to considerations related to the net neutrality principle and the development aspects.

3.2 Net Neutrality

During the past few years the principle of "net neutrality" has become a heatedly debated term which has also gained several meanings. Originally, net neutrality was seen as a domestic regulatory issue, but in the meantime, the global dimension of this principle—allowing users to access content, services and applications on the Internet without interference from network operators or by overbearing governance—is well accepted.

As a normative principle, net neutrality can have two meanings, namely the regulation of bandwidth and the focus on universal access to the resources connected to the Internet:

(i) The "net neutrality" principle seen in the context of bandwidth addresses the questions of whether network operators should get an indemnification for their investments (i.e. remuneration for transportation services) and whether differenti-

1008 DORIA/KLEINWÄCHTER, 91.
1009 WEBER, Regulatory Framework, 111.
1010 On the digital divide see below VI.E.

ated treatments of customers in respect to speed and other qualitative characteristics regarding the delivery of packets, could be justified. Since the potential for discriminatory misuse by network operators is substantial, the "neutrality" principle would favor a competitive environment.[1011]

Interpreting the term "neutrality" in a way that would concentrate its contents on the regulation of bandwidth leads to a notion addressing the issue in a problematically narrow way.[1012] According to such an interpretation, neutrality would lead to uniformity which contradicts the market-driven force of differentiation (for example regarding the speed with which packets are delivered) since interventionist policies would impede innovative processes and could become a technological straightjacket.[1013]

(ii) In the context of Internet governance, net neutrality should rather be understood as non-discriminatory, universal access to Internet resources. This approach of net neutrality means that private actors as well as governmental bodies should be prevented from blocking or filtering civil society's access to Internet content.

- As far as private actors are concerned, measures of vertical tying are to be excluded, i.e. the supply of bandwidth is not allowed to be tied to the supply of contents or service applications or terminal equipments; a corresponding risk is high if the provider of bandwidth is a monopolist or at least has a market dominant position.
- Regarding governmental bodies, blocking and filtering measures are often applied by introducing controlling regulations.
- Experience has shown that governmental blocking and filtering of Internet content has become increasingly common (for example in China or Singapore), even in some nominally democratic countries.[1014]

Vertical tying is a well-known problem in competition law. In case of a market dominant position a respective enterprise might be inclined to promote its own goods and services in a competitive market by having them tied to a good or service in a non-competitive market. An enterprise with significant market power (and in particular a monopoly) can use the broadband network service as a tying "product", for example by disabling features to prevent the customers from

1011 For further details see DANIEL J. WEITZNER, The Neutral Internet: An Information Architecture for Open Societies, available at <http://www.dig.csail.mit.edu/2006/06/neutralnet.html>.

1012 MUELLER, Net Neutrality, 3.

1013 MUELLER, Net Neutrality, 5.

1014 See the research done by the University-based Open Net Initiative, available at <http.//www.opennet.net>.

switching networks.[1015] Such behavior tends to increase costs and at the same time to decrease quality and innovation. Therefore, competition laws around the world usually do not accept vertical tying.

As far as regulations are concerned, civil society is called to introduce the net neutrality principle to domestic policy. In "The New Transnational Activism", SIDNEY TARROW catalogues the "diffusion" principle as one of the five main processes of transnational contention; it is defined as the imitation, adoption and adaptation of forms of contention in places different from their origin.[1016] Therefore, if net neutrality is successfully translated from the freedom of expression into modular, reproducible policies that work in various economic and institutional contexts, and if these policies have the beneficial societal, economic and innovative effects, then net neutrality can become successful in international institutions.[1017]

Such a concept would mean that the information flow on the given infrastructure would be driven by the end-users and not governed "from the middle"; an end-to-end-principle should thus be realized.[1018] In this sense, neutrality can be seen as public policy of the highest order.[1019] Summarizing the mentioned approach, the following three key items merit special attention:[1020]

- "Neutrality" should be seen as a global norm guiding Internet policies irrespective of their international or domestic implementation.
- "Neutrality" needs to be extended to the Internet's technical coordination functions, which are global in nature.
- "Neutrality" corresponds to the concept of "non-discriminatory access" and is also a central topic in free trade of goods and services.

3.3 Access and Development

As the discussions within IGF have shown, development issues remain a key concern.[1021] Despite the rapid spread of the Internet, 5 billion people still remain without access to this important network for economic growth and social development. Insofar, two aspects are of major importance, namely the availability and

1015 For further details see TIMOTHY S. WU, Wireless Carterfone, International Journal of Communication, Vol. 1, 2007, 389 ss.

1016 SIDNEY TARROW, The New Transnational Activism, Cambridge/Mass. 2005.

1017 MUELLER, Net Neutrality, 10; see also SOLUM, 88/89.

1018 See also the paper of MICHAEL PALAGE/AVRI DORIA, available at <http://www.kepp-the-core-neutral.org/files/keep_core_neutral.pdf>.

1019 MÜLLER, Net Neutrality, 13.

1020 MÜLLER, Net Neutrality, 2.

1021 See above III.D.

the affordability of the Internet.[1022] Access is a development issue which must be seen as a broad notion: Infrastructural access does not suffice if the end users do not have adequate access to content and services.[1023] Insofar, an obvious interplay among digital divide, multilingualism and access is noticeable; problems occur, for example with indigenous languages: the fact that they are often not written means that for the concerned people unconventional hardware and software solutions have to be realized.[1024]

A further area concerns the importance of open standards in maintaining the openness of the Internet. Stability, growth and global reach of the Internet require a coordinated development of resources, all of which should reinforce the long-standing custom of openness within the Internet technical community. In particular, open standards and respective transparent policies, which should not be tied to proprietary measures,[1025] can have significant positive network effects and make the Internet a powerful communication and collaboration tool.[1026] Openness is also in line with the principle of non-discrimination.[1027]

Furthermore, an important topic is the affordability of access to the Internet and its communication possibilities. Insofar, the existing dialectic between market efficiency and distributional equity must be overcome.[1028] Relevant aspects are international connectivity prices and costs; reasonable pricing is crucial for the successful implementation of the Internet and for maintaining its end-to-end-functionality; in less developed countries realizing Internet availability and reliability on a cost effective basis is issue number one.[1029] In other words, the costs associated with the building of networks and with access aspects as well as the associated revenues are to be distributed among the different players in a fair way. Compensation schemes among the providers carrying the traffic burden, merit special attention in the light of the affordability criterion of less developed countries. In this connection, regional multi-stakeholder collaboration needs to be improved by creating regional Internet Exchange Points and backbone networks.[1030]

In realizing the manifold possible efforts needed for improving access, one aspect should not be overlooked and that is that there is no "one size fits all" solution; however, knowing the "best practice" can help increasing access across the

1022 Doria/Kleinwächter, 77.
1023 Weber, Regulatory Framework, 111.
1024 Doria/Kleinwächter, 77.
1025 See also Weber, Regulatory Models, 109 ss.
1026 Doria/Kleinwächter, 78.
1027 This principle governs international trade rules according to the WTO legal principles.
1028 See also Mueller, in: Doria/Kleinwächter, 190.
1029 Doria/Kleinwächter, 77 and 286.
1030 See above VI.B.1.2 b) and Doria/Kleinwächter, 229 and 238.

world.[1031] Furthermore, the importance of knowledge enforcement should not be underestimated; in this respect, resources are available for less developed countries, for example "InfoDev", a multi-donor program which is housed at the World Bank and focusses on the facilitation of access for all to ICT, the mainstreaming of better ICT use in critical sectors (for example education, health), and the support of small and medium enterprises concentrating on ICT businesses and enabling ICT-driven innovation.[1032]

As far as the least developed countries are concerned, financial support from the developed countries seems to be unavoidable. To bridge the digital divide and direct accessibility towards the fulfillment of the Millennium Development Goals[1033], financial mechanisms are to be established in order to help these countries build up and implement the necessary infrastructure and thus give that part of civil society a voice and a means of participation. [1034]

C. Protection of Civil Liberties and Humanization of Internet Governance

An important aspect of Internet governance discussions concerns its "humanization". The promotion and protection of fundamental rights applicable in cyberspace is a matter which is addressed by different stakeholders in various settings. Subsequently, the focus will be directed towards the objective of developing a framework for a human rights-sensitive governing of the Internet.

1. Notion and Functions of Human Rights

A human society must be based on the values of human rights in all of their normative dimensions. The scope of these values is global and extends to the dignity of all people and their equal and inalienable rights; indeed, human rights provide for the only universally recognized system of values.[1035] Similarly, the Vienna Declaration and Programme of Action adopted at the 1993 World Conference on Human Rights refers to the "universal, indivisible, interdependent and interrelated" character of human rights.[1036] The core of human rights must remain un-

1031 Markus Kummer, in: Doria/Kleinwächter, 292.

1032 For further details see Valérie D'Costa, in: Doria/Kleinwächter, 282/83.

1033 Mouhamet Diop, in: Doria/Kleinwächter, 192.

1034 See below VI.E.

1035 Nowak, 1; to the historical background see Marzouki, 198 ss.

1036 UN Doc. A/CONF.157/23, para. 5.

changed and is not subject to political adaptation by governments or individuals, respectively. Therefore, the Vienna Declaration states that the "international community must treat human rights globally in a fair and equal manner, on the same footing and with the same emphasis".[1037]

Obviously, human rights are not unlimited since the exercise of a human right by an individual can interfere with the parallel human right of another individual; insofar, rights and freedoms are limited by the corresponding values of others.[1038] Furthermore, restrictions related to the exercise of human rights may also be imposed by the principle of morality or of public order as defined by the States: Each sovereign body wants to have some inalienable principles realized which are considered minimum standards of those citizens living together.[1039]

Originally and according to traditional doctrine of international law, States were conceived as the primary players and the only subjects of the international legal framework. In light of the origins of international law, the traditional concept of human rights was designed as merely addressing States; according to the doctrine of "negative", "vertical" or defensive human rights, only governments were internationally responsible for breaches against human rights. The later development and establishment of human rights—particularly in the aftermath of the atrocities committed during the Second World War—however, marked a shift in the perception towards acknowledging various "non-State actors" on the international stage and consequently challenging the understanding of "who" should be a legal subject under international law.[1040] In today's globalized world and connected with the slow but increasing appreciation of non-State actor's standing in international law, a gradual recognition is developing whereby the normative reference framework of human rights may also apply and thus oblige private persons just as it does legal entities.[1041]

1037 UN Doc. A/CONF.157/23, para. 5.

1038 This also corresponds with a KANTIAN liberalist perception of freedom.

1039 See also BENEDEK, Understanding, 23; MARZOUKI, 198, uses the term "guarantee rights".

1040 THÜRER, Changing Role of the State, 37; REINISCH, 37; CLAPHAM, 31; MALCOLM, Governance, 99–100; see also DRAKE/JØRGENSEN, 23.

1041 See below VI.C.3.2. Furthermore, the strict distinction between "negative" and "positive" rights is increasingly being assessed critically (see for example FREDMAN, 2; DRAKE/JØRGENSEN, 33/34). According to the tripartite terminology, State obligations exist "to respect, protect and fulfil human rights" (for a critical assessment of the tripartite typology see KOCH, 81 ss).

2. Existing Legal Framework for Human Rights

2.1 Global Level

Generally speaking, prior to World War II, issues of human rights were considered primarily a subject of domestic concern.[1042] This changed after the Universal Declaration of Human Rights came into existence on 10th December 1948. The Declaration universalized the global concern for a set of inalienable human rights, including, on the one hand, the so-called first generation of human rights, namely civil and political liberties aimed as defense rights against arbitrary use of governmental powers such as the basic right to life, the right to safety from unfair prosecution, the freedom of thought, expression and religion; on the other hand, the Declaration also encompassed the so-called second generation of rights, i.e. the economic, social and cultural rights pertaining, inter alia, to marriage, employment, education, and shelter.[1043]

Article 19 of the Universal Declaration of Human Rights (UDHR) is of particular importance in understanding global human rights in the context of the information society. This provision states that everyone has the right to "hold opinions without interference and to seek, receive and impart information and ideas through any media regardless of frontiers". It further stipulates that people should have the right to "the widest possible access to sources and information, to travel unhampered in pursuit thereof, and to transmit copy without unreasonable or discriminatory limitation, and should be guaranteed by action on the national and international plane".[1044]

The Universal Declaration of Human Rights had a strong impact on international law in general and considerably influenced the further developments of human rights in particular. However, the Declaration was conceived as a legally non-binding UN General Assembly Resolution, i.e. a "soft-law" framework. Attempts to establish legally-binding international agreements enshrining internationally

1042 For an overview on the history of human rights see TOMUSCHAT, 7–24 and NOWAK, 9–31; see also DRAKE/JØRGENSEN, 23 ss. However, the development of humanitarian law, the mandate system of the League of Nations, the acknowledgment of "public goods", as well as developments towards the establishment of a system for the protection of minorities and international labor regulations, provide for examples towards the gradual addressing of human rights at an international level.

1043 On the different generations of human rights see TOMUSCHAT 26–29; NOWAK, 23–25; DRAKE/JØRGENSEN, 9 ss. This subsection 2.1 partly follows WEBER, Legal Framework, 76–78.

1044 Universal Declaration of Human Rights, 10th December 1948, adopted by the General Assembly Resolution 217 (III), UN Doc. A/810 (1948), UN GOAR, 3rd Sess. Supp. No. 13, available at <http://un.org/Overview/rights/html>.

acknowledged human rights proved to be a rather difficult undertaking, particularly in light of the tensions between the Eastern and Western hemispheres during the Cold War. As a consequence, it took the world community almost another twenty years to finally sign and establish the International Covenant on Economic, Social and Cultural Rights (ICESCR) and the International Covenant on Civil and Political Rights (ICCPR), which both were adopted in 1966 and entered into force in 1976.[1045]

The two Covenants illustrate the distinction between two different "generations" or "dimensions" of human rights: The International Covenant on Economic, Social and Cultural Rights specifically protects second generation rights, i.e. right to live in conditions fit for human beings. It encompasses, for example, the rights of workers (to freely choose a job and to receive fair wages under appropriate conditions) and of families (paid leave for working mothers and appropriate protection of children, etc.), as well as the individual rights to health, to protection from discrimination (on the grounds of race, color, sex, language, religion, political or other opinion), and to an adequate standard of living. The International Covenant on Civil and Political Rights focuses on first generation rights and thus regulates rights associated with the protection of classic defensive rights of citizens against the State, such as rights protecting accused people and criminals, mobility rights, and civil rights, including the right not to be unfairly arrested or detained, the general right to free movement, the protection against torture, and the freedom of thought and of expression.

Compared to the UDHR, the two Covenants provide for a substantial progress in achieving protection of the individual according to the objective set in Article 1 paragraph 3 of the Charter of the United Nations,[1046] which aims at "promoting and encouraging respect for human rights and for fundamental freedoms for all without distinction as to race, sex, language, or religion." Furthermore, several conventions as well as resolutions adopted by the United Nation's General Assembly and the UN Human Rights Committee enhance human rights protection under the auspices of the United Nations.

As legally binding treaties both Covenants provide for particular reporting procedures to ensure their implementation: the Committee on Social Economic and Cultural Rights (CESCR)[1047] and the Human Rights Committee,[1048] respectively, adopt a monitoring function over the Member States' reports. Furthermore, the

1045 See also Brownlie, 562. For an overview on the different human rights standards see Brownlie, 555 ss.

1046 Charter of the United Nations, 26th June 1945, available at <http://www.un.org/aboutun/charter>.

1047 See Articles 16 and 17 ICESCR.

1048 See Article 40 ICCPR.

ICCPR acknowledges two main procedures for bringing complaints of human rights violations before the Human Rights Committee, namely State-to-State complaints according to Article 41 ICCPR and individual complaints according to the First Optional Protocol to the International Covenant on Civil and Political Rights.[1049]

In the field of the governing of the Internet, particularly the freedom of expression and information as well as privacy rights apply beyond the general guarantees of human dignity, integrity and equality. The information society provides individuals with unprecedented opportunities to exercise some of their most basic human rights, such as their free expression and information, as well as the guarantee of cultural rights, i.e. the communication possibilities introduced by the Internet enlarges the audience and increases the chances to get involved in information exchanges.[1050]

However, all these potential advantages and opportunities of information and communication technologies are of value only if the majority of the population has access to them. Access to information and the free flow of information must therefore be considered as one of the most fundamental human rights. It is much more than a technical issue—as often seen in the discussions of Internet governance experts;[1051] moreover, access includes financial dimensions (in the sense of affordability) and "human" elements.

Apart from the rights mainly addressing information and communication aspects, many other fundamental human rights play an important role in the Internet, such as the prevention of discrimination in various respects, the right to self-determination, the rights of minorities (indogenous people, women, children, older people, disabled people), the right to health, the right to fair working conditions, social welfare, progress and development, the right to marriage, the rights related to the administration of justice, the freedom of association as well as rights in the context of humanitarian law.[1052]

1049 Optional Protocol to the International Covenant on Civil and Political Rights, 16th December 1966, adopted and opened for signature by General Assembly Resolution 2200A (XXI), UN Doc. A/6316 (1966), 999 UNTS 302; it is interesting to note that on 10th December 2008, the UN General Assembly unanimously adopted an Optional Protocol to the ICCPR, which provides the Committee with the competence to receive and consider individual complaints; it is now opened for signing (see UN Doc. A/RE/63/117).

1050 See for example Lessig, Future of Ideas, 103 ss.

1051 See above III.D.

1052 See the extensive list of conventions, declarations recommendations and guidelines assembled by Drake/Jørgensen, 17 ss.

2.2 Regional Level

Additional regulatory frameworks relating to human rights exist on regional levels. The most prominent of these treaties is the European Convention for the Protection of Human Rights and Fundamental Freedoms of 1950 (ECHR).[1053] Most European countries have ratified this Convention, making its legal provisions directly applicable and enforceable before the European Court of Human Rights in Strasbourg; the claimant can be either a contracting State, by means of State application, or an individual claiming to be victim of a violation of the Convention, through an individual application. The European Court of Human Rights stands out as one of the most potent and effective international tribunals ensuring the respect of the individual's human rights by means of an independent jurisdictional system, it thus takes human rights protection a step further than under the UN Covenants.

The specific requirements necessary in the online world have led to further legislative activities, in particular at the European level. The Declaration on Freedom of Communication on the Internet, adopted by the Committee of Ministers of the Member States of the Council of Europe on 28th May 2003, can be seen as a first overarching document defining Internet-based human rights.[1054] This Declaration stipulates human rights principles and gives guidelines on how States should avoid interference in Internet freedom. In particular, lessons can be drawn from an analysis of the given principles in respect to the application of human rights in the communications technologies environment. The Declaration mainly refers to self-regulation[1055] due to the lack of specific Internet regulatory bodies, but it also encompasses co-regulation as a form of public-private "undertaking".[1056]

In 2005, the Council of Europe adopted the Declaration on Human Rights and the Rule of Law in the Information Society.[1057] This Declaration takes up self-regulatory and co-regulatory principles supporting the realization of a humanized online environment. Two years later, in 2007, a Recommendation on Measures to Promote the Public Service Value of the Internet was released by the Council of Europe;[1058] its Annex contains a number of guidelines related to human rights and democracy, access, openness, diversity and security which governments in cooperation with the private sector should achieve. At the occasion of the 1st Council of

---

[1053] European Convention for the Protection of Human Rights and Fundamental Freedoms, 4th November 1950, ETS No. 5, 213 UNTS 221.

[1054] Council of Europe, Declaration on Freedom of Communication on the Internet, 28th May 2003, H/Inf (2003) 7, available at <https://wcd.coe.int/ViewDoc.jsp?id=37031>.

[1055] See above I.C.2.

[1056] See also Benedek, Human Rights, 33.

[1057] CM Rec (2005) 56, 13rd May 2005.

[1058] CM Rec (2007) 16, 7th November 2007.

Europe Conference of Ministers responsible for Media and New Communication Services a political declaration and an action plan have been adopted, advocating for an improved implementation of human rights.[1059]

Recently, nine Members of the European Parliament submitted an initiative for the release of a Global Online Freedom Act, requiring better guarantees of Internet freedom.[1060] The objective of this Global Online Freedom Act consists in preventing limitations which can hinder the realization of the human rights introduced; for example, such is the case in countries that censor the flow of information and thus restrain the freedom of speech. In addition, the proposed Act not only seeks to encourage European companies, doing business in such countries, to show their disapproval of the censorship practiced but also wants to hold them accountable for their "compliancy" with authoritarian governments who suppress the freedom of speech.

On the other side of the Atlantic Ocean, on a national level, the encouragement of greater Internet freedom was addressed by the Global Internet Freedom Task Force (GIFT), an office of the US State Department. Furthermore, the draft Net Neutrality Bill presented to the US House of Representatives and the initiative of an Internet Freedom Preservation Act are to be mentioned as specific national initiatives with the purpose of preserving the Internet's democratic qualities such as the freedom of speech.[1061]

3. Characteristics of Human Rights Protection

3.1 Contents of Human Rights

A large number of human rights exists, most of which have a function in the online world.[1062] Some human rights have a special standing in the context of Internet governance matters and are to be addressed therefore.

a) Dignity, Integrity and Equality

Probably the core of all fundamental human rights must be seen in the dignity, integrity and equality of individuals. These basic human right positions relate to life and liberty and give equal rights and freedoms to all individuals.[1063]

1059 Rejkavik, 28th/29th May 2009, MCM (2009) 011.

1060 See http://www.eva-lichtenberger.eu

1061 Sec. 4 of the Internet Freedom Preservation Act of 2008.

1062 The following description only intends to convey the key message of a human right without going into the details of its legal "structure".

1063 See also Owens, 164–165.

Breaches against human dignity, integrity and equality may influence a person's genuine life in a particular way. If, as for example in the case of hate speech, freedom of expression of another individual is also involved, a balancing of different human rights becomes necessary.[1064]

b) Freedom of Expression and Information

Freedom of expression and freedom of information can be seen as the most fundamental co-existing human rights in the online world; legal frameworks must be designed in such a manner that any restrictions of freedom of expression and information serve legitimate purposes and do not go beyond what is necessary in a democratic society.[1065] Obviously the proper balancing of interests involved plays an increasingly important role in the context of the use of new technologies such as the Internet.[1066]

Freedom of expression on the Internet: In the past, freedom of expression and speech in the specific field of the press was considered very important.[1067] Today opinions can be easily expressed on the Internet in large parts of the world. While some States[1068] are still strengthening their systematic power through information control (protectionism), others are moved by reasons concerning further human rights, as is the case when "protecting minors from harmful content". Both forms of censorship entail the risk of breaching the right to free expression.[1069] Considerations of how to protect freedom of expression in the information society have thus become essential.[1070]

1064 See WEBER, Regulatory Models, 188–190.

1065 Council of Europe Contribution to the 2nd Preparatory Committee for the WSIS, Democracy, Human Rights and the Rule of Law in the Information Society, section 13.

1066 Hereinafter, the extent of the freedom of expression is not exemplified by a discussion of conflicting fields (such as hate speech, racism etc.), rather, the subsequent outline will focus on aspects of the humanization of the Internet; for further details see WEBER, Regulatory Models, 179–203.

1067 See also BENEDEK, Human Rights, 36 ss; LESSIG, version 2.0, 233 ss; to the filtering in general BENKLER, 183/84.

1068 Regarding the restrictions in China and Singapore see WEBER, Regulatory Models, 185/86; on the restrictions in China in particular see also GOLDSMITH/WU, 87 ss and DREZNER, 95 ss.

1069 According to the OpenNet Initiative of renowned universities (incl. Harvard, Oxford, Cambridge) filtering and censoring is on the rise in many countries (<http://opennet.net/about-filtering>).

1070 See Diverse Issues of Human Rights in the Information Society, section 1, para. 2, http://www.wsisasia.org/materials/patcha.doc; see also SUNSTEIN, 27/28, 141 ss, 145 ss and 151 ss.

Information sharing: Information sharing and the more transparent and accessible knowledge management systems are significant instruments for the functioning of the information society. In this context, maintaining a human rights point of view is of great importance; a fact which has become particularly apparent in the field of promoting and coordinating humanitarian aid. The new technologies play a crucial role, not only in disseminating information regarding human rights violations, but also in formulating this information, and determining how real world incidents can be communicated to the realm of factual, accessible information and data.[1071]

c) Privacy

The right to privacy means the protection of individual privacy free from national and international surveillance. The rapid progress made in the field of information technologies, and in particular, concerning developments such as fingerprinting, network monitoring, bio-awareness systems, electronic data processing, and creating extensive databases, have facilitated not only the collection and storage, but also the processing and interlinking of personal data.[1072]

These developments offer considerable advantages in terms of efficiency and productivity, but they also entail potential risks. Modern technology provides—within seconds—access to limitless quantities of personal data and establishes the possibility of creating "personality profiles" through the combination of different data files;[1073] this is facilitated by surveillance technology, potentially causing a considerable increase in individual privacy infringements.[1074]

In the information society the protection of personal data must be considered a key issue, in particular in view of the right to privacy.[1075] Data protection should be an essential guarantee for balancing between privacy (individual freedoms and security requirements) and the need for information exchange.[1076] One of the possibilities to protect privacy might be the establishment of counter-surveillance committees, which could mitigate national and private surveillance and help leg-

1071 See WEBER, Regulatory Framework, 79.

1072 Council of Europe Contribution to the 2nd Preparatory Committee for the WSIS, Democracy, Human Rights and the Rule of Law in the Information Society, section 16.

1073 Council of Europe Contribution to the 2nd Preparatory Committee for the WSIS, Democracy, Human Rights and the Rule of Law in the Information Society section 17.

1074 See also BENEDEK, Human Rights, 16 ss, 43 ss; HOSEIN, 138 ss; LESSIG, version 2.0, 200 ss.

1075 See also below VI.D.2.1.

1076 Council of Europe Contribution to the 2nd Preparatory Committee for the WSIS, Democracy, Human Rights and the Rule of Law in the Information Society, section 18; see also HOSEIN, 122 ss.

islate a privacy protection act.[1077] To be addressed is, furthermore, the difficulty of how netizens can be protected from the manifold threats to their privacy in the online world, which may come from both the States (for example, under security interests) as well as from private actors, in terms of economic or criminal interests.[1078]

3.2 Scope of Human Rights Application

According to the classical understanding of human rights the scope of protection is directed against States and governmental bodies which unduly interfere with fundamental rights of individuals. Consequently, human rights can only be protected from interference by non-State actors by way of exception, namely, if the relation between a State and an individual person can be analogously used regarding the relation between private individuals, and/or legal persons. Insofar, two possibilities exist under the international legal framework: (i) either non-State actors can be directly bound by human rights, which is sometimes known as "direct horizontal effect", or (ii) States can be obliged to protect human rights from violations committed by non-State actors.[1079]

(i) In general, multilateral agreements such as treaties encompassing human rights are subject to the interpretation rules of Articles 31–33 of the Vienna Convention on the Law of Treaties.[1080] According to Art. 31 of the Vienna Convention, "a treaty shall be interpreted in good faith in accordance with the ordinary meaning given to the terms of the treaty in their context and in the light of its object and purpose". In order to provide for effective human rights protection, treaties need to be interpreted dynamically, taking into account the changing social contexts in which they are applied.

The typical wording of an international convention is generally centered around the formulation "everyone has the right to" a particular freedom without holding anyone accountable. Nevertheless, some human rights provisions explicitly mention not only the State, but also the society or the family.[1081] A thorough study of the provisions of the freedom of expression in different human rights treaties

---

1077 See Diverse Issues of Human Rights in the Information Society, section 1, para. 4, available at <http://www.wsisasia.org/materials/patcha.doc>.

1078 See also Benedek, Human Rights, 40.

1079 The subsection 3.2 takes up the basic arguments discussed in more detail by Cheung/Weber, 418–423.

1080 Vienna Convention of 23rd May 1969, 1155 UNTS. 331, available at <http://untreaty.un.org/ilc/texts/intruments/english/conventions/1_1_1969.pdf>.

1081 See Cheung/Weber, 420 with further references. See for example Articles 23 and 24 ICCPR or Articles 17 and 19 of the American Convention on Human Rights (ACHR), 21st November 1969, OAS Treaty Series No. 36, 1144 UNTS 123, 9 ILM 99 (1969).

allows the conclusion that human rights obligations are not necessarily limited to State actors.[1082] The fact that non-State actors may not be made party to international procedures as well as the lack of specific sanctions does not stringently mean that non-State actors do not bear any legal obligations. Non-State actors can still be bound by the material provisions of a human rights treaty, regardless of whether and to which extent they have to fear legal consequences before an international institution.[1083]

In fact, rules which stipulate that no provisions may be interpreted to imply that any State, group, or person has a right to engage in any activity or to perform any act aimed at the destruction or limitation of the codified human rights may also be considered as an indication that non-State actors can be bound by them. This assumption is further supported by provisions which stipulate that any person whose human rights are violated should have an effective remedy, notwithstanding that the violation was committed by people acting in an official capacity.[1084]

Despite arguments in favor of acknowledging direct human rights obligations of non-State actors, the fact that according to the current international human rights regime in place, (still) only States may be addressed as direct violators of human rights, needs to be taken into account. The reconfiguration of the human rights framework and the paradigm shift endorsed by numerous human rights scholars remains subject to controversies.[1085]

(ii) A further differentiation concerns the question of whether there is an obligation of States to protect human rights from violations committed by non-State actors. If an international treaty is using the wording that a State has to "secure to everyone within the jurisdiction, the rights and freedoms", or the wording "undertakes to respect and to ensure" to all individuals the rights and freedoms recognized in the concerned document, a respective active obligation of a State must be assumed. In other words, States have to actively secure the protection of human rights in their territories as well as regard their general obligation to refrain from violating these provisions.[1086] To this extent, the classical "negative" perception of human rights and freedoms is complimented by positive obligations. The State is

---

1082 See CHEUNG/WEBER, 421 with further references. See in particular Articles 28 and 29 of the African (Banjul) Charter on Human and Peoples' Rights, 27th June 1981, OAU Doc. CAB/LEG/67/3 rev. 5; 1520 UNTS 217; 21 ILM 58 (1982). These articles even acknowledge duties for individuals to respect and consider their fellow beings and to preserve and strengthen the national community and society.

1083 CHEUNG/WEBER, 422.

1084 See CHEUNG/WEBER, 422.

1085 CHEUNG/WEBER, 437; for a thorough examination on human rights' application between non-State actors see CLAPHAM.

1086 CHEUNG/WEBER, 423.

obliged to balance the legally protected interests. Yet this interpretation does not allow for an expansion of these positive duties to a general governmental protection of private individuals from breaches by non-State actors.

Furthermore, the general responsibility of States for their internationally wrongful acts, regulated in the International Law Commission (ILC) Draft Articles on "Responsibility of States for Internationally Wrongful Acts"[1087] may be applied. A State can thus be held responsible for the conduct of an "entity which is not an organ of the State (…) but which is empowered by the law of that State to exercise elements of the governmental authority" considered an act of State (Art. 5), or if the entity is "in fact acting on the instructions of, or under the direction or control of, that State in carrying out the conduct" (Art. 8). Provided that the action of a private body can be attributed to a State and constitutes a breach of an international obligation, such as the violation of human rights, the State may be held liable.[1088]

3.3 Human Rights Transition from the Traditional to the New Online World

The transition from the traditional real world to a new online world also has consequences on the characteristics of the human rights protection. So far, legislators have been slow in addressing new issues which are paradigmatic in respect to the specific elements of cyberspace.[1089]

An important aspect concerns the fact that the relations between States and individuals are changing in the online world;[1090] some authors refer to a progressive subversion of hierarchies.[1091] An essential element which mainly is ascribed to the traditional world is human forgetfulness: An individual cannot easily keep in mind what another individual has done over the years; furthermore, the supervision of activities of an individual has its inherent limits. However, on the Internet, movements of individuals are easily discernable since data tracks are not very difficult to identify. In the real world,

> "privacy and anonymity towards State and corporate bodies are regularly granted and can only be lifted by considerable technical means or direct intervention. This situation is reversed in cyberspace. To go unnoticed on the Internet makes special

[1087] ILC Draft Articles on the Responsibility of States for Internationally Wrongful Acts, U.N.Doc. A/RES/56/83 (2001).

[1088] CHEUNG/WEBER, 423.

[1089] For a general overview see WEBER, Regulatory Models, 179 ss, and BENEDEK, Human Rights, 31 ss.

[1090] See BENKLER, 176 ss; MARZOUKI, 203/04; BENEDEK/KETTEMANN/SENGES, 2, 4/5.

[1091] See LOCKE/LEVINE/SEARLS AND BENEDEK/KETTEMANN/SENGES, 2.

> efforts necessary. This reversal situation provides the main reason for the necessity of a specific code of rules in Internet in order to protect the right to privacy and anonymity and therefore allowing for the basis of democratic expression and participation".[1092]

As mentioned in the legal doctrine, properties in the Internet are not "natural", but designed by humans and embedded in technical code and infrastructure.[1093] Consequently, human rights and the processes developed for protection need to address the specific challenges given in the online world. This also entails answering the question of whether new "digital rights" should be framed, i.e. existing human rights specified for the specific context of the Internet.[1094]

An obvious problem in the online world is the fact that impediments do exist in respect to human rights law enforcement, mainly due to the international character of the Internet and the emergence of human rights threats that are only gradually being conceptualized in the human rights vocabulary.[1095] The above mentioned conventions and declarations at the global and the regional levels do not adequately fulfil the requirements brought about by the new challenges, particularly in view of the increasingly menacing position which private players—such as Internet Services Providers—are acquiring.[1096] The reluctance of the United Nations human rights system to deal with the specific aspects of human rights in the online world might be a consequence of the UN System's partial lack of interest in the human rights dimension of the Internet governance process.[1097]

4. New Approaches for a Comprehensive Human Rights Architecture

4.1 Ongoing Activities

a) Context of the WSIS

It seems widely acknowledged that the issue of human rights should become one of the central points of discussion within the scope of the WSIS. Therefore, in preparation of the first WSIS (Geneva 2003) a special group of members of the

1092 CASACUBERTA/SENGES, 1.

1093 CASACUBERTA/SENGES, 2.

1094 See for example BENEDEK, Human Rights, 38/39.

1095 See also BENEDEK, Human Rights, 47/48; MÖLLER, 101/02.

1096 See also WEBER/CHEUNG, 475 ss.

1097 The Internet governance process is historically driven by the International Telecommunication Union and US-centered private bodies such as ICANN (see above III.B and III.C) which are not mainly concerned with human rights issues; see also BENEDEK, Human Rights, 42.

Human Rights in the Information Society (HRIS) Caucus was formed by civil society organizations attending the WSIS Preparatory Committee 1 (PrepCom 1) to ensure that human rights would duly be considered in the WSIS process by governments as well as by NGOs.[1098]

The HRIS Caucus delivered the recommendation that the international human rights adopted both in the ICCPR and the ICESCR should be translated—with reference to the particularities of information and communication technologies—into precise guarantees defined in the WSIS Declaration of Principles and the Action Plan. This embodies three main ideas, namely the need for a consistent articulation of rights, the recognition of information and communication as public common goods, and the development of mechanisms to ensure democratic governance and human rights enforcement.[1099]

Particularly relevant for the development of an information and communication society according to the HRIS Caucus is the reiteration of the following rights:

- the right to a fair trial, to the presumption of innocence and to equal treatment in law (Art. 14 and Art. 26 ICCPR);
- the right to privacy, especially protection against interference with private correspondence (Art. 17 ICCPR);
- the right to freedom of expression, to hold opinions without interference, and to seek, receive, and impart information and ideas of all kinds, regardless of frontiers, through any media (Art. 19 ICCPR);
- the right to be protected against any form of discrimination or incitement to hate (Art. 20 ICCPR);
- the right to peaceful assembly and freedom of association with others, including the right to form and join trade unions to protect one's own interests (Art. 21 and Art. 22 ICCPR);
- the right to take part in the conduct of public affairs (Art. 25 ICCPR);
- the right for minorities to enjoy their own culture and use their own language (Art. 27 ICCPR);

1098 Additionally, civil society formed a Civil Society Plenary group at the WSIS which was sub-divided into further self-organized caucuses and working groups. These included a regional caucus for each of the seven WSIS regions, two multi-stakeholder caucuses for gender and youth issues, as well as twenty-three thematic caucuses and working groups addressing thematic subjects such as education and academia, health, media and intellectual property rights. The caucus deemed of most relevance to the IGF was the Civil Society Internet Governance Caucus (CS-IGC), established during PrepCom 2 of the first phase of WSIS. For further information see Malcolm, Governance, 326 ss; Drake/Jørgensen, 28 ss.

1099 HRIS Caucus, Towards a Respectful Information and Communication Society, para. 6.

- the right for people to exercise self-determination, in particular to freely determine and pursue their economic, social and cultural development (Art. 1 ICESCR);
- the right for men and women to enjoy all economic, social and cultural rights equally (Art. 3 ICESCR);
- the right to form and join trade unions, to function freely as a trade union, and the right to strike (Art. 18 ICESCR);
- the right to education and knowledge (Art. 13 ICESCR);
- the right to participate in cultural life, to enjoy the advantages of scientific progress and its applications, to benefit from the protection of the moral and material interests resulting from any scientific, literary, or artistic production of which one is the author, to benefit from the development and the diffusion of science and culture, to benefit from respect of freedom and international cooperation indispensable for scientific research and creative activity (Art. 15 ICESCR).[1100]

The HRIS Caucus also gave an example of reaffirmation of rights in the WSIS context, in connection with the right to education and knowledge, with the following implications:

- Everyone should be able to acquire basic information and electronic education, in order to master social transformations in all their practical and civic aspects.
- The respect of intellectual property should not prevail over the right to education and knowledge, to be realized by the concept of fair use, i.e. use for non-commercial purposes, education, and research.
- Intellectual work and ideas, including programming methods and algorithms, should not be patentable; moreover, the production and use of free and open software and content should be encouraged and covered by public policy.
- Access to public data without charge is a necessary condition so that everyone has the means to exercise their citizenship.
- Access to infrastructure under acceptable economic conditions must be guaranteed, by supporting the possibility of being a provider as well as a consumer of information. This warranty implies the negotiation of agreements for contractual connections among different parts of the world and the realization of equitable cost sharing, thereby implying the existence and sustainability of local telecommunication operators.[1101]

1100 HRIS Caucus, Towards a Respectful Information and Communication Society, para. 7.
1101 HRIS Caucus, Towards a Respectful Information and Communication Society, para. 8.

In elaborating the legal framework specifically for the needs of the new information society, countries should be mindful of the common standards already elaborated for human rights and take these as a basis for future discussions. Art. 30 of the Universal Declaration of Human Rights says that no State, group, or person may claim any right under the Declaration "to engage in any activity or to perform any act aimed at the destruction of any of the rights and freedoms set forth" therein. It is thus important that the regulations adopted for the information society do not limit or interfere with the existing system of human rights.[1102]

The efforts of the NGOs were successful insofar as the central documents of the WSIS process now contain references to the importance of human rights. Para. 3 of the Geneva Declaration of Principles and para. 4 of the Tunis Commitment highlight the universality, indivisibility, interdependence and interrelation of all human rights and fundamental freedoms. In para. 1 of the Declaration and para. 2 of the Commitment, the States confirm their "desire and commitment to build a people-centered, inclusive and development-oriented Information Society." Civil society should be "premised on the purposes and principles of the Charter of the United Nations, international law and multilateralism, and respecting fully and upholding the Universal Declaration of Human Rights". Since the respect and guarantee of human rights is essential, the documents clarify "that people everywhere can create, access, utilize and share information and knowledge, to achieve their full potential and to attain the internationally agreed development goals and objectives, including the Millennium Development Goals".[1103] Apart from the right to development, the right to freedom of expression is particularly highlighted.[1104]

Following the two WSIS the Internet Governance Forum (IGF) became a new discussion platform for human rights issues in the field of the Internet. During the IGF 2006 in Athens several workshops focused on freedom of expression and human rights as well as on issues related to privacy and data protection. In Rio de Janeiro (2007) and Hyderabad (2008), the number of workshops and meetings addressing freedom of expression and the intensity of the discussion on a bill of rights increased further.[1105]

1102 WEBER, Legal Framework, 85. In light of such considerations, the claim to establish a new human right to communicate, which was promoted by the Communication Rights in the Information Society (CRIS) campaign, was appeased in favor of the objective of enforcing the existing human rights standards, see DRAKE/JØRGENSEN, 35/36.

1103 See para. 4 of the Geneva Declaration and para. 4 of the Tunis Commitment.

1104 See also BENEDEK, Human Rights, 33/34.

1105 See also BENEDEK, Human Rights, 34 and 37; see also BENEDEK/KETTEMANN/SENGES, 3/4.

b) Private Bodies

In the meantime, private bodies have recognized the importance of human rights and agreed to introduce basic rules at a self-regulatory level. In particular within the framework of the so-called Global Network Initiative many companies active in the information and communication field (such as Google, Microsoft, etc.), have agreed on a charter to protect and advance freedom of expression and privacy in information and communication technologies. This charter which entered into force in November 2008 contains the following sections on freedom of expression and on privacy:[1106]

> "(1) Freedom of opinion and expression is a human right and guarantor of human dignity. The right to freedom of opinion and expression includes the freedom to hold opinions without interference and to seek, receive and impart information and ideas through any media and regardless of frontiers.
>
> Freedom of opinion and expression supports an informed citizenry and is vital to ensuring public and private sector accountability. Broad public access to information and the freedom to create and communicate ideas are critical to the advancement of knowledge, economic opportunity and human potential.
>
> The right to freedom of expression should not be restricted by governments, except in narrowly defined circumstances based on internationally recognized laws or standards. These restrictions should be consistent with international human rights laws and standards, the rule of law and be necessary and proportionate for the relevant purpose.
>
> Participating companies will respect and protect the freedom of expression of their users by seeking to avoid or minimize the impact of government restrictions on freedom of expression, including restrictions on the information available to users and the opportunities for users to create and communicate ideas and information, regardless of frontiers or media of communication.
>
> Participating companies will respect and protect the freedom of expression rights of their users when confronted with government demands, laws and regulations to suppress freedom of expression, remove content or otherwise limit access to information and ideas in a manner inconsistent with internationally recognized laws and standards.
>
> (2) Privacy is a human right and guarantor of human dignity. Privacy is important to maintaining personal security, protecting identity and promoting freedom of expression in the digital age.
>
> Everyone should be free from illegal or arbitrary interference with the right to privacy and should have the right to the protection of the law against such interference or attacks.

1106 See <http//www.globalnetworkinitiative.org>.

> The right to privacy should not be restricted by governments, except in narrowly defined circumstances based on internationally recognized laws and standards. These restrictions should be consistent with international human rights laws and standards, the rule of law and be necessary and proportionate for the relevant purpose.
>
> Participating companies will employ protections with respect to personal information in all countries where they operate in order to protect the privacy rights of users.
>
> Participating companies will respect and protect the privacy rights of users when confronted with government demands, laws or regulations that compromise privacy in a manner inconsistent with internationally recognized laws and standards."

The actual implementation within the policies of the concerned enterprises needs to be observed during the coming months and years. Since self-regulatory measures constitute important guidelines for behavioral rules in the online world, a successful realization of these human rights principles could encourage further enterprises to subscribe to the charter.[1107]

4.2 Perspectives for a Humanization of Internet Governance

a) General Developments

The developments in cyberspace have led to a progressive shift towards the individualization and even "privatization" of international (human rights) law.[1108] Since a disintermediation of States has taken place, legal regimes tend to direct their focus on the individuals and consequently oblige them to comply with human rights standards. The multi-stakeholder structure in the Internet world has increased the volume and the extent of non-traditional norm-setting processes. As mentioned in the legal doctrine, individuals, through the power of their ideas[1109], have the possibility to influence the human rights dimension by way of participation in dynamic coalitions.

Human rights are often called the "missing link"[1110] between the technology-oriented and the value-oriented lines of thinking. Given the increasing need for guidance with regard to dealing with public issues, human rights approaches have to seize the multi-stakeholderism characteristics of the online world.[1111]

The described developments are associated with the philosophical discussions and dimensions of civil society's constitution in the online world. The mentioned

1107 See also above I.C.2.

1108 In general see DÖRR, 905 ss.

1109 In this sense the title of a book edited by KLEINWÄCHTER, Power of Ideas, 2007.

1110 See JØRGENSEN/MARZOUKI, 17.

1111 See also BENEDEK, Human Rights, 40.

concept of a social contract[1112] is based on the understanding (following JEAN-JACQUES ROUSSEAU) that members of civil society freely agree on coordinating their activities within a common framework. Realizing such a concept, implies that freedom, rules and power would coalesce in one and the same body according to the understanding of IMMANUEL KANT.[1113] Similarly, since the information society is structured in a decentralized way—i.e. on the basis of a complex network of interrelated system agents, without having a central regulatory power—the agreement of the members of civil society to comply with a volonté générale helps to realize a network of tolerance, or in other words, to avoid a network of ruthless intolerance as described by THOMAS HOBBES (homo homini lupus, i.e. "man is a wolf to man").[1114] Furthermore, by adopting JOHN RAWLS' image of a "veil of ignorance", it can be assumed that societies' representatives would opt for a social community adhering to the fundamental principles enshrined in human rights as a value basis.[1115]

Such a social contract within social networks or platforms would have to be user-directed and include a compliance function regarding the information uploaded to the networks or platforms.[1116] Obviously, tailor-made human rights protection for the specific field of the Internet cannot be realized with an immediate effect reaching beyond the already existing regulations which are in place. However, as the technical framework of the Internet is developed and designed, the involved principles of international human rights law and processes could also be included in the efforts. Importantly, the focus should be set on individuals as the relevant actors in the emerging Internet world.

b) Specific Initiatives

The process of strengthening human rights in the online world can also be illustrated by diverse efforts provided by manifold actors:

(i) Probably the most well known example[1117] of actors influencing the human rights developments with a non-traditional normative approach can be seen in

1112 See above IV.A.

1113 IMMANUEL KANT, Anthropologie in pragmatischer Hinsicht, 1798, AA VII.

1114 The concept is described by HOBBES in his seminal book Leviathan.

1115 RAWLS, para 24, 118 ss.

1116 Insofar, providers need to exercise a "medium" function; see on this aspect ROLF H. WEBER, Media Governance und Service Public, Zurich 2007, 9 ss.

1117 The number of dynamic coalitions in Internet governance can hardly be overlooked anymore. Examples are the Dynamic Coalition on Privacy, the Dynamic Coalition on Freedom of Expression and Freedom of the Media on the Internet (FOE online), the Dynamic Coalition on a Framework of Principles for the Internet, the Dynamic Coalition on Lingustic Diversity (Coalition Dynamique pour la Diversité Linguistique), the Dynamic Coalition on

the initiative of the dynamic coalition, i.e. a thematic network open to all stakeholders, for an Internet Bill of Rights (IBR).[1118] This project is based on the internationally accepted human rights expressed in the already mentioned Universal Declaration of Human Rights, the International Covenant on Economic, Social and Cultural Rights, and the International Covenant on Civil and Political Rights and its two Optional Protocols.[1119] The IBR initiative was founded in 2005 through a European attempt which was eventually endorsed by a wide number of eminent experts including US experts such as LAWRENCE LESSIG and RICHARD STALLMAN. A first appeal, based on a detailed project description, published in 2005 refers to the fact that in the online world "everybody can have their say, acquire knowledge, create ideas and not just information, exercise their right to criticize, to discuss, to take part in the broader political life, and thus to build a different world of which everybody can claim to be an equal citizen".[1120] The appeal also mentions the risks and dangers, occurring in case of short-sighted market approaches as well as in case of activities of authoritarian States trying to impose new forms of censorship.

After the initiative had been formally introduced into the discussions of the 2nd WSIS by the government of Italy, the Dynamic Coalition on an Internet Bill of Rights was created as part of the framework of the yearly Internet Governance Forum (IGF).[1121] In the subsequent years, the IBR promoters became an important dynamic coalition within the IGF. Since its incorporation in 2005, the IBR Dynamic Coalition has organized events in order to support the creation of and to deliberate various proposals on the concrete substance of the Bill of Rights. Subsequently, Italy and Brazil issued a joint declaration highlighting the fact that a "set of principles" is necessary to allow a democratic and inclusive development of the Internet.[1122]

In the course of 2008, the IBR became a multi-stakeholder coalition with far more than one hundred members. As a self-organized entity its mission is to build a platform to facilitate collaboration and dovetail the work of other dynamic coalitions especially as they relate to human rights on the Internet. The IBR Dynamic Coalition created a platform for debating on Internet rights (including human rights on the Internet), it established an Internet rights watch (implying the build-

---

an Internet Bill of Rights, the Dynamic Coalition on A2K@IGF, the Dynamic Coalition on Access and Connectivity for Remote, Rural and Dispersed Communities, the Dynamic Coalition on Open Standards.

1118 See <http://internet-bill-of-rights.org/en>.

1119 See above VI.C.2.1.

1120 See <http://internet-bill-of-rights.org/en>.

1121 See also BENEDEK, Human Rights, 38; BENEDEK/KETTEMANN/SENGES, 7.

1122 BENEDEK, Human Rights, 38.

up of a repository of precedents and coverage of Internet rights cases) and it developed standards which allow bringing Internet rights into "human readable" formats, enabling users and providers of services to become more aware of their applicable rights.[1123] In summer 2008, the coalition members adopted a specific charter which provided for a basis to create a steering committee and a chair coordinating and facilitating the discourse and other activities of the coalition. The IBR also established a new website which informs about new developments of the discussions and deliberations.[1124]

(ii) Another valuable approach was taken by a more scholarly based side: The Center for Innovation Law and Policy and the International Human Rights Clinic at the Faculty of Law at the University of Toronto have assumed the task to collaborate in defining and articulating a statement of recognized human rights; the developed document is understood as part of a longer process logically culminating in concrete steps for the vindication of these rights. The published Networked Communications Freedom Charter encompasses the following fundamental rights:[1125]

Article 1—Fundamental Human Rights and Freedoms

(1) Freedom to communicate is essential to a free and democratic society, and to the enjoyment of other fundamental human rights and freedoms.

(2) Communities of expression and knowledge made possible by networked communications technologies are integral to the modern global community, and they sustain the production and dissemination of ideas that promote our common humanity.

Article 2—Freedom of expression

(1) Everyone has the right to freedoms of thought, belief, opinion and expression. This right includes freedom to hold opinions without interference and to seek, receive and impart information and ideas through any networked communications technology, regardless of borders.

(2) Freedom of networked communication is both a fundamental human right in itself and an indispensable means of realising other fundamental human rights and freedoms.

Article 3—Freedom of association

(1) Everyone has the right to freedom of association within, and beyond, the communities created through networked communications technologies.

(2) Networked communities and their members must be free to use networked communications technologies to assemble and to engage in dialogue and debate.

1123 See <http://internet-bill-of-rights.org/en>.

1124 See <http://internet-bill-of-rights.org/en>.

1125 For more details see OWENS, 162 ss.

(3) Networked communities and their members must be free from interference and intervention, both through networked communications and beyond them.

(4) Freedom of association within and beyond the communities created by networked communications technologies is an essential aspect of the development of a free, open and democratic society.

Article 4—Equality

All human beings are born free and equal in dignity and rights. Everyone is entitled to all the rights and freedoms set forth in this Networked Communications Freedom Charter without distinction of any kind.

Article 5—Dignity, Integrity and Security of the Person

The rights and freedoms associated with networked communications and networked communications technologies should not impair the fundamental human rights to human dignity, bodily integrity or security of the person.

Article 6—Diversity of Expression

(1) Everyone has the freedom to participate in a diversity of networks of expression, networks of knowledge and networks of communities.

(2) Diversity of expression, as a means of literacy, education and participation, shall be directed to the full development of the human personality and to the strengthening of respect for human rights and fundamental freedoms.

Article 7—Access

Everyone has the right of access to networked communications technologies free from interference, intervention or restriction.

Article 8—Privacy

(1) Everyone has the right to privacy of networked communications, and the right not to be deprived thereof except in accordance with the principles of fundamental justice.

(2) The right to privacy of networked communications through networks of expression, networks of knowledge and networks of communities maintains the dignity and worth of the human person.

Article 9—International Cooperation

International cooperation, both public and private, should occur in a transparent, democratic and public manner in order to uphold the fundamental rights and freedoms engaged by networked communications technologies.

Article 10—Limitations

(1) The exercise of the rights contained herein may be subject to such formalities, conditions, restrictions or penalties as are prescribed by law and are necessary in a free and democratic society and consistent with the highest respect for human dignity and the effectuation of fundamental freedoms.

(2) Notwithstanding this section, the right to freedom of expression and access to networked communications technologies should be interpreted broadly and con-

strained only in exceptional situations in accordance with the terms set out in this document and consistent with the administration of justice.

This Charter project is now open for deliberation in the scholar community; it remains to be seen whether the Charter also finds its way into the coalitions driving the discussions within the IGF context.

c) Long-term Expectations

Assessed realistically, it cannot be expected that the international treaties encompassing fundamental human rights will be fully applied one-to-one to Internet matters. Apart from the extension of the scope of legally stated human rights (horizontal or indirect effects) which is in principle acknowledged by legal doctrine, jurisdictional problems can hardly be overcome: To what extent a national court may be competent to apply human rights to online matters, might often be quite uncertain.

For this reason, alternative approaches need to be thoroughly studied and followed with more emphasis:

(i) Self-regulatory efforts merit further support: The mentioned Networked Communications Freedom Charter[1126] can be considered a valuable legal framework which should be taken into account during the further elaboration of a humanized Internet governance. Correspondingly, the Global Network Initiative[1127] seems to be a reasonable step which could help make private enterprises comply with human rights.

(ii) The attempts to establish an Internet Bill of Rights[1128] are steps in a good direction which enable a gradual inclusion of human rights in the Internet governance process. The objective of this project could be strengthened by realizing the envisaged bill having it encompass human rights which are accepted as a "standard" and implemented through the Internet governing bodies. This would also foster a more comprehensive and harmonized approach in light of the manifold initiatives undertaken. In particular, the W3C is active in the creation of Internet standards; even if the respective activities had a main focus on technical issues, a slight change of approach in direction of human rights does not seem to be excluded. The standards of the W3C are not legally binding, but compliance with them is an aspect of good reputation.[1129] The experiences with the UN Global Compact morally binding large multinational enterprises show that soft law provisions do not remain without effect.

1126 See above VI.C.4.2 b) (ii).

1127 See above VI.C.4.1 b)

1128 See above VI.C.4.2 b) (i).

1129 See also BENEDEK/KETTEMANN/SENGES, 7.

(iii) Valuable inputs could stem from the perception of the information and communication infrastructure as based on scarce resources. Cyberspace can indeed be considered a part of the global commons, i.e. a public good which is not susceptible to State or private ownership or control. As a consequence, inspiration could be drawn from other legal frameworks on common resources.[1130] This aspect raises the myriads of questions linked to the endeavor of bridging the digital divide and thus ensuring access to the Internet in terms of a developmental goal.[1131] Furthermore, the objective of ensuring access would also have to focus on digitally disabled people in terms of a holistic approach, as well as take into account the corresponding challenges resulting from rapid technological developments.[1132]

(iv) Cooperation among the different stakeholders is an acknowledged principle for the governance of the Internet and should thus also extend to the specific human rights issues. This would entail a particular focus set on the linkage between human rights and Internet governance, not least within the agendas of the human rights bodies in place, for example under the auspices of the UN. The collaboration with these fora could provide for valuable inputs.[1133] In particular, the joint efforts undertaken in 2005 by the UN Special Rapporteur on Freedom of Opinion and Expression, the OSCE Representative for Freedom of the Media and the OAS Special Rapporteur on Freedom of Expression deserve mentioning.[1134]

(v) Human rights standards should similarly be developed with the objective of inducing registered organizations to comply with human rights best practices. Further input might be drawn from the ongoing deliberations on human rights within the IGF. Joint efforts of W3C and IGF could, for example, be worthwhile at the global architectural level, as well as at the level of services, particularly in view of the planned introduction of mechanisms to allow the development and implementation of practical solutions for the compliance with human rights. In addition, human rights considerations need to be included in the decision-making processes by establishing adequate participatory models.[1135]

1130 See also BENEDEK, Human Rights, 34.

1131 See WEBER/MENOUD, 4 ss. Indeed, some analysts would go as far as arguing that the failure to provide affordable access is inconsistent with human rights obligations (see DRAKE/JØRGENSEN, 30 ss).

1132 See also BENEDEK, Human Rights, 46.

1133 See also DRAKE/JØRGENSEN, 19/20.

1134 See International Mechanisms for Promoting Freedom of Expression, Joint Declaration of 21st December 2005, by the UN Special Rapporteur on Freedom of Opinion and Expression, the OSCE Representative on Freedom of the Media and the OAS Special Rapporteur on Freedom of Expression, available at <http://www.article19.org/pdfs/standards/three-mandates-dec-2005.pdf>. See also BENEDEK, Human Rights, 41/42.

1135 See above V.E.

(vi) A further topic concerns the "education" of the online community. Producers of online contents, services providers and users should become more aware of human rights protection in the online world. In particular sensitivity for human rights compliance ("e-literacy") appears to be an aspect which merits improval in order to achieve a more human rights-oriented online world.

In a nutshell, the gradual acknowledgment and consciousness of human rights issues in the field of Internet governance is a very welcome development. In order to avoid a dilution of such legal rights to mere "guidelines" and "values" for cyberspace, however, it is important to keep the juridical foundations of human rights in view. A comprehensive inclusion of the different aspects in question could be enhanced by a corresponding interdisciplinary approach to the subject of realizing human rights particularly for the information society in the virtual sphere.

D. Security: Assuring Safety, Trust, and Reliability

1. Safety

1.1 Security Threats

During the past few years experience has shown that hackers and attackers are breaking into vital portions of the global network infrastructure, causing problems and creating costs.[1136] Many incidents have shown that a threat—for example, the shut-down or attempt to shut down major sites used by an entire community to accomplish essential civil tasks—can go beyond a simple menace to economic safety and endanger national and international security.[1137] An umbrella term for such threats to infrastructure is "cyberterrorism", which is defined as an "extreme or intense force in an online setting, causing unexpected or unnatural results, and used for purposes of intimidating, coercing, or creating an atmosphere of anarchy, disorder, or chaos in a networked environment".[1138]

The online world is rich in possibilities; technical innovations and ingenuity allow the society to progress and prosper. However, regrettably, the development of new forms of technical activity can also potentially be misused. The following measures have played a role in practice:[1139]

1136 This subchapter mainly follows WEBER, Legal Framework, 105 ss.

1137 A detailed analysis is given by BIEGEL, 65 ss.

1138 BIEGEL, 232; in general to the problems of cyberterrorism see WONG, 199 ss.

1139 For further details see WEBER, Regulatory Models, 126/27.

- *Denial-of-Service Attacks:* Such activities consist of large streams of useless data directed towards particular network locations with the aim of overloading equipment and destroying its functionality. A denial-of-service attack does not steal passwords or manipulate data, but rather overloads the data traffic of certain systems (flood attack) or causes parts of the system's hardware or software to shut down. The following forms of denial-of-service attacks have been differentiated:
  - Flood attacks, such as mail-bombing, also known under the names of SYN Flood, Tribe Flood Network (TFN), TFN2K, Smurf, Trinoo;
  - Malformed packet attacks, also known under the names of Ping of Death, Teardrop, Land, WinNuke; and
  - Torpedo tactic.

  In so-called distributed denial-of-service attacks, the infringing person is able to manipulate the receiving computer to make its equipment participate in the attack.
- *Dissemination of Viruses:* A virus is a program that can copy itself, and is therefore attached to or inserted in data documents or the boot sector of the hard disk. A virus is often capable of deleting data or of invalidating certain functions of a computer's software, occasionally even its hardware.
- *Trojan Horses:* Those who place Trojan horses (for example, disguised as games) attempt to trigger the unauthorized execution of certain applications, such as the deletion of passwords, the disclosure of specific information, the manipulation of computer software, or the download of further Trojan horses.
- *Cracks:* In most cases, a person using software or techniques which circumvent or displace specific security measures, tries to change or delete specific data; if the targeted system is entered by use of a false identity, this is called "poofing".
- *Logical Bombs:* Programs that are attached to any other program and lead to the shutdown of the system are called logical bombs.
- *Sniffer:* Programs that are able to control data flow from one network to another are called sniffers; they usually attempt to steal user names and passwords.
- *Hacking:* The most serious technical attack is arguably the actual hacking into a communication system; the term "hacking" is often used for a broad range of illegal objectives and technical activities.

The above list of measures which endanger the security of networks is not exhaustive; moreover, with the development of new technologies new attacking tools and techniques are also regularly developed. Therefore, security (or more precisely cybersecurity) was already an important issue prior to the WSIS in Geneva[1140]

[1140] See BENDRATH/JØRGENSEN, 357.

and remained an active discussion topic in the debates of the WGIG and the second WSIS in Tunis.[1141] Subsequently, in the context of the IGF, security became a high-ranking issue[1142] and is thoroughly discussed at the annual IGF meetings.[1143]

1.2 Regulatory Framework

(i) The evaluation of possible rulemaking approaches should be based on general principles which are well identified or similarly established for situations regarding security threats. A uniform approach is reasonable in regulating aspects common and typical to all occurrences:

- *Consensus:* Civil society generally disapproves of the threats to security; it is commonly agreed that cyberterrorism is a problem and measures should be developed to counteract it[1144]. Unlike with many other topics of the online world (in particular aspects of content), a broad "moral" consensus exists with regard to security threats.
- *Conduct:* The actual conduct of cyberterrorists is not all that different from that of conventional terrorists; consequently, notions applied in "real world" situations can be transferred by analogy to the online world. However, the specific and unique characteristics of cyberspace—consisting particularly of the technical setting of the measures and features – should not be underestimated and call for the development of appropriate new solutions.[1145]
- *Jurisdiction and enforcement:* Cyberterrorism is a good example for activities which affect global networks, it also reveals many of the associated problems. Cyberterrorists are interested in reaching a wide online community; consequently, aspects of jurisdiction and enforcement are of utmost importance and require a greater degree of international cooperation than in other substantive areas of the online world.[1146]

(ii) Since online threats to infrastructure security are usually driven by a criminal intent, the main legal "tools" in place are the national governmental regulations which punish certain kinds of "computer misuse". Most developed countries already have criminal laws prohibiting, for example, the stealing of data or the changing of contents.[1147] Since developments in technology can cause legal gaps, it might be necessary to strengthen or update the relevant "rap and trace laws" and

1141 See BENDRATH/JØRGENSEN, 359, 362.
1142 DORIA/KLEINWÄCHTER, 73–76, 89–90.
1143 See DORIA/KLEINWÄCHTER, 167 ss, 322 ss.
1144 BIEGEL, 235.
1145 BIEGEL, 235.
1146 WEBER, Regulatory Models, 128; see also WONG, 200 ss.
1147 BIEGEL, 236 ss.

also consider stronger penalties from time to time. Nevertheless, the territorially limited application of national laws restricts a global approach and facilitates the work of people attacking infrastructure security[1148] and may thus not be overlooked.

Another difficult aspect concerns self-defense and counter-offense. It is generally accepted in the legal community for victims of an attack to use defensive measures to protect themselves. But because retaliatory actions in the online world can become volatile and arbitrary, it may be difficult for national legislators to strike a balance between justifiable protection and the avoidance of excessive self-defense.[1149]

Furthermore, law enforcement efforts should be strengthened in order to achieve a better implementation of legislative objectives and to deter people from even considering the undermining of infrastructure security. A certain degree of international harmonization of enforcement measures would also be appropriate.[1150]

(iii) The illegality of attacks against infrastructure security is universally accepted and is also recognized by the legal community worldwide.[1151] This common understanding, however, is not really reflected in legal agreements since a written harmonization of approaches against cyberterrorism is difficult to realize. Organizations and institutions are also confronted with the fact that there is no international "police" and that the existing international bodies are not equipped sufficiently to deal with illegal activities.[1152] However, the International Telecommunication Union (ITU) has now taken up the discussion by outlining a global cybersecurity agenda encompassing five pillars, namely legal measures, technical and procedural measures, organization structures, capacity building, and international cooperation.[1153] In particular, the ITU developed a "ITU Toolkit for Cybercrime Legislation" in 2009.[1154]

So far, only in geographically limited areas such as Europe has it been possible to agree on a Convention against Cybercrime.[1155] The Commission of the European Union also launched a strategy based on network security and on the establish-

1148 WEBER, Regulatory Models, 129.
1149 For more details see BIEGEL, 240 ss.
1150 BIEGEL, 246/47; WEBER, Regulatory Models, 130.
1151 WEBER, Regulatory Models, 66/67, 130.
1152 WEBER, Regulatory Models, 130; WONG, 222/23.
1153 International Telecommunication Union, Cybersecurity for All, Global Cybersecurity Agenda, Geneva 2009, 14 ss.
1154 See <http://www.itu.int/ITU-D/cyb/cybersecurity/legislation.html>
1155 Council of Europe, Convention on Cybercrime, Budapest, 23rd November 2001, ETS No. 185.

ment of a Cyber Security Task Force (CSTF).[1156] Recently, at the occasion of the 1st Council of Europe Conference of Ministers responsible for Media and New Communication Services a resolution has been adopted which states principles in anti-terrorism legislation.[1157]

Looking at the global threat of cyberterrorism, the question arises as to whether or not it would be useful to establish a new international agency addressing security issues. Such an agency could be formed under the auspices of an existing organization, such as the United Nations.[1158] The discussions within the framework of the IGF, however, have not yet revealed a high interest in such a new organization.[1159] So far, the technical standards of the ITU remain the only globally harmonized guidelines[1160].

(iv) From a regulatory point of view, an attempt should be made to adjust the technical framework to improve protection against cyberterrorism. Security experts and software engineers have already developed various code-based tools that can increase infrastructure stability. Some measures are not extremely difficult to achieve, for example the redesign of computer operating systems, but these can easily become vulnerable over time. Other measures, for example a change in Internet communication protocols, depend on the degree of international agreement and—as in the case of limiting anonymity—may cause basic legal problems.

The simplest code-based strategy available to participants in the online world is to rely on defensive software.[1161] Several products are available in the market, where software tries to develop an intelligent self-defense network or a reverse address look up. Nevertheless, people pursuing illegal activities in the Internet are often technically knowledgeable and able to circumvent firewalls and other protective measures. Moreover, not all defensive tools are equally effective against different kinds of attacks, and portable machines usually realize security objectives to a lesser degree.[1162]

1156 EU, Communication from the Commission to the Council, the European Parliament, the Economic and Social Committee and the Committee of Regions, eEurope 2005: An Information Society for All, Action Plan, 28th May 2002, COM (2002) 263 final, 15/16.

1157 Reykjavik, 28th/29th May 2009, Resolution MCM (2009) 011.

1158 Biegel, 249. Subsequent to the WTO Work programme on electronic commerce Biegel even suggested that such an agency could be established under the auspices of the World Trade Organization.

1159 See Doria/Kleinwächter, 232–234, 238.

1160 See International Telecommunication Union (fn. 1153), 43 ss.

1161 Biegel, 251/52.

1162 Biegel, 252.

Another software-based strategy consists in protecting computers from being used as unwitting agents.[1163] Technically, these solutions are relatively simple since computers secured in this way cannot be hijacked.[1164] In principle, two types of measures are possible, namely intrusion detection and personal firewalls. Many programs which help protect individual users are also available as free products or free advices that can be downloaded from the Internet.[1165] Nevertheless, experience has shown that demands for changes in the software industry practices are only acted on with some reluctance.[1166]

Software can also be designed so that attempted denial-of-service attacks are rerouted, turning the attack back on the perpetrators automatically. Technologically, however, establishing correct identification is not always easy, and practical obstacles can be difficult to overcome in daily application.[1167]

Some authors have proposed changing the architecture of Internet protocols and developing a new fundamental communication protocol that strengthens security by limiting anonymity. This would probably not prevent illegal attacks directly, but the perpetrators would become known.[1168] However, this approach not only involves substantial work at the international level, but could also raise legal questions, since anonymity is often a fundamental aspect of the right to privacy in national constitutions.[1169]

(v) A specific problem concerns the relation between security and privacy; a double-edged situation is given due to the fact that the strengthening of security regulations could jeopardize the privacy wishes.[1170] Insofar it is problematic that security and privacy are partly intermingled;[1171] at any rate, however, discussions on possible solutions and security issues must be pursued at the international level and particularly in the IGF context.[1172]

1163 BIEGEL, 252/53.

1164 The most common tools are TRIN00 and TFN (available at <http://www.nipc.gov>).

1165 See for example the Computer Emergency Response Team (<http://cert.org>), the International Computer Security Association (<http://www.icsa.net>), the Microsoft Security Adviser (<http://www.microsoft.com/security>), and the ZDNet's Security (<http://www.zdnet.com/enterprise/security>).

1166 BIEGEL, 256/57.

1167 BIEGEL, 254/55.

1168 BIEGEL, 255/56; DAVID P. HAMILTON, Redesigning the Internet: Can it be made less vulnerable?, Wall Street Journal, 14th February 2000.

1169 See BRANSCOMB, 1641 ss.

1170 On this problem in particular see below VI.D.2.1 c).

1171 This problem partly occurred in the preparations of the two WSIS (see BENDRATH/JØRGENSEN, 357 ss).

1172 See also DORIA/KLEINWÄCHTER, 322 ss.

2. Trust and Reliability

2.1 Privacy

a) Meaning and Functions of Privacy

Security and privacy have certain similarities, as "protection" is an important issue for both. In the case of security, protection aims at a suitable infrastructure to favor the safe execution of transactions, whereas in the case of privacy, the information itself is addressed.

The term "privacy" conveys a large number of concepts and ideas.[1173] Usually an individual wants to control access to his/her personal information.[1174] Three areas related to privacy can be identified:[1175]

- Physical space can be comprehended as a shield against unwanted objects or signals; in this sense, privacy is close to infrastructure security.
- Decision-making power may be required in relation to information flow: the objective here is the protection of a person's freedom to make self-defined choices in respect to data dissemination without State interference.
- Information privacy can be understood as an individual's control over processing: in this context, the acquisition, disclosure, and use of personal information is at issue.

Society has realized for quite some time now, that individuals' needs for privacy are at risk in the digital environment (as presaged in GEORGE ORWELL's "1984", and earlier in BENTHAM's "Panopticon"). Technological innovations, like quickstreams and cookies, can cause digital distress, and the large volumes of electronic transactions facilitate data warehousing.[1176] Privacy-destroying technologies may lead to ubiquitous surveillance.[1177] In this respect, three basic features of privacy should be considered:[1178]

- *Secrecy*, i.e. information known about an individual;
- *Anonymity*, i.e. attention paid to an individual;
- *Solitude*, i.e. access to an individual.

1173 SAMUEL D. WARREN/LOUIS D. BRANDEIS, The Right to Privacy, Harvard Law Review, Vol. 4, 1890, 193, 205 refer to the right "to be let alone." See also HOSEIN, 122 ss and 131 ss as well as LESSIG, version 2.0, 200 ss.

1174 WACKS, 235.

1175 KANG, 1202 ss.

1176 WEBER, Regulatory Models, 148/49.

1177 FROOMKIN, Privacy, 1475 ss.

1178 WACKS, 238.

Privacy is not a value in itself, but the decisive factor consists in the relation between a person and specific information.[1179] Particularly sensitive data vary in relevance depending on the person in question, since information always has a certain value in the information society.[1180] Furthermore, seen from a legal perspective, the fundamental right to privacy can contradict the (fundamental) freedom of speech. Ultimately, the most important objective of privacy is the prevention of improper use of personal information. Undue data dissemination can derail a fair process distributing benefits and burdens or making information vulnerable to unlawful acts and ungenerous practices.[1181]

Therefore, a number of general principles should be taken into account as milestones of an online privacy system:[1182]

- *Choice:* Individuals should have the choice of sharing or not sharing their information.
- *Ease of use:* The technical system should be designed so that the execution of choices by individuals is not too cumbersome in respect to privacy protection.
- *Notification:* Individuals whose information is used by third persons must be notified about such use.
- *Verification:* The legal framework should provide means to verify if the information is correct and if existing privacy policies are followed.
- *Enforcement and redress:* The legal framework should provide mechanisms which ensure compliance with privacy policies and give recourse for legal action.

Access to and control of own data can also be understood as a philosophical issue in terms of self-determination (in a KANTIAN use), or from a political stance, in terms of anti-totalitarianism, as well as in view of legal theory, i.e. as the fundamental rights stemming from human dignity and the moral values of each person.[1183]

Notwithstanding the fact that privacy constitutes a human right, there are certain countervalues that contradict individual control over personal information. Two aspects are noteworthy:

- Information privacy causes the risk of strict control by the information "owner" and can jeopardize the truthfulness of certain data.[1184] Criminal activities might

[1179] WEBER, Regulatory Models, 150.
[1180] REIDENBERG, 1323.
[1181] KANG, 1214/15.
[1182] BASHO, 1510.
[1183] WEBER, Regulatory Models, 150.
[1184] KANG, 1218/19.

even be hidden; RICHARD POSNER refers to the invasions of privacy as self-defense against deception.[1185]

- Information privacy may in the long term, but not necessarily, lead to informational quarantine; therefore the legal framework should be drafted in such a way that an individual can exercise control of data dissemination, however, within reasonable limits.[1186]

b) Regulatory Framework

An internationally binding agreement generally covering privacy and data protection does not exist. However, international human rights instruments usually embody the essence of privacy, at least to a certain extent.[1187] The International Covenant on Civil and Political Rights of the United Nations, the Convention on the Rights of the Child of the United Nations, and the European Convention on Human Rights address some matters related to privacy; for example, respect for private life is ensured, exposure to arbitrary or unlawful interference is rejected, and rules legally protecting privacy are introduced.[1188]

Further international instruments are the economically-oriented OECD Guidelines of 1980 entitled "Guidelines Governing the Protection of Privacy and Transborder Flows of Personal Data",[1189] the (regional) Convention for the Protection of Individuals with Regard to Automatic Processing of Personal Data of 1981 issued by the Council of Europe,[1190] and most comprehensively, the EC Directive on the Protection of Personal Data of 1995.[1191] The main principles of the EC Directive concern the proper collection of data, the observance of high data security standards, data integrity (purposeful use of data), and the proportionality of data collection.[1192]

Obviously, international cooperation or even co-regulation is needed to secure effective principles of privacy in the online world. The above mentioned conven-

---

1185 See RICHARD A. POSNER, The Right of Privacy, Georgia Law Review, Vol. 12, 1978, 393–422, 395.

1186 WEBER, Regulatory Models, 152.

1187 See also GREWLICH, Governance, 280/81.

1188 WEBER, Regulatory Models, 154.

1189 See OECD Guidelines Governing the Protection of Privacy and Transborder Flows of Personal Data, 23rd September 1980, available at <http://www.oecd.org/document/18/0,3343,en_2649_34255_1815186_1_1_1_1,00.html>.

1190 Convention for the Protection of Individuals with regard to Automatic Processing of Personal Data, 28th January 1981, ETS No. 108, 20 ILM 377 (1981).

1191 EC Directive 95/46/EC of the European Parliament and of the Council of 24th October 1995 on the Protection of Individuals with regard to the Processing of Personal Data and on the Free Movement of such Data, OJ 1995 L 281/31.

1192 See also WEBER, Regulatory Models, 155/56.

tions, primarily those dealing with human rights, contain a few provisions specifically supporting the notion of privacy. However, the background of these provisions lies in a constitutional approach, which is directed towards recognition of a human right and does not really deal with the justified allocation of information.[1193]

Because adequate legislation does not always exist, self-regulation has become an important mechanism for the protection of privacy. Possible elements of a self-regulatory scheme may include codes of conduct containing rules for best practices worked out in accordance with substantive data protection principles, the establishment of internal control procedures (compliance rules), the setting up of hotlines to handle complaints from the public, and transparent data protection policies.[1194] Many international instruments, such as the Guidelines of the OECD and Art. 27 of the EC Directive on the Protection of Personal Data, mention self-regulation as an appropriate tool. However, weaknesses in this approach can come from a lack of expertise and legal experiences with such processes, and from the risk that not all market participants are bound by private rules.[1195]

c) Relation between Security and Privacy

Privacy allows keeping certain information and data confidential. However, efforts to safeguard security might create barriers and roadblocks to others' freedom of action; shielding data from others eventually impinges on their ability to learn and to make decisions which protect their interests.[1196] Furthermore, extensive privacy might cause problems in case of criminal behavior of the concerned person and could even lead to an evasion of accountability for harm done to others. In particular, as far as the fight against cyberterrorism is concerned, governments need to have access to data and have to be enabled to collect the data necessary for the surveillance in the public interest. Obviously, due process must ensure that the collection of such data does not produce political abuses. Normally, in such situations, an interest balancing test should apply; however, the yardstick of such "trade-offs" is often rather discretionary. Therefore, attempts to bridge the wide discretion and to develop guidelines for an interests balancing test are of importance; in the context of the IGF, representatives from governmental bodies and the private sector have started to exchange ideas about possible common regulatory needs.[1197]

1193 WEBER, Regulatory Models, 165.

1194 For more details see WEBER, Regulatory Models, 167/68.

1195 BASHO, 1521/22; GREWLICH, Governance, 292/93.

1196 MUELLER, Securing Internet Freedom, 5.

1197 See BENDRATH/JØRGENSEN, 364, 367.

d) Future Approaches

The relation between the human right to privacy and the principle of free, transborder flow of information has not yet been discussed in depth.[1198] Additional efforts should thus be undertaken to reach a minimum harmonization of internationally applicable privacy standards.

(i) In developing the idea of minimum standards, the establishment of an intergovernmental "General Agreement on Information Privacy" could be considered, introducing an international organism which would build a high-level negotiating forum for consensus-based decisions.[1199] The substantive principles should cover the following issues:[1200]

- The data collector must be accountable for all personal information in its possession.
- Purposes for which the information is processed should be adequately identified.
- The information collection must be limited to the extent necessary for pursuing the identified purposes.
- The data collector should gather information with the knowledge and consent of the concerned individual.
- The information should only be used for the purposes specified and should be destroyed if no longer necessary.
- The data collector must ensure that personal information is kept accurate, complete, and up to date.
- The data collector is responsible for the appropriate security safeguards.
- Individuals must have access to their (collected) personal information, with a right to amend it if necessary.

Many national laws and regulations deal with the collection and use of personal information in private and in governmental matters. However, two major drawbacks of such an approach must be considered:

- The scope of application of national laws is restricted to the respective geographical territory. This limitation contradicts the borderless flow of information. The problem of adequate levels of protection in the various countries must

[1198] See also WEBER, Regulatory Models, 165.

[1199] REIDENBERG, 1360.

[1200] REIDENBERG, 1326/27; to possible privacy standards see also DREZNER, 103 ss and HOSEIN, 134.

then be dealt with by defining the limitations unanimously, a task which proves to be very difficult.[1201]

- As national laws often govern specific problems, a comprehensive approach is currently missing and regulatory gaps risk to be misused.[1202]

(ii) A harmonization approach must take into account the fact that in the context of the Internet, the traditional governmental domains such as security and crime prevention have moved away from State legislators and enforcers of rules to a less State-centric model. The governance of Internet security takes place by means of more informal, cooperative relationships among technical experts in the non-profit and private sectors.[1203] The steermen ("kybernetes") are mainly actors who have direct operational control of some form of access to the Internet (such as controllers of service, routers, bandwidth, domain names, i.e. generally non-State actors) and assume the functions within cooperative frameworks.

In view of this situation, self-regulation should play a more important role. Several elements can be combined to create a cooperative system of self-regulation, whereby substantive aspects (such as the protection of minors or the avoidance of illegal content) must be clearly distinguished from privacy aspects.[1204] Possible elements of a self-regulatory scheme may include the following:[1205]

- Codes of conduct for Internet privacy should be negotiated by market participants; preferably not only data collectors, but also users should have an influence.
- Such codes of conduct must contain rules for best practice,[1206] released in accordance with at least minimal substantive data protection principles.
- Data collectors should establish internal control procedures,[1207] to be in a position to continuously check compliance with the codes of conduct.
- Setting up hotlines to handle complaints from the public will help build confidence in self-regulation.
- The codes of conduct should be transparent and become a quality standard for good behavior.

Any new form of networked governance partly overcoming the limitations of territorial sovereignty must be thoroughly assessed. Relying on networked relations

1201 WEBER, Regulatory Models, 164.
1202 BASHO, 1519/20.
1203 MUELLER, Securing Internet Freedom, 15.
1204 This distinction is not made by GREWLICH, Governance, 267 ss, 294/95.
1205 The following bullet points are a summary of the considerations of GREWLICH, Governance, 294/95.
1206 For more details see GREWLICH, Governance, 301.
1207 For more details see GREWLICH, Governance, 300.

across organizational boundaries for security and crime prevention does not legitimize any authority of these organizations to act in relation to civil society or to an individual citizen. If, for example, the Anti-Phishing Working Group,[1208] a network organization devoted to fighting cybercrime, would take down websites containing contents of critical business activities, the occurrence of a mistake could not be excluded; if a website would erraneously be taken down, harm to innocent business is possible. Furthermore, the questions of to what extent such an organization should be entitled to release binding decisions and what rights the concerned people would have to proceed against such a decision, must be addressed.

(iii) Self-regulation can be monitored as appropriate, by bodies in the private or public sector. TRUSTe is an example of a program that imposes specific standards on organizations collecting personal data.[1209] Experience shows that the effectiveness of self-regulatory schemes varies depending on the private entities, organizational structures and governmental bodies involved. Codes of conduct could also be tailored to particular industries and evolve as technology develops. In fact, self-regulation is already a common tool, also supported by intergovernmental organizations such as the OECD.[1210] Correspondingly, Art. 27 of the Data Protection Directive of the European Union specifically refers to self-regulation. These practical examples demonstrate that the goals of appropriate data protection regimes cannot be achieved without self-regulatory efforts.

Weaknesses in self-regulation could come from a lack of expertise and legal experience with such processes, or from insufficiencies in the institutional framework for creating codes or substantive data protection principles.[1211] Furthermore, self-regulatory regimes can be one-sided if not all concerned market participants are allowed to contribute, or if their input is disregarded.[1212] Under such circumstances, self-regulation might lack the necessary legitimacy in the information society. These weaknesses, however, do not outweigh the advantages of self-regulation which remains a major tool in the field of privacy protection.

The fact that self-regulatory efforts merit to be supported is also underlined by the acceptance of privacy as a specific topic in the IGF discussion basket. Whereas privacy was almost replaced by security concerns at the beginning of the process,

1208 See <http://www.apwg.org>.

1209 Further details on the program TRUSTe are given, for example, by Froomkin, Privacy, 1525–27; Basho, 1522/23.

1210 See Grewlich, Governance, 292 Fn 86.

1211 On the weaknesses of self-regulation in the field of privacy particularly Basho, 1521/22, Grewlich, Governance, 292/93.

1212 See also above I.C.2.3 b).

it became a high-ranking issue over time,[1213] and during the annual conferences of the IGF, privacy is now a key discussion topic.[1214]

(iv) The last few years have experienced an increasing market demand for innovative, privacy-enhancing, user-empowering technologies,[1215] such as cryptographic methods and technology-based solutions for disclosure problems.[1216] The technical devices should be organizationally embedded into the system in order to protect personal identity by minimizing the collection of data that might identify an individual.[1217] Therefore, preference should be given to designs that can be integrated into the systems.[1218]

The technological architecture of global networks can assist users in developing self-help schemes, for example an encryption providing for user anonymity.[1219] Moreover, the application of a special icon could signal the observance and verification of privacy criteria.[1220] For the time being, however, such mechanisms still complicate the handling of electronic data transmission; thus, it cannot be expected for society as a whole to be willing or capable of applying the respective tools.[1221]

For this reason, privacy should be understood as a design philosophy that—as much as possible—encourages data collectors to remove identifiers linked to personal data in order to achieve an appropriate anonymity. Engineering specifications could embody policy rules for data protection in the online environment. The term "privacy enhancing technologies" (PETs) is typically used fur such systems; PETs can be subject-oriented, object-oriented, transaction-oriented, or system-oriented.[1222] By using the architecture of the infrastructure, technical solu-

---

1213 See BENDRATH/JØRGENSEN, 363.

1214 For further details see BENDRATH/JØRGENSEN, 365 ss.

1215 Sometimes, however, it is difficult to judge which applications are privacy-invasive and which are not (see THIMOTHY S. WU, Application-Centered Internet Analysis, Virginia Law Review, Vol. 85, 1999, 1163–1204, 1176/77).

1216 See REIDENBERG, Privacy, 1528/29.

1217 FROOMKIN, Privacy, 1528/29.

1218 In this sense also OECD, Privacy Protection in a Global Networked Society, available at <http://www.oecd.org/dsti/sti/it/secur/act/privatenote.htm>.

1219 See BASHO, 1524.

1220 GREWLICH, Governance, 279.

1221 See also PAUL M. SCHWARTZ, Beyond Lessig's Code for Internet Privacy: Cyberspace Filters, Privacy Control, and Fair Information Practices, Wisconsin Law Review, 2000, 743–788, 748 ss.

1222 For more details see SAMUELSON, 1167 ss; HARVARD LAW SCHOOL, 1645 ss; FROOMKIN, Privacy, 1528 ss.

tions are able to arbitrate divergences among national laws and may serve social innovation.[1223]

The main example in practice is the Platform for Privacy Preferences (P3P) initiated by the W3C.[1224] This technical solution is a server-based filtering tool that can be used to identify and protect against deviations from applicable codes of conduct in the privacy field.[1225] Intelligent agents are another means of achieving adequate protection of personal data and avoiding the secondary use of stored personal information.[1226] A further development of these technical solutions could politically be the easiest way forward to achieve an acceptable level of data protection.

The respective efforts are also supported by the Dynamic Coalition on Privacy being established as a stakeholder group in the context of the IGF process. The Dynamic Coalition on Privacy addresses emerging issues of Internet privacy such as digital identities, the link between privacy and development, and the importance of privacy and anonymity for freedom of expression.[1227] Apart from research work made available in draft form through the two co-leaders of the Coalition (Ralf Bendrath and Gus Hosein), modular human-readable privacy rights agreements are available for consultation.[1228] Since the IGF has now acknowledged the importance of privacy issues, the activities of the Dynamic Coalition on Privacy merit special attention[1229].

2.2 Data Security

a) General Guidelines

Specific requirements are usually stipulated in the data protection laws. As regards the automatic processing of personal data, the controller of the data files must follow those technical and organizational measures which are required to ensure appropriate data security. The following goals are at stake:[1230]

- *Access control*: Unauthorized people must be denied access to facilities where personal data are processed.

1223 See also Samuelson, 1169; Grewlich, Governance, 299.
1224 See <http://www.w3c.org>.
1225 For more details see Reidenberg, 1356/57.
1226 Reidenberg, Privacy, 1357.
1227 See <http://www.intgovforum.org/cms/index.php/dynamic-coations/69-privacy>.
1228 See <http://www.wiki.igf-online.net/wiki/Privacy-rights-agreements>.
1229 See also Malcolm, Governance, 82 ss.
1230 The mentioned principles correspond to Article 9 of the Swiss Ordinance of 14th June 1993 on the Federal Law on Data Protection (SR 235.11); see also Hosein, 134.

- *Personal data carrier control*: Unauthorized people are to be denied the possibility of reading, copying, altering, or removing data carriers.
- *Transport control*: Upon disclosure of personal data as well as during the transportation of data carriers, the unauthorized reading, copying, altering, or erasing of data must be prevented.
- *Control of release*: Recipients of data which disclose personal information must occur through identifiable devices for data transmission.
- *Storage control*: Unauthorized entries into storage as well as unauthorized alteration or erasure of stored personal data are to be excluded.
- *User control*: The unauthorized use of automatic data processing systems through devices for data transmission is to be prevented.
- *Access control*: Access by authorized people is to be limited to those needing the data to accomplish their tasks.
- *Entry control*: People having access to data must be identified in case of automatic systems.

b) Cryptography

Technical measures within the architecture of global networks can enhance security as systemic access mechanisms enable control over the information flow.[1231] For years now, password and serial number protection has been a common software-based tool in the digital environment. In the meantime, cryptographic technologies have become widely accepted as essential techniques for security and trust in open networks. The term "cryptography" can be used for two technological applications:[1232]

- Encryption helps to keep data and information confidential.
- Electronic signatures help to prove the origin of data (authentication) and verify if and to the extent of an alteration of data (integrity).

Encryption methods protect the contents of the transmitted information; an encryption algorithm transforms plain text into an unreadable ciphered text attached to the data.[1233] Encryption poses a regulatory problem because the technological measures can also be used for illegal purposes; for this reason, encryption regulations have continued to restrict the export of such programs or algorithms for years now.[1234] In the meantime, the legal underpinning of export control rules has in most cases elapsed. Nevertheless, some countries, such as the United States,

[1231] WEBER, Regulatory Models, 170/71.
[1232] GREWLICH, Governance, 173.
[1233] GREWLICH, Governance, 177.
[1234] GREWLICH, Governance, 182 ss.

still try to obligate market participants to deposit the source code for such programs or algorithms in advance.[1235] Such rules could come into conflict with liberal human rights, particularly the freedom of expression. In order to avoid restrictions of the transborder flow of information, international agreements such as the Cryptography Guidelines of the OECD are aiming at a minimum harmonization of encryption regulations.[1236]

Meanwhile, further cryptographic techniques have been developed. With digital watermarking, digital data is modified in order to insert a code that can be used to carry information (particularly image and digital video). Steganography, a special form of imperceptible photomarking, is a technique used to hide data in a work.[1237]

c) Electronic Signature

The regulatory framework related to electronic signatures puts in place a legal and technical regime that is based on a reliable infrastructure of two mathematically related keys for each communicating party (a public and a private key).[1238] Electronic signatures provide protection against unauthorized modification of information and allow for a reliable verification of the authenticity of the addresser. Additionally, electronic signatures also prevent the addresser from denying his authorship (so called non-repudiation).

Execution of the certification is done by independent third parties, usually called certification authorities or trusted parties. Many regulatory issues governing electronic signatures, such as requirements for certification authorities, technical conditions of electronic signature products, special liability rules, and the legal transborder recognition of electronic signatures,[1239] are subject to laws that have already been enacted. From a comparative legal perspective, the national laws on digital signatures in different countries have been fairly harmonized on the basis of the Model Law on Electronic Signatures prepared by UNCITRAL[1240]. This legal harmonization facilitates the cross-border application of electronic signature regulations and should help to increase the acceptability of this technical measure that cannot always be easily handled. At the European level, the Directive 1999 on

1235 WEBER, Regulatory Models, 171/72 with references.

1236 See OECD, Guidelines for Cryptography Policy, 19th December 1997, available at <http://www.oecd.org/document/11/0,3343,en_2649_34255_1814731_1_1_1_1,00.html>.

1237 WEBER, Regulatory Models, 172.

1238 GREWLICH, Governance, 174 ss.

1239 WEBER, Regulatory Models, 171.

1240 See UNCITRAL Model Law on Electronic Signatures, 5th July 2001, available at <http://www.uncitral.org/pdf/english/texts/electcom/ml-elecsig-e.pdf>.

Electronic Signatures[1241] harmonizes the conditions which had to be implemented into national law by the EU Member States until 2001.

E. Bridging the Digital Divide

Bridging the digital divide is not an issue which is limited to the Internet governance context, it has a much wider range. Nevertheless, the experience in the IGF process has shown that the notion of digital divide and the efforts of overcoming the respective problems have been lively debated;[1242] therefore, some general considerations are worth being mentioned hereinafter.

1. Introduction

So far, there is no single general abstract definition of the digital divide; it encompasses a wide spectrum of disparities and differences based on manifold factors. Broadly speaking, the perceived gap which surfaced between those who have access to information technology and those who do not, is referred to with the concept of digital divide.[1243] The term originated as a catch-phrase in US national studies of inequalities regarding access to information and communication.[1244] Afterwards, it quickly became so familiar that it entered every day political and societal debates. Mostly, the digital divide is understood as the "uneven diffusion of information and communication technology".[1245]

Digital divide should be perceived as a dynamic and multifaceted construct, which mainly depends on the factors and indices used to measure and analyze the inequalities in several ICT areas, such as ICT infrastructure, access or use.[1246] The International Telecommunication Union (ITU) and the United Nations Conference on Trade and Development (UNCTAD)—relying on their observance of the

1241 EC Directive 99/93 of the European Parliament and of the Council of 13th December 1999 on a Community Framework for Electronic Signatures, OJ 2000 L 13/12.

1242 See DORIA/KLEINWÄCHTER, 93/94, 404.

1243 For further details see WEBER/MENOUD, 4.

1244 See survey of the National Telecommunications and Information Administration (NTIA): Falling Through the Net: Defining the Digital Divide, Doc. SIN 003-000-00687-5, Washington D.C. 1999, available at <http://www.ntia.doc.gov/ntiahome/fttn99/>; see als YU, 2/3 with further references.

1245 UNITED NATIONS DEVELOPMENT PROGRAM (UNDP), Making New Technologies Work for Human Development, Human Development Report 2001, New York/Oxford 2001, 38.

1246 WEBER/MENOUD, 4; see also YU, 29, referring to the notion of an "ever-changing definition".

evolution of this gap in ICT access—have underlined basic elements which must be kept in mind when trying to frame the digital divide:[1247]

- The digital divide is a dynamic concept, which evolves over time;
- There is no single divide, but rather multiple divides are to be differentiated;
- The main factor causing theses divides is wealth.

The digital divide could also be understood through the closely-linked mirror-inverted concept of "digital opportunity". The first phase of the World Summit on the Information Society (WSIS), concluded with the adoption of the Geneva Principles, stated the participants' commitment towards "turning the digital divide into a digital opportunity for all".[1248] Information technology is no longer a luxury, but a development tool.[1249]

2. Digital Divide Problematic

2.1 Factual Situation

In 2007, the Information Economic Report of the United States related to the information and communication technologies (ICT) came to the conclusion that the ICT would have major implications for innovations and development policies. Such an approach can introduce a new paradigm for the configuration of economic activities encompassing the following topics:[1250]

- The economic impact of ICT could be more important in terms of externalities and spillovers through its use and applications in different sectors of the economy.
- ICT innovations provide new opportunities in favor of developing countries for their insertion into the global value chains and for diversifying production activities and exports.
- The rapid pace of innovation in the ICT sector itself considerably reduces the costs of access to ICT, allowing a democratization of ICT use and facilitating the adoption of ICT in poverty reduction programs.
- ICT is generating new services in form of e-commerce, e-finance, e-government, etc.; these new services can contribute to economic efficiency.

1247 ITU/UNCTAD, World Information Society Report 2007: Beyond WSIS, Geneva, June 2007.

1248 WSIS, Geneva Declaration of Principles, para. 10.

1249 See Yu, 16.

1250 United Nations, Information Economy Report, New York/Geneva 2007, 4/5.

- ICT require skills, i.e. education and training are ever more important in building a knowledge economy in which ICT represents an indispensable tool.
- ICT gives rise to new models of sharing collective production of ideas and innovations leading to "open access" models.

International statistical data, such as that provided by UNESCO or by ITU for example, expose sobering figures, revealing disquieting North-South inequalities in the proliferation of ICT. Only around 15% of the world's population have access to the Internet; the Internet users' rate tops at 76% of the population in Sweden, whereas it scarcely averages 4% on the African continent.[1251] There are around five times more fixed telephone lines in the developed countries than in developing ones.[1252] In remote areas people are not even linked to an electricity grid, which is a pre-condition for accessing most new ICT.[1253]

ICT divides also appear within developed countries and are revealed by factors such as income, gender, age and education; for example, 85% of the Swiss citizens with a university degree or equivalent use the Internet, whereas only 39% of the Swiss citizens with obligatory school education do; 52% of the Swiss households with a middle-level income (between CHF 3000 and CHF 5000 per month) possess a personal computer, whereas 93% of the households with a high-lever income (over CHF 9000) do.[1254]

For the purpose of measuring countries' digital opportunity level, ITU considers that, in an ideal world, digital opportunity implies the following:[1255]

- The whole population has access to ICT at affordable prices;
- All homes are equipped with ICT devices;
- All citizens have mobile ICT devices;
- Everyone uses broadband.

2.2 Relevant Aspects of the Digital Divide

The digital divide needs to be addressed at an international level. Efforts are to be taken in order to overcome the gap among individuals, households, businesses and geographic areas at different socio-economic levels with regard both to their

---

1251 ITU Statistics: The ITU ICT "eye", country data, available at <http://www.itu.int/ITU-D/icteye>.

1252 ITU, Building Digital Bridges, Geneva, November 2005, VIII, available at <http://www.itu.int/wsis/tunis/newsroom/stats/Building-digital-bridges_2005.pdf>.

1253 UNESCO, World Report: Towards Knowledge Society, Paris 2005, 29.

1254 See WEBER/MENOUD, 3 with further references.

1255 ITU, Digital Opportunity Index, available at <http://www.itu.int/doi>.

opportunities to access ICT and to their use of the Internet for a wide variety of activities.[1256] Generally, the main concerns of digital divide discussions focus on ICT; whereby two aspects are usually the subject of analysis: Telecommunication network access and Internet access. However, technologies concerned by distribution disparities are manifold and encompass various devices, such as televisions, radios, mobile phones, computers, Internet connections and digital switches.[1257] Therefore, the digital divide has to be understood as referring to a large scope of ICT consisting of "hardware, software, networks and media for the collection, storage, processing, transmission and presentation of information (voice, data, text, images), as well as related services".[1258] Consequently, the bridging of the access divide should encompass the filling of all technological gaps deserving public policy attention.[1259]

In order to systematically analyze the problem of the technological gap, PETER K. YU discusses five key prerequisites for bridging the digital divide:[1260]

- *Awareness:* Those who are not aware of the Internet and of the new communication technologies and those who are not aware of the benefits of computers and online access will not be able to benefit from the chances created by the new communication possibilities and to take advantage of the digital opportunities.
- *Access:* For obvious reasons, access to the Internet and the new communication technologies is paramount to survive personally and professionally, for example in view of daily communications, business transactions, entertainment, education, job search, research and information gathering, medical assistance and political participation; the Internet has also created many unprecedented opportunities for people with disabilities.
- *Affordability:* In many less developed countries, the costs of hardware and software and the interconnection fees are so high that Internet access remains out of reach for many people;[1261] the monthly income can certainly not be fully spent on using the Internet.
- *Availability:* Even if having Internet access, many people might not be able to find the information that is relevant to their lives and communities, i.e. to obtain the actually relevant information. An additional barrier to digital partici-

1256 See OECD, Understanding the Digital Divide, Paris 2001.

1257 WEBER/MENOUD, 5.

1258 See TASK FORCE ON FINANCIAL MECHANISMS FOR ICT FOR DEVELOPMENT (TFFM), Financing ICTD, Final Report, 22nd December 2004, available at <http://www.itu.int/wsis/tffm/final-report.pdf>, 22.

1259 See also above VI.B.3.

1260 YU, 8 ss.

1261 See above VI.B.1.2.

pation is language, even if the decision of ICANN of June 2008, to introduce other languages aside from English might have mitigated the problem to a certain extent;[1262] at least indigenous people who do not use written language cannot take advantage of Internet access.

- *Adaptability*: Access to information technology and Internet content is useful only if people are able to adapt to the changing technological environment and to use the new technological tools effectively. Computer illiteracy, technophobia, and cyberphobia have posed significant barriers to participation in the online world.[1263]

Based on these general thoughts on the digital divide, showing that the empowerment of civil society to become involved in information exchanges can create "soft power",[1264] the financing strategies are to be discussed hereinafter.

3. Financing Strategies

3.1 Financing Needs

Estimating the level of investment needed to achieve an inclusive civil society is difficult, mainly given its high complexity and the variety of components.[1265] On a global scale, bridging the digital divide in developing countries requires building sufficient basic infrastructures, maintaining ICT services, and reaching the necessary level of capacities at the same time.[1266] Moreover, ICT entail different elements, such as network infrastructure, hardware, software, and services; however, focusing on basic ICT infrastructure needs for investment purposes, a distinction can usually be made among the electric sector (which is the prerequisite for the implementation of any ICT), the fixed, and the mobile telecommunication sector.[1267] Besides the problem inherent to the complexity if ICT infrastructure components, it is difficult to take the impact of innovation and progress into account in the estimates, as technological change over the years may either raise or reduce investment needs: On the one hand, a new technology can be cheaper to install and may offer more opportunities, which would substantially reduce infrastructure costs; on the other hand, technology change could render the ICT

1262 See above III.C.5.

1263 See YU, 15/16.

1264 See ROBERT KEOHANE/JOSEPH NYE, Power and Interdependence, 3rd ed., New York 2001, 220.

1265 See following discussion is based on WEBER/MENOUD, 35/36.

1266 See PRADA, Mechanisms, 16–18.

1267 PRADA, Mechanisms, 17; FAY/YEPES, 2.

in place obsolete and require equipment renewal, which may eventually raise infrastructure costs.

The few estimations that have been attempted, particularly within the World Bank's research, show similar figures revealing that the level of investment needed in developing countries is huge: For instance, according to the study of MARIANNE FAY and TITO YEPES, developing regions would annually need around USD 325 billion in investments to generate electricity, install telephone mainlines, and mobile networks; this would solely meet consumers' and producers' demands (based on predictable GDP growth and without taking any social infrastructure optimum into account).[1268]

In 2005, the UK government released an impressive and comprehensive report, entitled "Our Common Interest: Report of the Commission for Africa",[1269] aiming at a better comprehension of the African Continent with a view on outlining growth strategies which would support the achievement of the Millennium Goals by 2015. The UK COMMISSION FOR AFRICA REPORT argues that "developed countries should provide an extra USD 10 billion a year up to 2010 and, subject to review, a further increase to USD 20 billion a year in the following five years" in order to support African infrastructure priorities ranging from building roads to ICT.[1270] The ongoing financial and economic crisis makes these figures even more illusory.

Although generally favoring a market-based approach, academics emphasize that, with regard to such high figures, the private sector is unlikely to be able to answer the financing needs of the developing world alone, without some support from the public sector. It is therefore paramount, on the one hand, that governments strive to provide the enabling environment and basic conditions for the private sector to play its growth-driving role by spending more GDP on infrastructure development[1271] and, on the other hand, that the international community commits itself to increased development aid.[1272] As the COMMISSION FOR AFRICA REPORT under-

[1268] FAY/YEPES, 11.

[1269] UK COMMISSION FOR AFRICA, Our Common Interest: Report of the Commission for Africa, March 2005 (COMMISSION FOR AFRICA REPORT).

[1270] COMMISSION FOR AFRICA, chapter 7 para. 67. The commissioned study by ESTACHE and YEPES estimates that Africa needs an additional expenditure of USD 20 billion a year to meet the expected demand at a 6% economic growth rate; however, the COMMISSION FOR AFRICA REPORT doubts that an increase of USD 20 billions could be easily and effectively absorbed over the next five years and therefore recommends a scaled approach.

[1271] FAY/YEPES, 12; COMMISSION FOR AFRICA REPORT, chapter 7 paras. 63–64.

[1272] UNCTAD, LDC Report 2007, 2007.

lines, "The promotion of growth is not a question of the State versus the private sector, but a question of how they combine to generate growth".[1273]

3.2 Political Initiatives

At different times and in various occasions, many international organizations have provided proposals to bridge the digital divide. However, concrete financing mechanisms have not been enacted yet. The question became particularly salient as the International Accounting Rate System (IARS), which was one of the main North-South financial resources for telecommunication development, was reformed in 1998, leaving a financial gap in developing countries' sources of revenue estimated between USD 5 and 10 billion per year.[1274]

The Geneva und Tunis phases of the WSIS undoubtedly lay the cornerstone of the financing debate. However, the first phase strongly relied on the Monterrey Consensus, calling for the conduction of a review and analysis regarding financial mechanisms to be carried out by an ad hoc task force, whereas the criticized second phase mainly welcomed the Digital Solidarity Fund "as an innovative financial mechanism", but did not otherwise provide concrete statements.

a) Monterrey Consensus

The International Conference on Financing for Development was held from 18th to 22nd March 2002, in Monterrey, Mexico, and was attended by around 800 delegates, among which 50 heads of State or government and over 200 ministers. The Conference resulted in the adoption of the Monterrey Consensus; the document sets out a new global approach to financing development, seeking to achieve internationally "agreed Development Goals, including those contained in the Millennium Declaration".[1275]

The Monterrey Conference was innovative and unique in many respects: For the first time in UN history, it allowed for quadripartite discussions among the governments, the private sector, civil society, and institutional stakeholders.[1276] Furthermore, the conference unveiled a change in the traditional development aid debates, showing concession-ready developed countries and realistic developing

1273 Commission for Africa Report, chapter 7 para. 31.

1274 See Weber/Menoud, 36.

1275 Development Goals are not detailed, but can be interpreted in the light of the first paragraph of the Monterrey Consensus which states: "Our goal is to eradicate poverty, achieve sustained economic growth and promote sustainable development, as we advance to a fully inclusive and equitable global economic system".

1276 Subedi, 52.

countries.[1277] The Monterrey Consensus reflects this evolution, calling for "a new partnership between developed countries and developing countries",[1278] in which the responsibilities for sustaining development are shared.[1279]

The Monterrey Consensus is organized around six "leading actions":[1280]

- The first set of recommendations is aimed at "ensuring the necessary internal conditions for mobilizing domestic savings".[1281]
- The second part focuses on international resources for development.[1282]
- The Monterrey Consensus reaffirms the importance of a "universal, rule-based, open, non-discriminatory and equitable multilateral trading system" and "meaningful trade liberalization" for stimulating development.[1283]
- Official Development Assistance (ODA)[1284] is seen as an essential complement to the primary private investment mechanisms and market forces, to which support is provided for, in the first three recommendations of the Monterrey Consensus.
- External debt issues are to be considered as important aspects.
- The final leading action stresses the "urgent need to enhance coherence, governance, and consistency of the international monetary, financial and trading systems".[1285]

The Monterrey Consensus sets a benchmark of financing for development, which is constantly referred to, as was the case at the WSIS. The outcome of the Monterrey Conference could be broadly summarized with three leading statements: The document calls for (i) increased mobilization of financial resources; (ii) coherent cooperation among the stakeholders; and (iii) a more central and effective leading role of the UN.[1286]

1277 HAQUE/BURDESCU, 221.

1278 Monterrey Consensus, para. 4.

1279 HAQUE/BURDESCU, 221.

1280 A more detailed description is contained in WEBER/MENOUD, 38–40.

1281 Monterrey Consensus, paras. 10–19.

1282 Monterrey Consensus, paras. 20–25.

1283 Monterrey Consensus, paras. 26–38.

1284 The term "Official Development Assistance" (ODA) applies to the official financing flow from the members of the OECD Development Assistance Committee (DAC) to developing countries listed in Part I of the List of Aid recipients. Grants and loans must fulfil three conditions to be considered as ODA: (1) They must be undertaken by the official sector; (2) have the promotion of economic development and welfare as main objective; (c) and be granted at concessional financial terms (i.e. a loan must have at least 25% of grant elements).

1285 Monterrey Consensus, paras. 52–67.

1286 Monterrey Consensus, notably paras. 38, 52, 61, 64, 67.

The Monterrey Consensus itself provides for a follow-up process in its last sections,[1287] which the UN has properly carried out. The intergovernmental follow-up should mainly take place within the UN General Assembly in the form of a High Level Dialogue on Financing for Development,[1288] held every two years, and in the Economic and Social Council (ECOSOC) whose High-Level Meetings with representatives of the Bretton Woods Institutions (World Bank Group, IMF) and of the WTO are held yearly.[1289] The Ad Hoc Group of Experts on International Cooperation in Tax Matters was renamed and reconstituted by the ECOSOC in 2004 in order to discuss the tax policy issues raised by the Monterrey Consensus on a yearly basis.[1290] The other major institutional stakeholders (IMF, World Bank Group, WTO, UNCTAD, and UNDP) have also adapted their organization and agenda to discuss development financing matters in committees, sub-commissions or intergovernmental bodies.

A follow-up international conference to review the implementation of the Monterrey Consensus was held from 29th November to 2nd December 2008 in Doha. It resulted in the adoption by consensus of the Doha Declaration on Financing for Development,[1291] which reaffirmed the goals and commitments of the Monterrey Consensus and focused on particular topics. Some of these specific topics were: the mobilizing of both domestic and international financial resources for development, the use of international trade as an engine for development, the increase in international financial and technical cooperation and development and the reduction of external debt. Further issues including the enhancement of coherence and consistency of the international monetary, financial and trading systems in support of development were also addressed. In addition, the Declaration also called for a United Nations Conference at the highest level with the mandate to examine the impact of world's financial and economic crisis on development.

1287 Monterrey Consensus, paras. 68–73.

1288 The High Level Dialogue on Strengthening International Cooperation for Development through Partnership has been reorganized to enable civil society and the private sector to participate and has the obligation to discuss the reports coming from the ECOSOC on development financing (UN, Resolution A/57/L.80, A/57/L.81 and A/57/L.82 of 8th August 2003).

1289 ECOSOC, Resolution E/2002/34 of 26th July 2002; the ECOSOC High-Level Meetings are also known as "Spring Meetings".

1290 ECOSOC, Resolution 2004/64 of 11th November 2004.

1291 Doha Declaration on Financing for Development, 29th November to 2nd December 2008, UN Doc. A/CONF.212/L.1/Rev.1.

b) World Summits on the Information Society

A major merit of the WSIS resides in the fact that it made governmental attention focus on the momentous issues surrounding Internet and ICT regulatory needs.[1292] However, the WSIS participants could not agree on an answer to the central question of how to bridge the digital divide. Indeed, the funding issue was the longest to resolve.[1293] Nevertheless, the below discussed Digital Solidarity Fund (DSF) proposal has become a successful approach in the WSIS context.

During the second meeting of the Preparatory Committee, the President of the Republic of Senegal, ABDOULAYE WADE, argued for the adoption of a concept of "digital solidarity" in the WSIS documents.[1294] His proposal aimed at reducing Southern countries' problems with interconnection, infrastructure and training partly through massive investments in the South, financed by countries of the North, and partly, through increased South-South cooperation. As a concrete mechanism to transfer resources from developed countries to developing ones, President WADE, drawing upon the monetary snake construct, proposed—with the help of statistical data provided by the ITU—the establishment of a similar "digital snake". Hereby countries whose Internet rate is situated in the upper fluctuation margin of the snake, help countries lying outside the snake to meet the lower margin limit by engaging in specified quantified action. Subsequently, many participants of the WSIS process took up the proposal during the discussions, but actual results have not yet been achieved. [1295]

Looking at the slow progress in the WSIS discussions, the cities and local authorities discussed and acknowledged the necessity to create a DSF at their World Summit of Cities and Local Authorities on the Information Society (Cities and Local Authorities Summit), held within the framework of the WSIS in Lyon on 4th and 5th December 2003. In their Declaration, the participants expressly invited cities and local authorities to actively commit to the DSF.[1296] Shortly afterwards, the mayors of Geneva and Lyon announced the creation of the Digital Solidarity Fund Foundation and an initial contribution from the cities of Geneva and Lyon and the Republic of Senegal.[1297] The WSIS members eventually endorsed the compromise

1292 SOUTER, 7.
1293 SOUTER, 10.
1294 WSIS, Statement by ABDOULAYE WADE, President of the Republic Senegal, Gap or worlds apart?, WSIS, Geneva PrepCom-2 document.
1295 For further details see WEBER/MENOUD, 44/45.
1296 World Summit of Cities and Local Authorities on the Information Society, Declaration of 5th December 2003.
1297 WSIS, Report from the Cities and Local Authorities in the IS, Statement of Mr. G. COLLEMB, Mayor of Lyon, and Mr. CH. FERRAZINO, mayor of Geneva, 12th December, 2003, available at <http://www.itu.int/wsis/geneva/coverage/statements/cities/s08-fr.pdf>, 3–4.

formulation which had been reached in the Preparatory Committees: "We recognize the will expressed by some to create an international voluntary «Digital Solidarity Fund», and by others to undertake studies concerning existing mechanisms and the efficiency and feasibility of such a Fund".[1298]

The Digital Solidarity Agenda, inserted into the Geneva Plan of Action, consists of two Subsections D1 and D2: Subsection D1 briefly states that two lines of action should govern the funding strategies of the international community: (i) At the national level, e-strategies[1299] should be integrated in national development plans, including poverty reduction strategies. (ii) Along these lines, at the international level, ICT should be included in ODA strategies. The second Subsection (D2) emphasizes the details of mobilizing resources for financing development.[1300] In addition, developing countries should endeavor to create a transparent stable and predictable investment environment in order to attract major private investments for ICT[1301] and the private sector is asked to contribute to the implementation of the Digital Solidarity Agenda.[1302]

Since no agreement could be reached on precise mechanisms to finance ICT development in the South, the Plan of Action resolved the establishment of a Task Force on Financial Mechanisms (TFFM) whose aim was to review available financial means, assess their adequacy, and propose innovation solutions. The creation of a DSF should then be examined by the TFFM along with other measures.[1303] The Plan of Actions delayed any decision-making on concrete financial issues at the second phase of the WSIS for which the report of the TFFM served as a discussion basis.[1304]

Later, in the context of the second WSIS, relying on the findings and conclusions of the TFFM Report, the Tunis Commitment and the Tunis Agenda reflected

[1298] WSIS, Geneva Declaration of Principles, para. 61.

[1299] "E-strategies" are not expressly defined in the WSIS documents. However, elements of the definition can be found scattered in the Plan of Action and in other ITU documents. National e-strategies are defined as national development strategies which aim at developing technical ICT infrastructure and capacity building responding to the communities' individual needs (ITU, E-strategies: Empowering Development, Geneva 2006). The Plan of Action identifies ten indicative basic targets which may be taken into consideration when establishing national e-strategies; these can be grouped in three goal categories: (1) connection; (2) access; (3) content (WSIS, Geneva Plan of Action, Section A, para. 6). On how a country should establish and implement its e-strategy, see World Bank, Information and Communications for Development (2006), 87–104.

[1300] For further details see Weber/Menoud, 46/47.

[1301] WSIS, Geneva Plan of Action, Section D2 (d) (i).

[1302] WSIS, Geneva Plan of Action, Section D2 (d) (iii).

[1303] WSIS, Geneva Plan of Action, Section D2 (f).

[1304] For further details on the TFFM-Report see Weber/Menoud, 47–52.

slightly more agreement than the Geneva Documents and, with respect to financing, adopted some timid, but promising statements, among which three can be mentioned: Firstly, the Tunis Agenda welcomes the DSF

> "as an innovative financial mechanism of a voluntary nature open to interested stakeholders with the objective of transforming the digital divide into digital opportunities for the developing world by focusing mainly on specific and urgent needs at the local level and seeking new voluntary sources of «solidarity» finance. The DSF will complement existing mechanisms for funding the Information Society, which should continue to be fully utilized to fund the growth of new ICT infrastructure and services".[1305]

Secondly, the Tunis Agenda recognizes that "market forces alone cannot guarantee the full participation of developing countries in the global market for ICT-enabled services", which gives a spur to explore alternative solutions.[1306] In this respect, the Tunis Agenda encourages the public sector and multilateral institutions to allocate more funding to ICT infrastructure and capacity development.[1307] Thirdly, great prominence is given to multi-stakeholder initiatives, which are seen as "indispensable if the fruit of the Information Society are to benefit all".[1308] Following the mandate of the Tunis Agenda, in particular the ITU took some actions in multi-stakeholder data collection platforms.[1309]

A further discussion forum established after the Tunis Summit is the Global Alliance for ICT and Development (GAID), housed at the United Nations in New York.[1310] This body has the objective to deliberate on the relevant development issues and to support less developed countries in the improvement of ICT structures.

3.3 Financial Mechanisms

Discussions around ICT financing strategies rely on two basic premises. These have been outlined and recognized by the international community:

- The market alone does not suffice to ensure equitable, fair and adequate ICT development; this is particularly true for rural areas and low income popula-

[1305] WSIS, Tunis Agenda, para. 28.
[1306] WSIS, Tunis Agenda, para. 18.
[1307] WSIS, Tunis Agenda, paras. 20–21.
[1308] WSIS, Tunis Commitment, para. 37; see also WSIS, Tunis Action Plan, para. 27(b); the Tunis Agenda, for instance, invites the UN agencies to be organized so as to improve involvement of relevant stakeholders (WSIS, Tunis Agenda, para. 103).
[1309] See WEBER/MENOUD, 53/54.
[1310] See <http://www.un-gaid.org>

tions.[1311] Thus, a strong case for national and international intervention exists to ensure that financing for ICT development is forthcoming.

- Substantial elements of the knowledge provision process (ICT, networks, connectivity, Internet) have global public good qualities that make ICT development desirable and important to the whole international community, and enhancing ICT infrastructure and access is part of the Millennium Development Goals.[1312]

Relying on these assumptions, basic principles which ICT development financing strategies should meet, can be outlined as follows:[1313]

(i) Identify the Various ICT Areas Requiring Financing

The first step when establishing a financing strategy is necessarily to identify the areas that need additional financing. This implies carrying out a survey of local existing and missing facilities and needs in order to assess where the private sector alone has not provided for adequate funding. Such areas are typically backbone expansion, interconnectivity development, services to low income and remote populations, broadband and human resource capacities, as well as content and applications building.[1314]

(ii) Improve the Leveraging and Mobilization of Existing Financial Sources

To draw the best out of existing financial resources and ensure their availability, it is paramount that leveraging and mobilization mechanisms be improved. As suggested by the Global Public Goods (GPG) Task Force with respect to the provision of public goods, new funding models seeking to consolidate financing predictability and replenishment should be elaborated.[1315] At a global level, when multilateral financing is sought through international organizations, it is crucial that broad participation be ascertained and that the financial burden be fairly shared.[1316] Having such precise and adapted mechanisms in place could, on the one hand, give countries sufficient incentives to contribute the individually pledged amount and, on the other hand, provide an effective lever to the international community to encourage the fulfillment of the agreement.

1311 TFFM Report, 21.

1312 See UN, Millennium Declaration, para. 20.

1313 These principles are drawn from the recommendations of the TFFM Report, 92–94 and from the observations of the GPG Task Force, Final Report, 108–114; see also Weber/Menoud, 56–58.

1314 TFFM Report, 21; WSIS, Tunis Agenda, para. 23.

1315 GPG Task Force, Final Report, 109.

1316 See the study of ITU, World Telecommunication/ICT Development Report 2006: Measuring ICT for social and economic development, 8th ed., Geneva 2006.

(iii) Explore and Mobilize New and Alternative Sources for Financing

Particularly within the WSIS, there has been a call for innovative financing sources, which would go beyond traditional assistance and conventional public finance. New mechanisms that could answer the broad scope of needs across the developing world for sustained and predictable financial flow should be explored. The international community has examined and partly implemented a wide range of innovative instruments which could help financing different Millennium Development Goals.

(iv) Work with the Private Sector and Market

Market forces can provide considerable resources through private investments and specialized knowledge. Governments should thus work towards putting incentives and enticing conditions in place and providing the necessary sound regulatory framework.

(v) Work with Developing Countries

It is paramount that developing countries and least developed countries be assisted by developed countries, international organizations and civil society bodies in the development of new ICT policy models adapted to their needs, in order to eventually attract financial investment. This assistance goes beyond financial support and aims to address the interests of all ICT stakeholders fairly through exchange of views, sharing of effective practices and resources and technical assistance.[1317]

3.4 Financing Strategies' Legal Framework

Financial mechanisms should be conceived within a sound supporting framework in order to be able to take all stakeholders' interests into account and to maximize their efficiency. Manifold regimes, norms, standards and institutions still need to be created and consolidated in order to provide a sound framework to support ICT financing strategies. A new system should incorporate all the identified elements of ICT development, namely (i) stakeholders' and actors' interests and influence; (ii) infrastructure and means of access; (iii) capacity building, contents and applications. These elements should be implemented congruently at all levels of the international policy-making process.[1318]

1317 WSIS, Tunis Agenda, para. 87.
1318 See also WEBER/MENOUD, 58.

In providing for the implementation and follow-up of the WSIS, the Tunis Agenda sets out the basis of this threefold layered approach for building digital inclusion and puts forward critical recommendations for the national, regional, and international levels:[1319]

(i) At the national level, governments are encouraged:

- to integrate national e-strategies within their development plans and poverty reduction strategies, aiming at achieving the Millennium Development Goals and other internationally agreed development targets;
- to mainstream ICT into their Official Development Assistance strategies through improved information sharing and cooperation;
- to assist other governments in their implementation efforts through existing bilateral and multilateral technical assistance programs;
- to introduce a component for ICT development in their Country Assessment reports.

(ii) At the regional level, WSIS Member States can request:

- that regional intergovernmental organizations, in collaboration with other stakeholders, carry out WSIS implementation activities, by exchanging information and best practices and facilitating policy debate;
- that UN Regional Commissions organize regional WSIS follow-up activities, collaborating with other regional organizations and assisting WSIS Member States with technical and relevant information.

(iii) WSIS implementation and follow-up at the international level should be realized by taking its multi-stakeholder and intergovernmental components into account.

Discussions about the attempts to institutionalize relations between the global sphere and the national interests are not new. Similar patterns have already been discussed in other fields. In particular, standardizations in the telecommunication markets, but also in the energy markets, are driven by similar incentives.[1320] Furthermore, multilateral banks and United Nations' agencies have adopted and reinforced the use of different mechanisms designed to improve the telecommunication infrastructures by investing financial resources and applying technical cooperation.

The agreements and contracts among the different network domains need to make sure that global policies and in particular global standardization are effectively implemented on the regional/national/local level. Thereby, international under-

---

1319 WSIS, Tunis Agenda, paras. 100, 101 and 102; see also WEBER/MENOUD, 59.

1320 On the standardization issue see WEBER, Regulatory Models, 118–124.

standings should pave the way towards setting up a global framework of norms and regulatory activities.[1321] Consequently, it is important to ensure the provision of supporting activities through the participation of experts in the discussions, especially on behalf of the less developed countries: Concrete instruments can include technical cooperation, improvement of capacity building,[1322] and specific support funds for participation in the form of universal access funds with mobilization schemes or other participation models of capital markets.[1323] Mechanisms to mobilize financial resources for the development of technologies at reasonable costs or programs to build local capacities should be prioritized.

An international agreement can achieve the best legal quality if it is adopted by sovereign States or international organizations within the scope of their competences; such agreements are legally binding. However, experience has shown that it could be quite difficult to establish and actually implement international binding agreements and that such an approach is usually rather time-consuming.[1324] Obstacles to the creation of more international legal agreements seem to be more structural and organizational than substantive in nature, since—despite all differences in culture and value-making-processes—it might be easier to establish substantive minimum rules than to implement a new international organization.[1325]

Furthermore, the importance of "soft law" should not be underestimated since it has a special legal relevance in the field of good faith and with regard to the interpretation of international law. "Soft law" can also play a major role in legal orders' development: At the international level, it often represents a step in the evolving process of international law, whereas at a national level it can be an important source of inspiration.[1326] Self-regulation in particular, has the advantage that rules created by the participants of a specific community are usually efficient because they respond to real needs and mirror the technology available; meaningful self-regulation also provides the opportunity to adapt the legal framework to changing technologies in a flexible way. Furthermore, self-regulation can usually be implemented at reduced costs (costs-saving effects) and effective self-regulation induces the concerned people to be open to a permanent consultation process.[1327]

Therefore, it could be worthwhile to think of a new self-regulation body starting the activities on an informal and private law based framework and to consider an

---

1321 PRADA, Vision, 56.

1322 On respective programs see above VI.B.3.3.

1323 See also the chart offered by PRADA, Mechanisms, 27.

1324 See above I.C.1.

1325 See WEBER, Regulatory Models, 77–79.

1326 See WEBER/MENOUD, 61; on "soft law" regulation see also above I.C.2.2 b).

1327 See above I.C.2.

eventual "conversion" of this structure into a set of international binding rules at a later stage.[1328]

4. Outlook

Finding financial means that would provide sufficient resources for achieving global access can appear to be a daunting task. Leveraging and mobilizing the instruments at disposal requires a focused and strong international consensus that is not always present. However, there are many financial mechanisms in place, which could, with few amendments and betterments, make substantial flow available to invest in ICT projects. No instrument alone is able to contribute sufficient resources; however, several mechanisms combined could, together, supply the necessary funding and answer developing countries' needs with respect to ICT infrastructure and services development:[1329]

Official Development Assistance

- The Official Development Assistance (ODA) target of 0.7% of GNP to developing countries and 0.15 to 0.20% to least developed countries should be reached as committed in the Monterrey Consensus.
- ODA's governance must be improved notably by making more coordination and disclosure efforts.
- National ODA strategies are to be streamlined in order to give more attention to ICT infrastructure within the Millennium Development Goals.
- Investments in ICT aspects that cannot be left to the market are necessary, such as the development of expertise and technological innovation, "first-phase" installations in particularly remote and disadvantaged areas and the fostering of international cooperation.
- Projects formulated to involve empowerment of the developing countries after their pilot stage merit to be supported.

Private Investment Support

- Market-friendly policies ensuring an enabling investment climate, notably implying the removal of restrictions on admission, on establishment, and on the operations of direct investors, the implementation of the non-discrimination and Most Favored Nation principles, the clarifications of nationalization and

[1328] See WEBER/MENOUD, 62.
[1329] This sub-section is taken and shortened from WEBER/MENOUD, 179–182.

expropriation policies, and the establishment of efficient dispute settlement procedures, need to be endorsed.

- Governmental plans to increase local capabilities, skills and facilities in terms of administration, institutions and personnel should be implemented.
- Engagement in the conclusion of flexible International Investment Agreements or Bilateral Investment Treaties arranging for possibilities to take into account the needs of development promotion through special and preferential treatment or specific measures is necessary.
- Possible betterments in investment risk or export risk guarantee schemes of developed countries must be examined.
- Guarantee mechanisms in host developing countries to support domestic investments need to be set up.
- The possibility of establishing an additional insurance within the Multilateral Investment Guarantee Agency of the World Bank Group for covering investors against commercially motivated governmental measures in particularly volatile developing regions should be assessed.

Public-Private Partnership Schemes

- The engagement in public-private partnership (PPP) if they are a warranted option in the light of the particularities of the project at hand, meaning if they deliver more value for money than traditional state-undertaken initiatives, merit further support.
- The clarity and certainty of governmental policies relating to PPP by developing a sound legal framework governing PPP should be increased, either in the form of a special law or by undertaking legislative amendments in the various legal areas that impact on PPP.
- Governance principles and standards, transparency requirements, and accountability disciplines to giva a framework to private partners, while assessing in each case the necessity to arrange for fees and tariffs set in advance or subjected to governmental approval must be nailed down.
- The shortcomings of PPP, for instance their punctual and geographically limited range of action, are to be compensated by working closely with regional or international coordination and assistance agencies.

Global Digital Solidarity Fund

- Adherence to the Digital Solidarity Fund (DSF) and examination of the possibility to endorse the 1% digital solidarity principle at a national, regional and local level is worthwile.

- The adoption of a legal basis enabling local authorities to engage in decentralized cooperation if the legal system in force does not permit it, thus making the implementation of the 1% digital solidarity principle possible at regional and local levels should be considered.
- The ways to include the digital solidarity clause within public bids without contravening fundamental requirements of national contract and public procurement law should be examined.
- Structures and capabilities of the DSF Foundation according to the increasing number of its members while answering developing countries' concerns regarding their representation within the DSF are to be adapted.

Besides pursuing discussions at local, regional and national levels, it is paramount to spur the current international debate. There is a need for increased financing resources for ICT development that can only be met with more engaged international cooperation. Ongoing international talks within the framework of the Monterrey Conference follow-ups, the revisions of the IMF and the World Bank Group, the Doha Round, and the further developments of the DSF and its 1% digital solidarity clause offer valuable opportunities to take decisive legislative steps towards ensuring a more inclusive ICT access.

VII. Concluding Observations

Internet governance is work in progress. The project, having seen daylight less than five years ago, is still very much in its infancy. Multifaceted, interdisciplinary approaches try to get hold of the main topics and issues designing an adequate concept of Internet governance.

Undoubtedly, traditional forms of international regulation cannot suffice all requirements of the online world anymore. Alternative forms of regulation and enforcement need to be applied at the global level.[1330] Thereby, epistemic communities have to be included in the legal framework. Since the digitization lowers the importance of territorial limits, new regulatory regimes can no longer rely on the concept of territoriality, but should transcend geographical boundaries.

A key focus of the intensive ongoing discussions about Internet governance in international organizations, non-governmental organizations, private entities and spontaneous dynamic coalitions concerns organizational aspects. The rapid growth and expansion of the Internet provide for constant challenges in respect to organizations concerned with the Internet such as the ICANN, the IETF, the ISOC, the W3C etc. The ability to absorb technologies such as television, radio and telephone is a prominent model of the Internet's potential applications that might only be at the beginning of exploration. The development of the Internet, its increasing access speeds, and its growing user population will continue to challenge the preservation of accessibility, renderability, and interpretability of increasing amounts of information on the Internet in the future. In particular, new challenges in connection with the adoption of different alphabets that are not based on the Latin script will have to be tackled.

The phenomenon of electronic information and communication exchanges should also lead to an increased participation of civil society. This fact causes a certain fragmentation of knowledge and power and provokes a concept of decentralization as regulatory functions spread out from a previously controlling body to a larger number of actors. Such kind of distribution of regulatory functions also calls for an increased responsibility of the different stakeholders within a multi-stakeholderism concept. Because civil society as the most active user of the Internet needs to be included in the participatory and decision-making processes of its governance, additional regulatory elements are to be tackled, encompassing for example legitimacy, transparency, accountability, stability and sustainability of participants' activities.

[1330] Similarly, Solum, 86/87, refers to "hybrid models".

Copyright © Schulthess Juristische Medien AG, Zurich – Basel – Geneva 2009.
Published by Springer-Verlag GmbH Berlin Heidelberg 2010. All Rights Reserved

The inclusion of civil society requires the implementation of a bottom-up process allowing responsiveness of the concerned actors in a rational discourse which improves democratic quality of the structures. In practice, e-inclusion must be enhanced at all levels; this means, among other things, that approaches with e-voting should be revitalized in an improved way, that discussion fora need to be implemented, and that the building of new coalitions merits to be tested. Thereby policy and legal decisions are to be accompanied by empirical investigations based on a solid research methodology.

Internet governance must address central questions such as: Who rules the Internet, in whose interests, by which mechanisms and for which purposes? Particularly with the growing influence that some Internet organizations feature, questions on their legitimacy arise. The envisaged realization of a concept of "multi-stakeholder in governance", perceived as the new way forward in favor of the inclusion of the whole of society, goes beyond the scope of traditional governance theories, which generally pursued an approach strictly distinguishing the State (public law) from society (civil law). Such a development challenges the traditional international legal and political understanding of legitimacy and makes it necessary to tackle the general question of, who could be a legitimate stakeholder. Whether concepts such as "social contract" or "transnationalism" are applied or other approaches to international governance endorsed, the fundamental "democratic" question—as inherent in any approach to legitimacy—is at stake as to which the governed "demos" forms the basis that is in the position to decide on legitimacy.

Consequently, architectural principles are to be developed and compiled in an international legal framework governing the Internet and consensus should be secured regarding the way in which the players effectively representing the multi-stakeholders within the different organizational structures are to receive a legitimizing background. In order to ensure legitimate decision-making, the processes of consensus-making need to come under scrutiny. Representation only has a legitimizing effect, if the outcome reflects the values of the represented stakeholders. In particular, such a comprehension calls for procedures that establish equal bargaining powers and fair proceedings, as well as enhanced transparency and review mechanisms which enable the allocation of accountability. In this regard, the mentioned elaboration of architectural principles can have a legitimizing effect by providing for certain criteria for the assessment of Internet governing decisions.

The medium of the Internet itself offers valuable opportunities for transparent communication. In fact, in order to achieve transparency in the regulatory process, the Internet could be used to achieve open access to negotiations, collect proposals and statements from the various stakeholders concerned, present the decisions and results, and thereby enhance and facilitate communication and dialogue between the different Internet governance-regulated institutions and the interested parties. Open access to negotiations and information can also promote the mobilization of new actors and help them play their part in Internet governance. The Internet Governance Forum (IGF) is a prominent and valuable example for such enhancement of dialogue. Transparency also influences the architectural and constitutional principles of the Internet, such as flexibility and openness. The achievement of a greater degree of clarity and predictability also fosters the stability of the legal framework. Furthermore, the open communication by the Internet governing bodies improves the stakeholders' confidence in the cross-border nature of the Internet. Transparent minimum quality standards also enhance the Internet`s conditions and the assessment of performance and accountability, as well as facilitate the coordination of Internet governance related regulations. Transparent procedures allow for a certain level of "democratic" legitimization and credibility through active involvement of citizens as well as through certain control over the decision-making processes.

Accountability is regularly called for to improve the governance regimes of organizations in the field of the Internet. Even if multi-stakeholderism leads to diverse constitutions of the accountees and therefore accountability mechanisms should reflect the different particularities in the various segments of civil society, accountability in Internet governance could be improved if standards would be harmonized in a way which makes governing bodies accountable, at least at the organizational level; accountability-holders must also be able to impose some sort of sanction in case of non-compliance with accountability criteria. Standards could help implement legitimizing structures and a guideline for Internet governance in general; they would be suitable to entail significant self-constraints for the policy-making institutions, and, hence, move towards substantiating the realistic implementation of accountability.

As mentioned, civil society should be included in the decision-making processes. Inputs from civil society have to be taken into account and reasons need to be given if the governing bodies diverge from the opinion of the public. Internet organizations and other bodies dealing with online matters should become responsible for the introduction of self-regulatory mechanisms allowing participation of civil society, in particular for their implementation and enforcement. The inclusiveness and quality of Internet governance could be improved and the effective participation of more stakeholders would be facilitated by more transparent decision-making processes. Rules which serve as a benchmark for public participation, access to information and transparency in Internet governance as well as the building of a common understanding of the respective principles and their practice, help to design a democratic environment.

The number of regulatory issues in Internet governance is almost unlimited as the discussions during the last four years have shown. Many issues have an overarching meaning, encompassing online aspects as well as elements of the physical world. For example, Internet governance must play an important role in the allocation of critical Internet resources: In particular, an equitable and non-discriminatory use should be achieved by the allocation of such resources which are limited due the technical restrictions. The law is called upon to establish a framework allowing the implementation of a fair resource allocation management. Similarly, access to infrastructure and realization of open standards are of utmost importance. A crucial aspect of Internet governance discussions also concerns its "humanization". The promotion and protection of fundamental rights applicable in cyberspace is a matter which merits more attention by different stakeholders in various settings. A human society must be based on the values of human rights in all of their normative dimensions. The scope of these values is global and extends to the dignity of all people and their equal and inalienable rights; indeed, human rights provide for the only universally recognized system of values. In particular, freedom of expression and freedom of information should be seen as main fundamental human rights in the online world, but also the right of privacy which calls for the protection of individuals against national and international surveillance needs to be realized in the digital environment. The new approaches for a comprehensive human rights' architecture are to be supported and the gradual acknowledgement and consciousness of human rights issues in the field of Internet governance is a very welcome development since human rights can be seen as the missing link between the technology-oriented and the value-oriented lines of thinking. The strengthening of safety, trust and reliability must also attract better attention in order to avoid extensive privacy infringements.

Bridging the digital divide is not an issue which is limited to the Internet governance context. However, the experience in the IGF process has shown that the notion of digital divide and efforts of overcoming the respective problems need to have an appropriate multi-stakeholder forum. Estimating the level of investments needed to achieve an inclusive civil society is difficult, mainly given its high complexity and variety of components. On a global scale, bridging the digital divide in developing countries requires building sufficient basic infrastructures, maintaining ICT services and reaching the necessary level of capacity at the same time. Nevertheless, financial mechanisms must be conceived within a sound supporting framework in order to be able to take all stakeholders into account and to maximize their efficiency. Leveraging and mobilizing the instruments at disposal requires a focused and strong international consensus, willing to improve financial mechanisms in place by amendments and betterments; no instrument alone is able to contribute sufficient resources, however, several mechanisms combined could, together, supply the necessary funding and answer developing countries' needs with respect to ICT infrastructure and services developments (for example compliance with Official Development Assistance undertaking, involvement of International Monetary Fund and World Bank Group, improvement of private investment support and public-private partnership schemes or Global Digital Solidarity Fund).

A study on Internet governance is now and also for the coming years only a "spotlight", sheding some light on ongoing lively discussions. The outcome of the process can hardly be forecasted; indeed, nothing may really be considered as established except the fact that the online world will certainly change. The final, but challenging observation is therefore very short: *panta rhei.*

Index

A

Aarhus Convention 149–172, 174, 183
Access 69/70, 151–162, 171/72, 176, 178, 180, 196/97, 201–207, 229, 245, 251, 270
Accountability 78, 98/99, 120, 132–148, 269
Anonymity 218/19, 237
Architecture 49, 89–91, 119, 188, 194, 236, 244, 268, 269
Aristocracy 77
Aristotle 77, 112
ARPANET 51
Autonomy 17

B

Backbone 179, 180, 206
Bandwidth 178, 180, 203/04
Bottom-up (*see* also self-regulation) 77/78, 92, 111

C

Capacity building 207, 231
ccTLD *see* top-level domains
Censorship 97, 101, 204, 214
Children 185, 239
Civil society 34, 68, 74–88, 92, 108, 113, 117/18, 132, 137, 139, 140–142, 147, 148–174, 180, 199, 202/03, 204, 205, 207, 224/25, 233, 252, 254, 267, 269
Code 4, 19/20, 92, 98, 174, 242, 243
Compatibility 194/195
Competition 196/97, 203, 204
Constitution 89–91, 118
Consultation *see* participation
Convergence 203
Co-regulation 3, 5, 18/19, 202, 239
Cosmopolitanism 115
Critical Internet resources 69/70, 175/76, 176–186, 269/70
Cryptography 244, 246/47
Culture *see* diversity
Customary rules 14/15
Cybercrime (*see* also terrorism) 173, 183/84, 188, 231–236
Cyberlaw 2

Copyright © Schulthess Juristische Medien AG, Zurich – Basel – Geneva 2009.
Published by Springer-Verlag GmbH Berlin Heidelberg 2010. All Rights Reserved

Cybersecurity (*see* also terrorism) 5, 67, 101, 231–233
Cyberspace 1–3, 4/5, 28, 94, 111, 218, 230

D

DARPA 48, 51
Data protection *see* privacy
Decentralisation 92, 267
Decision-making 73, 78, 79/80, 81, 83, 84, 94, 100, 118, 122, 132, 141/42, 144, 148–151, 162–174, 237, 269
Deliberative democracy *see* democracy
Democracy 3, 62/63, 78, 82, 84, 91, 96–98, 107, 109–120, 132, 133, 137/38, 152, 165, 171, 198, 268, 269
Dependence 62, 97
Digital divide 9/10, 108, 155, 199, 206/07, 229, 248–266, 270
– Definition 248, 251
– Factual situation 249/50
– Financial mechanisms 259–261
– Financial needs 252–254
– Legal framework 261–266
– Political initiatives 254–259
Digital signature *see* encryption
Disaggregation 115/16
Discourse 110/11, 118
Discrimination 86, 204, 205, 206
Diversity 69/70, 83, 91, 176, 185/86, 228
Domain names (*incl.* DNS) 4, 28, 51, 52/53, 61, 66, 106/07, 127, 177, 178, 181, 187, 192, 197/98
DSF (Digital Solidarity Fund) 86, 201, 254, 257–259, 265/66, 270
Dynamic coalitions 70/71, 225/26, 245, 267

E

E-commerce (*incl.* e-trade) 4, 132, 195, 249
E-democracy *see* voting
E-government 249
Elections *see* voting
E-literacy 231
Encryption *see* cryptography
Environmental law 148–174
Essential facilities doctrine 196/97
EuroDig 71/72
Equity (*incl.* equality) 16, 86, 206, 213/14, 228

F

Fairness 86/87, 103, 113, 118, 134
Financing mechanisms 199–202, 259–261
Freedom of expression 97, 101, 149, 209, 211, 214/15, 220, 224, 226, 227, 238, 270
Fundamental rights *see* human rights
FSB (FSF) 100

G

GAID 259
GATS 124/25
Geneva Principles 31–33, 64, 66/67, 90/91, 102, 107, 119, 222, 249, 258
Globalization 5, 93, 94
Global Network Initiative (GNI) 98, 223/24, 229
Global village 9
Governance (general principles) 2/3, 4/5, 7/8, 71, 94, 115–120
Government networks 94–96, 116
gTLD *see* top-level domains

H

Hacking 232
Hierarchy 145, 218
Hobbes 225
HRIS Caucus 220/21
Human rights 84–87, 91, 207–231, 238, 239/40, 270
– Characteristics 213–219
– Global agreements 209–211
– Regional agreements 212/13
– Scope of application 216–218

I

IAB 43, 44, 52, 59, 89, 173, 188, 197
IAHC 52
IANA 28, 29, 52–54
ICANN 29/30, 35, 39, 51–66, 68, 82, 85, 88, 91, 92, 96–103, 106–111, 126, 127–130, 134–140, 143/44, 148, 153/54, 160/61, 165, 168, 172, 173, 179, 181, 187/88, 192, 196, 197/98, 267
– Accountability 134/35
– ALAC 59, 63, 97, 108, 145
– Board of Directors 55–57

– ccNSO 60, 146
– GAC 30, 58, 63, 103, 128
– GNSO 60, 146
– Green Paper 53
– JPA 29, 62, 99, 134, 136
– Membership 54/55
– Organizational Structure 55–60
– RALO 59, 146
– Transparency 127–129
– White Paper 53
ICC 116, 195
ICT 9, 67, 89, 180, 190–192, 194/95, 200/01, 207, 248–252, 257–259, 259–261, 262, 264, 266, 270
IETF 39, 42/43, 44, 68, 92, 106, 117, 130, 134, 139, 173, 191/92, 195, 197, 267
IGF 35–37, 46, 65, 66–71, 87, 97/98, 101, 108, 117, 131, 144, 148, 171, 173, 175/76, 177, 202, 205, 222, 226, 230, 233, 235/36, 240, 245, 268, 276
ILO 185
IMF *see* World Bank
Inclusiveness *see* civil society
Information society (*see* also civil society) 9/10, 32, 67, 222
Intergovernmental organization 39, 92, 98, 205, 263
International convention 13, 16, 181–186, 209–213, 216, 220–222, 226, 239, 263, 267
International Court of Justice 13, 14
International law 11–17, 94, 181–186, 208
International organizations 34, 39, 92, 98, 205, 263
International relations 11
Internet
– Bill of Rights 91, 225–227, 229
– Exchange Points (IXP) *see* backbone
– Governance 4/5, 7/8, 31–37, 60/61, 66–72, 76–84, 88–103, 105–174, 175–266, 267/68
– Naming and numbering *see* critical Internet resources
– Standards development *see* standardization
– Technical coordination *see* Internet Protocol
Internet Protocol 28, 29, 42, 51, 60, 89, 187/88, 190–192, 198, 236
– Addresses (*see* also domain names) 28, 90, 130, 197
– IPv4 47, 66, 175/76, 181, 186–202
– IPv6 47, 66, 90, 175/76, 177, 178, 181, 186–202
– Management *see* RIRs
Interoperability 89, 119, 191/92, 200

ISOC 29, 42, 43–47, 52, 58, 92, 134, 139, 173, 197, 267
ISPs 99, 198, 219, 231
ITU 27, 31, 32, 39, 40–42, 52, 59, 64, 234/35, 248, 250, 257, 259

J

Justice 171/72

K

Kant 74/75, 84/85, 225, 238
Kyoto Protocol 182

L

Language *see* multilingualism
Legitimacy 62/63, 78, 96–98, 105–120, 140, 243, 268
Lex mercatoria (general legal principles) 15–17
Liberalism 94/95
Locke 15, 74

M

MacBride Report 25–28
Mass Media Declaration 26
Memorandum of Understanding 29, 52, 54, 62, 99, 173/74
Millennium Development Goals 207, 222, 254, 260, 261
Monterrey Consensus 201, 254–256
Montesquieu 16, 113
Multiculturalism *see* diversity
Multilateralism 34, 92
Multilingualism 32, 66, 160, 178, 206
Multi-Stakeholderism 34, 65, 69–71, 73, 83, 87, 88–103, 105, 108, 116/17, 120, 147, 199, 224/25, 226, 262, 267–269

N

NCSG 60
Net neutrality 203–205
Networked Communications Freedom Charter 227–229
New World Information Order 25
NGOs 82, 95, 117, 220, 222, 267

O

ODA 201, 255, 258, 262, 264, 270
OECD 239/40, 243, 247
Ombudsman 58
Open society 78/79
Openness 69/70, 79, 81, 89, 90, 119, 131, 134, 176, 206, 269
OSCE 184, 230

P

P3P 245
Parliament 113
Participation 82–84, 102/03, 118, 120, 132, 135, 140–142, 144, 148–151, 162–174, 202, 207, 230, 269
PETs 244/45
Philosophy 73–103, 110/11, 224/25
PIC 106
Plato 15
Pluralism 79
PrepCom 31/32, 89, 220, 257/58
Privacy 215/16, 218/19, 220, 223/24, 228, 236, 237–245, 270
– Functions 237/38
– Principles 241/42
– Regulation 239/40
Protocol *see* Internet Protocol
Public-private partnership 201, 265, 270

R

Rawls 75, 225
Registrars/Registries *see* RIRs
Regulation (*see* also rule-making, self-regulation) 11–23, 239/40
Representation 63, 77–79, 91, 112, 117, 268
RFCs 43, 89, 188, 190
RIRs 54/55, 194, 198
Root server 179
Routing 177, 191, 196
Rousseau 74–76, 81, 84–87, 112, 225
Rule-making (*see* also regulation, self-regulation) 78, 92–95, 109, 111, 132

S

Safety 230–236, 270
Security 69/70, 130, 176, 191/92, 230–237, 240, 243/44, 245–248
Self-regulation (*see* also regulation, rule-making) 17–23, 61/62, 111, 134, 151, 154, 173/74, 198, 229, 240, 242, 243, 263
– Forms 18/19
– Legal quality 20
– Strengths/weaknesses 21–23
Social contract 20, 73–88, 112, 113, 120, 268
Soft law (*see* also self-regulation) 20, 39, 173/74, 209, 263
Software 235/36
Spam 130, 173, 188
Stakeholders (*see* also multi-stakeholderism) 20, 22, 84, 117, 119, 135, 194/95
Standardization 4, 41, 42/43, 59, 190/91, 262

T

Technology *see* ICT
Terrorism (*see* also cybercrime, cybersecurity) 5, 101, 231–234
Telecommunication (*see* also ITU) 203
Top-level domains 30, 51/52, 54, 61, 66, 102, 130, 146, 161, 188
Transgovernmentalism 3
Transnationalism 95/96, 115/116, 120, 205, 268
Transparency 22, 73, 78, 98/99, 118, 120, 121–132, 134/35, 141, 203, 268/69
TRUSTe 92, 243
Tunis Agenda 35/36, 65, 67/68, 175/76, 177, 258/59, 262

U

UDRP 30, 62, 103, 127
UN (*see* also UNCITRAL, UNCTAD, UNDP, UNESCO) 31, 36, 66, 68, 98, 114, 219
UNCITRAL 247
UNCTAD 39, 248, 256
UNDP 39, 256
UNESCO 25–28, 39, 185, 250

V

Viruses 232
Volonté générale 80/81
Voting 63, 77, 82, 87, 98, 103, 108, 112, 143, 165

W

W3C 47–50, 59, 106, 134, 139, 229, 230, 267
WGIG 33–35, 64, 80, 102, 143, 175/76, 233
WIPO 39, 52, 53
World Bank (*incl.* IMF) 39, 86, 100, 125/26, 137, 201, 256, 265, 266, 270
World Wide Web 29, 47/48, 52, 106, 111, 120
WSIS 27, 30, 31–37, 46, 64, 66–71, 89, 107, 119, 144, 174, 219–222, 232/33, 249, 254, 255, 257–259, 261, 262
WTO 39, 98, 114, 116, 124/25, 256

Publikationen aus dem Zentrum für Informations- und Kommunikationsrecht der Universität Zürich

erschienen bei Schulthess Juristische Medien AG, Zürich

Band 1 **Neues Fernmelderecht – Erste Orientierung**
WEBER ROLF H. (Hrsg.),
mit Beiträgen von Fischer Peter R., Geiser Jean-Maurice, Gunter Pierre-Yves, Haag Marcel, Hoffet Franz, Maurer François, Ramsauer Matthias, Rieder Pierre, Stampfli Katharina und Weber Rolf H., Zürich 1998

Band 2 **Symposium Schluep – Querbezüge zwischen Kommunikations- und Wettbewerbsrecht**
WEBER ROLF H. (HRSG.),
in Zusammenarbeit mit von der Crone Hans Caspar, Forstmoser Peter, Zäch Roger und Zobl Dieter,
mit Beiträgen von von der Crone Hans Caspar/Groner Roger, Mestmäcker Ernst-Joachim, Nobel Peter, Schwarz Mathias/Klingner Norbert und Weber Rolf H., Zürich 1998

Band 3 **Informatik und Jahr 2000 – Risiken und Vorsorgemöglichkeiten aus rechtlicher Sicht**
WEBER ROLF H.
Zürich 1998

Band 4 **Daten und Datenbanken – Rechtsfragen zu Schutz und Nutzung**
WEBER ROLF H./HILTY RETO M. (Hrsg.),
mit Beiträgen von Druey Jean Nicolas, Gaster Jens-L., Hilty Reto M., Kemper Kurt, Sieber Ulrich und Weber Rolf H., Zürich 1998

Band 5 **Neustrukturierung der Rundfunkordnung**
WEBER ROLF H.
Zürich 1999

Band 6 **Rechtsschutz von Datenbanken (EU – USA – Schweiz)**
KÜBLER PHILIP
Zürich 1999

Band 7 **Informationsqualität – Ein Beitrag zur journalistischen Qualitätsdebatte aus der Sicht des Informationsrechts**
ZULAUF RENA
Zürich 2000

Band 8 **Werbung im Internet – Rechtsvergleichende, lauterkeitsrechtliche Beurteilung von Werbeformen**
JÖHRI YVONNE
Zürich 2000

Band 9 **Rechtlicher Regelungsrahmen von raumbezogenen Daten**
WEBER ROLF H.
Zürich 2000

Band 10 **Geschäftsplattform Internet – Rechtliche und praktische Aspekte**
WEBER ROLF H./HILTY RETO M./AUF DER MAUR ROLF (Hrsg.)
Zürich 2000

Band 11 **Finanzierung der Rundfunkordnung**
WEBER ROLF H.
Zürich 2000

Band 12 **Der Softwarepflegevertrag**
WIDMER MICHAEL
Zürich 2000

Band 13 **Datenschutzrecht vor neuen Herausforderungen**
Marketing – E-Commerce – Virtuelle Bank – Sachdaten
WEBER ROLF H.
Zürich 2000

Band 14 **Geschäftsplattform Internet II – Rechtliche und praktische Aspekte**
WEBER ROLF H./HILTY RETO M./AUF DER MAUR ROLF (Hrsg.)
Zürich 2001

Band 15 **Digitale Verbreitung von Rundfunkprogrammen**
und Meinungsvielfalt – Entwicklungen, Probleme, Lösungen
WEBER ROLF H./DÖRR BIANKA S.
Zürich 2001

Band 16 **Die Übernahme von Allgemeinen Geschäftsbedingungen in**
elektronisch abgeschlossene Verträge
SCHWAB KARIN
Zürich 2001

Band 17 **Geschäftsplattform Internet III – Kapitalmarkt – Marktauftritt – Besteuerung**
WEBER ROLF H./HILTY RETO M./AUF DER MAUR ROLF (Hrsg.)
Zürich 2002

Band 18 **Rechtliche Rahmenbedingungen für verwaltungsunabhängige**
Behördenkommissionen – Untersuchung am Beispiel der geplanten
Fernmelde- und Medienkommission
WEBER ROLF H./BIAGGINI GIOVANNI
Mitarbeit: Dörr Bianka S./Peduzzi Roberto
Zürich 2002

Band 19 **Elektronische Signaturen**
SCHLAURI SIMON
Zürich 2002

Band 20 **Zugang zu Kabelnetzen – Spannungsfeld zwischen**
Netzbetreiberfreiheit und offenem Zugang
WEBER ROLF H.
Zürich 2003

Band 21 **Elektronische Signaturen und Haftung der Anbieter von Zertifizierungsdiensten – Eine Darstellung am Beispiel der Regelungen in der EU, Deutschland, Grossbritannien und der Schweiz**
Dörr Bianka S.
Zürich 2003

Band 22 **Geschäftsplattform Internet IV**
Weber Rolf H./Berger Mathis/Auf der Maur Rolf (Hrsg.)
Zürich 2003

Band 23 **IT-Outsourcing**
ICT: Rechtspraxis I
Weber Rolf H./Berger Mathis/Auf der Maur Rolf (Hrsg.)
Zürich 2003

Band 24 **Rechtsfragen rund um Suchmaschinen**
Weber Rolf H.
Mitarbeit: Spacek Dirk
Zürich 2003

Band 25 **Schweizerisches Filmrecht**
Weber Rolf H./Unternährer Roland/Zulauf Rena
Zürich 2003

Band 26 **Kinofilmverwertung in der Schweiz**
Unternährer Roland
Zürich 2003

Band 27 **E-Health und Datenschutz**
Berger Kurzen Brigitte
Zürich 2004

Band 28 **Unternehmensinformation und Recht – Eine Übersicht**
Stückelberger Balz
Zürich 2004

Band 29 **Schutz von TV-Formaten – Eine rechtliche und ökonomische Betrachtung**
Spacek Dirk
Zürich 2005

Band 30 **Kulturquoten im Rundfunk**
Weber Rolf H./Rossnagel Alexander/Osterwalder Simon/
Scheuer Alexander/Wüst Sonia
Zürich 2006

Band 31 **Zugang zu Premium Content**
Weber Rolf H./Osterwalder Simon
Zürich 2006

Band 32 **Sorgfaltspflichten bei der Datenübertragung**
Favre Katia
Zürich 2006

Band 33 **IT-Sicherheit und Recht – Grundlagen eines integrativen Gestaltungskonzepts**
WEBER ROLF H./WILLI ANNETTE
Zürich 2006

Band 34 **Privatvervielfältigung im digitalen Umfeld**
BAUMGARTNER TOBIAS
Zürich 2006

Band 35 **Das Recht der personenbezogenen Information**
WEBER ROLF H./SOMMERHALDER MARKUS
Zürich 2007

Band 36 **Staatliche Massnahmen gegen Medienkonzentration**
KELLERMÜLLER HANSPETER
Zürich 2007

Band 37 **Der Mehrwertdienst im Fernmelderecht**
HUBER KARIN
Zürich 2007

Band 38 **Telecommunications Competition and Its Driving Force**
WU JUN
Zürich 2008

Band 39 **Media Governance und Service Public**
WEBER ROLF H.
Zürich 2007

Band 40 **The Information Society and the Digital Divide Legal Strategies to Finance Global Access**
WEBER ROLF H./MENOUD VALÉRIE A.
Zürich 2008

Band 41 **Netzzugang in der Telekommunikation**
AMGWERD MATTHIAS
Zürich 2008

Band 42 **IT-Governance als Aufgabe des Verwaltungsrates – Kriterien einer sorgfältigen Pflichterfüllung unter Berücksichtigung der strategischen Rolle der IT im Unternehmen**
WILLI ANNETTE
Zürich 2008

Band 43 **Der ASP-Vertrag**
CHRISTIAN M. IMHOF
Zürich 2008

Band 44 **Zivilrechtliche Haftung von Internet-Providern bei Rechtsverletzungen durch ihre Kunden**
PHILIPP FRECH
Zürich 2009

Band 45 **Public Key Infrastructure**
DANIEL MARKWALDER
Zürich 2009

Ausserdem erschienen:

Regulatory Models for the Online World
WEBER ROLF H.
Zürich 2002

Towards a Legal Framework for the Information Society
WEBER ROLF H.
in collaboration with Roduner Xenia
Zürich 2003

FSC
www.fsc.org
MIX
Papier | Fördert
gute Waldnutzung
FSC® C083411

Kolibri 360 GmbH
Ferdinand-Jühlke-Straße 7
99095 Erfurt, Deutschland
produktsicherheit@kolibri360.de